VEGETARIAN JOURNAL'S

GUIDE TO

NATURAL FOODS RESTAURANTS

IN THE U.S. AND CANADA

FOREWORD BY LINDSAY WAGNER

D1118433

THE VEGETARIAN RESOURCE GROUP

AVERY PUBLISHING GROUP INC.

Garden City Park, New York

Information compiled by: Sally Clinton and Deborah Wasserman
Cover Design: Ann Vestal and Rudy Shur
In-House Editor: Linda Comac
Typesetter: Bonnie Fried

Library of Congress Cataloging-in-Publication Data

Vegetarian journal's guide to natural foods restaurants in the U.S. and
    Canada / by the Vegetarian Resource Group.
      p.   cm.
    ISBN 0-89529-571-7 (pbk.)
      1. Vegetarian restaurants—United States—Guidebooks.   2. Natural
    food restaurants—United States—Guidebooks.   3. Vegetarian
    restaurants—Canada—Guidebooks.   4. Natural foods restaurants-
    -Canada—Guidebooks.   I. Vegetarian Resource Group.   II. Vegetarian
    journal.   III. Title: Guide to natural foods restaurants in the U.S.
    and Canada.
    TX907.2.V44   1993
    647.9573—dc20   93-23984
                                                        CIP

Printed in the United States of America

10   9   8   7   6   5   4   3   2

CONTENTS

Natural Foods Restaurants in Canada

Acknowledgments

As you can imagine, putting together a natural foods restaurant guide of this proportion is a tremendous task. Sally Clinton's huge job would have been impossible without the help of many individuals. A very grateful "thank you" to these members of The Vegetarian Resource Group and readers of *Vegetarian Journal* who recommended restaurants for inclusion in this guide:

E.S. Wilson, Libby Williams, Ann and Wes Weaver, Mr. and Ms. Wayman, Gail Watson, Salli Vogler, Karla Verbeck, the Vaupels, Lauren Turner, Carol Tracy, Judy Terry, Joe Taksel, Ziona and Tom Swigart, Patricia Swanson, Maxine and Stuart Stahler, Wayne Smeltz, Geri Singer, John Lowell Simcox, Eve Sicurella, Keith Seifert, Brad Scott, Susan Havrilla Schneider, David Schneider, Marianne Sanford, Judith Ruiz, Wendy Rozov, John Rouse, Denise Rosen, Mark Rolloson, S. Reilly, Jennifer Raymond, Sheila Pierson, Melinda Kjarum Peterson, Marcia Pearson, Patti Park, Sally Nelson, Valerie Mortensen, Margaret Moran, Becky Moody, Lila Moffitt, Judith Miner, Thomas Mills, Lynn Tschantre-Mills, Dorothy Millard, M. McMahon, Marianne Matte, Reed Mangels, Marlene Mannella, Helen Mader, Eric Lynn, Barbara Lovitts, Atsuko Livernois, Ellen Levy, Pat LeBlanc, Kate Lawrence, the Landens, Kathryn Lance, T. Kramer, Stacey Koltonow, Celeste Knofczynski, Robert and Roberta Kalechofsky, Sharon Jonas, Jolene Johnson, Elizabeth Jennings, Matthew Jaquith, J.D. Jackson (*Bunny Huggers' Gazette*), Charlene Inglis, Nancy Howerter, Marilyn Havill, Juliana Harrison, Alison Harlow, Kimberly Hardy, Carole Hamlin, Shari Greenfield, Gigi Green, the Gouldings, Janet Gotlieb, Chris Goss, Shari Goodman, Sheree Gonzalez, Sharlene Goldberg, Amy Gilliland, Peter Gilder, The Fund For Animals, Inc., South Central Regional Office, Barbara Fontaine, Dan Flaherty, Mary Faith, Alice Espey, Cate Eisenberg, Pat Ehlinger, M. Drummond, Matt and Jean Craig, Carmen Corbeil, S. Conroy, Brenda Collins, Suzanne L. Cole, Bill and Ginger Clinton, Mary Clifford, Joan Chowdhury, Bob Chorush (Animal-Free Trade),

Elizabeth Caro, Mary Beth Burgmeier, Patti Breitman, Parris Boyd, Marilyn Berry, Dr. Richard Berman, Andrea Bennington, Robert Beaumont III, R. Baumgarten, Marcia Anderson, Arnie Alper, Aleithia's Kennels.

Special thanks to Brad Scott, Jennifer Raymond, Jon and Kathleen Shoemaker, Ann Truelove, and Ziona Swigart who helped us meet the deadline of this book. Our appreciation to Rudy Shur of Avery Publishing Group for having a personal interest in this project and to Linda Comac of Avery for editing the final manuscript.

Debra Wasserman
Charles Stahler
Editors of *Vegetarian Journal*,
Coordinators of The Vegetarian
Resource Group

FOREWORD

I am so excited to be writing a foreword for an entire book of restaurants in the United States that cater to vegetarians. I may seem easily pleased. However, I've been a performer struggling to maintain a vegetarian lifestyle for almost twenty years. Here's what a good number of those years on the road looked like . . .

Limousine drives up to the Ritz-Carlton. Chauffeur opens the door. Doorman approaches. "Welcome, Ms. Wagner, glad to have you with us." The Bellman leads the way to the luxurious suite. "Where shall I put the bags?" I reply, "Those three go in the bedroom. THAT BAG stays here." After lifting THAT BAG off the trolley, the bellman is clearly relieved it isn't going very far. And there I am, on location for a film and in one of the finest hotels in the country unpacking THAT BAG. Out comes my two-burner hot plate, two stainless steel pans, brown rice, adzuki beans, tamari sauce, Bragg's amino acid, whole-wheat tortillas and, of course, the ever-present cayenne pepper.

Life was rough in the '70s and '80s for vegetarians on the road. Eventually I learned to inquire (first thing) about the ethnic restaurants in town. (Most other countries around the world seem to understand nutrition without such a heavy carnivorous bent.) That made life much easier and resulted in setting off far fewer smoke alarms.

I now can take my *Guide to Natural Foods Restaurants* with me (in a much smaller bag) and know that my children and I will have a much easier time traveling and working in a healthy, sated way.

God bless the *Guide to Natural Foods Restaurants*!

Lindsay Wagner

Lindsay Wagner

Introduction

One of the aspects of traveling I most treasure is stumbling upon the many wonderful vegetarian or natural foods restaurants in the most unexpected places. Wherever the restaurant happens to be, it seems like an oasis, and the food tastes better than any food you've ever had. Not too long ago, the search for good vegetarian food while traveling did seem comparable to seeking a lake in a desert—an oasis of healthy foods amidst the desolate menus of mainstream eateries. While the United States had been a culinary desert for vegetarians in the past, today it is being reclaimed by health food delis, juice bars, and vegetarian and natural foods restaurants. These eateries are springing up like puddles, and are being joined by numerous mainstream restaurants that are expanding their menus to include options for vegetarians.

A survey conducted by Gallup for the National Restaurant Association in 1991 indicated that when eating out, 20 percent of American adults are likely or very likely to look for a restaurant that serves vegetarian items. This same study revealed that 30 percent or more are likely to order specific vegetarian items. Almost any vegetarian, by personal experience alone, can tell you that these trends are reflected in what is offered at restaurants today, and that the acceptability and availability of vegetarian foods is greater than ever before. Numerous restaurants have "heart-healthy" or "light" menu items and still others are willing to accommodate special diets. With all of these factors combined, it seems that now vegetarians often have several options, and no longer have to subsist on steamed vegetables and bread. Now, we more frequently have the opportunity to explore the vast array of creative and delicious tastes, textures, and flavors that are prevalent in the world of healthy, vegetarian cuisine.

In compiling this restaurant guide, we've tried to map out as many vegetarian-oriented treasures as we could find, as well as list the long-established vegetarian oases that have been both welcoming to and appreciated by health-conscious individuals for decades. The information is very usable, listed alphabetically by state, then city, then restaurant. At the beginning of the description of each restaurant, an italicized phrase indicates the type of restaurant (eg., *Italian* or *health-food-store deli*); this is followed by whatever detailed information we can provide. Each listing concludes with a quick reference section in bold that provides some of the basic information you may need. This includes hours or days the restaurants are open; type of service (full, limited, or cafeteria style); availability, if known, of vegan (dairyless) or macrobiotic options; beverages including fresh squeezed juices, espresso/cappuccino, non-alcoholic beer and wine, and wine, beer, and alcohol; provision for take-out; accepted credit cards; and the price range, which is explained in the key box on page 5 and on the bottom of various pages throughout the restaurant listing.

We have tried to make this guide as thorough as possible, but in many cases the information listed is limited by what was provided to us. We wrote to every restaurant requesting that our survey be completed and returned with a copy of the restaurant's menu. Sometimes, however, we did not receive a copy of the menu or the survey was incomplete; consequently, there are some gaps in the information provided. So if "vegan options" or credit card information isn't provided in this publication, you should call the restaurant with your questions. In general, it is wise to check first, especially if you are traveling a good distance to visit a restaurant. Restaurant hours and menus change frequently so there is no guarantee the information listed will remain the same.

We were also limited in our ability to ascertain which menu items are vegan. A listing of "vegan options" may only indicate that our review of the menu led us to the conclusion that vegan options are available. Once again, you might want to double-check to be sure.

While the availability of vegetarian foods certainly has increased significantly, there are still some places where you'll feel as though you're in a desert. In these areas, the selections we have listed may not make your taste buds jump for joy, but there will be options that let you get by. If there aren't any listings for your locality, check out any ethnic restaurants you can find. You can almost always find something to eat at Asian, Indian, Italian, Ethiopian, Mexican, and Middle Eastern eateries. You can also try calling a local health food store, if there is one, and asking for the recommendation of a place to dine. If you are really having trouble, we have listed some local contacts (see page 254) and resources that might be able to help you. We have also included a "vegetarian vacation guide" that lists camps, resorts, spas, bed-and-breakfasts, and tour services that cater to vegetarians.

Finally, if you do find a place we've missed, please let us know!! We never would have been able to compile this guide without the help of vegetarian groups and health-conscious eaters around the country, and we'd love your help in keeping the listing current. For your convenience, a form is included in the back of the book for your replies.

Thank you for thinking and caring about what you eat. I hope this guide makes your travels more enjoyable. And I hope you always find yourself in an oasis of delicious vegetarian foods!

Sally Clinton
The Vegetarian Resource Group,
publisher of *Vegetarian Journal*

NATURAL FOODS RESTAURANTS

Below are the symbols and primary abbreviations that will provide you with important information about each entry.

> ❧ Reviewers' choice
> • Vegetarian restaurant
> •• Vegan restaurant
> $ less than $6
> $$ $6–$12
> $$$ more than $12
> AMX—American Express accepted
> MC—MasterCard accepted
> DISC—Discover Card accepted
> DC—Diner's Club accepted
> VISA—Visa Card accepted
> BYOB—Bring Your Own Bottle
> Non-alc.—Non-alcoholic
> Fresh juices—freshly squeezed in
>   the restaurant, e.g., carrot juice

An abbreviated version of the above codes can be found on the bottom of various pages throughout the guide.

In addition, at the beginning of a number of the larger city entries, there appears a listing of towns, suburbs, and/or localities that are in close proximity to the respective city. The names within these listings can be used to locate additional restaurants in these neighboring areas.

ALABAMA

BIRMINGHAM

• Golden Temple Natural Grocery & Cafe
1901 11th Ave. S., Birmingham, AL 35205   **(205) 933-6333**
Vegetarian. Sandwiches, salads, drinks, and daily specials are offered at this quick-service vegetarian cafe. Low-salt, low-fat meals are also available. **Open Monday through Saturday. Limited service, vegan options, fresh juices, take-out, VISA/MC, $**

HOOVER

Custom Foods International
3309 Lorna Rd., Hoover, AL 35216   **(205) 823-7002**
Natural foods. Located inside Golden Temple, this eatery opened late in 1992 and offers an eclectic mixture of everything from the "Deep South to the French Alps." **Cafeteria style, fresh juices, take-out, $**

ALASKA

ANCHORAGE

The Marx Brothers Cafe
627 W. 3rd Ave., Anchorage, AK 99501   **(907) 278-2133**
Regional. Some vegetarian options are offered at Marx Brothers, which is also willing to prepare special meals for vegetarians. Herbs, spices, lettuce, and edible flowers are grown on the premises in the summer. **Open for dinner Monday through Saturday. Full service, wine/beer, VISA/MC, $$$**

FAIRBANKS

Cafe de Paris
801 Pioneer Rd., Fairbanks, AK 99701   **(907) 456-1669**
International. Located in a sixty-year-old Victorian house with a beautiful redwood deck, Cafe de Paris serves a wide variety of foods using only the freshest ingredients available. Lettuce and most fresh vegetables are grown for the restaurant by a local gardener. A large variety of European desserts and pastries is served. **Lunch only. Closed Sunday. Full service, cappuccino/espresso, take-out, VISA/MC/AMX/DC, $$**

Gambardella's Pasta Bella
706 2nd Ave., Fairbanks, AK 99701   **(907) 456-3417**
Italian. The Gambardellas pride themselves on generations of fabulous Italian food. Vegetarian entrees are conveniently indicated on the menu. Examples include Pasta Marinara, Fettucini Alfredo, Eggplant Parmesan, Pesto Pasta, and Gourmet Pizza. **Open Monday through Saturday and on Sundays in summer. Full service, cappuccino/espresso, wine/beer, take-out, VISA/MC, $—lunch, $$—dinner**

JUNEAU

Fiddlehead Restaurant & Bakery

429 W. Willoughby Ave., Juneau, AK 99801   **(907) 586-3150**

Natural foods. Fiddlehead offers full gourmet natural foods. Breakfast, lunch, and dinner menus include salads, omelettes, sandwiches, soups, bean burgers, and entrees. Local artwork is displayed, and there is live piano music evenings with a weekend jazz club. The upstairs dining room offers a view of Mt. Juneau. No smoking. **Open daily. Full service, vegan options, fresh juices, wine/beer/alcohol, take-out, VISA/MC/AMX, $$**

PETERSBURG

Helse Restaurant

#17 Sing Lee Alley, Petersburg, AK 99833   **(907) 772-3444**

Natural foods. Helse's reputation is based on its soup and homemade bread special offered every day except Monday. Helse offers three vegetarian sandwiches (two of which are vegan), tofu salad, and a garden salad in addition to various seafood and meat sandwiches. A natural foods store is located adjacent to the restaurant. **Open every day except Sunday. Full service, vegan options, cappuccino/espresso, take-out, $$**

ARIZONA

FLAGSTAFF

Cafe Espress

16 N. San Francisco, Flagstaff, AZ 86001   **(602) 774-0541**

Natural foods. A cafe, bakery, and gallery all in one, with a menu that's actually a little newspaper with ads and interesting info, Cafe Espress can feed your body and mind a variety of vegetarian foods and facts about the area. Options include salads, soups, sandwiches, chili, and hot entrees plus a salad bar. Fresh baked breads, pastries, and desserts. **Open for three meals daily. Full service, vegan options, fresh juices, wine/beer, take-out, VISA, $**

Dara Thai Restaurant

1612 E. Santa Fe Ave., Flagstaff, AZ 86001   **(602) 774-0047**

Thai. Dara Thai serves delicious vegetarian food from either its regular menu or a separate sheet of additional dishes that includes Veggie Rolls and several tofu specials. The restaurant is also willing to make a vegetarian version of any meat dish. **Open daily except Mondays in winter. Full service, vegan options, alcohol, take-out, VISA/MC, $$**

PRESCOTT

Lynette's . . . Enchanted Cafe

111 Grove Ave., Prescott, AZ 86301   **(602) 778-3616**

Natural foods. Located in a Victorian building, this natural foods restaurant offers several vegetarian options and a few vegan selections as well as egg-free, wheat-free, and sugar-free bakery products. **Open for breakfast and lunch daily. Full service, vegan options, fresh juices, take-out, $**

• Super Carrot Natural Food Market & Cafe

236 S. Montezuma, Prescott, AZ 86303   **(602) 776-0365**

Vegetarian. Daily specials instead of a set menu are offered at the Super Carrot. **Closed Sundays. Very casual, vegan options, limited service, fresh juices, $**

SCOTTSDALE

Marche Gourmet

4121 N. Marshall Way, Scottsdale, AZ 85251   **(602) 994-4568**

Natural foods. Breakfast, lunch, and dinner menus include vegetarian items. Pasta, salads, couscous, and five tofu dishes are offered. **Open daily but closed Sunday evenings. Breakfast offered until 2 P.M. Full service, vegan options, take-out, $$**

SEDONA

La Mediterranee

Atop the Quality Inn, 771 Hwy. 179, Sedona, AZ 86339   **(602) 282-7006**

Lebanese. Vegetarian selections include Falafel, Stuffed Grape Leaves, Hummus, a vegetarian combination plate, Stuffed Zucchini, homemade bread, plus much more. **Open daily for lunch and dinner. Full service, fresh juices, wine/beer/alcohol, VISA/MC/DISC, $$**

Oaxaca Restaurant & Cantina

231 N. Hwy. 89A, Sedona, AZ 86336   **(602) 282-4179**

Mexican. Oaxaca offers regional and Southwestern entrees, featuring blue-corn and whole-wheat tortillas. Heart-healthy dishes and vegetarian meals are planned by a registered dietitian. All food is prepared fresh daily without additives or animal fat. **Open every day. Full service, cappuccino/espresso, wine/beer/alcohol, take-out, VISA/MC/DISC, $$**

Sedona Salad Co.

2370 W. Hwy. 89A, Sedona, AZ 86336   **(602) 282-0299**

American. The Sedona Salad Co. boasts a salad bar with over sixty items, some of which are organic. Sandwiches and potato bar, soup bar, and regular menu. **Limited service, take-out, $**

TEMPE

Gentle Strength Deli

234 W. University, Tempe, AZ 85282   **(602) 968-4831**

Natural foods. The Gentle Strength Deli is located within a cooperatively owned natural food store. The deli strives to provide vegetarian, vegan, and macrobiotic choices in a healthy, pleasing atmosphere. Featured are award-winning muffins, noteworthy soups, fresh sandwiches, daily specials, and desserts. **Open daily.**

Sunday brunch only. Limited service, vegan/macrobiotic options, take-out, VISA/MC, $

Healthy Heart
6340 S. Rural Rd., Tempe, AZ 85283 (602) 831-6464

Natural foods. Healthy Heart restaurant offers low-fat, low-cholesterol food. Meat is offered on the menu, but there is a good selection of vegetarian fare. No nitrates, citrates, or MSG is used. **Closed on Sundays. Self-service, vegan options, take-out, no credit cards, $**

TUCSON

El Adobe Mexican Restaurant
40 W. Broadway, Tucson, AZ 85701 (602) 791-7458

Mexican. Located in the historic Charles O. Brown House, one of Tucson's oldest structures, El Adobe features Sonoran style "heart-healthy Mexican food." Butter, lard, MSG, and sulfites are never used. All of the traditional Mexican dishes include beans or vegetable fillings as options. **Full service, vegan options, iced cappuccino, non-alc. beer, wine/beer/alcohol, take-out, VISA/MC/AMX/ DISC/DC, $$**

Good Earth Restaurant & Bakery
6366 E. Broadway, Tucson, AZ 85710 (602) 745-6600

American. The restaurant features an extensive menu offering pasta and vegetarian entrees as well as soups, salads, sandwiches, entrees, and desserts. Breads, pastries, and desserts are baked on the premises. Premium wine and beer are served by the glass. **Open daily for breakfast, lunch, and dinner. Full service, fresh juices, espresso/cappuccino, wine/beer, take-out, no credit cards, $$**

La Indita
622 N. 4th Ave., Tucson, AZ 85705 (602) 792-0523

8578 E. Broadway, Tucson, AZ 85701 (602) 886-9191

Mexican. "La Indita," an affectionate term for a little female Indian in Spanish, features the unique recipes of its own "little Indian woman," Maria Garcia, a Tarascan Indian from Michoacan, Mexico. The restaurant offers a mixture of traditional Mexican food, popular Indian fry breads, and Maria Garcia's own family recipes. No lard is used and vegetarian items are indicated on the menu. Outdoor patio at 4th Ave. location. **Open daily. Full service, vegan options, fresh juices, wine/beer, take-out, $**

Selamat Makan Restaurant
3502 E. Grant Rd., Tucson, AZ 85716 (602) 325-6755

Malaysian. Vegetarian dishes are available. **Full service, wine/beer, take-out, VISA/MC/AMX/DISC, $$**

➤ Reviewer's choice   ● Vegetarian restaurant   ●● Vegan restaurant
$ less than $6 $$ $6–$12 $$$ more than $12
VISA/AMX/MC/DISC/DC—credit cards accepted
Non-alc.–Non-alcoholic   Fresh juices—freshly squeezed

ARKANSAS

Dairy Hollow House
515 Spring St., Eureka Springs, AR 72632   **(501) 253-7444**
Natural foods. This is an award-winning country inn and restaurant. Seven nights a week from April 1 through December 31 and on weekends during February and March, dinner is served at one seating, 7 P.M. The vegetarian owners make sure the soups are vegetarian, and there is always at least one vegetarian selection for the main course. They are willing to accommodate vegans with notice. **Reservations required. Formal, full service, VISA/MC/AMX/DISC/DC/Carte Blanche, $$$**

Beans, Grains, & Things
300 S. Rodney Parham Rd., Little Rock, AR 72205   **(501) 221-2331**
Natural foods deli. This deli is located in a health food store. **Open daily. Self-service, VISA/MC, $**

CALIFORNIA

Alisan Restaurant
115 W. Katella Ave., Anaheim, CA 92802   **(714) 772-4160**
Mandarin/Taiwanese. Specializing in unique and interesting vegetarian dishes, Alisan has a menu that lists more than twenty-five vegetarian items on the back page. Included are many tofu dishes, mushroom creations, and noodle entrees. No MSG or eggs are used. Alisan Restaurant is within walking distance of both Disneyland and the Anaheim Convention Center. **Open daily. Dinner served only on Sundays. Full service, vegan options, wine/beer, take-out, $$**

•• Gourmet Vegetarian
1314 S. Magnolia Ave., Anaheim, CA 92804   **(714) 827-8867**
Vegan. Gourmet Vegetarian offers a vegan buffet in addition to a completely vegan menu. Specializing in home cooking, the restaurant does not use MSG or preservatives in the food. Vegan foods are sold in a grocery. **Open daily; dinner served only on Sundays. Full service, completely vegan, catering, take-out, $**

The Greenery Natural Kitchen
323 So. Magnolia Ave., Anaheim, CA 92804   **(714) 761-8103**
Natural foods. The Greenery features lacto-vegetarian dishes. **Full service, take-out, $–$$**

Sitar Indian Restaurant
2632 W. La Palma Ave., Anaheim, CA 92801   **(714) 821-8333**
Indian. More than ten vegetarian entrees are offered. **Open daily for lunch and dinner. Full service, vegan options, wine/beer/alcohol, take-out, VISA/MC/ AMX, $$**

ARCATA

Casa de Que Pasa
854 9th St., Arcata, CA 95521   **(707) 822-3441**
Mexican. Heart-healthy dishes that are approved by the American Heart Association are clearly indicated on the menu. Vegetarian soups and other vegetarian Mexican dishes are available. "Vegerito" is a featured item—a whole-wheat flour tortilla filled with beans (vegetarian), broccoli, mushrooms, zucchini, tofu, sunflower seeds, walnuts, and sesame seeds in a tomato sauce, topped with guacamole, cheese (optional), and salsa. **Almost always open for lunch and dinner. Limited service, vegan options, wine/beer, local beers on tap, take-out, $–$$**

Spoons Take-Out Kitchen
Arcata Co-op, 811 I St., Arcata, CA 95521   **(707) 822-5947**
Natural foods deli. Spoons is a deli-style kitchen in a natural foods co-op supermarket. Ethnic foods, salads, and entrees are offered, most of which are meatless. Locally grown organic foods are used in preparation whenever possible. **Deli style, vegan options, fresh juices, wine/beer in store, take-out, $**

• The Tofu Shop
768 18th St., Arcata, CA 95521   **(707) 822-7409**
Vegetarian. Arcata's Tofu Shop is modeled after the traditional neighborhood tofu shops in Japan. Fresh tofu is made daily, and a wide variety of tofu entrees, salads, and desserts are offered on the menu. Organic and locally produced ingredients are used when possible. **Open daily. Closed on major holidays. Cafeteria style, vegan options, take-out, $**

• Wildflower Cafe and Bakery
1604 G St., Arcata, CA 95521   **(707) 822-0360**
Macrobiotic/vegetarian. Wildflower features gourmet vegetarian and macrobiotic foods, using local organic fruits and vegetables when possible. The fresh baked breads and sweets are excellent. Families are welcome. **Open Monday through Saturday for breakfast, lunch, and dinner; Sundays from 10 A.M. to 2 P.M. Full service, vegan/macrobiotic options, fresh juice, catering, no credit cards, $**

AUBURN

Latitudes
130 Maple St. #11, Auburn, CA 95603   **(916) 885-9535**
Natural foods. Offering multicultural cuisine with an excellent vegetarian selection, Latitudes has a tropical decor with indoor and outdoor dining. It features an extensive micro-brewery and California wine selection. Families are welcome. **Lunch Monday through Friday, dinner Monday and Thursday through Saturday, brunch Sunday. Full service, vegan options, fresh juice, catering, take-out, VISA/MC/AMX, lunch/brunch—$$, dinner—$$$**

BERKELEY

Blue Nile
2525 Telegraph Ave., Berkeley, CA 94704   **(510) 540-6777**
Ethiopian. The Blue Nile of Berkeley serves authentic Ethiopian cuisine in a warm and inviting environment. Vegetarian dishes are clearly indicated and described. **Open daily. Full service, vegan options, wine/beer, take-out, VISA/ MC, $–$$**

Brick Hut
3222 Adeline, Berkeley, CA 94703   **(510) 658-5555**
Natural foods. Waffles, omelettes, tofu burgers, chili, and salads are featured. **Open daily for breakfast and lunch. Full service, take-out, $$**

Cafe Intermezzo
2442 Telegraph Ave., Berkeley, CA 94704   **(510) 849-4592**
Natural foods. This restaurant serves mostly vegetarian food. Soups, salads, and sandwiches are featured. **Open daily. Full service, fresh juices, wine/beer, take- out, $**

Elmwood Natural Foods
2944 College Ave., Berkeley, CA 94705   **(510) 841-3871**
Natural foods deli. This organic grocery offers soup, sandwiches, and take-out macrobiotic meals. Non-dairy, whole-grain desserts and baked goods made without refined sugar are also available. **Open daily. Counter service, macrobiotic, take-out, VISA/MC, $**

• Govinda's
2334 Stuart St., Berkeley, CA 94705   **(510) 644-2777**
Vegetarian. Govinda's offers a vegetarian all-you-can-eat buffet. **Closed Sunday and Monday. $**

Long Life Vegi House
2129 University Ave., Berkeley, CA 94704   **(510) 845-6072**
Chinese. The Vegi House menu has more than forty vegetarian entrees including mock chicken, beef and pork, tofu and vegetarian soups, and appetizers such as Pot Stickers or Fresh Garlic Seaweed Salad. Even the pickiest eaters should find something they like here! Upon request, no MSG is used. **Open daily. Full service, vegan options, wine/beer, catering, take-out, VISA/MC, $$**

Maharani
1025 University Ave., Berkeley, CA 94710   **(510) 848-7777**
Indian. This Indian restaurant has an extensive vegetarian menu. **Open daily. Full service, vegan options, wine/beer, take-out, VISA/MC/AMX/DISC, $$**

Petrouchka
2930 College Ave., Berkeley, CA 94705   **(510) 848-7860**
Russian. Vegetarian options are available. **Full service, wine/beer, take-out, VISA/MC, $$$**

• Smokey Joe's Cafe
1620 Shattuck, Berkeley, CA 94709 **(510) 548-4616**
Vegetarian. Vegetarian fast food includes Falafel and Hash Browns. **Open daily. $**

Vasiliki Restaurant & Bakery
2175 Allston Way, Berkeley, CA 94704 **(510) 649-1160**
Greek/American. A salad bar with more than fifty items is augmented by pasta, Greek specialties, fresh baked breads, and fresh juices. **Open daily. Full service, fresh juices, espresso, wine/beer, VISA/MC/AMX/DISC, $$**

• Vegi Food, Inc.
2083 Vine St., Berkeley, CA 94709 **(510) 548-5244**
Vegetarian. **Open daily, Mondays for dinner only. Full service, $**

Whole Foods Market
3000 Telegraph Ave., Berkeley, CA 94705 **(510) 649-1333**
Natural foods deli. **Cafeteria style, fresh juice, take-out, VISA/MC, $–$$**

BEVERLY HILLS

• Akasha's Vegetarian Cuisine
9348 Civic Center Dr., Ste. 101, Beverly Hills, CA 90210 **(310) 201-0429**
Vegetarian catering. This vegetarian delivery service uses only fresh ingredients. Foods are delivered to home or office for individuals, private parties, or conventions. **Monday, Wednesday, Friday delivery. Delivery only, vegan options, $$**

•• Orean . . . The Health Express
9667 1/2 Wilshire Blvd., Beverly Hills, CA 90212 **(310) 247-1819**
Vegan. The menu at Orean's proclaims it "The First Vegetarian Fast Food Take-out." This vegan establishment prepares dishes without eggs, milk, cheese, or refined sugar. Veggie Burgers, Pizza, Chili, and Mexican dishes make up this fast-food menu. On weekends, Orean is an open coffeehouse with stand-up comedians and music. Patio seating. **Cafeteria style, completely vegan, take-out, $**

•• Vegé Gourmet
231 N. Beverly Dr., Beverly Hills, CA 90210 **(310) 276-1400**
Vegan. The gourmet vegan cuisine includes international creations. Add Veggie Burgers and more classic dishes such as Chili and Lasagna and deciding what to order becomes a challenge. Desserts, smoothies, and fresh juices tempt your sweet tooth. No artifical ingredients, processed sugar, or salt is used. **Open daily. Completely vegan, take-out, VISA/MC, $$**

BRENTWOOD

A Votre Santé
13016 San Vicente, Brentwood, CA 90049 **(310) 451-1813**
Natural foods. Salads, pasta, and Mediterranean cuisine are featured. **Full service, vegan options, fresh juices, wine/beer, take-out, VISA/MC/AMX, $$**

BURLINGAME

•• Sebastian's Takeoutrageous
1207 Capuchino Ave., Burlingame, CA 94010   **(415) 348-8015**
Vegan. You can dine on pasta, soups, salads, Veggie Burgers, burritos, and more.
Closed Sunday. Counter service, vegan, fresh juices, take-out, $

CALISTOGA

• Seed Time & Harvest Restaurant & Bakery
1226 Washington St., Calistoga, CA 94515   **(707) 942-5512**
Vegetarian. Foods are primarily vegan but some breakfast dishes use eggs and many
items include soy cheese that may contain dairy derivatives. The fresh ground-
wheat breads, many cakes, cookies, and muffins are made without dairy, refined
sugar, or oil. Outdoor dining in courtyard. **Open for breakfast, lunch, and dinner
Sunday through Friday; closed Saturday. Full service, vegan options, fresh juices,
take-out, $$**

CAMPBELL

Bread of Life
1690 S. Bascom Ave., Campbell, CA 95008   **(408) 371-5000**
Health-food-store deli. Bread of Life offers a salad bar with more than forty items
including sushi, quiche, and cakes. Also available are more than thirty salads,
twenty desserts, and twenty sandwiches. **Limited service, fresh juices, take-out,
VISA/MC/DISC, $**

Royal Taj India Cuisine
1350 Camden Ave., Campbell, CA 95008   **(408) 559-6801**
Indian. Thirteen vegetarian specialties are available at this restaurant offering
authentic Indian cuisine at five locations. Pakora, samosa, Dahl Soup, salads, and
many Indian breads are also on the menu. **Open daily for lunch and dinner. Full
service, vegan options, wine/beer, take-out, VISA/MC/AMX/DISC, $**

CANOGA PARK

• Follow Your Heart
21825 Sherman Way, Canoga Park, CA 91303   **(818) 348-3240**
Vegetarian. This classic vegetarian restaurant offers an excellent selection of
natural foods—salads, sandwiches, entrees with vegetarian (rennet-free) cheese,
tofu dishes, and other vegetarian favorites. The beverages consist of juices, teas,
raw milk, and shakes. The full breakfast menu, weekend brunch, and all dishes are
vegetarian without eggs, sugar, or harmful additives. Heart-healthy items are
indicated on the menu. **Open for three meals daily. Full service, vegan options,
fresh juices, organic coffee, BYOB, take-out, VISA/MC, $$**

⇘ Reviewers' choice   • Vegetarian restaurant   •• Vegan restaurant
$ less than $6 $$ $6–$12 $$$ more than $12
VISA/AMX/MC/DISC/DC—credit cards accepted
Non-alc.—Non-alcoholic   Fresh juices—freshly squeezed

CAPITOLA

Book Cafe
1475 41st Ave., Capitola, CA 95010 **(408) 462-4415**
Natural foods. The Book Cafe features Lasagna, soups, deli salads, and pastries. **Closed Sunday. Counter service, $**

• Dharma's Restaurant
4250 Capitola Rd., Capitola, CA 95010 **(408) 462-1717**
Vegetarian. A smiling cow wearing dark sunglasses graces the front of Dharma's menu. This is followed by statistics on the number of rainforest acres and cows saved by eating Dharma's vegetarian burgers. No bull! A serious mission with a sense of humor and excellent food is a combination worth exploring. Dharma's offers a wide range of international vegetarian dishes including Mexican, Italian, Chinese, Japanese, and Thai in addition to the old American stand-bys, great muffins, and desserts. The majority of the foods are organic. **Open for three meals daily. Cafeteria style, limited service, many vegan options, fresh juices, espresso, wine/beer, take-out, $**

CARMEL

Royal Taj India Cuisine
230 Crossroads Blvd., Carmel, CA 93923 **(408) 624-9110**
Indian. See entry under Campbell, CA.

CERRITOS

• Madhu's Dasaprakash
11321 E. 183rd St., Cerritos, CA 90701 **(310) 924-0879**
Vegetarian/Indian. South Indian vegetarian cuisine is featured at this all-vegetarian restaurant. The usual vegetarian Indian dishes are available, such as samosas, pakodas, and poories, and there are many more unique dishes featuring crêpes and stuffed patties. **Closed on Monday. Full service, vegan options, wine/beer, take-out, VISA/MC, $**

CHICO

• Cafe Sandino
817 Main St., Chico, CA 95928 **(916) 894-6515**
Vegetarian. Home of "Today's Tomales," Cafe Sandino is a vegetarian restaurant that strives to use organically grown ingredients, and uses unrefined canola and olive oils. **Lunch Monday through Saturday, dinner Wednesday through Saturday. Full service, vegan options, organic juice, organic coffee, wine/beer, take-out, $–$$**

CORONADO

Stretch's Coronado Cafe
943 Orange Ave., Coronado, CA 92118 **(619) 435-8886**
Natural foods. Stretch's takes pride in the quality of the food and the variety offered to both vegetarians and non-vegetarians. All food is prepared fresh daily. **Self-serve, fresh juices, wine, take-out, $**

Tiffiny's Deli-Juice Bar
1120 Adella Ave., Coronado, CA 92118   **(619) 437-1368**
Natural foods. Amidst old-fashioned decor, this deli-juice bar offers sandwiches and smoothies. Open daily for breakfast, lunch, and dinner. **Counter service, vegan options, beer/wine, catering, take-out, VISA/MC, $**

CORTE MADERA

Moondoggies
119 Town Center Dr., Corte Madera, CA 92626   **(415) 924-6261**
Fast foods. Moondoggies features Veggie Burgers. **Open daily. Counter service, vegan options, take-out, $**

COSTA MESA

Forty Carrots
South Coast Plaza Mall, Bristol at 405
Costa Mesa, CA 92626   **(714) 556-9700**
Natural foods. Forty Carrots serves pasta, Mexican foods, soups, and salad. **Open daily. Full service, wine/beer, VISA/MC/AMX, $$**

Mother's Market & Kitchen
225 E. 17th St., Costa Mesa, CA 92627   **(714) 631-4741**
Natural foods. Mother's has a vegetarian menu except for tuna. Centrally located within the natural foods store, the restaurant offers a wide assortment of delicious appetizers, salads, entrees, pastas, sandwiches, and ethnic and side dishes. A children's menu is available. **Full service, fresh juices, non-alc. wine/beer, take-out, $**

COTATI

Markey's Cafe & Coffee House
8240 Old Redwood Hwy., Cotati, CA 94931-5208   **(707) 795-7868**
Natural foods cafe/bakery. The majority of the menu items are vegetarian and include sandwiches, tempeh burgers, soups, salads, entrees, smoothies, and desserts. **Open daily. Cafeteria style, vegan options, cappuccino/espresso, wine/beer, VISA/MC, $**

CULVER CITY

• Govinda's Restaurant
9624 Venice Blvd., Culver City, CA 90230   **(213) 836-1269**
Vegetarian. Govinda's features international dishes and a la carte items. **Closed on Sundays. Limited service, vegan options, take-out, VISA/MC, $$**

CUPERTINO

Bread of Life
10983 N. Wolfe Rd., Cupertino, CA 95014   **(408) 257-7000**
Health-food-store deli. See entry under Campbell, CA.

The Good Earth
20807 Stevens Creek Blvd., Cupertino, CA 95014   **(408) 252-3555**

Natural foods. Enjoy wok dishes, Vegetarian Scramble, Tofu Scramble, Vegetarian Burger, burritos, tostadas, Eggplant Sandwich, salads, Pasta Primavera, Walnut Mushroom Au Gratin, Guatamalan Rice and Tofu. **Open daily. Full service, wine/beer, VISA/MC/AMX, $$**

Hobee's Restaurant
21267 Stevens Creek Blvd., Cupertino, CA 95014   (408) 255-6010
Restaurant chain. Mexican favorites, Veggie Patty, Black Bean Chili, and a salad bar make up the vegetarian options at Hobee's. **Open daily. Full service, fresh juices, wine/beer, take-out, VISA/MC, $$**

DAVIS

• The Blue Mango
330 G St., Davis, CA 95616   (916) 756-2616
Vegetarian. A cooperatively run restaurant, Blue Mango features burritos, tostadas, sandwiches, salads, and Indian entrees. Enjoy indoor and outdoor seating, and live entertainment. **Full service, vegan options, $**

DEL MAR

•• Garden Taste
1555 Camino Del Mar #101A, Del Mar Plaza, Del Mar, CA 92014   (619) 793-1500
Vegan. All organic, this restaurant offers raw soups, sprouted salads, non-wheat, non-dairy pizza, and sprouted veggie burgers. No oil, sugar, or salt is used. **Open daily, full service, completely vegan, fresh juices, take-out, $**

Souplantation/Sweet Tomatoes
Corporate offices in Del Mar, CA 92014   (619) 792-0713
Restaurant chain. An extensive salad bar includes fresh bakery items, a vegetarian soup option, fresh fruits, and desserts. There are twenty-six locations in Northern California. **Closed Sunday. Buffet style, take-out, $–$$**

DUNCAN MILLS

The Blue Heron
1 Steelhead Blvd., Duncan Mills, CA 95430   (707) 865-2269
Ethnic foods. Ethnic dishes, salads, and pasta dishes are featured. **Open daily in summer. Hours vary in winter. Wine/beer/alcohol, take-out, VISA/MC, $$$**

EL CAJON

• L'Chaim Vegetarian Cafe
134 W. Douglas Ave., El Cajon, CA 92020   (619) 442-1331

Reviewers' choice   • Vegetarian restaurant   •• Vegan restaurant
$ less than $6 $$ $6–$12 $$$ more than $12
VISA/AMX/MC/DISC/DC—credit cards accepted
Non-alc.–Non-alcoholic   Fresh juices—freshly squeezed

Vegetarian. "Wonderful vegan selections and great soups, salads and carrot juice," writes one local patron. You might have to search a little for L'Chaim as it is difficult to find. It faces on an alley instead of the street. **Full service, vegan/macrobiotic options, fresh juice, $$**

EMERYVILLE

Hobee's Restaurant
5765 Christie Ave., Emeryville, CA 95608   **(415) 652-5944**
Restaurant chain. See entry under Cupertino, CA.

ENCINITAS

Colors Cafe
745 First St., Encinitas, CA 92024   **(619) 944-1447**
Natural foods. Located on the old coast highway, this casual, up-scale restaurant features organic salads and juices. Vegetarian and non-dairy menu items are clearly marked. Vegan appetizers are served. Inside and patio dining. **Full service, fresh juices, wine/beer, take-out, VISA/MC/AMX/DISC/DC, $$**

• Fountain of Juice
1163 First St., Encinitas, CA 92024   **(619) 944-0612**
Vegetarian. This vegetarian restaurant offers a wide variety of entrees including Curried Vegetables, Black Bean Burritos, and mock meat dishes. Open daily. **Counter service, vegan options, espresso/cappuccino, smoothies, catering, take-out, $**

• Roxy Restaurant and Ice Cream
517 First St., Encinitas, CA 92024   **(619) 436-5001**
Vegetarian. International dishes are featured. **Open daily. Full service, take-out, fresh juices, wine/beer/alcohol, VISA/MC/AMX/DISC, $$**

Star of India Restaurant
927 First St., Encinitas, CA 92024   **(619) 632-1113**
Indian. Rated among the top ten restaurants in San Diego, Star of India features a large vegetarian selection. **Open daily for lunch and dinner. Full service, wine/beer/alcohol, catering, take-out, VISA/MC/AMX/DISC/DC, $$**

EUREKA

• East West Center
1122 M St., Eureka, CA 95501   **(707) 445-2290**
Vegetarian. On Thursday nights only, Meredith McCarty, author of *Innovative Gourmet Macrobiotic*, runs a wonderful four- to six-course feast including fresh market produce, organic grains and beans, and great desserts. Reservations are required by Wednesday; call weekdays from 10 A.M. to 4 P.M. **Open Thursday only. Reservations required. Limited service, macrobiotic options, $$**

Tomaso's Tomato Pies
216 E St., Eureka, CA 95501   **(707) 445-0100**

Italian. Tomaso's serves Spinach Pies, Spinzones, vegetarian soups, salads, Whole-Wheat Pizza, and various vegetarian entrees. **Full service, wine/beer, take-out, VISA/MC/AMX/DISC, $$**

Tomo Japanese Restaurant
2120 4th St., Eureka, CA 95501   **(707) 444-3318**

Japanese. Tomo serves Japanese country-style whole food, and traditional and non-fish sushi. Most entrees are available without meat. **Full service, wine/beer, macrobiotic, VISA/MC/DISC, $$**

FAIR OAKS

• Sunflower Natural Foods Drive In
10344 Fair Oaks Blvd., Fair Oaks, CA 95628   **(916) 967-4331**

Vegetarian. Vegetarian fast food—including burgers, burritos, Chili, and sandwiches—is made primarily on the premises with an emphasis on raw foods. Sunflower is adjacent to a park. **Open daily in summer. Closed Sunday and Monday in winter. Limited service, take-out, VISA/MC, $**

FOSTER CITY

Joy Restaurant
1495 Beach Park Blvd., Foster City, CA 94404   **(415) 345-1762**

Mandarin/Szechuan. Several statements on Joy's menu assure vegetarians they are welcome and encouraged to request any special vegetarian dish they would like. Any type of meatless "chicken" is available, and cooking without meat and eggs is not a problem here. Vegetarian appetizers, soup, and entrees are offered. **Open daily. Full service, vegan options, wine/beer, take-out, VISA/MC/AMX, $$**

FREMONT

Hobee's Restaurant
39222 Fremont Blvd., Fremont, CA 94538   **(510) 797-1244**

Restaurant chain. See entry under Cupertino, CA.

• Manju Farsan House
Freemont Shopping Center
40645 Fremont Blvd., Fremont, CA 94538   **(510) 656-2336**

Vegetarian/Indian. Indian vegetarian fast-food items are offered including samosas and many entrees. **Open daily for lunch and dinner. Full service, vegan options, catering, take-out, $**

FULLERTON

Rutabegorz
211 N. Pomona, Fullerton, CA 92632   **(714) 871-1632**

International. Specializing in homemade food, this bohemian-style coffeehouse has an extensive coffee menu as well as Veggie Burritos, pastas, Spinach Lasagna, Stuffed Mushrooms, etc. **Closed Sundays. Full service, vegan options, fresh juices, wine/beer/alcohol, $$**

GARBERVILLE

Woodrose Cafe
911 Redwood Dr., Garberville, CA 95440   **(707) 923-3191**
Natural foods. The many vegetarian options contain a lot of cheese and eggs. Organic and local ingredients are used. **Open for breakfast daily; open for lunch Monday through Friday. Full service, vegan options, fresh juices, non-alc. beer, wine/beer, take-out, $**

GARDEN GROVE

New Moon II Healthfood Store & Lunch Bar
12792 Valley View St. #D, Garden Grove, CA 92645   **(714) 893-0301**
Health-food-store deli. New Moon II offers soups, sandwiches, and non-dairy frozen desserts. Open for lunch daily. **Limited service, vegan options, take-out, VISA/ MC, $**

GLENDALE

• Glendale Adventist Medical Center
1509 Wilson Terrace, Glendale, CA 91206   **(818) 409-8090**
Vegetarian. **Open for three meals daily. Cafeteria style, take-out, $**

GOLETA

Good Earth
5955 Calle Real, Goleta, CA 93117   **(805) 683-6101**
Natural foods. This restaurant offers soups and salads, casseroles, stir-fries, and Mexican specialties. **Open daily for three meals. Full service, wine/beer, catering, take-out, VISA/MC/AMX/DISC, $$**

HALF MOON BAY

• Healing Moon Health Foods
523 Main St., Half Moon Bay, CA 94019   **(415) 726-7881**
Health-food-store deli. Entrees include soups, brown rice dishes, pasta, tofu, Veggie Burgers, and salads. All foods are organic, and soy cheese is used. **Open daily. Counter service, vegan options, take-out, $**

HARBOR CITY

Siam Clift Cuisine of Thailand
1605 W. Pacific Coast Hwy. #106, Harbor City, CA 90710   **(310) 325-0844**
Thai. Enjoy Thai curry, stir-fried entrees, and various specials in a beautiful dining room. Closed Sunday. **Full service, wine/beer, catering, take-out, VISA/MC/ AMX, $**

ɬ Reviewers' choice   • Vegetarian restaurant   •• Vegan restaurant
$ less than $6 $$ $6–$12 $$$ more than $12
VISA/AMX/MC/DISC/DC—credit cards accepted
Non-alc.—Non-alcoholic   Fresh juices—freshly squeezed

HERMOSA BEACH

• The Spot Natural Food Restaurant
110 Second St., Hermosa Beach, CA 90254 (310) 376-2355

Vegetarian. This friendly, "local" beach restaurant offers only vegetarian fare with many vegan items. Specialities include burritos, Veggie Burgers, and steamed vegetable plates ("Steamers") with tasty sauces. **Open daily. Full service, vegan options, fresh juices, wine/beer, take-out, $$**

HOLLYWOOD

Flowering Tree
8253 Santa Monica Blvd., W. Hollywood, CA 90046 (213) 654-4332

Natural foods. Flowering Tree features Veggie Burgers, Baked Sesame Tofu, and other delicious entrees. **Open late daily. Counter service, vegan options, non-alc. beer, take-out, $**

Gengis Cohen
740 N. Fairfax Ave., Hollywood, CA 90046 (213) 653-0640

Chinese. No MSG is used, but be sure to request no chicken broth. An acoustic music showroom is featured. **Open for lunch Monday through Friday, dinner daily. Full service, vegan options, wine/beer/alcohol, take-out, VISA/MC/ AMX/DC, $$**

• Parus Indian Vegetarian Restaurant
5140 Sunset Blvd., Hollywood, CA 90027 (213) 661-7600

Vegetarian/Indian. Most of the main dishes are non-dairy, corn oil is used for cooking, and exotic Indian beverages are available. A brunch special is offered on Saturday and Sunday. Patio service is available. **Full service, wine/beer, take-out, VISA/MC, $$**

The Source Restaurant & Sidewalk Cafe
8301 Sunset Blvd., W. Hollywood, CA 90069 (213) 656-6388

Natural foods. This is "the place to see and be seen" says *The Source.* The natural foods menu includes some gourmet vegetarian dishes such as Whole-Wheat Lasagna, Mother's Eggplant, and Cheese and Walnut Loaf. There is only one vegan entree on the menu, however. Sandwiches, appetizers, and salads make up the rest of the menu. Outdoor patio. **Breakfast served every day. Full service, fresh juices, espresso/cappuccino, take-out, VISA/MC/AMX/DC, $$**

HUNTINGTON BEACH

• Eight Immortals of Tao
8841 Adams Ave., Huntington Beach, CA 92646 (714) 965-8894

Vegetarian. Enjoy creative, unusual, and tasty vegetarian dishes including tofu, vegetables, and mock meat plus six appetizers and seven soups. **Open daily for lunch and dinner. Full service, vegan options, take-out, $–$$**

Mother's Market & Kitchen
19770 Beach Blvd., Huntington Beach, CA 92648 (714) 963-6667

Natural foods. See entry under Costa Mesa, California.

The Wok Chinese Restaurant
7572 Edinger Ave., Huntington Beach, CA 92648   (714) 842-5698
Mandarin/Szechuan Chinese. The Wok serves natural and fresh Chinese food without MSG. Vegetarian dishes are available. **Open daily. Full service, vegan options, wine/beer, take-out, VISA/MC, $**

IRVINE

Clay Oven
15435 Jeffrey Rd., Irvine, CA 92714   (714) 552-2851
Indian. Clay Oven, which takes a healthy approach to Indian cooking, offers nine vegetable entrees. **Full service, vegan options, wine/beer, VISA/MC/AMX/DISC, $$**

Harvest Restaurant & Bakery
4127 Campus Dr., Irvine, CA 92715   (714) 725-9184
Mexican/health foods. The menu includes appetizers, salads, dressings, entrees, hot and cold sandwiches, burgers, and desserts with many vegetarian options. Harvest, with five locations in Colorado, specializes in low-fat, low-cholesterol, low-salt items for breakfast, lunch, and dinner. Healthful items are indicated by the Healthmark (HM). **Open for three meals daily. Full service, vegan options, fresh juice, wine/beer, take-out, VISA/MC/AMX, $**

LA JOLLA

• Ché Café
**UCSD, 9500 Gilman Dr., Student Ctr., 0323-C
La Jolla, CA 92093   (619) 534-2311**
Vegetarian. This is a not-for-profit vegetarian collective on the UCSD campus. Ché Café serves mostly vegan foods. Live music shows are held most weekends. **Always open Wednesday; call for other times and information. Limited service, take-out, $**

Star of India Restaurant
1025 Prospect St. #100, La Jolla, CA 92037   (619) 459-3355
Indian. See entry under Encinitas, CA.

LAGUNA BEACH

• Cafe Zinc
350 Ocean Ave., Laguna Beach, CA 92651   (714) 494-6302
Vegetarian. Cafe Zinc offers salads, soups, mini- and full-sized pizzas. Indoor and outdoor seating are available. **Hours vary. Call for information. Counter service, wine/beer, take-out, $**

• Guaranga's
285 Legion St., Laguna Beach, CA 92651   (714) 497-9707
Vegetarian. If you're hungry, Guaranga's all-you-can-eat vegetarian buffet might be just what you need. The steam table includes two soups, brown and basmati rice, steamed veggies, pasta and sauce, mixed Indian-style veggies, and entrees that vary daily. Tuesday and Thursday entrees are vegan. No eggs are used. **Closed Sunday. Cafeteria style, vegan options, take-out, $**

•• The Downtown Stand
347 Mermaid St., Laguna Beach, CA 92651　　　　**(714) 494-9499**
Vegan. See next entry.

•• The Stand Natural Foods Restaurant
238 Thalia St., Laguna Beach, CA 92651　　　　**(714) 494-8101**
Vegan. If you're looking for a restaurant with a commitment to quality and excellent vegan food, then The Stand is for you. In business for more than twenty-one years, The Stand offers a wide selection of international salads, sandwiches, side orders, burritos, tamales, main dishes, and treats. All foods are vegan and made without refined sugar, salt, or artificial ingredients. **Open daily. Limited service, completely vegan, fresh juices, take-out, $**

LARKSPUR

•• Garden of Eatin' Cafe
474 Magnolia Ave., Larkspur, CA 94939　　　　**(415) 927-7611**
Vegan. Eden may be a ways from Larkspur, California, but the Garden of Eatin' does offer a bit of heaven for vegans and others who want healthful, high quality fast food in a charming environment. Located in a historic building in downtown Larkspur, the Garden offers sandwiches, veggie hot dogs, burgers, oil-free fries, salads, and rolls with some ethnic options. Customers can eat inside or outside on the patio in the herb and flower garden. No sugar, white flour, preservatives, or artificial ingredients are used; honey is used in some items. Organic goods are used when possible. **Open Monday through Saturday. Deli counter, vegan options, fresh juices, organic coffee, catering, take-out, $**

LOMA LINDA

• Loma Linda University Medical Center Cafeteria
Anderson and Barton Rds., Loma Linda, CA 92354　　　**(714) 824-4365**
Vegetarian. The cafeteria offers soups, salads, casseroles, and mock meat dishes. **Open daily. Cafeteria service, vegan options, take-out, $**

LOS ANGELES

(For restaurant listings in the surrounding areas, see Anaheim, Beverly Hills, Brentwood, Canoga Park, Costa Mesa, Culver City, Fullerton, Garden Grove, Glendale, Harbor City, Hermosa Beach, Hollywood, Huntington Beach, Irvine, Laguna Beach, Marina Del Rey, Monterey Park, Newport Beach, Northridge, Norwalk, Orange, Pasadena, Redondo Beach, Riverside, Rosemead, Santa Ana, Santa Monica, Sherman Oaks, South Pasadena, Studio City, Tarzana, Topanga Canyon, Tustin, Venice, Ventura, and Westlake Village.)

A Votre Santé
345 N. LaBrea, Los Angeles, CA 90036　　　　**(213) 857-0412**
Natural foods. See entry under Brentwood, CA.

Artful Balance
525$^1/_2$ N. Fairfax Ave., Los Angeles, CA 90036   **(213) 852-9091**
Natural foods. Specials that change daily are offered in a comfortable atmosphere. Vegetarian options are available. **Open Tuesday through Saturday. Full service, VISA/MC, take-out, $$**

Beverly Hills Juice Club
8382 Beverly Blvd., Los Angeles, CA 90048   **(213) 655-8300**
Juice bar. Enjoy fresh juices and some foods prepared from local organic produce. Shakes and wheatgrass are made to order. Tahini, Sauerkraut, Hummus, sushi, Applesauce, Dairy-free Ice Cream, and other treats are prepared on the premises. **Open Monday through Saturday. Fresh juices, take-out only, $**

• The Bodhi Garden Vegetarian Restaurant
1498 Sunset Blvd. #2, Los Angeles, CA 90026   **(213) 250-9023**
Vegetarian/Chinese. Many appetizers, lunch specials, soups, and entrees are offered. **Closed Tuesday. Full service, vegan options, take-out, $**

• Country Life Vegetarian Buffet
888 S. Figueroa St., Los Angeles, CA 90017   **(213) 489-4118**
Vegetarian. International vegetarian cuisine is offered in a contemporary setting with a pleasant atmosphere. The buffet is composed of creative entrees that rotate daily, including Nutty Tofu Croquettes and Vegetable Pocket Quiches. There are also desserts and home-baked goods such as Tofu Cheesecake, and a full salad and fruit bar. **Open for lunch Monday through Friday. Buffet, vegan options, fresh juices, catering, take-out, $**

Don's Fountain of Health
3606 W. 6th St., Los Angeles, CA 90020   **(213) 387-6621**
Natural foods. Sample the Veggie Burgers, Chili, freshly squeezed juices, and cakes and cookies made on the premises. **Open daily. Full service, fresh juices, catering, take-out, $**

Erewhon Foods Deli
7660 Beverly Blvd., Los Angeles, CA 90048   **(213) 937-0777**
Health-food-store deli. The menu features Stir-Fried Veggies, Steamed Veggies, Millet Loaf, lentil dishes, and Spinach Lasagna. **Open daily. Counter service, VISA/MC, $$**

• Fragrant Vegetable
11859 Wilshire Blvd., Los Angeles, CA 90025   **(310) 312-1442**
Vegetarian/Chinese. Mock meat, mock poultry, and mock fish dishes made with tofu and wheat gluten are featured. **Open daily. Full service, reservations recommended, vegan options, wine/beer, take-out, VISA/MC/AMX, $$**

ᴎ Reviewers' choice   • Vegetarian restaurant   •• Vegan restaurant
$ less than $6 $$ $6–$12 $$$ more than $12
VISA/AMX/MC/DISC/DC—credit cards accepted
Non-alc.—Non-alcoholic   Fresh juices—freshly squeezed

The Good Earth
11819 Wilshire Blvd., Los Angeles, CA 90025   **(310) 479-0177**
Natural foods. This restaurant offers Vegetarian Lasagna, stir-fries, Tofu Burgers, soups, and salads. **Open daily. Full service, wine/beer, take-out, VISA/MC/ AMX/DISC, $$**

• Govinda's
9624 Venice Blvd., Los Angeles, CA 90232   **(310) 836-1269**
Vegetarian. Govinda's specializes in natural foods, featuring a variety of ethnic cuisines. Dairy products are used, but no eggs. **Closed on Sunday. Full service, catering, take-out, VISA/MC, $**

•• I Love Juicy
7174 Melrose Ave., Los Angeles, CA 90025   **(213) 935-7247**
Vegan juice bar. This is more than just a juice bar. Fresh soups, appetizers, salads, sandwiches, and quite a few entrees are available. **Open daily. Counter service, vegan, fresh juices, take-out, $$**

Inaka Natural Foods Restaurant
131 S. La Brea Ave., Los Angeles, CA 90036   **(213) 936-9353**
Macrobiotic/natural foods. No eggs or dairy products are used, and foods are vegetarian except for some fish plates. Brown rice and different beans are featured with vegetables. **Closed Sunday; open for dinner Monday through Saturday and for lunch Monday through Friday. Full service, vegan options, take-out, $$**

India's Cuisine
5947 W. Pico Blvd., Los Angeles, CA 90035   **(213) 936-2050**
Indian. Fresh clay-oven-baked breads are the specialty here. India's Cuisine has a vegetarian section on the menu plus vegetarian appetizers such as samosas and Onion Balls. **Open daily. Full service, vegan options, wine/beer, take-out, VISA/ MC, $**

Kukatonor African Restaurant
2616 Crenshaw Blvd., Los Angeles, CA 90016   **(213) 733-3171**
African/American. At Kukatonor (meaning "We are one"), African masks, plants, and the echoing drums of African music provide an authentic atmosphere in which to sample African cuisine. Kukatonor offers a good range of unique, tasty, and filling vegetarian foods that are traditional Liberian dishes. A local member recommends the "Fufu," a dumpling-like staple, with Palava Sauce or Groundnut Stew. **Open daily. Full service, vegan options, fresh juices, wine/beer, take-out, VISA/MC, $$**

• Mani's Bakery
519 S. Fairfax Ave., Los Angeles, CA 90036   **(213) 938-8800**
Vegetarian bakery/coffeehouse. Try Mani's Bakery for after-dinner treats such as turnovers, deep dish pies, and truffles. **Open late daily. Counter service, take-out, VISA/MC/AMX/DISC, $**

Mother Earth Restaurant
11277 National Blvd., Los Angeles, CA 90064   **(213) 477-0555**

Natural foods. Ten vegetarian entrees are listed on Mother Earth's menu. The vegan options include Fried Tofu, Steamed Vegetable and Brown Rice Platter, and Stuffed Cabbage Rolls with Vegetables. No preservatives, added sugar, or salt is used. **Open for lunch and dinner every day except Sunday. Full service, vegan options, fresh juices, wine/beer/alcohol, take-out, VISA/MC, $–$$**

• Naturally Fast
11661 Santa Monica Blvd., Los Angeles, CA 90025   (310) 444-7886
Vegetarian. This natural fast-food restaurant features inexpensive soups, salads, baked potatoes, sandwiches, burgers, hot entrees, daily vegan specials, and desserts without eggs or sugar. **Open daily. Full service, vegan options, take-out, $**

• Nora's
9340 W. Pico Blvd., W. Los Angeles, CA 90035   (310) 273-8088
Vegetarian/Indian. Try the Masala Dosa (an Indian crêpe filled with potato curry) or sample other dishes that range from mildly spicy to extra hot per the customer's request. **Closed Monday. Full service, fresh juices, take-out, VISA/MC, $$**

Nowhere Cafe
8009 Beverly Blvd., Los Angeles, CA 90048   (213) 655-8895
Gourmet natural foods. With its gourmet natural cuisine, Nowhere will take your taste buds where they've never been before. Next door to the Nowhere natural foods market, the cafe takes extra measures to utilize fresh, organic produce in its dishes, which are often free from fats, oils, preservatives, sugar, and dairy products. Nowhere caters to special diets. **Open daily. Full service, vegan options, fresh juices, espresso/cappuccino, wine/beer, catering, take-out, VISA/MC/AMX/DISC, $$**

Osteria Romana Orsini
9575 W. Pico Blvd., Los Angeles, CA 90035   (310) 277-6050
Italian. Osteria features a large selection of meatless items. **Open Monday through Saturday for lunch and dinner. Closed Sunday. Full service, wine/beer/alcohol, take-out, VISA/MC/AMX, $$–$$$**

La Salsa
Corporate office   (213) 857- 1275 or (800) La Salsa
Restaurant chain. This Mexican food restaurant chain has many locations throughout California and gladly accommodates vegetarian requests. Call for locations. **Open daily. Full service, take-out, $**

•• Shantis Vegetarian
6382 Hollywood Blvd., Los Angeles, CA 90028   (213) 462-8624
Vegan/Indian. Shantis is totally vegan except for one item. **Open daily. Full service, vegan, take-out, $–$$**

Shekarchi Restaurant
1712 Westwood Blvd., Los Angeles, CA 90024   (310) 474-6911
Persian. Several vegetarian plates are featured. **Open daily. Full service, catering, take-out, VISA/MC/AMX, $$**

La Toque
8171 Sunset Blvd., Los Angeles, CA 90046 **(213) 656-7515**
French. Fine dining at this French restaurant always includes vegetarian options. The menu changes daily, and reservations are required. **Full service, fresh juices, non-alc. beverages, wine/beer/alcohol, VISA/MC/AMX, $$$**

Tulipe
8360 Melrose Ave., Los Angeles, CA 90069 **(213) 655-7400**
French. Imaginative classic and regional dishes are offered in an elegant setting. **Open for lunch and dinner Monday through Saturday, only for dinner on Sunday. Full service, wine/beer, catering, take-out, VISA/MC/AMX, $$$**

White Memorial Medical Center Cafeteria
1720 Brooklyn Ave., Los Angeles, CA 90025 **(213) 268-5000 x 1318**
Hospital cafeteria. This cafeteria is in a Seventh-day Adventist hospital. **Open daily. Cafeteria style, take-out, $$**

LOS GATOS

• Richard's Natural Foods
111 E. Main St., Los Gatos, CA 95032 **(408) 354-0588**
Vegetarian health-food-store deli. Enjoy soups, an organic salad bar, and dairyless cakes and pies. **Closed Sunday. Counter service, take-out, VISA/MC, $**

Rooh's Cafe Salsa
New Town Center, 15525 Los Gatos Blvd.
Los Gatos, CA 95032 **(408) 358-ROOH**
Mexican/restaurant chain. Entrees include Enchilada de Rooh's featuring lentils, and pancake pizzas. Rooh's uses no lard, no sugar, no preservatives, and no MSG. Nutritional fact sheets about the food are available. **Open daily. Limited service, take-out, VISA/MC, $**

MARINA DEL REY

Akbar Cuisine of India
590 Washington Blvd., Marina Del Rey, CA 90292 **(310) 822-4116**
Indian. Akbar serves authentic Indian cuisine. **Open for dinner daily, for lunch Monday through Friday, and for brunch on Sunday. Full service, wine/beer/alcohol, catering, take-out, VISA/MC/AMX/DISC, $$**

MENLO PARK

Flea Street Cafe
3607 Alameda de la Pulgas, Menlo Park, CA 94025 **(415) 854-1226**
Natural foods. The chef at this very fancy and formal restaurant will improvise to accommodate vegans. Organic produce is used. **Open daily for lunch and dinner, weekends for brunch. Full service, vegan options, wine/beer, take-out, VISA/MC, $$$**

Fresh Choice
600 Santa Cruz Cove, Menlo Park, CA 94025   (415) 323-4061
American. The salad selection is extensive and there is always one vegetarian soup and usually at least one vegetarian pasta. Fixed price includes everything including bread and dessert. **Open daily. Cafeteria style, wine/beer, VISA/MC, $$**

Late for the Train
150 Middlefield Rd., Menlo Park, CA 94025   (415) 321-6124
Natural foods. This country-style restaurant prepares food to order, and serves meals in the "wholest form possible." Produce is organic when available. Chemicals, preservatives, and artificial coloring are not added. Most of the vegetarian dishes include dairy. There's a full breakfast menu. **Open daily but hours vary. Full service, espresso/cappuccino, wine/beer, take-out, VISA/MC, $$**

• Peninsula Macrobiotic Community
St. Bede's Church, 2650 Sandhill St.
Menlo Park, CA 94025   (415) 599-3320
Macrobiotic/vegetarian. A full-course dinner—even dessert— is served every Monday evening. After-dinner speakers are often featured. The gourmet macrobiotic and dairy-free meals include many organic ingredients. Dine with the friendly macro folks or take dinner with you. **Monday only. Reservations encouraged. Limited service with one menu, take-out, $$**

MONTEREY

Amarin Thai Cuisine
807 Cannery Row, Monterey, CA 93942   (408) 373-8811
Thai. Enjoy authentic Thai cuisine in an informal Thai atmosphere. Tofu can be substituted for the meat in any dish. **Open daily for lunch and dinner. Full service, wine/beer, take-out, VISA/MC/AMX/DISC, $$**

MONTEREY PARK

• Merit Grove Vegetarian Restaurant
206 S. Garfield Ave., Monterey Park, CA 91754   (818) 280-7430
Vegetarian/Chinese. Don't be fooled by the meat dishes listed on the menu. It's all soy protein. More than eighty main dishes are offered; a few list oyster sauce. **Open daily. Limited service, vegan options, take-out, VISA/MC/DISC, $$**

MORENO VALLEY

Dragon House Restaurant
22456 Alessandro Blvd., Moreno Valley, CA 92507   (714) 653-1442
Chinese. Dragon House features a complete vegetarian menu including "vegetarian meats" made from soybean protein so don't be surprised when you see chicken, beef, and scallop dishes on the vegetarian menu. **Open daily for lunch and dinner. Full service, vegan options, wine/beer/alcohol, take-out, VISA/MC/AMX, $$**

MOUNTAIN VIEW

Country Gourmet
2098 El Camino Real, Mountain View, CA 94040 (415) 962-0239
Natural foods. Enjoy Veggie Burritos, Taco Salad, and pasta dishes. **Open daily. Counter service, wine/beer, take-out, VISA/MC/DISC, $$**

Hobee's Restaurant
2312 Central Expressway, Mountain View, CA 94040 (415) 968-6050
Restaurant chain. See entry under Cupertino, CA.

Rooh's Cafe Salsa
650 Castro St., Mountain View, CA 94041 (415) 969-6393
Mexican/restaurant chain. See entry under Los Gatos, CA.

NEEDLES

Irene's Drive Inn
703 Broadway, Needles, CA 92363 (619) 326-2342
Fast food. This is a typical fast-food hamburger place that has window service. From a distance, there is no indication of the wonderful, large vegetarian tacos and burritos that are also available on the menu. Vegetarian food is available because, historically, there has been a Seventh-day Adventist community in the area. This is certainly an oasis in the desert! You can buy food to eat in your car or at the picnic table outside. **Open daily. Window service, fresh juices, take-out, $**

NEVADA CITY

• Earth Song Market & Cafe
727 Zion St., Nevada City, CA 95959 (916) 265-8025
Vegetarian. Located adjacent to a natural foods market in the Sierra Nevada foothills, this vegetarian restaurant offers salads, Veggie Burgers, sandwiches, and entrees using fresh organic vegetables and grains when available. Several soups and specials are prepared each day. **Open daily. Full service, vegan/macrobiotic options, fresh juices, take-out, VISA/MC, $**

NEWPORT BEACH

Far Pavillions
1520 West Coast Hwy., Newport Beach, CA 92663 (714) 548-7167
Indian. This restaurant is located along the Pacific coast. The menu has a vegetable section that features twelve vegetarian dishes plus traditional appetizers such as samosas and pakoras. **Full service, vegan options, $$**

ᴂ Reviewers' choice • Vegetarian restaurant •• Vegan restaurant
$ less than $6 $$ $6–$12 $$$ more than $12
VISA/AMX/MC/DISC/DC—credit cards accepted
Non-alc.—Non-alcoholic Fresh juices—freshly squeezed

Royal Thai Cuisine

4001 W. Pacific Coast Hwy., Newport Beach, CA 92663   (714) 650-3322

Thai. Royal Thai offers nine vegetarian entrees plus appetizers, soups, and salads. **Open Monday through Friday for lunch, Saturday and Sunday for dinner. Sunday Brunch. Full service, wine/beer/alcohol, VISA/MC/AMX/DISC, $$**

NORTHRIDGE

Canopy of the Sky

9351 Reseda Blvd., Northridge, CA 91325   (818) 885-1875

Gourmet natural foods. Recommended by a member, this small restaurant has a wonderful hand-painted decor. Each meal is prepared individually so be prepared for leisurely dining. Delicious nut-vegetable and vegetable soups. **Open daily. Reservations recommended. Full service, vegan options, wine/beer, take-out, VISA/MC/AMX/DISC, $$–$$$**

• Paru's

9545 Reseda Blvd., #16, Northridge, CA 91324   (818) 349-3546

Indian/vegetarian. Paru's features South Indian cuisine without preservatives or additives and mostly non-dairy. This is a tiny restaurant with delightful service and delicious food. **Closed Monday. Full service, vegan options, take-out, VISA/MC, $$**

NORWALK

• Our Daily Bread Bakery

12201 Front St., Norwalk, CA 90650   (310) 863-6897

Vegetarian/deli. The entree menu rotates every twenty-one days, and there are twelve different soups, breads, cookies, Macaroni and Cheese, Stuffed Peppers, enchiladas, and quiche. **Open Monday through Thursday late morning and afternoon, and Friday morning. Counter service, vegan options, $**

OAKLAND

Granny Feels Great

5020 Woodminster Lane, Oakland, CA 94602   (510) 530-6723

Natural foods. Granny's primarily offers sandwiches. Vegetarian options using cheese or dairy are available. The menu also lists a salad plate, Potato Salad, and Carrot-Raisin Salad. **Closed Sunday. Deli style, fresh juices, take-out, $**

Holyland Kosher Foods

677 Rand Ave., Oakland, CA 94610   (510) 272-0535

Kosher. Enjoy salads and Hummus, Tabouleh, Falafel, and Stuffed Grape Leaves. Indoor and outdoor seating. **Open Sunday through Thursday afternoon and evening; open Friday until noon. Closed Saturday. Full service, fresh juices, wine/beer, catering, take-out, $**

• Macrobiotic Grocery/Organic Cafe

1050 40th St., Oakland, CA 94608   (510) 653-6510

Vegetarian/macrobiotic. Gourmet macrobiotic food is prepared with organic ingredients by a team of internationally trained macrobiotic cooks. Every meal is unique.

Desserts are made without refined sugars, honey, eggs, or dairy products. **Open for three meals daily. Full service, vegan/macrobiotic options, catering, take-out, $$**

Nan Yang Rockridge
6048 College Ave., Oakland,CA 94618   **(510) 655-3298**
Burmese. The wide variety of vegetarian dishes includes Fried Tropical Squash, Hot and Sour Soup, Stir-fried Brussels Sprouts and Baby Corn, Stir-fried Jicama, Burmese Cold Noodles, and more. Savor curry, black, coconut, or chili rice. **Open Tuesday through Sunday. Full service, vegan options, wine/beer, take-out, VISA/MC, $$**

Organic Cafe
1050 40th St., Oakland, CA 94609   **(510) 653-6510**
Macrobiotic. There is a fixed macrobiotic menu each day. **Open daily. Limited service, macrobiotic options, amazake, take-out, $$**

OJAI

• Govinda's Vegetarian Buffet
1002 E. Ojai Ave., Ojai, CA 93023   **(805) 646-1133**
Vegetarian. Each day, Govinda's offers a different buffet menu including two entrees, two soups, basmati and brown rice, steamed veggies, and dessert. There's also a complete salad bar plus egg-, dairy-, and sugar-free cakes. Enjoy family dining and an early dinner special. **Open Tuesday through Saturday and holidays for dinner. Cafeteria style, vegan options, fresh juices, take-out, $$**

ORANGE

The Healthy Gourmet Cafe & Restaurant
3505 E. Chapman Ave. #E, Orange, CA 92669   **(714) 771-1993**
Natural foods. Vegetarian and "California Lite" cuisines characterize the creative and nutritional cooking. Low-fat and high-energy foods are offered for well-being and weight management. No smoking. **Open daily. Full service, vegan options, fresh juices, non-alc. beer, espresso/cappuccino, take-out, VISA/MC/DISC, $$**

Tandoor Cuisine of India
1132 E. Katella Ave., Orange, CA 92667   **(714) 538-2234**
Indian. Minutes from Disneyland and the Anaheim Convention Center, Tandoor has a good selection of vegetarian Indian specialties including appetizers, salad, rice dishes, and entrees that taste excellent! **Open daily. Full service, vegan options, take-out, $$**

OROVILLE

Vega Macrobiotic Center
1511 Robinson St., Oroville, CA 95965   **(916) 533-7702**
Macrobiotic. Vega offers a variety of macrobiotic meals ranging from simple to international gourmet, depending on which cooking course is in progress on the day you eat there. **Open Monday through Friday. Reservations required. Limited service, take-out, VISA/MC/AMX, $$–$$$**

Tillie Gort's Cafe & Restaurant

111 Central, Pacific Grove, CA 93950   **(408) 373-0335**

Natural foods. Tillie Gort's restaurant/coffeehouse and impromptu art gallery has been a fixture on Central Ave. in Pacific Grove for twenty-three years. Tillie's serves a wide variety of foods including some that qualify as "health food" and organic. Many vegetarian options are offered, including the No Meat Loaf, Veggie Pasta, and Eggplant Parmesan. **Open for three meals daily. Full service, vegan options, fresh juices, espresso/cappuccino, wine/beer, take-out, VISA/MC, $$**

• Let's Get Juiced

651 N. Palm Canyon Dr., Palm Springs, CA 92262   **(619) 327-9112**

Vegetarian. According to the menu at this coffeehouse/juice bar/gallery, "Real Food for Real People" is offered at "a meeting place for artists, musicians, yogis, cyclers, storytellers, recyclers, writers, neo-bio-revolutionaries and other assorted friends of the universe." Not only does the food sound great, the menu is fun to read; it made me smile. Menu sections include Get Juiced, Smoothies, Outrageous Salads, Sandwiches, Soups and Pleasant Lunches, Vegetable Dinners, Side Orders, and Desserts. No animal products are used except for milk and half-and-half. Organic ingredients are used whenever feasible. **Open daily. Closes early on Tuesdays for community educational events. Closed in August. Full and self service, vegan options, fresh juices, organic coffee and tea, espresso/cappuccino, take-out, $–$$**

Bombaywala

421 Alma, Palo Alto, CA 94301   **(415) 323-1195**

Indian. Enjoy a small Indian-food buffet with Bombay-style cuisine that uses no oil and emphasizes vegetarianism. **Closed Sunday. Limited service, take-out, $**

Country Sun Natural Foods Deli

440 California Ave., Palo Alto, CA 94306   **(415) 328-4120**

Health-food-store deli. The Country Sun deli offers breakfast and lunch every day with a variety of vegetarian options. Organically grown grains, beans, fruits and vegetables are used whenever possible. The menu features homemade vegetarian pizza, a wide variety of salads, hot entrees, vegetarian burgers, and sandwiches. **Open daily. Deli style, vegan/macrobiotic options, fresh juices, limited seating, take-out, $**

Fresh Choice

Stanford Shopping Center, Palo Alto, CA 94304   **(415) 322-6995**

American. See entry under Menlo Park.

Gaylord India Restaurant

317 Stanford Shopping Center, Palo Alto, CA 94304   **(415) 326-8761**

Indian. "Vegetarian selections as extensive as the delicate spices which are added to taste. When we say vegetarian menu, we mean more than steamed broccoli."

Eleven vegetarian entrees are offered. **Open daily. Reservations accepted. Formal, full service, vegan options, wine/beer/alcohol, take-out, VISA/MC/AMX/DC/Carte Blanche, $$–$$$**

The Good Earth
185 University Ave., Palo Alto, CA 94301 (415) 321-9449

Natural foods. Enjoy wok dishes, Vegetarian Scramble, Tofu Scramble, vegetarian burger, burritos, tostadas, Eggplant Sandwich, salads, Pasta Primavera, Walnut Mushroom Au Gratin, Guatamalan Rice and Tofu. **Open daily. Full service, wine/beer, VISA/MC/AMX, $$**

Hobee's Restaurant
4224 El Camino Real, Palo Alto, CA 94306 (415) 854-6124

67 Town & Country Village, Palo Alto, CA 94301 (415) 327-4111

Restaurant chain. Mexican favorites, veggie patties, Black Bean Chili, and a salad bar make up the vegetarian options at Hobee's. **Open every day. Full service, fresh juices, wine/beer, take-out, VISA/MC, $$**

Nataraja Indian Cuisine
117 University Ave., Palo Alto, CA 94301 (415) 321-6161

Indian. "Walk in and get the feeling of being transported into another culture far, far away with ambience, aroma, and gracious hospitality"; so reads the front of Nataraja's menu. Vegetarian entrees are limited, but there are vegetarian appetizers such as samosas and pakoras in addition to eleven "country-style side orders." Fresh vegetables are used in all veggie entrees. Extremely pricey. **Closed Monday. Full service, wine/beer/alcohol, VISA/MC/AMX, $$$**

Tokyo
448 University Ave., Palo Alto, CA 94301 (415) 325-1605

Ethnic. Enjoy tempura tofu dishes and mock (gluten) meats. **Open daily. Full service, beer/wine, VISA/MC, $$**

Whole Foods Market & Deli
774 Emerson St., Palo Alto, CA 94301 (415) 326-8676

Natural foods deli. This gourmet natural foods deli offers thirty-five all natural and organic salads. Specialty items include homemade vegetable knishes, pizzas, and vegetable sushi. There are also hot food selections including vegan entrees, vegetable lasagna, and two daily soups. Breakfast is served and box lunches to go are available. **Open daily. Deli style, vegan options, fresh juices, wine/beer, catering, take-out, VISA/MC, $**

PALOMAR MOUNTAIN

• Mother's Kitchen
Junction of S6 and S7, Palomar Mountain, CA 92060 (619) 742-4233

Vegetarian/juice bar. Any visitor to San Diego who drives up the mountain to see the famous Mt. Palomar telescope will drive right past Mother's. It's the only eatery on the mountain. In this rustic mountaintop cabin, you'll find soups, salads, sandwiches, nutburgers, and fruit smoothies. **Closed Tuesday and Wednesday. Full service, fresh juices, wine/beer, take-out, $$**

PARADISE

• # Feather River Hospital Cafeteria
5974 Pentz Rd., Paradise, CA 95969   **(916) 877-9361**
Vegetarian. Sample the Spinach Tortellini or Spaghetti, Mushroom Loaf, Zucchini Quiche, Enchilada, Garbanzo Casserole, salad bar, pizza bar, and veggie burger bar. **Open daily for lunch and dinner. Cafeteria style, take-out, $**

PASADENA

The Good Earth
257 N. Rosemead Blvd., Pasadena, CA 91107   **(818) 351-5488**
Natural foods. Good Earth offers Walnut Mushroom Casserole, Eggplant Parmesan, soups, salads, etc. **Open daily. Full service, fresh juices, wine/beer, take-out, VISA/MC/AMX, $$**

PETALUMA

Markey's Cafe
316 Western Ave., Petaluma, CA 94952   **(707) 763-2429**
Natural foods. See entry under Cotati, CA.

REDONDO BEACH

• # MT Plate
403 N. Pacific Coast Hwy., Redondo Beach, CA 90277   **(310) 318-8558**
Vegetarian/international. "Extremely gourmet" and "artfully prepared" are phrases the owners use to describe the dishes offered at MT Plate. Recipes have been gathered during travels around the world, and foods from such countries as Greece, Mexico, Italy, and Thailand are offered in addition to some American classics. The menu includes appetizers, salads, pizza, entrees, and pasta. "Flavors beyond belief and beef!" **Open daily for dinner. Full service, vegan options, fresh juices, wine/beer, catering, take-out, VISA/MC, $$–$$$**

REDWOOD CITY

Joy Meadow
701 El Camino Real, Redwood City, CA 94063   **(415) 365-3550**
Natural foods. In the relaxing atmosphere of Joy Meadow, you can enjoy a variety of unique vegetarian dishes such as Nepal Loaf, Golden Chalice (stuffed eggplant), and Enchanted Forest (tofu marinated in plum sauce with broccoli). They have an extensive vegetarian menu section plus a Light and Tasty section that includes many vegetarian and vegan options. Next door to the restaurant is the Harmony Bookshop, part of Joy Meadow Inc., featuring New Age books and related items. **Open daily for lunch and dinner. Reservations accepted. Full service, vegan options, espresso/cappuccino, wine/beer, take-out, VISA/MC/AMX/DISC, $$**

๛ Reviewers' choice   • Vegetarian restaurant   •• Vegan restaurant
$ less than $6 $$ $6–$12 $$$ more than $12
VISA/AMX/MC/DISC/DC—credit cards accepted
Non-alc.—Non-alcoholic   Fresh juices—freshly squeezed

RIVERSIDE

Dragon House Restaurant
10466 Magnolia Ave., Riverside, CA 92505 **(714) 354-2080**
Chinese. See entry under Moreno Valley, CA.

ROSEMEAD

Chameli
8752 Valley Blvd., Rosemead, CA 91770 **(818) 280-1947**
Ethnic. You'll eat ethnic foods while listening to classical Indian sitar. **Closed Tuesday. Full service, wine/beer, catering, take-out, VISA/MC/AMX, $$**

SACRAMENTO

Eat Your Vegetables
1841 Howe Ave., Sacramento, CA 95825 **(916) 922-8454**
American. A mega salad bar includes soup, salad, baked potato, pasta, breads, and desserts. **Open daily. Cafeteria style, VISA/MC, $$**

Good Earth
2024 Arden Way, Sacramento, CA 95616 **(916) 920-5544**
Natural foods. Food is prepared without artificial ingredients or preservatives. Wok dishes, Mexican cuisine, and casseroles are among the offerings. **Open daily for three meals. Full service, vegan options, fresh juices, non-alc. beer, wine/ beer, VISA/MC, $$**

Juliana's Kitchen
1401 G St., Sacramento, CA 95814 **(916) 444-0966**
Middle Eastern/natural foods. Juliana's Kitchen specializes in a variety of vegetarian pita bread sandwiches from the Middle East along with a daily Middle Eastern special. Salads, desserts, and organic juice sections are also on menu. **Limited service, vegan options, wine/beer, take-out, $**

•• Marline's Vegetable Patch
1119 8th St., Sacramento, CA 95814 **(916) 448-3327**
Vegan. Marline's completely vegan menu features Mexican dishes with soy cream; vegan sandwiches such as the Tomacado Nut Burger and the "So-Cal" Sub served on whole-wheat buns, bread or pita; and several side orders. Delicious fruit smoothies and fresh fruit juices are also available. **Open for lunch Monday through Friday. Limited service, vegan, fresh juices, take-out, VISA/MC/AMX/ DISC, $**

• Mums
2968 Freeport Blvd., Sacramento, CA 95818 **(916) 444-3015**
Vegetarian. Mums has a cozy dining room, and outside seating in the summertime. Eggs are used only in omelettes. Dishes that can be prepared without eggs or wheat are clearly indicated on the menu, which includes salads, appetizers, and children's dinner, lunch and brunch sections. **Closed Monday; only brunch is served Sunday. Full service, vegan options, fresh juices, wine/beer, limited catering, take-out, VISA/MC/AMX, $$**

Sacramento Natural Foods Co-op
1900 Alkambra Blvd., Sacramento, CA 95818   (916) 455-COOP
Deil/juice bar. This co-op features many vegan options. **Open daily. Vegan options. $**

Taj Mahal
2355 Arden Way, Sacramento, CA 95825   (916) 924-8378
Indian. Vegetarian curry and tandoori dishes are featured at Taj Mahal. **Open daily for lunch and dinner. Full service, wine/beer, VISA/MC/AMX/DC, $$**

SAINT HELENA

• St. Helena Health Center Dining Room
650 Sanitarium Rd., St. Helena, CA 94576   (707) 963-6214
Vegetarian. The food service is for participants at the health center, but non-participants can be accommodated with reservations. **Open daily for three meals. Reservations required. Cafeteria style.**

SAN BRUNO

Hobee's Restaurant
#12 Bayhill Shopping Center, San Bruno Ave.
San Bruno, CA 94066   (415) 588-9662
Restaurant chain. See entry under Cupertino, CA.

SAN DIEGO

(For more restaurant listings in the surrounding areas, see Coronado, Del Mar, El Cajon, Encinitas, La Jolla, Palomar Mountain [on the way from L.A.], and Solana Beach.)

Cafe Greentree
3560 Mt. Acadia Blvd., San Diego, CA 92111   (619) 560-1975
Natural foods. Cafe Greentree has an extensive vegetarian menu. **Open daily. Full service, VISA/MC, $**

Casa De Pico
2754 Calhoun St., San Diego, CA 92110   (619) 296-3267
Mexican. Located in the heart of Bazaar Del Mundo Shopping Complex in old-town San Diego's historic state park, Casa De Pico offers many vegetarian options. A special menu for the health-conscious offers foods low in salt, fat, and cholesterol. Enjoy live mariachi music nightly on an open air patio. **Open daily. Full service, wine/beer/alcohol, take-out, VISA/MC/AMX/DISC, $-$$**

• Faque Burgers
6109 University Ave., San Diego, CA 92115   (619) 583-9520
Vegetarian. Faque Burgers is a fast-food joint for vegetarians, complete with drive-thru window and homemade fries. Vegan burgers and dairy-free shakes can be enjoyed on an outdoor patio. **Open Sunday through Thursday 10 A.M. until 1 A.M., Friday until 4 P.M. only, Saturday 8:30 P.M. to 2 A.M. Limited service, vegan options, take-out, $**

La Fresqueria
1125 Suite B 6th Ave., San Diego, CA 92116 **(619) 235-0655**
Health-food-store deli. Healthy fresh foods with a Latin influence are offered on a limited menu featuring sandwiches and salads. Seasonal fruit salads and smoothies are also available. **Open Monday through Friday. Limited service, fresh juices, espresso/cappuccino, take-out, no credit cards, $**

• Gelato Vero Cafe
3753 India St., San Diego, CA 92103 **(619) 295-9269**
Vegetarian. The menu is limited at this coffeehouse cafe—soup, salad, and fresh bread. **Open every evening. Counter service, fresh juices, take-out, AMX, $**

• Govinda's
3102 University Ave., San Diego, CA 92104 **(619) 284-4826**
Vegetarian/international. Govinda's features different international menus daily. One price includes soup, fresh vegetable salad bar, and hot entrees such as Cabbage Peanut Rastafel, Govinda's Pot Pie, and Kofta Balls in Tomato Sauce. Non-dairy dishes are offered every day. **Closed Sunday. Buffet, vegan options, fresh juices, reservations accepted, take-out, $–$$**

Greentree Farms
3560 Mt. Acadia, San Diego, CA 92111 **(619) 560-1975**
Natural foods deli. Vegetarian and non-vegetarian options are available at this full-service health-food-store deli. **Full service, take-out, $**

• Jimbo's Vegetarian Restaurant
3910 30th St., San Diego, CA 92104 **(619) 294-9611**
Vegetarian. The back of Jimbo's menu states, "By supporting organic agricultural techniques, we hope to have a positive impact on the environment, our own health, and the health of others," which of itself is an excellent reason to patronize this restaurant. Jimbo's takes extra measures to create healthy dishes using only organic whole-wheat flour, filtered water, and sea salt. Jimbo's features primarily whole-wheat pizza but also offers vegetable and BBQ burgers, an organic salad bar, and an a la carte menu of rice, beans, and tofu meatballs. For vegans, Jimbo's prepares its own totally dairy-free (no casein!) tofu cheese. **Open Wednesday through Sunday. Full service, vegan options, fresh juice, organic coffee, non-alc. beer, beer/organic wine, $–$$**

Jyoti Bihanga
3351 Adams Ave., San Diego, CA 92116 **(619) 282-4116**
Natural foods. Jyoti Bihanga offers excellent vegetarian and macrobiotic foods in a peaceful, serene atmosphere with a fountain, high arched ceiling, and fifteen-foot windows. Sample daily specials, homemade soups and desserts, and an all-you-can-eat Saturday breakfast buffet. **Closed Sunday. Full service, vegan/macrobiotic options, fresh juices, take-out, no credit cards, $–$$**

• Kool Korner
3896 Fifth Ave., San Diego, CA 92103 **(619) 298-3155**
Vegetarian/juice bar. The menu changes daily and includes burgers, curries, stews, and salads. **Open daily. Counter service, fresh juices, take-out, $**

• Kung Food

2949 Fifth Ave., San Diego, CA 92103   **(619) 298-7302**

Vegetarian. Kung Food has been serving gourmet international vegetarian cuisine since 1975. The varied and extensive menu includes "Enchanting Desserts" with vegan options. Entrees include Layered Tofu Supreme, Greek Spinach Pie, and Spaghetti with Mock Italian Sausage. Dishes are prepared from scratch without the use of refined white or brown sugar. Most of the cheese is raw, vegetarian (rennetless), and undyed. The restaurant is located near Balboa Park and features an intimate dining room and garden patio. **Open daily. Full service, vegan options, wine/beer, take-out, VISA/MC/DISC, $**

Lotsa Pasta

1726 Garnet Ave., #7, San Diego, CA 92109   **(619) 581-6777**

Italian. Many different pastas are cut to order and served with different sauces for a total of more than 500 combinations. **Open daily. Full service, take-out, VISA/MC/AMX/DISC, $$**

• Lux Kahv'e

728 Fifth St., San Diego, CA 92101   **(619) 232-7700**

Vegetarian/bistro. This urban-style coffeehouse and sidewalk cafe has music every night as well as sandwiches, salads, Falafel, pasta, Hummus, blended juices (e.g., honeydew strawberry), and desserts. **Call for current hours. Full service, vegan options, blended juices, espresso/cappuccino, non-alc. beer and wine, beer/wine, take-out, VISA/MC/AMX/DISC/DC, $$**

Mandarin Plaza

3760 Sports Arena Blvd., San Diego, CA 92110   **(619) 224-4222**

Mandarin/Cantonese Chinese. Mandarin Plaza's menu has both vegetable and special diet sections that include some unique dishes such as Braised Squash and Mushrooms and Subgum Vegetables. No MSG is used. **Open daily. Full service, vegan options, wine/beer, take-out, VISA/MC /AMX/DISC, $-$$**

Maria Isabella

1830 Sunset Cliffs Blvd., San Diego, CA 92107   **(619) 298-2860**

Mexican. A vegetarian menu is available. **Open daily. Limited service, vegan options, fresh juices, beer, take-out, $**

•• Ocean Beach People's Natural Foods Market & Deli

4765 Voltaire St., San Diego, CA 92107   **(619) 224-1387**

Vegan deli. This deli in a health food store features vegan and raw foods. A great selection of organic produce and green salads, cold salads, soups, entrees, sandwiches, baked goods, and desserts are limited to take-out. **Open daily. Vegan options, fresh juices, take-out only, $**

Pasta Time Cafe

1417 University Ave., San Diego, CA 92103   **(619) 296-2425**

Italian. Pasta Time takes pride in creating dishes that are healthful and delicious. The menu lists twelve entrees, five of which are vegetarian. All of the sauces, soups, salads, and desserts are made from scratch. Daily pasta specials are joined by a different soup each day. No smoking. **Limited service, vegan options, non-alc. beer, take-out, $**

Skinny Haven
4344 Convoy St., San Diego, CA 92111 **(619) 560-8151**
American. Skinny Haven features a vegetable platter, Quesadilla, Lasagna, a salad bar, and sandwiches. **Closed Sunday. Full service, take-out, VISA/MC, $**

SAN FRANCISCO

(For more restaurants in the surrounding areas, see Berkeley, Burlingame, Campbell, Corte Madera, Cupertino, Emeryville, Foster City, Fremont, Larkspur, Los Gatos, Menlo Park, Mountain View, Oakland, Palo Alto, Redwood City, San Bruno, San Jose, San Rafael, San Clara, Saratoga, and Sunnyvale.)

A.J.'s Falafel King
420 Geary St., San Francisco, CA 94102 **(415) 776-2683**
Middle Eastern/kosher. Enjoy Falafel, Hummus, soups, salads, etc. **Open Sunday through Thursday all day, Friday morning and early afternoon. Counter service, take-out, $**

All You Knead
1466 Haight St., San Francisco, CA 94117 **(415) 552-4550**
American. Pasta, pizza, and soup are available. **Open Sunday through Saturday. $$**

• Amazing Grace
216 Church St., San Francisco, CA 94114 **(415) 626-6411**
Vegetarian. Sundry and simple vegetarian dishes include soups, baked potatoes, sandwiches, and a salad bar. The menu changes each day. **Closed Sunday. Cafeteria style, vegan options, fresh juices, $**

• Ananda Fuara
3050 Taraval St., San Francisco, CA 94102 **(415) 621-1994**
Vegetarian. This Sri-Chimnoy restaurant offers sandwiches, BBQ tofu burger, pizza, a curry dish, salads, and smoothies, plus a breakfast menu. The food has received an excellent rating from one of our members. **Open Monday through Saturday 7 A.M to 7 P.M, except Wednesday until mid-afternoon. Full service, vegan/macrobiotic options, fresh juices, take-out, $–$$**

Cornucopia
114 Columbus, San Francisco, CA 94133 **(415) 398-1511**
Deli. No meat stock is used in the soups. Rigatoni Salad, Buckwheat Noodles, and Pasta Salad are also offered. **Open weekdays only. Cafeteria style, wine/beer, take-out, no credit cards, $**

➤ Reviewers' choice   ● Vegetarian restaurant   ●● Vegan restaurant
$ less than $6 $$ $6–$12 $$$ more than $12
VISA/AMX/MC/DISC/DC—credit cards accepted
Non-alc.–Non-alcoholic   Fresh juices—freshly squeezed

Diamond Street Restaurant
737 Diamond St., San Francisco, CA 94114   (415) 285-6988
American. Diamond Street has some vegetarian options. **Open daily. Reservations accepted. Full service, wine/beer, take-out, VISA/MC/AMX, $$–$$$**

• The Ganges Restaurant
775 Frederick St., San Francisco, CA 94117   (415) 661-7290
Vegetarian/Indian. The vegetarian offerings are light but exotic, with distinct flavors from Gujarat, India. You can go à la carte or choose a special combination plate from the Ganges menu, which features dahl, curries, Saffron Rice, and other classic Indian appetizers. Enjoy a vegan dessert and, Thursday through Saturday, live Indian music. **Open for dinner Tuesday through Saturday. Full service, vegan options, wine/beer, take-out, $$**

Gaylord's India Restaurant
1 Embarcadero, San Francisco, CA 94111   (415) 397-7775
Indian. Gaylord's offers world-renowned Indian cuisine with bread baked fresh in clay ovens. Vegetarian appetizers and meatless specialties are listed on the menu. **Open daily for lunch and dinner. Full service, vegan options, fresh juices, wine/beer, take-out, VISA/MC/AMX/DISC, $$**

• Greens Restaurant
Fort Mason Building A, San Francisco, CA 94123   (415) 771-6222
Vegetarian. Greens is located in an old army warehouse with beautiful views of the San Francisco Bay and the Coastal Mountain Range. **Reservations required. Full service, limited vegan options, fresh juice, wine/beer, VISA/MC, $$$**

Haven Restaurant
One Post St., San Francisco, CA 94104   (415) 397-1299
Health food store. **Open daily 7 A.M. to 3 P.M. Fresh juices, wine/beer, catering, take-out, $**

• Josie's Cafe and Juice Joint
3583 16th St., San Francisco, CA 94114   (415) 861-7933
Vegetarian. Salads, soups, quiche, veggie burger, tofu burgers, tempeh burgers, and baked goods are offered. This is a vegetarian restaurant during the day and a cabaret after 8 P.M. **Open daily. Counter service, fresh juices, take-out, $**

Joy Chinese Restaurant
3258 Scott St., San Francisco, CA 94123   (415) 922-0270
Szechuan/Mandarin. See entry under Foster City, CA.

Just Like Home
1924 Irving St., San Franciso, CA 94122   (415) 681-3337
Mediterranean. Enjoy Baba Ghanouj, Hummus, Falafel, Dolma, and Tabouleh. **Open daily for lunch and dinner. Limited service, beer, take-out, $**

• Lotus Garden ☙
532 Grant Ave. (between California and Pine)
San Francisco, CA 94108   (415) 397-0707

Vegetarian/Chinese. It is worth visiting this restaurant with its wide selection of vegetarian items ranging from Asparagus with Stewed Bean Gluten Puff to Vegetarian Won Ton to Almond Vegetarian Chicken Dices. The management is very supportive of vegetarian organizations. **Closed Monday. Full service, vegan options, wine/beer, VISA/MC/AMX, $$**

• Lucky Creation Vegetarian Restaurant
854 Washington St., San Francisco, CA 94108   **(415) 989-0818**

Vegetarian/Chinese. The phrase "Health is Wealth" is featured on the menu to let customers know Lucky Creation serves only vegetarian food because it is concerned about customers' health. The take-out menu is divided into appetizers, soups, entrees, clay pot dishes, pan fried noodles, noodles in soup, and rice plates. Entrees include Sauteed Black Mushrooms with Chinese Greens and Meatless Diced Almond Chicken, plus twenty-three other items. **Closed Wednesday. Full service, vegan option, wine/beer, take-out, $**

Maharani
1122 Post St., San Francisco, CA 94109   **(415) 775-1988**

Indian. See listing under Berkeley, CA.

Real Good Karma
501 Delores, San Francisco, CA 94110   **(415) 621-4112**

Natural foods. Partake of various stir-fry dishes, salads, batter dipped entrees, and fresh pasta with an Asian influence. Dine in a simple sunny room with a piano open to anyone who is inspired to play. **Open daily for lunch and dinner. Full service, vegan/macrobiotic options, fresh juices, beer, take-out, $–$$**

Red Crane
1115 Clement, San Francisco, CA 94118   **(415) 751-7226**

Chinese. Mock meat entrees are featured. **Open daily. Full service, wine/beer, take-out, VISA/MC, $**

• Shangri-La
2026 Irving St., San Francisco, CA 94122   **(415) 731-2548**

Vegetarian/Northern Chinese. Eggs are used in some dishes, but no dairy. **Open daily. Full service, wine/beer, take-out, VISA/MC, $**

Silver Moon Vegetarian and Seafood Restaurant
2301 Clement St., San Francisco, CA 94121   **(415) 386-7852**

Chinese. The menu at Silver Moon is divided in half with vegetarian on one side and seafood on the other. The vegetarian section features categories such as Soups, Appetizers, Gluten Puff, Vegetarian Pork, Sweet & Sour Vegetables, Chow Mein, Fried Rice, and Imitation Duck, Chicken, and Shrimp. **Open daily. Formal, full service, vegan options, wine/beer, take-out, VISA/MC/DISC, $$**

Tai Chi
2031 Polk St., San Francisco, CA 94109   **(415) 441-6758**

Chinese. Tai Chi features Spring Rolls, Chinese Pancakes, Vegetable Stir-Fry, Hot and Sour Cabbage, and Dry Braised Green Beans. **Open daily. Full service, wine/beer, take-out, VISA/MC/ AMX, $**

Taiwan Restaurant
445 Clement St., San Francisco, CA 94118   **(415) 387-1789**
Chinese. Enjoy vegetarian dishes such as Steamed Dumplings, Hot and Sour Fried
Rice, Sweet and Sour Mock Pork, and other mock meat dishes. **Open daily for
lunch and dinner. Full service, wine/beer, take-out, VISA/MC/AMX, $$**

Tortola
3521 20th Ave., San Francisco, CA 94132   **(415) 566-4336**

3640 Sacramento St., San Francisco, CA 94118   **(415) 929-8181**
Mexican. Features vegetarian tacos, burritos, and tostadas. No lard is used in the
beans. **Sacramento St. closed Monday; 20th Ave. open daily. Full service, wine/
beer, full bar at Sacramento St., take-out, $$**

• Vegi Food
1820 Clement St., San Francisco, CA 94121   **(415) 387-8111**
Vegetarian/Chinese. No eggs, garlic, onions, or MSG is used in the varieties of mock
meats. **Open Tuesday through Sunday for lunch and dinner. Full service, take-
out, $–$$**

Vicolo Pizzeria
201 Ivy St., San Francisco, CA 94102   **(415) 863-2382**
Pizza. This pizzeria features corn-meal-crust pizza, wonderful salads, and vegetarian soups. **Open daily for lunch and dinner. Limited service, non-alc. beer,
wine/beer, take-out, $–$$**

Wu Kong Restaurant
101 Spear St., San Francisco, CA 94105   **(415) 957-9300**
Chinese. "Vegetable Goose" (tofu stuffed with mushrooms) and various other bean
curd and vegetable dishes are among the vegetarian options offered. **Full service,
take-out, VISA/MC/AMX, $$**

SAN GABRIEL

• Diwana Restaurant
1381 E. Las Tunas Dr., San Gabriel, CA 91775   **(818) 287-8743**
Vegetarian/Indian. Diwana offers a unique dining experience—authentic Indian
vegetarian dishes from all parts of India. Only the finest ingredients are used.
Dishes are adapted from recipes handed down through generations. **Closed
Tuesday. Full service, fresh juice, wine/beer, take-out, VISA/MC, $$**

SAN JOSE

The Crêpe Shoppe
86 N. Market St., San Jose, CA 95113   **(408) 978-3633**
French. This romantic bistro serves many kinds of crêpes for breakfast, lunch, and
dinner, plus salads, onion soup, and dessert crêpes. The Shoppe is located two
blocks south of the Fairmont Hotel. **Open daily. Reservations accepted. Full
service, espresso bar, wine/beer, VISA/MC/DISC, $$**

Fresh Choice
1600 Saratoga Ave., San Jose, CA 95125 **(408) 866-1491**
American. The salad selection is extensive, and there is always one vegetarian soup and usually at least one vegetarian pasta. A fixed price includes everything from bread to dessert. **Open daily. Cafeteria style, wine/beer, VISA/MC, $$**

Hobee's Restaurant
920 Town & Country Village
Stevens Creek Blvd., San Jose, CA 95128 **(408) 244-5212**
Restaurant chain. See entry under Cupertino, CA.

Rooh's Cafe Salsa
Metro Plaza, 25 Metro Drive, San Jose, CA 95110 **(408) 441-ROOH**
Mexican/restaurant chain. See entry under Los Gatos, CA.

Royal Taj India Cuisine
118 E. Santa Clara Street, San Jose, CA 95112 **(408) 993-0661**
Indian. See entry under Campbell, CA.

• White Lotus ﷼
80 N. Market St., San Jose, CA 95113 **(408) 977-0540**
Vegetarian/ethnic. Mock meats make up a lot of the menu at this restaurant, so don't be surprised when you see beef, chicken, duck, pork, and fish dishes listed. Extremely flavorful fare, the foods are drawn from several cultures, especially Vietnamese, and White Lotus utilizes many Eastern herbs and spices. The menu is mostly vegan. Absolutely no smoking. **Closed Monday. Full service, vegan options, take-out, VISA/MC/AMX, $$**

SAN JUAN CAPISTRANO

Natural Offering Cafe
San Juan Capistrano, CA **(714) 472-1721**
This restaurant had yet to open at press time.

SAN LUIS OBISPO

Hobee's
212 Madonna Rd., San Luis Obispo, CA 93401 **(805) 549-9186**
Restaurant chain. One vegetarian and one vegan soup are offered daily. You can also partake of tofu burgers, Tofu Scramble, four vegetarian dinner specials daily, seven vegan veggie sautees with rice, Black Bean Chili, a salad bar, and baked goods. **Open daily. Full service, vegan options, fresh juice, wine/beer, take-out, VISA/MC/AMX, $$**

SAN RAFAEL

Bangkok Thai Express
809 Fourth St., San Rafael, CA 94901 **(415) 453-3350**
Thai. Bangkok Thai calls its vegetarian menu section "Vegie Deluxe" and offers twelve vegetarian options including curries, noodle dishes, and veggies with various Thai

seasonings. The restaurant is small, seating fifteen, and the prices are low. **Closed Sunday. Full service, vegan options, take-out, VISA/MC, $**

Healthy Gourmet Cafe
1132 4th St., San Rafael, CA 94901   **(415) 457-0132**
Natural foods. Enjoy freshly made soups, salads, sandwiches, muffins, daily specials, and a juice bar. **Open Monday through Saturday. Cafeteria style, fresh juices, take-out, VISA/MC/DISC, $**

•• Milly's ?▲
1613 Fourth St., San Rafael, CA 94901   **(415) 459-1601**
Vegan. I haven't yet had the pleasure of sampling the gourmet vegan cuisine at Milly's, but it's definitely on my list of places to feast due to the rave reviews from various readers of *Vegetarian Journal.* One local patron of Milly's writes, "This is the finest, healthful, gourmet, low-fat, delicious food restaurant I have experienced in twenty years of vegetarian restaurant hunting around the world!" **Full service, casual to formal, completely vegan, catering, take-out, $$–$$$**

Szechuan Village Restaurant
720 "B" St., San Rafael, CA 94901   **(415) 454-2828**
Szechuan Chinese. Szechuan Village serves fresh vegetable pot stickers, spring rolls, assorted vegetarian soups, tofu salad, garlic and sweet and sour dishes. **Open daily. Full service, vegan options, wine/beer, take-out, VISA/MC/AMX, $**

SANTA ANA

Niki's Tandoori Express
3705 S. Bristol St., Santa Ana, CA 92704   **(714) 838-7615**

2031 E. 1st St., Santa Ana, CA 92705   **(714) 542-2969**
Indian. Niki's is a new concept in Indian fast food. Some vegetarian options are available. **Open daily. Cafeteria style, wine/beer, take-out, $–$$**

The Village Farmer
South Coast Plaza Village
3810 S. Plaza Dr., Santa Ana, CA 92704   **(714) 557-8433**
American. Vegetarian options are offered. **Open daily. Wine/beer, take-out, VISA/MC/AMX, $$**

SANTA BARBARA

• Follow Your Heart
19 S. Milpas, Santa Barbara, CA 93103   **(805) 966-3694**
Vegetarian. See entry under Canoga Park, CA.

Main Squeeze Cafe & Juice Bar
138 E. Canon Perdido, Santa Barbara, CA 93101   **(805) 966-5365**
Natural foods/macrobiotic. Homemade soups, salads, sandwiches, Mexican specialties, and daily pasta specials are offered in addition to a vegetarian menu. Fresh squeezed juices, smoothies, shakes, and an espresso bar with fresh, homebaked

desserts are also available. **Open daily. Limited service, vegan options, fresh juices, wine/beer, take-out, $**

Sojourner Restaurant & Coffeehouse
134 E. Canon Perdido St., Santa Barbara, CA 93101   (805) 965-7922
Natural foods. Vegetarian options are interspersed throughout the menu, which also includes non-vegetarian dishes. Some international themes are favored such as the Mediterranean plate, curries, and Mexican fare. The Sojourner is now using vegetarian (rennetless) jack and cheddar cheese. Non-alcoholic specialty drinks such as Mocha Frosted and Carob Supreme are offered. Entirely non-smoking. **Open daily. Full service, vegan options, espresso/cappuccino, wine/beer, take-out, $$**

SANTA CLARA

Fresh Choice Restaurants
Corporate Offices
2901 Tasman Dr., Suite 225, Santa Clara, CA 95054   (408) 986-8661
American. There are eighteen Fresh Choice Restaurants in California. Call for locations. An extensive salad selection is complemented by one vegetarian soup and usually at least one vegetarian pasta. A fixed price includes everything—even bread and dessert. **Open daily. Cafeteria style, wine/beer, VISA/MC, $$**

The Good Earth
2705 The Alameda, Santa Clara, CA 95050   (408) 984-0960
Natural foods. Enjoy wok dishes, Vegetarian Scramble, Tofu Scramble, Vegetarian Burger, burritos, tostadas, Eggplant Sandwich, salads, Pasta Primavera, Walnut Mushroom Au Gratin, Guatamalan Rice and Tofu. **Open daily. Full service, wine/beer, VISA/MC/AMX, $$**

Pasand India Cuisine
3701 El Camino Real, Santa Clara, CA 95051   (408) 241-5150
Indian. Authentic South Indian food is prepared with spices and herbs imported from India. Almost half of the menu lists various kinds of vegetarian dishes. Live classical Indian music is featured on Friday and Saturday evenings. **Open daily. Full service, vegan options, wine/beer, catering, take-out, VISA/MC/AMX/DISC/DC, $$**

Rooh's Cafe Salsa
2777 El Camino Real, Santa Clara, CA 95051   (408) 985-ROOH

University Plaza,
1171 Homestead, Santa Clara, CA 95050   (408) 246-2455
Mexican/restaurant chain. See entry under Los Altos, CA.

SANTA CRUZ

The Bagelry
320 A Cedar St., Santa Cruz, CA 95060   (408) 429-8049

1636 Seabright Ave., Santa Cruz, CA 95060   (408) 425-8550
Bagel shop. Twenty kinds of bagels are baked daily. Dairy and non-dairy sandwiches are made with bagels and there are soups, salads, cookies, and a full selection of

hot and cold beverages. Outdoor dining. **Open for three meals daily. Counter service, vegan options, fresh juices, take-out, $**

• Guaranga's
503 Water St., Santa Cruz, CA 95060   **(408) 427-0294**

Vegetarian. This vegetarian self-service restaurant features an all-you-can-eat salad bar and entrees. An entree (choice of four), soup (choice of two), vegetables, bread, and dessert can be had for one low price. Some entrees are vegan, and there is a vegan night three times a week. **Open Monday through Saturday for lunch and dinner. Cafeteria style, vegan options, catering, take-out, $**

Hobee's Restaurant
The Galleria de Santa Cruz
740 Front St., Santa Cruz, CA 95060   **(408) 458-1212**

Restaurant chain. See entry under San Luis Obispo, CA.

India Joze Restaurant
1001 Center St., Santa Cruz, CA 95060   **(408) 427-3554**

Natural foods. On the menu, vegetarian selections are scattered amidst non-vegetarian dishes. The completely vegetarian category includes seven options such as Tempeh Goreng and Coptic Chickpeas. India Joze hosts special food events including "Fungi Festival" in January, "International Chickpea Festival" in February, and "Buddha's Birthday Celebration" in April. Patio seating. **Open for lunch and dinner. Brunch on weekends. Full service, vegan options, fresh juices, wine/beer, take-out, VISA/MC, $$–$$$**

• Indian Summer Deli
2724 Soquel Ave., Santa Cruz, CA 95062   **(408) 476-9840**

Macrobiotic/vegetarian. This seasonal vegetarian, macrobiotic, and, oftentimes, vegan restaurant uses locally grown organic products when available. Little salt and no white sugar is used, even in the homemade desserts and breads. The foods do not contain dairy products, which are available upon request. Indian Summer features The Square Meal, comprised of soup, grain, and beans cooked with kombu. **Open Monday through Saturday afternoon. Limited service, fresh juices, vegan options, catering, take-out, $**

Linda's Seabreeze Cafe
542 Seabright Ave., Santa Cruz, CA 95062   **(408) 427-9713**

American. Called a great restaurant by one of our reviewers, Linda's is a charming place for breakfast or lunch on the way to the Santa Cruz beach. Breakfast features pancakes, Tofu Scramble, and home fries. **Open daily for breakfast and lunch only. Full service, vegan options, take-out, $**

New Leaf Deli
2351 Mission St., Santa Cruz, CA 95060   **(408) 425-1306**

ᐂ Reviewers' choice   • Vegetarian restaurant   •• Vegan restaurant
$ less than $6 $$ $6–$12 $$$ more than $12
VISA/AMX/MC/DISC/DC—credit cards accepted
Non-alc.—Non-alcoholic   Fresh juices—freshly squeezed

Health-food-store deli. While dining outdoors, you can enjoy approximately twenty sandwiches plus hot foods, cold deli salads, soups, and green salads. **Open daily. Cafeteria style, vegan options, fresh juices, wine/beer, take-out, VISA/MC, $**

•• Restaurant Keffi ❧

2-1245-B East Cliff Dr., Santa Cruz, CA 95062 (408) 476-5571

Vegan. "Keffi" is a Greek word that shows you are enjoying the spirit of living; the restaurant aims to help you do that by offering healthy, gourmet vegetarian fare. The menu features appetizers, soups, salads, entrees, desserts, special drinks, and many vegan options. Portions tend to be small but artfully prepared. There's live music Wednesday through Sunday. **Brunch on Sunday. Closed Monday. Full service, vegan options, fresh juices, catering, take-out, $-$$**

Royal Taj India Cuisine

270 Soquel Ave., Santa Cruz, CA 95062 (408) 427-2400

Indian. See entry under Campbell, CA.

Saturn Cafe

1230 Mission St., Santa Cruz, CA 95060 (408) 429-8505

American. The cafe has its own bakery and serves soups, salads, burgers, sandwiches, chili, and ratatouille. **Open daily until midnight. Counter service, vegan options, espresso, wine/beer, take-out, $**

• Staff of Life Natural Foods Market

1305 Water St., Santa Cruz, CA 95062 (408) 423-8041

Vegetarian deli. This market includes a deli that offers burritos, falafels, sandwiches, and soups. The featured entree changes daily and is usually rice- or pasta-based. Some vegan options are available, and various salads and other items may be purchased separately. **Open daily. Cafeteria style, vegan options, fresh juices, take-out, $**

Whole Earth

University of California, Redwood Tower Bldg.
Santa Cruz, CA 95064 (408) 426-8255

Natural foods. Partake of muffins, scrambled tofu, soups, salads, and many vegan options. **Open daily. Cafeteria style, vegan options, take-out, $**

SANTA MONICA

Bistro of Santa Monica

2301 Santa Monica Blvd., Santa Monica, CA 90404 (310) 453-5442

Italian. The Bistro is a European-style restaurant featuring northern Italian cuisine. All items are prepared from scratch without salt, sugar, or preservatives. Vegetarian selections are offered in addition to items for guests with special dietary requirements. Fifteen types of pasta can be combined with numerous sauces listed under tomato, cream, olive oil, and specialty headings. **Open daily. Full service, vegan options, fresh juices, espresso/cappuccino, wine/beer/alcohol, take-out, VISA/MC/AMX/DISC, $$-$$$**

Get Juiced
1423 Fifth St., Santa Monica, CA 90401   **(310) 395-8177**
Juice bar. You can get fresh fruit and vegetable juices, wheatgrass, frozen fruit creams, and custom gift baskets. **Closed Sunday. Deli, fresh juices, VISA/MC/AMX**

News Room Es-press-o Cafe
530 Wilshire Blvd., Santa Monica, CA 90401   **(310) 319-9100**
Natural foods. This cafe always has vegetarian specials including burritos, soups, sandwiches, and salads. There is also a vegan frozen dessert. **Open daily for three meals. Limited service, fresh juices, non-alc. beer, espresso, take-out, $**

Shambala Cafe
607 Colorado Ave., Santa Monica, CA 90401   **(310) 395-2160**
Ethnic. Sandwiches, pita, and pizza offerings are augmented by an international selection of Japanese, Mexican, Chinese, and Indian dishes. **Open daily. Cafeteria style, take-out, $$**

Zabie's
3003 Ocean Park Blvd., Santa Monica, CA 90405   **(310) 399-1150**
Natural foods. The menu is Provencal French and Italian with a Mediterranean influence. Zabie's daily fare is chosen from a list of seasonal dishes for breakfast, lunch, and dinner. The restaurant has its own bakery and uses organic produce and flours when available. **Open Monday through Saturday. Limited service, vegan options, fresh juices, espresso/cappuccino, wine/beer, catering, take-out, $$**

SANTA ROSA

Fresh Choice
277 Santa Rosa Plaza, Santa Rosa, CA 95401   **(707) 525-0912**
American. See entry under Menlo Park, CA.

• Jump Start
1195 W. College Ave., Santa Rosa, CA 95401   **(707) 578-6151**
Vegetarian/deli. The food—soups, salads, breads, hot entrees, Vegetable Pot Pie, Lasagna, African Squash Stew, and Barley Loaf—meets McDougall guidelines. Jump Start also conducts cooking classes. **Open Monday through Saturday afternoon and evening. Deli/bakery, vegan options, fresh juices, catering, take-out, VISA/MC, $$**

• Revelation Original Sandwiches
645 Fourth St., Santa Rosa, CA 95404   **(707) 526-2225**
Vegetarian. Sandwiches, soups, and salads are available. **Open Monday through Saturday for breakfast and lunch. Counter service, take-out, $**

Ristorante Siena
1229 N. Dutton Ave., Santa Rosa, CA 95401   **(707) 578-4511**
Italian/natural foods. The menu for Ristorante Siena includes Antipasti, Insalata, Pasta/Polenta/Pizza (the three P's), Griglia (don't ask me), and specials. Lunch selections also include salads and sandwiches. Patio seating. **Open weekdays for**

lunch and dinner, weekends for brunch and dinner. **Full service, VISA/MC/ AMX/DISC, $$**

Rooh's Cafe Salsa
3082 Marlow Rd., Santa Rosa, CA 95403   **(707) 544-ROOH**
Mexican/restaurant chain. See entry under Los Gatos, CA.

SARATOGA

Hobee's
14550 Big Basin Way, Saratoga Village, CA 95071   **(408) 741-1989**
Restaurant chain. See entry under Cupertino, CA.

Rooh's Cafe Salsa
18832 Cox Ave., Saratoga, CA 95070   **(408) 374-2227**
Mexican/restaurant chain. See entry under Los Gatos, CA.

SEBASTOPOL

• Nancy's Vegetarian
6970 McKinley St., Sebastopol, CA 95472   **(707) 829-6627**
Vegetarian. Vegetarian food is prepared without the use of eggs, white sugar, or preservatives; organic produce is used when available. Nancy's also features low-fat entrees. Soups and desserts are always dairy-free, and desserts are sweetened with barley malt, honey, date sugar, or Sucanat. Selections include grilled tofu, tempeh, or seitan; a nice variety of Mexican options; a veggie roll wrapped in whole-wheat tortilla; and steamed veggies over rice. **Open daily except Wednesday afternoon and evening. Vegan/macrobiotic options, organic coffees, fresh juices, $–$$**

SHERMAN OAKS

Foods for Health
14543 Ventura Blvd., Sherman Oaks, CA 91403   **(818) 784-4033**
Natural foods. Enjoy healthy foods at low prices. Zesty salads, sandwiches, melts, and soups are made fresh every day. Fruit and vegetable juices, and protein drinks are available. **Closed Sunday. Full service, vegan options, fresh juices, take-out, VISA/MC, $**

SOLANA BEACH

Chung King Loh
552 Stevens Ave., Solana Beach, CA 92075   **(619) 481-0184**
Mandarin/Szechuan Chinese. An extensive vegetarian menu is offered at Chung King Loh with more than twenty veggie entrees plus appetizers and soups. Entrees include Broccoli and Carrots in Hot Peanut Sauce, Bean Curd with Ginger and Green Onions, and Mung Bean Noodle with Black Mushrooms. No MSG is used. Dishes made without oil, sugar, and salt are available upon request. **Open daily. Full service, vegan options, wine/beer/alcohol, take-out, VISA/MC/AMX/ DISC/DC/Carte Blanche, $$**

SOQUEL

The Bagelry
4763 Soquel Dr., Soquel, CA 95073   **(408) 462-9888**
Bagel shop. See entry under Santa Cruz, CA.

Tortilla Flats
4724 Soquel Dr., Soquel, CA 95073   **(408) 476-1754**
Mexican. Rice, beans, or the "Flatland Mix" (made from a nut mixture) can be substituted for meat in the burritos and tostadas. **Open daily. Full service, wine/beer, take-out, VISA/MC, $–$$**

SOUTH LAKE TAHOE

Grass Roots Natural Foods Cafe
2040 Dunlap Dr., S. Lake Tahoe, CA 96150   **(916) 541-7788**
Natural foods. Hot and cold sandwiches, Mexican specialties, spuds and fixin's, and soups and salads make up the Grass Roots menu. Fresh juices, smoothies, Aloe Blast, protein drinks, and shakes make up the beverage selection. Cafe, store, and bakery are all at the same location. Seating is limited to fifteen. **Open daily. Limited service, vegan options, fresh juices, take-out, $**

SOUTH PASADENA

Grassroots Natural Food Market and Kitchen
1119 Fair Oaks Ave., South Pasadena, CA 91030   **(818) 799-0156**
Natural foods. Fast and fresh healthy food is made daily—from scratch. There's an unusual variety of salads, dairy-free soups, tasty hot entrees, sandwiches, and a tempting selection of homemade muffins. **Closed Sunday. Cafeteria style, vegan options, fresh juices, take-out, VISA/MC/AMX, $**

STUDIO CITY

•• Vege Gourmet
11288 S. Ventura Blvd., Studio City, CA 91604   **(818) 761-7100**
Vegan. This is gourmet vegan cuisine. Deciding what to order is a challenge; international vegan creations are joined by Veggie Burgers and more classic dishes such as Chili and Lasagna. No artificial ingredients, processed sugar, or salt is used. Desserts, smoothies, and fresh juices tempt your sweet tooth. **Open daily. Completely vegan, take-out, VISA/MC, $$**

SUNNYVALE

The Country Gourmet & Co.
1314 S. Mary Ave., Sunnyvale, CA 94087   **(408) 733-9446**
Natural foods. The Country Gourmet features fresh baked goods, an extensive salad collection, and entrees that change daily. Everything is prepared from fresh ingredients with no preservatives or MSG. A couple of vegetarian entrees are featured nightly in addition to the regular menu selection, and there is a children's menu. No smoking. **Limited service, vegan options, fresh juices, wine/beer, take-out, VISA/MC, $$**

Dahlak Restaurant

1009 Duane Ave., Sunnyvale, CA 94086   **(408) 732-8444**

Eritrean. Low-fat dishes are a specialty of foods from Eritrea (formerly a region of Ethiopia). All dishes—including homemade breads and strict vegetarian offerings— are preservative- and additive-free. A special flax dressing is used on salads. **Closed Sunday. Full service, buffet lunches, vegan options, wine/beer/alcohol, VISA/ MC/AMX**

Royal Taj Indian Cuisine

889 E. El Camino Real, Sunnyvale, CA 94087   **(408) 720-8396**

Indian. See entry under Campbell, CA.

TARZANA

Armen & Salpy's

19014 Ventura Blvd., Tarzana, CA 91356   **(818) 343-1301**

Ethnic/natural foods. Falafel and salads are among the foods prepared daily for this smoke-free restaurant. **Closed Sunday. Full service, wine/beer, take-out, $$**

India's Cuisine

19006 Ventura Blvd., Tarzana, CA 91356   **(818) 342-9100**

Indian. See entry under Los Angeles, CA.

TOPANGA CANYON

Inn of The Seventh Ray

128 Old Topanga Rd., Topanga, CA 90290   **(310) 455-1311**

Gourmet Californian. This up-scale natural foods restaurant is willing to accommo- date special requests. No smoking. **Open daily for dinner, Monday through Friday for lunch, Saturday and Sunday for brunch. Full service, wine/beer, non-alc. wine/beer, take-out, VISA/MC, $$$**

TUSTIN

Rutabegorz

158 W. Main St., Tustin, CA 92680   **(714) 871-1632**

International. See listing under Fullerton, CA.

UKIAH

Earthly Delight

538 E. Perkins St., Ukiah, CA 95482   **(707) 462-4970**

Health-food-store deli. Located in the Pear Tree Shopping Center, Earthly Delight offers homemade bread and soups, and sugar-free frozen yogurt. **Fresh juice, take-out, $**

✎ Reviewers' choice   • Vegetarian restaurant   •• Vegan restaurant
$ less than $6 $$ $6–$12 $$$ more than $12
VISA/AMX/MC/DISC/DC—credit cards accepted
Non-alc.—Non-alcoholic   Fresh juices—freshly squeezed

VENICE

The Dandelion Cafe
636 Venice Blvd., Venice, CA 90291   **(310) 821-4890**
American/Californian. Vegetarians can dine on Vegetarian Chili Tostada, quiche, Vegetable Garden Melt (with cheese), fresh fruit, and Avocado Melt at this patio restaurant with a nice ocean breeze. **Open daily for breakfast and lunch. Full service, vegan options, wine/beer/alcohol, VISA/MC/A MX/DISC, $$**

Fig Tree Cafe
429 Ocean Front Walk, Venice, CA 90291   **(310) 392-4937**
Natural foods. Any dish can be made vegetarian, or choose from Spinach Nutburger, Roasted Eggplant and Peppers, Santa Fe Tostada, and Stir Fry Pizzete (chapati pizza). **Open daily. Full service, wine/beer, VISA/MC/AMX/DISC, $$**

•• I Love Juicy
826 Hampton, Venice, CA 90291   **(310) 399-1318**
Vegan/juice bar. Located on the west side of Los Angeles, this is a casual, cafeteria-style deli and juice bar. All food is vegan with a wonderful array of chilled salads. Hot entree specials are also available. **Open daily from 9 A.M. until midnight. Counter service, fresh juices, catering, take-out, $**

A Votre Santé
1025 Abbott Kinney Blvd., Venice, CA 90291   **(310) 314-1187**
Natural foods. See entry under Brentwood, CA.

VENTURA

Classic Carrot
1847 E. Main St., Ventura, CA 93001   **(805) 643-0406**
Natural foods. Enjoy international ethnic daily specials, homemade soups, vegetarian chili, and sandwiches in a casual, friendly atmosphere. Garden, brick patio, and indoor dining areas feature the work of local artists. All-weather patio dining. **Open for three meals daily. Limited service, vegan options, fresh juices, espresso/cappuccino, wine/beer, take-out, VISA/MC/AMX, $**

•• Garden Fresh
2833 A East Main St., Ventura, CA 93003   **(805) 643-5627**
Vegan/organic. At press time, this restaurant was up for sale. Call before going. Homemade soups, salads, desserts, and non-dairy dessert drinks had been available. Organic produce and purified water were used. **Open Monday through Saturday afternoon and early evening. Full service, fresh juices, take-out, VISA/MC, $**

Tipps Thai Cuisine
512 East Main St., Ventura, CA 93001   **(805) 643-3040**
Thai. Tipps has a full vegetarian menu featuring more than twenty entrees plus appetizers, soups, and salads. Entrees include standard vegetable dishes, mock meats, curries, and noodle and rice dishes. No MSG is used. **Open Monday through Saturday for lunch and dinner. Full service, vegan options, wine/beer, take-out, VISA/MC/AMX, $$**

WALNUT CREEK

Pita King

1607 Palo Verdes Mall, Walnut Creek, CA 94596   (510) 945-0386
Middle Eastern/pita bread bakery. Pita King serves falafel and other vegetarian sandwiches. **Open Monday through Saturday for breakfast and lunch. Counter service, take-out, $**

WESTLAKE VILLAGE

India House Restaurant

860 Hampshire Rd., Ste. 2, Westlake Village, CA 91362   (805) 373-6266
Indian. India House grinds its own spices, in addition to making its own cheese,
yogurt, and breads. Only vegetable oil is used for cooking and no preservatives.
The menu includes appetizers, clay oven entrees, curries, eight vegetarian items,
breads, rice dishes, desserts, and beverages. **Closed Monday. Full service, vegan
options, wine/beer, take-out, VISA/MC, $–$$**

WILLITS

• Harvest Bounty

39 S. Main, Willits, CA 95490   (707) 459-9647
Vegetarian. Fresh baked cornbread complements homestyle meals, and organic
produce is used in salads. **Open for lunch. Full service, fresh juices, $**

Tsunami Restaurant

50 S. Main St., Willits, CA 95490   (707) 459-4750
Japanese/international. Dinner and lunch menu headings include Sushi, Salads,
Side Orders, Grilled, Cajun, Colache, and Tempura. All categories list vegetable, tofu, fish, and chicken selections, and vegetarian specials are also offered.
Dishes are all carefully prepared from scratch with natural ingredients, and
most vegetables are locally and organically grown. Dessert selections are
prepared without dairy, sugar, or eggs. Beverages include local micro-brewery
beers, coffee, and wine. Dine on the patio amidst Japanese maple trees, plum
trees, and flowers. **Closed Sunday. Reservations recommended. Full service,
wine/beer, take-out, $$**

YREKA

Yreka Cafe

322 W. Miner, Yreka, CA 96097   (916) 842-6010
Natural foods. Fettucine, salads, and omelettes are featured. **Closed Sunday. Full
service, take-out, $**

COLORADO

Carnitas
529 Main St., Alamosa, CO 81101   **(719) 589-0475**
Southwestern. Carnitas features Southwestern and traditional Spanish cuisines with vegetarian options. Blue-corn or whole-wheat pancakes, posale, and many standard dishes that emphasize low-fat and whole-grain foods appear on the menu. **Open for three meals daily. Full service, vegan options, fresh juice, take-out, $$**

• Explore Coffeehouse
221 E. Main St., Aspen, CO 81611   **(303) 925-5336**
Vegetarian. This sophisticated gourmet vegetarian restaurant and European-style coffeehouse is located under the same roof as a contemporary bookstore. Each week, a different ethnic specialty is featured in addition to the standard offerings of soups, salad bar, tofu burger, and steamed veggies. **Open daily for lunch and dinner. Full service, children's menu, vegan options, take-out, VISA/MC, $$**

Denver Salad Co.
14201 E. Public Market, Aurora, CO 80012   **(303) 750-1339**
American. Features seventy-item salad bar, fresh soups, potato bar, and sandwiches. **Open daily. Cafeteria service, wine/beer, take-out, VISA/MC, $$**

Fong Lynn
1780 S. Buckley Rd., Aurora, CO 80017   **(303) 745-9111**
Chinese. Fong Lynn features tofu dishes. **Open daily for lunch. Full service, wine/ beer/alcohol, take-out, VISA/MC/AMX, $**

Wild Oats Market
12131 East Iliff Ave., Aurora, CO 80014   **(303) 695-8801**
Health-food-store deli. Wholesome vegetarian dishes feature ethnic foods that are prepared locally, salads, and baked goods. Wild Oats has recently added an espresso/juice bar. **Open daily. Deli service, fresh juices, espresso, take-out, VISA/MC/DISC, $**

Alfalfa's Market
1651 Broadway, Boulder, CO 80302   **(303) 442-0909**
Natural foods. Sandwiches, salads, and fresh baked goods are offered. **Open daily. Cafeteria style, catering, vegan options, take-out, VISA/MC, $**

Attusso's Italian Cafe
1739 Pearl St., Boulder, CO 80302   **(303) 442-2262**

Italian. Imported pasta with fresh, organic veggies and everything else on the menu is made to order. **Open daily for dinner. Full service, wine/beer/alcohol, take-out, VISA/MC/AMX/DISC, $$$**

Boulder Salad Co.

2595 Canyon Blvd., Boulder, CO 80302   **(303) 447-8272**

American. Features seventy-item salad bar, fresh soups, potato bar, and sandwiches. **Open daily. Cafeteria service, wine/beer, take-out, VISA/MC, $$**

Cafe Central

2100 Central Ave., Boulder, CO 80301   **(303) 443-8855**

Cafeteria. Cafe Central is an up-scale cafeteria serving pastries, salads, soups, specials, and sandwiches prepared fresh daily. Vegetarian options. Carryout breakfast and box lunches are available. **Open Monday through Friday for breakfast and lunch. Cafeteria style, fresh juice, wine/beer/alcohol, take-out, VISA/MC, $**

• Creative Cafe ✿

1837 Pearl St., Boulder, CO 80302   **(303) 449-1952**

Vegetarian. Home-cooked foods are made with organic vegetables when in season. The atmosphere is charming and the portions are good-sized. **Open daily. Sunday brunch. Full service, take-out, VISA/MC, $$**

Dot's Diner

799 Pearl St., Boulder, CO 80302   **(303) 449-1323**

Natural foods. Dot's bases its reputation on its homestyle breakfasts, which are served through lunchtime every day. The lunch menu includes daily specials, Mexican dishes, grilled sandwiches, and a variety of vegetarian entrees. **Open daily for breakfast and lunch. Full service, fresh juice, espresso/capuccino, take-out, no credit cards, $**

Golden Buff

1725 28th St., Boulder, CO 80301   **(303) 442-2800**

Natural foods. **Open for three meals daily. Full service, fresh juice, wine/beer, take-out, VISA/MC, $-$$**

Harvest Express

2006 Broadway, Boulder, CO 80304   **(303) 449-6225**

Health-food-store deli. Harvest Express serves nutritious and delicious soups, salads, snacks, sandwiches, entrees, and fresh baked breads and other baked goods. Lots of smoothies and shakes as well. **Open daily. Cafeteria style, fresh juices, espresso/capuccino, take-out, $**

Harvest Restaurant & Bakery

1738 Pearl St., Boulder, CO 80302   **(303) 449-6223**

Mexican/healthy foods. The menu includes appetizers, salads, dressings, entrees, hot and cold sandwiches, burgers, and desserts with many vegetarian options. Harvest Restaurant specializes in low-fat, low-cholesterol, low-salt items for breakfast, lunch and dinner. Healthful items are indicated by the Healthmark (HM). In-house bakery. **Open for three meals daily. Full service, vegan options, fresh juice, wine/beer, take-out, VISA/MC/AMX, $$**

Healthy Habits
4760 Baseline, Boulder, CO 80303   **(303) 733-2105**
American. The restaurant features an extensive salad bar, with three vegetarian soups and three veggie pasta sauces that change daily, along with bread, muffins, and desserts. **Open daily. Cafeteria service, wine/beer, take-out, VISA/MC/AMX, $$**

Himalaya's
2010 14th St., Boulder, CO 80302   **(303) 442-3230**
International. The cuisine here includes Indian, Nepali, and Tibetan food. Fresh breads are baked in the restaurant's Tandoor oven. Lunch is a buffet with four vegetarian dishes. **Open daily. Full service, wine/beer, take-out, VISA/MC, $$**

José Muldoon's
1600 38th St., Boulder, CO 80301   **(303) 449-4543**
Mexican. Blue corn, Santa Fe-style vegetarian and authentic Mexican fare includes appetizers, soups, salads, sandwiches, burgers, tostada bar, and vegetarian specials. Patio dining. **Open daily for lunch and dinner. Sunday brunch. Full service, vegan options, wine/beer/alcohol, take-out, VISA/MC/AMX, $–$$**

Nancy's
825 Walnut St., Boulder, CO 80302   **(303) 449-8402**
American/ethnic. Saturday and Sunday breakfast at Nancy's is a Boulder tradition. The restaurant also serves lunch and dinner, and in 1992 introduced four-course vegetarian specials nightly. **Open daily. Full service, vegan options, fresh juices, wine/beer/alcohol, take-out, VISA/MC/AMX, $–$$**

Narayan's Nepal Restaurant
921 Pearl St., Boulder, CO 80302   **(303) 447-2816**
Nepalese. A full menu of fine Nepali entrees is geared to the vegetarian diet. The menu includes vegetable curry, stuffed jumbo roti, pakodas, samosas, etc. **Full service, vegan options, wine/beer/alcohol, take-out, VISA/MC/AMX, $**

Pablo's New Mexican Cafe
2865 Baseline Rd., Boulder, CO 80303   **(303) 442-7512**
Mexican. Seven vegetarian options are on the menu at Pablo's. Tofu and tempeh are used in some of these dishes. Heart-healthy dishes are indicated on the menu by the Healthmark (HM). **Open daily. Full service, vegan options, fresh juice, wine/beer/alcohol, take-out, VISA/MC/AMX, $$**

Rocky Mountain Joe's Cafe & Espresso Bar
1410 Pearl St., Boulder, CO 80302   **(303) 442-3969**
Natural foods. Tempeh and garden burgers, vegetarian chili, salads, and some breakfast items make up the vegetarian offerings on Rocky Joe's menu. **Open daily for breakfast and lunch. Full service, fresh juice, espresso/cappuccino, take-out, VISA/MC, $**

Rudi's Restaurant
4720 Table Mesa Dr., Boulder, CO 80303   **(303) 494-5858**
Natural foods. Extended gourmet vegetarian menu along with ethnic specialties.

All food is fresh and homemade. Bakery, cafe, coffee, fruit and juice bar. **Open daily for lunch and dinner. Weekend brunch. Full service, fresh juices, wine/beer, VISA/MC/DISC, $$**

Siamese Plate & Sumida's Sushi Bar
1575 Folsom, Boulder, CO 80302 (303) 447-9718

Thai. The vegetarian menu has a good selection of appetizers, soups, and entrees. Vegetarian versions of many of the regular menu items are available as well. **Open daily for lunch and dinner. Full service, wine/beer/alcohol, take-out, $$**

Walnut Cafe
3073 Walnut, Boulder, CO 80301 (303) 447-2315

Natural foods. Whether you're in the mood for a Boulder-sized muffin, Huevos Rancheros, or a Veggie Burger, the "Nut" has what you're looking for. The cafe cooks up a special soup, quiche, and omelette every day and has an espresso menu with sixteen drinks. No smoking. **Open daily for breakfast and lunch. Dinner served Thursday through Sunday. Full service, fresh juices, espresso/cappuccino, take-out, VISA/MC/DISC, $**

Wild Oats Market
2584 Baseline, Boulder, CO 80303 (303) 499-7636

Health-food-store deli. Features Tabouleh, Hummus, Pasta Salad, and soup, with a full dinner menu. Some non-vegetarian items. **Open daily. Counter service, vegan options, take-out, VISA/MC/DISC, $**

• Wild Oats Vegetarian Market
1825 Pearl St., Boulder, CO 80302 (303) 440-9599

Vegetarian/health-food-store deli. Same as Wild Oats Market (above), except all vegetarian.

Young's Place Asian Cuisine
1083 14th St., Boulder, CO 80302 (303) 447-9837

Asian. Korean, Japanese, Chinese, and Mongolian cuisines are served at Young's Place. The Mongolian barbecue has tofu and vegetable options, and there are some other vegetarian selections. **Closed Sunday. Full service, take-out, $**

BRECKENRIDGE

Amazing Grace Natural Foods
213 Lincoln Ave., Breckenridge, CO 80424 (303) 453-1445

Health-food-store deli. Located in a historic building, Amazing Grace has a chalkboard menu that lists a soup du jour, veggie sandwiches, smoothies, garden salads, and fresh juice. **Open daily for lunch and dinner. Deli service, fresh juices, take-out, $**

ᨠ Reviewers' choice • Vegetarian restaurant •• Vegan restaurant
$ less than $6 $$ $6–$12 $$$ more than $12
VISA/AMX/MC/DISC/DC—credit cards accepted
Non-alc.–Non-alcoholic   Fresh juices—freshly squeezed

The Red Orchid
206 N. Main St., Breckenridge, CO 80424   **(303) 453-1881**
Chinese. Szechuan, Hunan, and Mandarin cuisines are offered at the Red Orchid. Some vegetarian dishes include Braised Bean Curd, Moo Shu Vegetables, and Szechuan Eggplant. **Open daily for lunch and dinner. Full service, deck dining, vegan options, wine/beer/alcohol, take-out, VISA/MC, $$**

CHERRY CREEK

Alfalfa's
201 University, Cherry Creek, CO 80209   **(303) 442-0909**
Natural foods. See description under Boulder, CO.

COLORADO SPRINGS

Dale Street Cafe
115 E. Dale St., Colorado Springs, CO 80903   **(719) 578-9898**
Natural foods. All natural freshly prepared foods include appetizers, salads, pasta, and some Mediterranean dishes. **Open daily for lunch and dinner. Full service, non-alc. beer, wine/beer/alcohol, take-out, VISA/MC, $$**

Golden Dragon Restaurant
903 S. 8th St., Colorado Springs, CO 80906   **(719) 632-3607**
Chinese/American. Vegetarian appetizers, soup, and entrees are available at the Golden Dragon. No MSG is used and the restaurant is willing to accommodate special diets (may require advance notice). **Open daily for lunch and dinner. Full service, vegan options, wine/beer/alcohol, take-out, VISA/MC/AMX/DISC, $$**

José Muldoon's
222 N. Tejon St., Colorado Springs, CO 80903   **(719) 636-2311**
Mexican. See description under Boulder, CO.

The Olive Branch
333 N. Tejon St., Colorado Springs, CO 80903   **(719) 475-1199**
Natural foods. Vegetarian, "heart healthy," and other items are served. **Open for three meals daily. Full service, fresh juices, take-out, VISA/MC/AMX, $**

The Olive Branch
2140 Vickers Dr., Colorado Springs, CO 80918   **(719) 593-9522**
Natural foods. See previous listing for description. **Breakfast and lunch only.**

DENVER

(For more restaurant listings in the surrounding areas, see Aurora, Englewood, Littleton, Westminster, and Wheatridge.)

Beau Jo's Pizza
2700 S. Colorado Blvd., Denver, CO 80222   **(303) 758-1519**
Pizza restaurant. Enjoy delicious pizza—sixteen vegetarian toppings and a vegan pizza topped with tofu and whatever else you'd like! A soup and salad bar is also

available. **Open daily for lunch and dinner. Full service, vegan options, wine/beer/alcohol, take-out, VISA/MC/AMX/DISC, $**

City Spirit Cafe
1434 Blake St., Denver, CO 80202   **(303) 575-0022**
Natural foods. Everything served here is made from scratch. Organic items are available. The use of fats is minimal. Entrees include organic tamales, Cityburritas, and Urbanachos. Live music on weekends. **Open late daily. Full service, vegan options, wine/beer/alcohol, take-out, $**

Delhi Darbar
1514 Blake St., Denver, CO 80202   **(303) 595-0680**
Indian. Buffet lunch every day features primarily vegetarian foods, and the extensive vegetarian dinner menu includes fresh baked breads. **Open daily for lunch and dinner. Full service, wine/beer/alcohol, take-out, VISA/MC/AMX/ DISC, $$**

Denver Salad Co.
2700 S. Colorado Blvd., Denver, CO 80207   **(303) 691-2050**
American. See description under Aurora, CO.

Golden Tempura Bowl
1448 Market St., Denver, CO 80202   **(303) 534-3370**
Japanese. Healthy Japanese food is served efficiently in a fast-food-restaurant atmosphere. **Closed Sunday. Counter service, BYOB, take-out, $**

Good Friends
3100 E. Colfax Ave., Denver, CO 80206   **(303) 399-1751**
Natural foods. "Fern bar" from the '70s offers a wide selection of moderately priced foods. Over half of the menu is vegetarian including dishes such as eggplant salad, stir-fry, Mexican food without lard, and salads. **Open daily for lunch and dinner. Full service, wine/beer/alcohol, take-out, VISA/MC/AMX/DISC, $–$$**

• Govinda's Vegetarian Buffet
1400 Cherry St., Denver, CO 80220   **(303) 333-5462**
Vegetarian buffet. Here's an all-you-can-eat vegetarian buffet in the Govinda's tradition. No eggs are used and only vegetarian (rennetless) cheese is served. Thursday is vegan day—all items are non-dairy. Salad bar, rice, breads, and steamed vegetables round out the international entrees. **Closed Sunday. Buffet, vegan options, take-out, VISA/ MC, $**

Greens Natural Foods Cafe
320 E. Colfax Ave., Denver, CO 80203   **(303) 831-1315**
Natural foods. Greens features fresh, seasonal dishes cooked to order. Organic ingredients are used when possible. The menu includes salads, sandwiches, and hot plates. **Open daily. Full service, vegan options, wine/beer, take-out, VISA/ MC/AMX, $$**

Harvest Restaurant & Bakery
430 S. Colorado Blvd., Denver, CO 80222   **(303) 399-6652**

5056 S. Wadsworth, Denver, CO 80123   **(303) 933-2011**
Mexican/healthy foods. See entry under Boulder, CO.

Healthy Habits
865 S. Colorado Blvd., Denver, CO 80206   **(303) 733-2105**
American. See description under Boulder, CO.

Jerusalem Restaurant
1890 E. Evans Ave., Denver, CO 80210   **(303) 777-8828**
Middle Eastern. The Middle Eastern food offered at this restaurant includes many vegetarian appetizers and a couple of "combo" dishes that make a satisfying meal. A special section of the menu lists the vegetable dishes. **Open daily, 24 hours on Friday and Saturday. Full service, vegan options, take-out, VISA/MC/AMX, $**

Josephina's
7777 E. Hampden Ave. #120, Denver, CO 80231   **(303) 750-4422**
Italian. Josephina's serves Northern and Southern Italian foods plus heart-healthy and vegetarian dishes. Heart-healthy items are indicated on the menu. **Open daily. Full service, vegan options, wine/beer/alcohol, take-out, VISA/MC/AMX/ DISC, $$**

Mediterranean Health Cafe
2817 E. 3rd Ave., Denver, CO 80206   **(303) 399-2940**
Kosher/Mediterranean. Various Middle Eastern vegetarian foods are available from the primarily vegetarian menu. Fish is the only non-vegetarian food served. On the menu are Falafel, Hummus, Veggie Burger, Vegetarian Chili, and sandwiches. The editors of the *Vegetarian Journal* give the food rave reviews. **Open daily. Full service, kosher, vegan options, take-out, VISA/MC/AMX, $**

Paul's Place
Cherry Creek Shopping Center
3000 E. 1st Ave., #115, Denver, CO 80206   **(303) 321-5801**
Gourmet fast food. This fast-food restaurant offers a wide selection of vegetarian and vegan dishes including veggie burgers and hot dogs, sandwiches, tamales, burritos, chili, baked potatoes, and tacos. **Open Monday through Saturday for three meals. Counter service, vegan options, catering, take-out, VISA/MC/DISC, $**

• Rosewood Cafe
Porter Hospital, 2525 S. Downing St., Denver, CO 80210   **(303) 778-5881**
Vegetarian. The Rosewood Cafe offers an exciting, varied menu that changes daily. Most food, including baked goods, is freshly prepared. The public is welcome! **Open every day. Cafeteria Style, kosher, some vegan options, fresh juice, take-out, no credit cards, $**

Seoul Food
701 E. 6th Ave., Denver, CO 80203   **(303) 837-1460**
Korean. Seoul Food serves authentic Korean cuisine with vegetarian and health-oriented selections. **Open daily for lunch and dinner. Full service, wine/beer, take-out, VISA/MC, $**

T-WA Inn Vietnamese Restaurant
555 S. Federal Blvd., Denver, CO 80219   **(303) 922-4584**
Vietnamese. Special vegetarian section on menu features fourteen entree options

including Vegetables with Rice Noodles, Tofu with Lemongrass, curry, and egg-plant dishes. **Open daily for lunch and dinner. Full service, vegan options, wine/beer/alcohol, VISA/MC/AMX, $$**

Walnut Cafe
338 E. Colfax Ave., Denver, CO 80203   **(303) 832-5108**
Natural foods. Open for breakfast and lunch. Tofu available as a meat, cheese, or egg substitute. **Open daily. Full service, take-out, $**

Wolfe's Barbecue
333 E. Colfax Ave., Denver, CO 80203   **(303) 831-1500**
Barbecue. Traditional hole-in-the-wall (their words, not ours!) barbecue offering vegan BBQ entrees and side dishes. Wolfe's even has coleslaw without mayonnaise! **Open Monday through Friday for lunch and dinner. Limited service, take-out, VISA/MC, $**

ENGLEWOOD

Paul's Place
Southgate Shopping Center
6818 S. Yosemite, Englewood, CO 80237   **(303) 771-8855**
Gourmet fast food. This fast-food restaurant offers a wide selection of vegetarian and vegan fast dishes including veggie burgers and hot dogs, sandwiches, tamales, burritos, chili, baked potatoes, and tacos. **Open daily for breakfast, lunch, and dinner. Counter service, vegan options, catering, take-out, VISA/MC/DISC, $**

Twin Dragon Restaurant
3021 S. Broadway, Englewood, CO 80110   **(303) 781-8068**
Mandarin/Szechuan. Extensive menu offers approximately fifteen vegetable and tofu options. **Open daily for lunch and dinner. Full service, vegan options, wine/beer/alcohol, take-out, VISA/MC/AMX/DISC, $$**

ESTES PARK

Molly B's
200 Moraine Ave., P.O. Box 3280, Estes Park, CO 80517   **(303) 586-2766**
Natural foods. Vegetarian selections are available for both lunch and dinner. Examples include pasta, stir-fry, and lasagna. Various specials are offered daily. Baked goods are prepared on the premises. **Full service, vegan options, fresh juices, wine/beer, take-out, VISA/MC/AMX, $$**

EVERGREEN

River Sage Restaurant
4651 S. Hwy. 73, Evergreen, CO 80439   **(303) 674-2914**
Natural foods. The cuisine is described as "exuberant Rocky Mountain," and you can dine indoors surrounded by wonderful artwork, or on the streamside deck. Featured are homemade entrees such as Rainbow Garden Skillet for breakfast, Vegi Burritos and Southwestern Tempeh Sauté for lunch, and Oriental Nine Vegetable Wok or Indian Vegetable Curry for dinner. **Open daily. Full service, vegan options, wine/beer, take-out, VISA/MC, $$**

FORT COLLINS

Chow's Garden
23 Old Town Square #100, Fort Collins, CO 80524   **(303) 484-6142**
Chinese. There's a vegetarian section on the menu with nine selections including eggplant and tofu dishes. **Full service, wine/beer/alcohol, take-out, VISA/MC/AMX/ DISC, $–$$**

Cozzola's Pizza
241 Linden, Fort Collins, CO 80524   **(303) 482-3557**
Pizza restaurant. Cozzola's offers gourmet pizza with whole-wheat, herb, or white crusts plus a variety of sauces and toppings—even soy cheese! Some of the sauces do contain cheese, so vegans should inquire first. **Closed Monday. Full service, vegan options, take-out, no credit cards, $**

Cuisine! Cuisine!
130 S. Mason, Fort Collins, CO 80524   **(303) 221-0399**
International. Chalkboard menu changes daily, featuring regional and international theme weeks such as French, Caribbean, Southwestern, Pacific Northwest, Cajun, and Southeast Asian. There are vegetarian options. **Closed Mondays. Full service, formal, vegan options, take-out, VISA/MC/AMX, $$$**

Fort Collins Food Co-op
250 E. Mountain Ave., Fort Collins, CO 80524   **(303) 484-7448**
Natural foods deli. This small take-out deli is in a natural foods market. **Open Monday through Friday. Deli service, fresh juice, take-out, no credit cards, $**

Rainbow Ltd.
212 W. Laurel, Fort Collins, CO 80521   **(303) 221-2664**
Natural foods. **Open daily. Full service, wine/beer, take-out, VISA/MC, $**

Rio Grande Mexican Restaurant
143 W. Mountain Ave., Ft. Collins, CO 80524   **(303) 224-5428**
Mexican. Rio Grande serves authentic Mexican foods with sauces made fresh daily. All bean dishes are made with black beans and without lard. **Open daily. Full service, vegan options, wine/beer/alcohol, take out, VISA/MC/DISC, $$**

Spudworks Restaurant
626 S. College Ave., Fort Collins, CO 80524   **(303) 484-5400**
American. Spudworks offers more than thirty toppings for potatoes, half of which are vegetarian. It also has soups, salads, sandwiches, and homemade desserts. **Closed Sunday. Full service, vegan options, wine/beer, take-out, VISA/MC, $**

GRAND JUNCTION

Good Pastures Restaurant & Lounge
733 Horizon Dr., Grand Junction, CO 81506   **(303) 243-3058**
International. Good Pastures takes pride in serving as natural a product as possible and therefore avoids using chemicals, dyes, and preservatives. The menu is varied and geared to please any appetite. **Open for three meals daily. Full service, vegan options, fresh juices, wine/beer/alcohol, take-out, VISA/MC/AMX/DISC, $$**

River City Cafe & Bar
748 North Ave., Grand Junction, CO 81501 (303) 245-8040
Natural foods. The menu features pasta, bean burgers, bean burritos, and enchiladas. **Open daily. Full service, vegan options, non-alc. beer, wine/beer/alcohol, take-out, VISA/MC/AMX/DISC, $$**

• Sundrop Grocery
741 Main St., Grand Junction, CO 81501 (303) 243-1175
Vegetarian deli. The fare here is pre-made sandwiches including tofuna, guacamole, veggie pita, bagel sandwiches and more. **Closed Sunday. Take-out only, vegan options, $**

GREENWOOD VILLAGE

Harvest Restaurant & Bakery
7730 E. Belleview, Greenwood Village, CO 80111 (303) 779-4111
Mexican/healthy food. See Boulder, CO, listing for description.

IDAHO SPRINGS

Beau Jo's Pizza
1517 Miner St., Idaho Springs, CO 80452 (303) 567-4376
Pizza. A visit to Beau Jo's will undoubtedly be worth the trip, whether you eat or not. Seventeen years' worth of napkin art is displayed at the restaurant. But if you do want to eat, the pizza options are just as interesting. Sixteen vegetarian toppings are offered plus a tofu pizza, which is vegan. There is also a soup and salad bar. **Open daily for lunch and dinner. Full service, vegan options, wine/beer/alcohol, take-out, VISA/MC/AMX/DISC, $$**

LAFAYETTE

Efrain's Mexican Restaurante & Cantina
101 E. Cleveland, Lafayette, CO 80026 (303) 666-7544
Mexican. Mexican food is prepared fresh daily, and vegetarian items are indicated on the menu. **Open daily for lunch and dinner. Full service, vegan options, take-out, VISA/MC, $**

LITTLETON

Alfalfa's
5910 S. University, Littleton, CO 80121 (303) 798-9699
Natural foods/juice bar. A natural foods store with deli, bakery, pizza bar, and juice bar. **Open daily for three meals. Cafeteria style, fresh juices, cappuccino, take-out, catering, VISA/MC/DISC, $$**

◆ Reviewers' choice • Vegetarian restaurant •• Vegan restaurant
$ less than $6 $$ $6–$12 $$$ more than $12
VISA/AMX/MC/DISC/DC—credit cards accepted
Non-alc.–Non-alcoholic Fresh juices—freshly squeezed

Denver Salad Co.
2010 E. County Line Rd., Littleton, CO 80126   **(303) 798-3453**
American. See description under Aurora, CO.

Harvest Restaurant & Bakery
5056 S. Wadsworth Blvd., Littleton, CO 80123   **(303) 933-2011**
Natural foods. See description under Boulder, CO.

LONGMONT

Ichi Ban Japanese Restaurant
1834 N. Main St., Longmont, CO 80501   **(303) 772-6882**
Japanese. Ichi Ban features authentic Japanese foods with vegetarian options such
as Egg Rolls, Vegetable Tempura, and noodle dishes. **Open Tuesday through
Saturday. Full service, wine/beer, take-out, VISA/MC, $$**

LOUISVILLE

Karen's Kitchen
700 Main St., Louisville, CO 80027   **(303) 666-8020**
Natural foods. Features Eggplant Parmesan, burritos, Lasagna, and salads. **Open
daily, only brunch served on Sunday. Full service, vegan options, wine/beer,
take-out, $$**

MANITOU SPRINGS

Adam's Mountain Cafe
733 Manitou Ave., Manitou Springs, CO 80829   **(719) 685-1430**
Natural foods. This award-winning restaurant features Southwestern entrees including a breakfast burrito. Other dishes include the Small Planet Burger and
Vegetarian Colorado. Scenic location. **Open daily. Full service, vegan options,
wine/beer, take-out, $$**

TELLURIDE

Athenian Senate
123 S. Spruce, Telluride, CO 81435   **(303) 728-3018**
Greek/Italian. This is a friendly and comfortable family restaurant. Many Greek
and pasta dishes are suitable for vegetarians. Children's menu. **Open daily. Full
service, vegan options, wine/beer/alcohol, take-out, VISA/MC/AMX, $$$**

Gregor's Bakery & Cafe
217 E. Colorado Ave., Telluride, CO 81435   **(303) 728-3334**
Natural foods. This restaurant serves a variety of creative vegetarian foods and
features a bakery. **Open daily. Limited service, beer, take-out, $$**

Natural Source
124 E. Colorado Ave., Telluride, CO 81435   **(303) 728-4833**
Health-food-store deli. Features soups, sandwiches, and salads, and two hot entrees
daily, which are usually vegan. **Open daily. Take-out service only, vegan options,
VISA/MC/AMX, $**

WESTMINSTER

La Casa Loma Cafe
710 W. 120th St., Westminster, CO 80234   **(303) 450-6906**
Mexican/American. La Casa Loma's menu features low-cholesterol foods that include many Mexican and American dishes. No lard is used in the beans or green chili. Vegetarian options are on the menu, and the restaurant is willing to accommodate special diets. **Closed Sunday. Full service, vegan options, wine/ beer/alcohol, take-out, VISA/MC, $**

WHEATRIDGE

Gemini Restaurant
4300 Wadsworth Blvd., Loehmann's Plaza
Wheatridge, CO 80033   **(303) 421-4990**
Natural foods/ethnic. Extensive menu offers appetizers, salads, soups, sandwiches, quiche, pasta, and Mexican dishes—vegetarian and non-vegetarian foods. Children's menu. **Open for three meals daily, weekend brunch. Full service, vegan options, fresh juice, wine/beer/alcohol, take-out, VISA/MC, $$**

CONNECTICUT

BRIDGEPORT

• Bloodroot ૨ક
85 Ferris St., Bridgeport, CT 06605   **(203) 576-9168**
Vegetarian. Situated on an inlet in Long Island Sound, Bloodroot is "a feminist restaurant and bookstore with a seasonal vegetarian menu." This menu changes every three to four weeks to take advantage of foods in season. Outdoor dining on the herb terrace. **Open Tuesday and Thursday through Sunday. Limited service weekdays, full service on weekends, vegan options, wine/beer, no credit cards, $$**

CANTON

Tangiers Mediterranean Cafe
140 Albany Turnpike, Canton, CT 06019   **(203) 693-6668**
Middle Eastern. Savor vegetarian Middle Eastern specialties. **Closed Tuesday. Full service, vegan options, fresh juice, take-out, VISA/MC, $$**

DANBURY

Sesame Seed
68 W. Wooster St., Danbury, CT 06810   **(203) 743-9850**
Natural foods. Middle Eastern dishes, Broccoli Strudel, Spinach Dumplings, and Vegetable Pie are featured at Sesame Seed. **Closed Sunday. Full service, non-alc. beer, wine/beer, take-out, $–$$**

HARTFORD

Cafe at Reader's Feast
529 Farmington Ave., Hartford, CT 06105 **(203) 232-3710**

Cafe and bookstore. Various international menu items and sandwiches are served. Breakfast includes granola, eggs, French toast, and omelettes. Reader's Feast has a monthly art exhibit by local artists, and readings on most Sundays. Menu changes seasonally. **Open for breakfast, lunch, and dinner Monday through Saturday; only for brunch on Sunday. Full service for dinner, cafeteria style for lunch, vegan options, wine/beer, take-out, VISA/MC, $-$$**

Congress Rotisserie
7 Maple Ave., Hartford, CT 06114 **(203) 560-1965**

Bistro. A stir-fry and a pasta dish make up the vegetarian selection on the menu at this bistro, but the restaurant notes that special diets can be accommodated. In general, the menu features eclectic fish and chicken dishes. **Open daily. Full service, wine/beer/alcohol, take-out, VISA/MC/AMX, $$**

Kashmir Restaurant
481 Wethersfield Ave., Hartford, CT 06114 **(203) 296-9685**

Indian. Sample classic Moghul cooking plus a wide variety of authentic dishes from various Indian traditions. The menu includes appetizers, soups, side dishes, entrees, breads, and desserts, all of which are prepared without artificial ingredients, additives, or saturated fats. **Full service, vegan options, take-out, $$**

MIDDLETOWN

•• It's Only Natural Restaurant
686 Main St., Middletown, CT 06457 **(203) 346-9210**

Vegan. This is a vegan restaurant serving international gourmet vegetarian and macrobiotic meals, and featuring fresh baked bread and desserts. **Open Tuesday through Saturday. Full service, completely vegan, fresh juices, catering, take-out, AMX, $$**

NEW HAVEN

Avanti's
45 Grove St., New Haven, CT 06511 **(203) 777-3234**

Italian. Avanti's is an Italian restaurant and pizzeria with several vegan options. **Closed Sunday. Full service, vegan options, espresso/cappuccino, wine/beer, take-out, VISA/MC, $$**

Claire's CornerCopia
1000 Chapel St., New Haven, CT 06510 **(203) 562-3888**

International. Claire's offers meatless Mexican, Italian, and Jewish fare. The wide variety of baked goods is made on the premises. **Open daily. Limited service, vegan options, fresh juices, take-out, no credit cards, $-$$**

Edge of the Woods
379 Whalley Ave., New Haven, CT 06511 **(203) 787-1055**
Health-food-store deli. Partake of vegetarian fare with some vegan choices and baked goods. **Open daily. Sunday brunch. Cafeteria style, fresh juices, take-out, $**

House of Chao
898 Whalley Ave., New Haven, CT 06515 **(203) 389-6624**
Chinese. House of Chao offers many vegan options and is accustomed to adjusting the menu for vegetarians. **Open daily for lunch and dinner. Full service, vegan options, take-out, $$**

India Palace
65 Howe St., New Haven, CT 06511 **(203) 776-9010**
Indian. There's a vegetarian menu section plus vegetable pakora, samosas, soup, breads, and desserts. **Open daily for lunch and dinner. Full service, vegan options, wine/beer, take-out, VISA/MC, $$**

Mamoun's Falafel Restaurant
85 Howe St., New Haven, CT 06511 **(203) 562-8444**
Middle Eastern. Traditional Middle Eastern foods such as Hummus, Falafel, Baba Ghanouj, salads, and pastries are served. **Open daily. Limited service, vegan options, take-out, $**

Rainbow Garden
1022 Chapel St., New Haven, CT 06511 **(203) 777-2390**
Natural foods. Hot and cold vegetarian sandwiches along with ethnic entrees, daily specials, and soups are available at Rainbow Garden. Menu changes daily and has many vegan entrees. Smoke- and alcohol-free environment. **Open daily. Self-serve, vegan options, take-out, VISA/MC/AMX, $**

• State Your Grain
1012 State St., New Haven, CT 06511 **(203) 865-5370**
Vegetarian. This is a small vegetarian restaurant with some vegan options. The latest menu includes a veggie burger, hot and cold sandwiches, plus fresh home-made soups, specials and desserts daily, non-dairy, oil-free, low-salt, and sugar-free items. **Open daily. Full service, vegan options, fresh juices, take-out, $**

SIMSBURY

Panda Valley Chinese
570 Hopmeadow St., Simsbury, CT 06070 **(203) 651-8700**
Chinese. Twelve vegetarian entrees along with some appetizers and vegetarian soup are offered at Panda Valley. **Open daily. Full service, vegan options, wine/beer/alcohol, take-out, VISA/MC/AMX, $$**

ᏍᏛ Reviewers' choice • Vegetarian restaurant •• Vegan restaurant
$ less than $6 $$ $6–$12 $$$ more than $12
VISA/AMX/MC/DISC/DC—credit cards accepted
Non-alc.—Non-alcoholic Fresh juices—freshly squeezed

SOUTHBURY

Natural Merchant Cafe
142 Main St., Southbury, CT 06488   **(203) 264-9954**
Natural foods. Located in a historic building, this restaurant is accompanied by a natural foods store and offers soups, sandwiches, salads, quiche, and fresh baked desserts and muffins. Two entrees are offered daily. **Open daily for lunch. Fresh juices, BYOB, take-out, VISA/MC/AMX, $–$$**

WEST HARTFORD

Pacific Restaurant
206 Park Rd., West Hartford, CT 06119   **(203) 236-6639**
Vietnamese. Pacific Restaurant offers vegetarian fare and does not use MSG in the preparation of its meals. **Open daily for lunch and dinner. Full service, vegan options, take-out, VISA/MC/AMX, $**

Tapas
1150 New Britain Ave., West Hartford, CT 06040   **(203) 521-4609**
Mediterranean. Platters, eclectic pizzas, side orders, salads, and daily specials for lunch and dinner are offered at Tapas. Patio dining. **Open daily. Full service, vegan options, wine/beer, take-out, VISA/MC/AMX, $$**

DELAWARE

DOVER

El Sombrero
655 N. D Hwy., Dover, DE 19901   **(302) 678-9445**
International. Vegetarian menu includes vegetable fajita, lasagna, samosa, and other items. **Open daily for lunch and dinner. Vegan options, wine/beer/alcohol, take-out, VISA/MC/AMX/DISC, $$**

HOCKESSIN

Capriotti's
120 Lantana Square Shopping Center, Route 7 & Valley Rd.
Hockessin, DE 19707   **(302) 234-2322**
Deli. Capriotti's is more than just a regular deli as it features several options for vegetarians, including vegetarian turkey and ham hoagies, veggie burgers and hot dogs, and veggie tuna for subs and sandwiches. **Deli, vegan options, take-out, $**

NEW CASTLE

Capriotti's
708 W. Basin Rd., New Castle, DE 19720   **(302) 322-6797**
Deli. See description under Hockessin, DE.

Tribeni Indian Restaurant
216 N. Dupont Hwy., New Castle, DE 19720 **(302) 322-2260**
Indian. This friendly, family-owned restaurant takes special measures to offer fresh and healthful Indian food. All of the food is prepared with 100-percent vegetable oil and is free from preservatives. A large vegetarian selection is available and on Sundays, a complete vegetarian dinner buffet is offered. Enjoy excellent food and friendly service. **Closed Monday. Full service, vegan options, take-out, VISA/ MC/DISC, $$**

NEWARK

Capriotti's
614 Newark Shopping Ctr., Newark, DE 19711 **(302) 454-0200**
Deli. See description under Hockessin, DE.

King's Chinese Restaurant
2671 Kirkwood Hwy., Newark, DE 19711 **(302) 731-8022**
Chinese. Chef and owner Bob Chang invites you to explore his new menu of homemade soups, tasty appetizers, and vegetarian entrees. King's extensive vegetarian menu features many Chinese dishes including mock meat and exotic mushroom entrees. The restaurant is very flexible and willing to prepare whatever you request. King's is located in the Meadowood Shopping Center but is difficult to see from the highway as you must drive around to the side of the shopping center to find it. **Open daily for lunch and dinner. Full service, vegan options, wine/beer/alcohol, take-out, VISA/MC/AMX/DISC, $$**

Newark Co-op
280 East Main St., Newark, DE 19711 **(302) 368-5894**
Food co-op with deli. This successful food co-op offers a small deli where you can purchase pre-made cold salads and sandwiches. **Closed Sunday. Vegan options, take-out, $**

REHOBOTH BEACH

• Health-O-Rama Restaurant
10 Shoppes of Camelot, Route 1
Rehoboth Beach, DE 19971 **(302) 227-3814**
Vegetarian/ethnic foods. Enjoy lentil soup served in a bowl made of bread, salads with locally grown vegetables, sandwiches, and generous portions for dinner entrees. Vegan options are offered, but be sure to be specific when asking about ingredients. **Open daily for lunch and dinner. Full service, vegan options, fresh juice, take-out, $–$$**

WILMINGTON

Capriotti's
510 N. Union St., Wilmington, DE 19805 **(302) 479-9818**

2124 Silverside Rd., Barba Plaza, Wilmington, DE 19810 **(302) 454-0200**
Deli. See description under Hockessin, DE.

DISTRICT OF COLUMBIA

(For more restaurant listings in the surrounding areas, see Arlington and Falls Church in Virginia; Bethesda, Capital Heights, College Park, Gaithersburg, Greenbelt, Olney, Riverdale, Rockville, Silver Spring, Spencerville, Tacoma Park, and Wheaton in Maryland.)

Aditi Indian Cuisine
3299 M St., NW, Washington, DC 20007   **(202) 625-6825**
Indian. Sample vegetarian appetizers, soup, entrees, breads, and dessert. **Open Tuesday through Sunday for lunch and dinner and on Monday for dinner only. Full service, vegan options, fresh juices, wine/beer/alcohol, take-out, VISA/ MC/AMX/DISC, $$**

• Agradut-Hiya-Rabi
3000 Connecticut Ave., NW, Washington, DC 20008   **(202) 332-8989**
Vegetarian. International vegetarian cuisine is served at Agradut-Hiya-Rabi or Pioneer-Heart-Sun, a vegetarian cafe. This Sri Chinmoy restaurant offers a peaceful atmosphere with an outdoor cafe. Menu selections include the special Peace Pies. **Open daily for three meals. Cafeteria style, vegan options, fresh juices, take-out, $**

• Balajee
1379 K St., NW, Washington, DC 20005   **(202) 682-9090**
Vegetarian/Indian. Partake of a wide variety of vegetarian Indian dishes. **Open daily for lunch and dinner. Cafeteria style, vegan options, fresh juices, take-out, $–$$**

The Bombay Club
815 Connecticut Ave., NW, Washington, DC 20006   **(202) 659-3727**
Indian. Regional Indian cuisine is served in clublike ambiance. Varied vegetarian dishes from all of India. **Open daily for lunch and dinner. Full service, wine/ beer/alcohol, take-out, VISA/MC/AMX, $$**

City Cafe
2213 M St., NW, Washington, DC 20037   **(202) 797-4860**
Natural foods. The City Cafe serves multi-ethnic new American cuisine using all organic ingredients. Vegetarian appetizers, salads, and entrees are offered. Menu changes seasonally. **Closed Sunday. Open Monday through Friday for lunch and dinner and on Saturday for dinner only. Full service, vegan options, fresh juices, wine/beer/alcohol, take-out, VISA/MC, $$–$$$**

City Lights of China
1731 Connecticut Ave., NW, Washington, DC 20009   **(202) 265-6688**
Hunan/Szechuan. Request the special vegetarian menu at City Lights, and you'll be pleased to find a wide assortment of delicious vegetarian appetizers, entrees, and soups that include mock meat dishes as well as other vegetarian Chinese foods. **Open daily for lunch and dinner. Full service, vegan options, wine/beer/ alcohol, take-out, VISA/MC/AMX, $$**

• Eat For Strength Vegetarian Cafe

1917 9th St., NW, Washington, DC 20001   **(202) 332-7604**

Vegetarian. Entrees, soups, side orders, "pitawiches" (pita bread sandwiches), eggless egg rolls, and salads priced per pound make up the offerings at the Eat For Strength Cafe. The food is mostly dairyless with a wide variety of tasty vegetarian dishes. Seven entrees and eight soups are listed on the menu. **Closed Saturday. Buffet, vegan options, fresh juices, take-out, $**

Fasika's Ethiopian Restaurant

2447 18th St., NW, Washington, DC 20009   **(202) 797-7673**

Ethiopian. Fasika's has a vegetarian menu section featuring salads, vegetable, and grain dishes. **Open daily for dinner. Full service, vegan options, wine/beer/alcohol, take-out, VISA/MC/AMX/DC, $$**

Food for Thought

1738 Connecticut Ave., NW, Washington, DC 20009   **(202) 797-1095**

Natural foods. The extensive menu features a wide assortment of creative sandwiches, salads, soups, light fare, and desserts. Several dinner entrees and daily specials are also available. Live music nightly. **Open Monday through Saturday for lunch and dinner; Sunday, dinner only. Full service, vegan options, fresh juices, wine/ beer/alcohol, winter beverages, take-out, VISA/MC/AMX, $$**

Good Health Natural Foods

325 Pennsylvania Ave., SE, Washington, DC 20003   **(202) 543-2266**

Natural foods/macrobiotic. Macrobiotic and vegetarian sandwiches, soups, salads, and snacks are available for take-out at Good Health Natural Foods. Menu items include sushi, soba, hijiki, chiraci, various bean and grain soups, and veggie burgers. **Closed Sunday. Vegan options, take-out only, VISA/MC, $**

Ice In Paradise

615 Pennsylvania Ave., SE, Washington, DC 20003   **(202) 547-1554**

International deli. Various sandwiches, subs, entrees, and soups with an international flair are available at Ice In Paradise. **Open daily for lunch and dinner (call on Sunday). Cafeteria style, vegan options, take-out, $**

India Gate Restaurant

2408 18th St., NW, Washington, DC 20009   **(202) 332-0141**

Indian. Enjoy various vegetarian appetizers, soups, entrees, homemade breads, and salads. **Open daily for lunch and dinner. Full service, vegan options, wine/beer/alcohol, take-out, VISA/MC/AMX/DC, $$**

• Indian Delight

1100 Pennsylvania Ave., NW, Washington, DC 20004   **(202) 371-2295**

Union Station Food Court, 50 Massachusetts Ave., NE, Washington, DC 20002   **(202) 842-1040**

2815 M St., NW, Washington, DC 20007   **(202) 338-6450**

Vegetarian/Indian. Eleven vegetarian entrees plus appetizers, soup, salad, and desserts are offered on the Indian Delight menu. Daily specials are also available.

The Pennsylvannia Ave. restaurant is located inside an old post office, and the Georegetown restaurant (M St.) is next to Biograph Theater. **Open daily for lunch and dinner. Cafeteria style, vegan options, take-out, no credit cards, $**

Indian Kitchen
3506 Connecticut Ave., NW, Washington, DC 20008   (202) 965-2541
Indian. Indian cuisine with South Indian and exotic dishes of India is featured. Appetizers, vegetable entrees, special dishes, and breads are included on the menu. Indoor and outdoor seating. **Open daily for lunch and dinner. Limited service, vegan options, take-out, $**

Kalorama Cafe
2228 18th St., NW, Washington, DC 20009   (202) 667-1022
Natural foods. This natural foods restaurant with an ethnic flair offers Italian-style pastas, pizza, and vegetarian dishes. Kalorama is happy to cater to special diets such as low-salt, low-fat, and low-sugar. **Open Tuesday through Saturday. Full service, fresh juices, wine/beer, take-out, no credit cards, $$**

Lebanese Taverna
2641 Connecticut Ave., NW, Washington, DC 20008   (202) 265-8681
Lebanese. Various Middle Eastern appetizers and salads plus approximately four vegetarian entrees are available. Outdoor cafe. **Full service, $$–$$$**

Madras Restaurant
3506 Connecticut Ave., NW, Washington, DC 20008   (202) 966-2541
Indian. This is a mostly vegetarian Indian restaurant. **Open daily for lunch and dinner. Cafeteria style, take-out, VISA/MC/AMX/DISC/DC, $**

• Madurai Vegetarian Room
3318 M St., NW, Washington, DC 20002   (202) 333-0997
Vegetarian/Indian. Madurai specializes in appetizers and soups. Eggs are not used. **Open daily, buffet on Sunday. Full service, VISA/MC/AMX, $$**

Paru's Indian Vegetarian Restaurant
2010 S St., SW, Washington, DC 20009   (202) 483-5133
Indian. Paru's is all vegetarian (except for one chicken dish) and features masala dosa in an inexpensive, informal atmosphere with a few tables. **Closed Sunday. Counter service, take-out, $$**

Red Sea Ethiopian Restaurant
2463 18th St., NW, Washington, DC 20009   (202) 483-5000

🍴 Reviewers' choice   • Vegetarian restaurant   •• Vegan restaurant
$ less than $6 $$ $6–$12 $$$ more than $12
VISA/AMX/MC/DISC/DC—credit cards accepted
Non-alc.—Non-alcoholic   Fresh juices—freshly squeezed

Ethiopian. Red Sea uses a rich variety of native herbs and spices to flavor the authentic Ethiopian cuisine. Diners eat in the traditional manner, using fingers and pieces of the Ethiopian bread, injera, in which to wrap and eat food. Menu clearly explains the various dishes. Seven vegetable entrees are offered. **Open daily for lunch and dinner. Full service, vegan options, wine/beer/alcohol, take-out, VISA/MC/AMX, $$**

Restaurant Nora
2132 Florida Ave., NW, Washington, DC 20008   **(202) 462-5143**

Natural foods. Restaurant Nora is an organic and biodynamic restaurant serving multi-ethnic new American cuisine. The menu changes daily. Every evening, an organic, vegetarian plate is offered. There also is a selection of vegetarian appetizers and salads, and the restaurant is willing to accommodate special diets. **Open Monday through Saturday for dinner. Reservations recommended. Formal but no dress code, full service, fresh juices, wine/beer/alcohol, VISA/MC, $$$**

Sarinah Satay House
1338 Wisconsin Ave., NW, Washington, DC 20007   **(202) 337-2955**

Indonesian. Sarinah serves the internationally known Gado-Gado, a vegetarian dish with a special peanut butter sauce. Other vegetarian dishes include tofu and tempeh, noodles, and fried rice. **Closed Monday. Full service, vegan options, wine/beer/ alcohol, take-out, VISA/MC/AMX/DC/Carte Blanche, $$**

Skewers
1633 P St., NW, Washington, DC 20036   **(202) 387-4005**

Middle Eastern. Skewers features Vegetable Kabobs, Falafel, Hummus. **Open daily. Full service, vegan options, wine/beer/ alcohol, take-out, VISA/MC/AMX, $$**

Stoup's of Athens
1825 Eye St., NW, Washington, DC 20006   **(202) 223-1169**

Greek. Authentic Greek cuisine is served along with vegetarian dishes such as Vegetable Platter, Spinach Pie, Stuffed Cabbage, and soups. **Closed Sunday. Vegan options, wine/beer, take-out, no credit cards, $**

Taj Mahal
1327 Connecticut Ave., NW, Washington, DC 20036   **(202) 659-1544**

Indian. Washington's oldest Indian restaurant has been serving the nation's capital since 1965. Vegetarian cuisine from North India is offered in a special section of the menu. Vegetarian appetizers, soup, and dessert are also on the menu. **Open daily for dinner, Monday through Friday for lunch. Full service, vegan options, wine/beer/alcohol, take-out, VISA/MC/AMX/DISC, $$**

Yes! Natural Gourmet
1825 Columbia Rd., NW, Washington, DC 20009   **(202) 462-5150**

3425 Connecticut Ave., NW, Washington, DC 20008   **(202) 363-1559**

Natural foods. Soups, sandwiches, and fresh-squeezed juices are featured. **Open daily. Take-out service only, fresh juices, VISA/MC/AMX, $**

Your's Naturally Health Food Center & Deli
1523 L St., NW, Washington, DC 20005   **(202) 628-1865**
Health-food-store deli. This deli specializes in raw foods and juices. **Deli, vegan options, fresh juices, take-out, VISA/MC/AMX, $**

Zed's Ethiopian Cuisine
3318 M St., NW, Washington , DC 20007   **(202) 333-4710**
Ethiopian. As is customary with Ethiopian foods, no utensils are used at Zed's, and the meal is eaten with the traditional bread, injera, which is used to pick up the food. Various vegetarian options are available. **Open daily. Full service, vegan options, wine/beer/alcohol, take-out, VISA/MC/AMX, $**

Zorba's Cafe
1612 20th St. NW, Washington, DC 20009   **(202) 387-8555**
Greek. Enjoy a variety of ethnic vegetarian dishes such as Fasolakia, Falafel, Spanakopita, and Fasolia. **Open daily for lunch and dinner. Deli style, vegan options, wine/beer, take-out, $**

FLORIDA

ALTAMONTE SPRINGS
Chamberlin's Natural Foods
Goodings Plaza, 1086 Montgomery Rd.
Altamonte Springs, FL 32714   **(407) 774-8866**
Natural foods. Salad bar, vegetarian deli, smoothies, homemade soup and veggie chili, frozen yogurt, hot and cold sandwiches, and hot vegetarian entrees are offered. **Open daily. Counter service, vegan options, fresh juices, take-out, no credit cards, $**

CASSELBERRY
Chamberlin's Natural Foods
1271 Semoran Blvd., Ste. 105, Lake Howell Square
Casselberry, FL 32707   **(407) 774-8866**
Natural foods. See description under Altamonte Springs, FL.

CLEARWATER
Bunny Hop Cafe
1408 Cleveland St., Clearwater, FL 34615   **(813) 443-6703**
Natural foods. Located inside Nature's Food Patch, the Bunny Hop Cafe serves international vegetarian and macrobiotic foods in a casual atmosphere. High-fiber, low-fat cooking, fresh veggies and fruit, salad bar, veggie burgers, stir-fry, smoothies, desserts, and more are offered. **Closed Sunday. Full service, vegan options, fresh juices, take-out, VISA/MC, $–$$**

COCONUT GROVE

The Last Carrot
3133 Grand Ave., Coconut Grove, FL 33133 **(305) 445-0805**
Natural foods/juice bar. Sandwiches, spinach pies, salads, and various fresh juices and smoothies are served. **Open daily for lunch and dinner. Deli style, vegan options, fresh juices, take-out, $**

Oak Feed Market & Restaurant
2911 Grand Ave., Coconut Grove, FL 33133 **(305) 448-7595**
Natural foods/macrobiotic. Oak Feed is a full-service restaurant featuring vegetarian and macrobiotic specialties plus a full range deli and bakery. **Open daily. Full service, vegan options, fresh juices, wine/beer/alcohol, take-out, VISA/MC/ AMX, $$**

FORT LAUDERDALE

(For more restaurant listings in the surrounding areas, see Hollywood.)

Bread of Life Market and Restaurant
2388 N. Federal Hwy., Fort Lauderdale, FL 33305 **(305) 565-7423**
Natural foods. This gourmet natural foods restaurant and juice bar provides a beautiful art-deco, no-smoking environment. Bread of Life is willing to cater to special diets such as macrobiotic, fat-free, salt-free, etc. There's live jazz on Friday and Saturday nights. **Open daily for lunch and dinner. Full service, vegan options, fresh juices, wine/beer, VISA/MC/DISC/AMX, $$**

Nature Boy Health Foods
220 East Commercial Blvd., Fort Lauderdale, FL 33308 **(305) 776-4696**
Natural foods. Vegetable and fruit salads, sandwiches, soups, side orders, smoothies, and juices are served. **Open Monday through Saturday for lunch. Full service, limited vegan options, fresh juices, take-out, VISA/MC, $**

Nature's Delights
1544 E. Commercial Blvd., Fort Lauderdale, FL 33334 **(305) 776-7321**
Natural foods. The menu includes natural style sandwiches, salads, soups, and dinner specials. **Closed Sunday. Full service, fresh juices, take-out, VISA/MC, $**

FORT MYERS

Sangeet of India Restuarant
12375-25 S. Cleveland Ave., Villas Plaza
Fort Myers, FL 33907 **(813) 278-0101**

🍓 Reviewers' choice • Vegetarian restaurant •• Vegan restaurant
$ less than $6 $$ $6–$12 $$$ more than $12
VISA/AMX/MC/DISC/DC—credit cards accepted
Non-alc.—Non-alcoholic Fresh juices—freshly squeezed

Indian. Featured are appetizers such as samosas, pakoras, and mixed vegetable curries. All menu items can be made vegetarian upon request. Also offers Jewish menu on Jewish holidays. **Closed Monday, open Tuesday through Friday for lunch and dinner, dinner only on weekends. Full service, non-alc. wine/beer, wine/beer/alcohol, take-out, VISA/MC/AMX/DISC/DC, $$**

GAINESVILLE

(For more restaurant listings in the surrounding areas, see High Springs)

Falafel King Sandwiches
12 NW 13th St., Gainesville, FL 32601   **(904) 374-9830**

3252 SW 35th Blvd., Gainesville, FL 32608   **(904) 375-6342**
Middle Eastern. Middle Eastern specialties are provided in a deli-like atmosphere. Falafels, gyros, tabouleh, and other sandwiches are available for take-out. **Counter service, vegan options, take-out, $**

Ivey S. Grill
3303 W. University Ave., Gainesville, FL 32607   **(904) 371-4839**
Natural foods. Progressive menu with vegetarian entrees including tofu and pasta is featured. **Open for three meals Monday through Saturday, Sunday brunch. Full service, vegan options, fresh juices, wine/beer, VISA/MC/AMX, $$**

HIGH SPRINGS

The Great Outdoors Cafe
65 N. Main St., High Springs, FL 32643   **(904) 454-2900**
Natural foods. Located just off I-75 in north Florida, this cafe offers an eclectic array of foods: fresh salads, pastas, vegetarian entrees, and desserts. There is also a bed-and-breakfast inn serving vegetarian foods. Non-smoking. **Open daily. Full service, vegan options, wine/beer, take-out, VISA/MC/DISC/AMX, $$**

HOLLYWOOD

Harvest Village Natural Foods
1928 Harrison St., Hollywood, FL 33020   **(305) 921-5149**
Juice bar. Fruit and vegetable salads, sandwiches, and fresh fruit and vegetable juice are available. **Closed Sunday. Counter service, vegan options, take-out, VISA/MC, $**

MELBOURNE

Natureworks! Deli
461 N. Harbor City Blvd., Melbourne, FL 32935   **(407) 242-0772**
Natural foods. This is a mostly vegetarian deli. Natureworks! features a daily hot entree, soup, vegetarian chili, salad bar, and hot and cold sandwiches. The deli also offers vegetarian cooking classes and monthly vegan potluck dinner. **Closed Sunday. Limited service, vegan options, fresh juices, take-out, VISA/MC/AMX/DISC, $**

MIAMI

(For more restaurant listings in the surrounding areas, see Coconut Grove, Miami Beach, and Miami Springs.)

Granny Feelgood's
111 NW 1st. Street, Metro Dade Bldg., Miami, FL 33128   (305) 579-2104

190 SE 1st Avenue, Miami, FL 33131   (305) 358-6233
Natural foods. Granny Feelgood's makes a special effort to offer the freshest, healthiest foods available. Organic produce is offered and the menu selections (sandwiches, soups, salads, desserts, and international entrees) emphasize low-fat, low-cholesterol, and low-sodium foods. **Open Monday through Friday. Full service, vegan options, fresh juices, take-out, $**

Namaskar Health Food Restaurant
7921 SW 40th St., Miami, FL 33155   (305) 262-2054
Natural foods. Namaskar offers new Latin-flavor natural foods—low fat, low sodium, no frying. The menu is in Spanish and English and includes appetizers, soups, sandwiches, salads, à la carte dishes, beverages, and desserts. **Closed Sundays. Limited service, vegan options, fresh juices, take-out, VISA/MC/AMX/DISC, $$**

Natural Eats
Dadeland Plaza, 9477 S. Dixie Hwy., Miami, FL 33156   (305) 665-7807

Kendall Town & Country, 8720 Mills Dr., Miami, FL 33176   (305) 271-7424
Natural foods. The Natural Eats menu is ahead of its time with a nutritional breakdown of the menu items. This rarely seen feature is quite handy and may be a more common addition to menus in the future. All foods are prepared with fresh ingredients and without refined sugar, saturated fats, preservatives, or chemicals. Salads, sandwiches, a veggie burger, and desserts are offered. Vegan muffins as well! **Open daily. Full service, fresh juice, take-out, $**

•• Natural Foods Express
Delivery Only   (305) 672-FOOD
Vegan/delivery only. Although not a restaurant, this establishment delivers vegan meals in the Dade County area. Dishes include soups, whole-grain and bean dishes, seitan stew, stuffed butternut squash, salads, desserts, etc. **Delivery only; $37-minimum order**

MIAMI BEACH

Artichoke's Natural Cuisine
3055 NE 163rd St., N. Miami Beach, FL 33160   (305) 945-7576

૨&> Reviewers' choice   • Vegetarian restaurant   •• Vegan restaurant
$ less than $6 $$ $6–$12 $$$ more than $12
VISA/AMX/MC/DISC/DC—credit cards accepted
Non-alc.—Non-alcoholic   Fresh juices—freshly squeezed

International natural foods. Vegetarian, macrobiotic, and Pritikin dishes are served at this popular "neighborhood-type" restaurant. The menu includes appetizers, salads, entrees, and desserts. **Open for dinner nightly. Full service, vegan options, fresh juices, wine/beer, take-out, VISA/MC, $$**

Kebab Indian Restaurant
514 NE 167th St., N. Miami Beach, FL 33162   (305) 940-6309
North Indian. Kebab is recommended by the Vegetarian Gourmet Society in Florida as serving "the best Indian vegetarian foods that we have ever tasted." Dishes are made fresh and special diets are accommodated. **Open daily. Full service, vegan options, wine/beer, take-out, VISA/MC/AMX, $$**

•• Our Place
830 Washington Ave., Miami Beach, FL, 33139   (305) 674-1322
Vegan. Our Place features four or more daily specials, soups, and a wide variety of burgers and veggie sushi. **Open daily for lunch and dinner. Full service, vegan, wine/beer, take-out, VISA/MC, $–$$**

Pineapples
530 Arthur Godfrey Rd., Miami Beach, FL 33140   (305) 532-9731
Natural foods. This gourmet vegetarian and natural foods restaurant and market offers daily specials for lunch and dinner, weekend breakfast, and weekend brunch. **Open daily. Vegan options, take-out, $**

Unicorn Village
3565 NE 207th St., N. Miami Beach, FL 33180   (305) 933-8829
Natural foods. This three-story waterfront restaurant offers many vegetarian dishes including several creative salads, Spinach Lasagna, Roasted Eggplant, pasta, pizzas made with soy cheese, and a Veggie Burger. The chef tries to use as many organic ingredients as possible. **Open daily for lunch and dinner. Full service, fresh juices, organic wine/beer/alcohol, take-out, VISA/MC, $**

MIAMI SPRINGS

The Garden Restaurant
17 Westward Dr., Miami Springs, FL 33166   (305) 887-9238
Natural foods. A wide variety of appetizers, soups, salads, pastas, entrees, sandwiches, and burgers are listed on The Garden Restaurant menu. Many vegetarian options are offered including a Veggie Burger, Vegetable Tempura, Zucchini Melt, and Tofu Marinara. **Open daily for lunch and dinner. Full service, vegan options, fresh juices, wine/beer, take-out, VISA/MC/AMX, $$**

ORLANDO

(For more restaurant listings in the surrounding areas, see Altamonte Springs, Casselberry, and Winter Park.)

Bee Line Diner
9801 International Dr., Peabody Hotel, Orlando, FL 32819   (407) 352-4000
International. This diner features a vegetarian section on the menu that includes Chili,

Lasagna, Falafel, and Veggie Burgers. **Open 24 hours daily. Full service, non-alc. wine/beer, wine/beer/alcohol, take-out, VISA/MC/AMX/DISC/DC, $$**

Chamberlin's Natural Foods
Colonial Plaza Shopping Center
38 Colonial Plaza Mall, Orlando, FL 32803   **(407) 894-8452**

The Marketplace
7600 Dr. Phillips Blvd., Orlando, FL 32819   **(407) 352-2130**
Natural foods. See description under Altamonte Springs, FL.

• Florida Hospital Cafeteria
601 E. Rollins St., Orlando, FL 32803   **(407) 897-1793**
Vegetarian cafeteria. Deli and taco bar, soup and salad bar are featured; low-fat and low-salt entrees are available. **Open 24 hours every day. Cafeteria service, take-out, $**

4, 5, 6
657 N. Primrose Dr., Orlando, FL 32803   **(407) 898-1899**
Chinese. Vegetarian egg rolls, soups, and twenty non-dairy vegetarian dishes with brown rice are available. MSG is not used. **Open daily for lunch and dinner. Full service, vegan options, wine/alcohol, take-out, VISA/MC, $$**

Green Earth Health Foods
2336 W. Oakridge Rd., Orlando, FL 32809   **(407) 859-8045**
Natural foods. The cafe offers fresh soups, chili, sandwiches, salads, and smoothies. It is "dedicated to serving wholesome foods with no chemicals or preservatives" and uses organic products when possible. All food is prepared on the premises and is low-salt and low-fat. Green Earth is located in Oakridge Plaza. **Open Monday through Friday. Limited service, vegan options, fresh juice, VISA/MC, $**

Passage to India
5532 International Dr., Orlando, FL 32819   **(407) 351-3456**

845 Sand Lake Rd., Orlando, FL 32809   **(407) 856-8362**
Indian. The menu features vegetarian appetizers, soups, and twelve vegetarian entrees. **Open daily for lunch and dinner. Full service, non-alc. wine/beer, wine/beer, take-out, VISA/MC/AMX/DISC, $$**

PALM BEACH

• Sunrise Natural Foods
233 Royal Poinciana Way, Palm Beach, FL 33480   **(407) 655-3557**
Vegetarian/macrobiotic. Selections include soup, egg rolls, spinach pies, and artichoke pasta. **Open for lunch. Closed Sunday. Take-out only, non-alc. beer/wine, VISA/MC/AMX, $**

SARASOTA

• Froggy's
3025 North Tamiami Trail, Sarasota, FL 34234   **(813) 359-VEGE**

Vegetarian. This relatively new fast-food vegetarian restaurant is a must to visit if you find yourself along the Gulf Coast of Florida. The food is wonderful. The owners opened this restaurant due to their desire to help the environment and to promote low-fat eating. In fact, the local heart association recommends its patients dine at this establishment. Items featured on the menu include a wide variety of vegetarian burgers, sandwiches, delicious air-fried potatoes, burritos, and non-dairy banana smoothies. Saturday evenings there's a coffeehouse. **Open daily for lunch and dinner. Counter service, $**

Wildflower
5218 Ocean Blvd., Sarasota, FL 34242   **(813) 349-1758**
Macrobiotic. Diners enjoy a casual atmosphere near the beach. Daily specials include soups and creative vegetarian entrees. **Open daily for lunch and dinner. Full service, fresh juices, wine/beer, take-out, VISA/MC, $$**

TAMPA

The Natural Kitchen, Inc. (The N.K. Cafe)
4100 W. Kennedy Blvd., Tampa, FL 33609   **(813) 287-1385**
Natural foods. Originally a vegetarian restaurant, the N.K. Cafe now offers meat and fish. There is still a decent selection of vegetarian fare, however, particularly for salads and sandwiches. There are three vegetarian entrees and many desserts. **Open Monday through Friday. Cafeteria style, limited vegan options, fresh juices, wine/beer, take-out, VISA/MC/AMX, $–$$**

WINTER PARK

Chamberlin's Natural Foods Restaurant
Winter Park Mall, 430 N. Orlando Ave.
Winter Park, FL 32789   **(407) 647-3330**
Natural foods. See description under Altamonte Springs, FL.

The Power House
111 E. Lyman Ave., Winter Park, FL 32789   **(407) 645-3616**
Natural foods. Enjoy sandwiches, salads, soup, vegetarian chili, and a wide variety of shakes and smoothies. **Open daily. Limited service, vegan options, $**

GEORGIA

ATHENS

Bluebird Cafe
493 E. Clayton St., Athens, GA 30601   **(706) 549-3663**
Natural foods. Vegetarian dishes with a Mexican flair are included on the Bluebird Cafe menu. Entrees such as burritos, quesadilla, enchiladas, plus salads, quiche, sandwiches, and desserts are offered. **Open daily. Full service, vegan options, take-out, no credit cards, $**

ATLANTA

(For more restaurant listings in the surrounding areas, see Decatur.)

Eat Your Vegetables
438 Moreland Ave., NE, Atlanta, GA 30307 **(404) 523-2671**
Natural foods. Vegetarian and macrobiotic specials are available every day in addition to the vegetarian entrees on the menu. **Full service, take-out, $$**

Lettuce Souprise You
Corporate offices in Atlanta, GA **(404) 955-3999**

Loehmann's Plaza
2470-47 Briarcliff Rd., Atlanta, GA 30329 **(404) 636-8549**

Sandy Springs
5975 Roswell Rd., Atlanta, GA 30328 **(404) 874-4998**

Rio Mall
595 Piedmont Ave. #D200.1, Atlanta, GA 30308 **(404) 874-4998**

1109 Cumberland Mall, Atlanta, GA 30339 **(404) 438-2288**

245 Pharr Rd., Atlanta, GA 30305 **(404) 841-9583**
American/restaurant chain. All-you-can-eat salad-bar chain in the Atlanta area also has muffins, soups, baked potatoes, and fresh fruit. Smoking is not allowed. **Open daily; some locations closed Sundays. Buffet style, take-out, $–$$**

Nuts 'N Berries
4274 Peachtree St. NE, Atlanta, GA 30319 **(404) 237-6829**
Natural foods. This whole foods restaurant offers home-baked goods, sandwiches, salads, and side dishes, chili, and soup. **Open daily. Limited service, vegan options, fresh juices, take-out, VISA/MC, $**

Rio Bravo Cantina
3172 Roswell Rd., Atlanta, GA 30305 **(404) 262-7431**
Mexican. The cantina has an extensive Mexican menu offering appetizers, soups, salads, sandwiches, specials, Mexican favorites, and vegetable entrees. Only pure (100-percent) vegetable oil is used in cooking. **Open daily for lunch and dinner. Full service, vegan options, fresh juices, wine/beer/alcohol, take-out, $$**

Shipfeifer on Peachtree
1814 Peachtree St., Atlanta, GA 30309 **(404) 875-1106**
Mediterranean. Wraps, salads, platters, side dishes, Mediterranean pizza, and desserts are included on the Shipfeifer menu. All food is prepared fresh to order. Outdoor patio dining. **Open daily for lunch and dinner. Full service, vegan options, wine/beer, take-out, VISA/MC/AMX/DISC, $–$$**

•• Soul Vegetarian Restaurant
879 Abernathy Blvd., SW, Atlanta, GA 30310 **(404) 752-5194**

Vegan. Soul has its own unique gluten creation called "Kalebone" that is made into burgers, "furters," steaks, and salads. Soul's many other original dishes—soups, lentil burgers, veggie patties, tofu filet, veggie gyros, salads, and desserts—are sure to keep your veggie taste buds happy. Children's dinner available. **Open daily for lunch and dinner. Full service, totally vegan, fresh juice, catering, take-out, VISA/MC/AMX, $**

•• Veggieland
211 Pharr Rd., NE, Atlanta, GA 30305   **(404) 231-3111**

220 Sandy Springs Cir., NW, Atlanta, GA 30328   **(404) 252-1165**
Vegan. This totally vegan restaurant features delicious low-salt, low-calorie, sugar-free foods. Filtered water is used even for the ice cubes! Menu consists of starters, salads, veggie burgers and sandwiches, pasta, stir-fry, desserts, and specials. **Full service, completely vegan, fresh juices, take-out, $$**

COLUMBUS

• Country Life Vegetarian Restaurant and Health Food Store
1217 Eberhart Ave., Columbus, GA 31906   **(706) 323-9194**
Vegetarian. A buffet lunch and a soup and salad bar are available Sunday through Thursday. The fare here is "Healthy foods that taste good" with a menu that changes daily. **Open for lunch Sunday through Thursday. Limited service, vegan options, take-out, VISA/MC, $**

DECATUR

Rainbow Natural Foods
2118 N. Decatur Rd., NE, Decatur, GA 30033   **(404) 636-5553**
Natural foods. Sandwiches and soups are featured along with daily special entrees. **Open daily for lunch and dinner. Sunday brunch. Full service, fresh juice, take-out, $**

DULUTH

Lettuce Souprise You
Gwinnett Esplanade
3525 Mall Blvd., Bldg. 6, Duluth, GA 30136   **(404) 418-9969**
American/restaurant chain. See entry under Atlanta.

ROSWELL

Lettuce Souprise You
Holcomb 400
1474 Holcomb Bridge Rd., #155, Roswell, GA 30076   **(404) 642-1601**
American/restaurant chain. See entry under Atlanta.

HAWAII

Chiang Mai Thai Restaurant
2239 S. King St., Honolulu, HI 96826 (808) 941-1151

Thai. Here you will find exotic northern Thai cuisine with a full vegetarian menu (and we mean full!). The front of the menu says, "Vegetarians Welcome," and what's offered on the inside reflects this. Appetizers, salads, soups, noodle and rice dishes, and other entrees of tofu and vegetables make up an excellent selection for vegetarians. **Open daily for lunch and dinner. Full service, vegan options, wine/beer, take-out, VISA/MC/AMX, $**

Crêpe Fever Restaurant
Ward Centre, 1200 Ala Moana Blvd.
Honolulu, HI 96822 (808) 521-9023

Natural foods. Crêpe Fever features an eclectic mixture of dishes for breakfast, lunch, and dinner. Salads, crêpe, sandwich, and croissant specialties are joined by soups, stir-fry, and side orders. **Open daily. Limited service, vegan options, fresh juices, espresso/cappuccino, wine/beer/alcohol, take-out, VISA/MC, $–$$**

• Down To Earth Deli
2525 S. King St., Honolulu, HI 96826 (808) 947-7678

Vegetarian. **Open daily. Cafeteria style, vegan options, fresh juices, take-out, VISA/MC, $**

• Guaranga's Vegetarian Dining Club
51 Coelho Way, Honolulu, HI 96817 (808) 595-3947

Vegetarian. Located on a lovely three-acre estate in the hills of Nuvano, Guaranga's is accompanied by the largest banyan tree on the island. The club features a full salad bar, homemade whole-grain bread, fresh baked cookies, mung dahl soup, brown and jasmine rice, and more. There are ethnic themes for each night. **Open for lunch and dinner Monday through Saturday. Buffet, vegan options, fresh juices, take-out, no credit cards, $$**

India Bazaar Madras
2320 S. King St., Honolulu, HI 96826 (808) 949-4840

Indian. India Bazaar features South Madras-style Indian cuisine. **Closed Sunday. Cafeteria style, BYOB, take-out, $**

Keo's Thai Cuisine
625 Kapahulu Ave., Honolulu, HI 96815 (808) 737-8240

1200 Ala Moana Blvd., Honolulu, HI 96814 (808) 533-0533

1486 S. King St., Honolulu, HI 96814 (808) 947-9988

Thai. Gourmet Thai cuisine is served in a casually elegant, tropical garden setting. Vegetarian appetizers, salads, entrees, and curry dishes are available on the menu. Any item can be made vegetarian because all food is cooked to order. **Dinner** served nightly. **Full service, vegan options, wine/beer/alcohol, take-out, VISA/ MC/AMX/DC/Carte Blanche, $$**

La Salsa Rita's
500 Ala Moana Blvd., Honolulu, HI 96813   **(808) 536-4828**
Mexican. Homemade tortillas, beans without lard, Mexican tofu, and meatless items make it easy for vegetarians to find a satisfying meal at La Salsa Rita's. **Open daily for lunch and dinner. Full service, vegan options, wine/beer/alcohol, take-out, VISA/MC/AMX, $$**

Mekong Restaurant
1295 S. Beretania St., Honolulu, HI 96814   **(808) 521-2025**
Thai. The oldest Thai restaurant in Hawaii, Mekong includes vegetarian dishes on the menu. No smoking. **Open daily for dinner, lunch Monday through Friday. Full service, BYOB, take-out, VISA/MC/AMX/DC, $-$$**

Pineland Chinese Restaurant
1236 Keeaumoku St., Honolulu, HI 96814   **(808) 955-2918**
Chinese. Pineland features a special vegetarian menu with dishes such as Hot and Sour Noodles in Soup, Fried Bean Curd with Szechuan Orange Flavor, and Eggplant with Spicy Hunan Garlic Sauce. **Open for dinner daily except Sunday. Full service, vegan options, BYOB, take-out, $**

Yen King Chinese Restaurant
4211 Waialae Ave., Kahala Mall, Honolulu, HI 96816   **(808) 732-5505**
Chinese. Szechuan, Mandarin, and Shanghai cuisines are featured. The back page of the Yen King menu lists thirty vegetarian dishes including soups, assorted vegetable and noodle entrees, mock meat, and gluten dishes. **Open daily. Full service, vegan options, wine/beer/alcohol, take-out, VISA/MC/ AMX, $$**

KAILUA

Something Good
301 B Hahani St., Kailua, HI 96734   **(808) 262-8792**
Natural foods. Something Good offers frozen dessert and a few entree items. **Open 24 hours daily. Limited service, limited vegan options, fresh juices, take-out, $$**

The Source Natural Foods & Juice Bar
32 Kainehe St., Kailua, HI 96734   **(808) 262-5604**
Natural foods. All salads, burgers, sandwiches, soups, and entrees are fresh and made to order. The Source serves a wide selection of vegetarian options, including chili, veggie burgers, sushi, and Mexican dishes. **Open daily. Limited service, vegan options, fresh juices, BYOB, take-out, no credit cards, $**

😋 Reviewers' choice   ● Vegetarian restaurant   ●● Vegan restaurant
$ less than $6 $$ $6–$12 $$$ more than $12
VISA/AMX/MC/DISC/DC—credit cards accepted
Non-alc.–Non-alcoholic   Fresh juices—freshly squeezed

KAUAI

International Museum & Cafe
9875 Waimea Rd., Waimea, Kauai, HI 96796   **(808) 338-0403**
International. If you're looking for something unique, try this museum, where eating and drinking is not only allowed but encouraged. The menu is primarily vegetarian with appetizers, sandwiches, beverages, and desserts. You'll also enjoy the full Asian-Hawaiian museum, jewelry, clothing, and antiques for sale. No smoking. **Hours are seasonal. Full service, fresh juice, wine/beer/alcohol, take-out, AMX, $$**

Koloa Ice House & Deli
(Across from post office)
P.O. Box 1326, Koloa Town, Kauai 96756   **(808) 742-6063**
Natural foods. For fourteen years, Koloa Ice House has been working hard to spread aloha spirit with fresh sandwiches, salads, homemade soups, lasagna, quiche, and many other specialties. It also serves delicious smoothies and frozen desserts as well as homemade cookies. Outside dining. **Open daily. Counter service, fresh juices, take-out, AMX, $**

KEAAU TOWN

•• Tonya's Vegetarian Cafe
Across from Keaau Post Office, Keaau Town, HI 96749   **(808) 966-8091**
Vegetarian. An island-style vegetarian cafe with an international flair, this almost completely vegan cafe serves such items as tempeh burgers, varying international specials, and seasonal Hawaiian fruits and vegetables. **Closed Saturday and Sunday. Counter service, vegan options, BYOB, catering, $**

MAUI

Cheese Burger in Paradise
811 Front Street, Lahaina, Maui, HI 96761   **(808) 661-4855**
American. From the sound of its name, you would never expect Cheese Burger in Paradise to offer vegetarian food. But it does offer two vegetarian burgers, a tofu burger, and a spinach nut burger, as well as Lahaina Grilled Cheese. This restaurant is located on the beach and offers live music during the evening. **Open daily for lunch and dinner. Full service, fruit smoothies, beer, take-out, $$**

Royal Thai Cuisine
Azeka Shopping Center, Kihei, Maui, HI 96761   **(808) 874-0813**
Thai. Although not a vegetarian restaurant, Royal Thai Cuisine offers more than twenty-five vegetarian entrees. **Open daily for dinner, Monday through Friday for lunch. Full service, take-out, VISA/MC/AMEX, $–$$**

Saeng's Thai Cuisine
1312 Front Street, Lahaina, Maui, HI 96761   **(808) 244-1567**
Thai. Saeng's offers more than ten vegetarian entrees including several tofu dishes. **Open daily for lunch and dinner. Full service, take-out, $$**

Thai Chef Restaurant
Lahaina Shopping Center, Lahaina, Maui, HI 96761   (808) 667-2814
Thai. Authentic Thai cuisine is offered in a relaxed, cozy atmosphere. Thirteen
vegetarian entrees including tofu, curry, and vegetable dishes are on the menu.
The chef is willing to accommodate special diets and can prepare any of the regular
dishes without meat. **Open seven days. Full service, vegan options, take-out,
VISA/MC/DISC, $$**

PAIA

•• The Vegan Restaurant
115 Baldwin Ave., Paia, HI 96779   (808) 579-9144
Vegan. All of the vegan Thai food here is homemade. **Closed Monday. Limited
service, completely vegan, fruit juices, non-alc. beer, take-out, VISA/MC, $$**

IDAHO

COEUR D'ALENE

Coeur d'Alene Natural Foods Store and Cafe
301 Lakeside Ave., Coeur d'Alene, ID 83814   (208) 664-3452
Health-food-store cafe. **Open for lunch Monday through Saturday. Cafeteria style,
fresh juices, take-out, VISA/MC, $**

ILLINOIS

ARLINGTON HEIGHTS

• Chowpati Vegetarian Restaurant
1035 S. Arlington Heights Rd., Arlington Heights, IL 60005   (708) 640-9554
Vegetarian/ethnic. This family-owned vegetarian restaurant serves international fare—
American, Italian, French, Mexican, and Middle Eastern dishes. **Closed Monday.
Open for lunch and dinner. Full service, vegan options, fresh juices, non-alc.
beer/wine/champagne, catering, take-out, VISA/MC/AMX/DISC/DC, $**

CHAMPAIGN

Fiesta Cafe
216 S. First St., Champaign, IL 61820   (217) 352-5902
Mexican. **Open daily for lunch and dinner. Full service, wine/beer/alcohol,
take-out, VISA/MC/AMX/DISC, $**

CHICAGO

(For more restaurants in the surrounding suburbs, see Arlington Heights,

Downers Grove, Evanston, Glen Ellen, Oak Park, Palatine, Rolling Meadows, St. Charles, Skokie, Villa Park, W. Dundee, and Westmont.)

A Natural Harvest
7122 S. Jeffery Blvd., Chicago, IL 60649　　　　　**(312) 363-3939**
Natural foods. Soups, salads, sandwiches, and other entrees are prepared on-site daily. The restaurant specializes in vegetable proteins; vegetarian burgers, steak-lets, and hot dogs are sold by the pound. **Closed Sunday. Limited service, fresh juices, take-out, VISA/MC/AMX/DISC, $**

The Bread Shop
3400 N. Halsted, Chicago, IL 60657　　　　　　**(312) 528-8108**
Natural foods bakery and deli. This full-line bakery, grocery, and deli is famous for its whole-grain pizza and burritos. Menu changes. **Open daily. Cafeteria style, vegan options, fresh juices, take-out, no credit cards, $**

• Cafe Voltaire
3231 N. Clark St., Chicago, IL 60657　　　　　　**(312) 528-3136**
Vegetarian. A very small vegetarian restaurant that stays open late, the cafe occasionally features plays in a downstairs room. **Open daily for lunch and dinner. Full service, espresso/cappuccino, non-alc. beer, wine/beer, VISA/MC, $$**

• The Chicago Diner
3411 N. Halsted, Chicago, IL 60657　　　　　　**(312) 935-6696**
Vegetarian restaurant/juice bar. The Chicago Diner serves an eclectic assortment of international vegetarian fare without preservatives, processed, or artificial foods. Fresh organic produce is purchased whenever possible. The owners have traveled extensively and are dedicated to promoting healthy eating for the sake of humans, the planet, and animals. The diner serves delicious vegetarian fare and is the hub for the animal rights movement in the Midwest. Breakfast menu and kid's menu. Patio dining in summertime. **Open daily. Full service, vegan options, fresh juices, non-alc. beer, beer/organic wine, take-out, VISA/MC/AMX/ DISC, $$**

Gaylord India Restaurant
678 N. Clark St., Chicago, IL 60610　　　　　　**(312) 664-1700**
Indian. Indian food is freshly prepared using no canned or processed ingredients. **Open daily for lunch and dinner. Full service, vegan options, wine/beer/alcohol, take-out, VISA/MC/AMX, $$**

• Govinda's Vegetarian Buffet & Salad Bar
1716 W. Lunt Ave., Chicago, IL 60626　　　　　　**(312) 973-0900**
Vegetarian buffet. Consistent with Govinda's fashion, the buffet has a monthly menu with a different entree daily that is accompanied by bread, two types of rice, two vegetable dishes, a bean dish, large salad bar, ice cream, and sweets. All for one low price!! Vegan entrees are indicated on monthly menu. **Open Wednesday through Saturday for dinner. Buffet, vegan options, take-out, $**

Heartland Cafe
7000 N. Glenwood, Chicago, IL 60626　　　　　　**(312) 465-8005**
Natural foods. "Good wholesome foods for the mind and body" are served in a comfortable environment. Starters, soups and salads, sandwiches, various entrees,

and vegetarian specialties feature many Mexican and international dishes. There is late night music and dancing on winter weekends and outdoor dining during warm months. The cafe is accompanied by a general store that features wholistic and political magazines, and merchandise. **Open daily. Full service, vegan options, fresh juices, wine/beer/alcohol, take-out, VISA/MC/AMX, $$**

The Magical Tortoise
1600 W. Morse Ave., Chicago, IL 60626

Juice bar/coffeehouse. Recommended by a local patron, the Magical Tortoise is a combination coffee house/juice bar with organic whole-grain muffins and fresh baked goods. **Cafeteria style, $**

Mama Desta's Red Sea
3216 N. Clark St., Chicago, IL 60657   **(312) 935-7561**

Ethiopian. The restaurant is decidedly decorated to create an African ambiance with crafts and paintings from Africa plus bamboo-and-reed-covered walls. **Open daily for lunch and dinner. Full service, wine/beer/alcohol, take-out, VISA/MC/AMX, $$**

• Natraj India Restaurant
2240 W. Devon Ave., Chicago, IL 60659   **(312) 274-1300**

Vegetarian/Indian. Natraj is a family restaurant with an emphasis on quality food. The menu includes a wide assortment of vegetarian appetizers, soups, salads, entrees, breads, rice, and desserts. **Open daily. Full service, vegan options, BYOB, catering, take-out, VISA, MC, $$**

The Original Mitchell's Restaurants
101 W. North Ave., Chicago, IL 60610   **(312) 642-5246**

Natural foods. Mitchell's prides itself on its delicious breakfasts known nationwide for such foods as vegetarian sausage, non-dairy whole-wheat pancakes, giant homemade muffins, and omelettes. Mitchell's has daily vegetarian lunch and dinner specials as well. **Open daily. Full service, vegan options, fresh juices, wine/beer, take-out, VISA/MC, $**

Pattie's Heart-Healthy
520 N. Michigan, Chicago, IL 60614   **(312) 645-1111**

Heart-healthy fast food. Grams of fat and calories are listed for each menu item. Sandwiches, soups, pizza, calzones, vegetarian specials, and sweets are included on the menu. Breakfast menu, too. **Open daily. Counter service, vegan options, fresh juices, espresso/cappuccino, take-out, no credit cards, $**

Pegasus
130 S. Halsted, Chicago, IL 60606   **(312) 226-4666**

Greek. A local patron recommends Pegasus' excellent all-vegetable entrees and mentions that the restaurant has "more vegan selections than any other restaurant in Greek town." **Full service, $$**

•• Soul Vegetarian
205 E. 75th St., Chicago, IL 60619   **(312) 224-0164**

Vegan. Various ethnic dishes are featured at Soul Vegetarian, including African,

Middle Eastern, and American fare. Examples include Vegetarian Ribs, Tofu Fish, Sunflower-Seed Burger, and Split Pea and Chickenless Noodle Soup. **Open daily. Reservations accepted. Full service, vegan options, fresh juices, take-out, VISA, $$**

Star of Siam
11 E. Illinois St., Chicago, IL 60611 (312) 670-0100
Thai. All dishes can be prepared without meat or with tofu or veggie substitutes. **Open daily for lunch and dinner. Full service, vegan options, wine/beer/alcohol, take-out, VISA/MC/AMX/DISC, $**

DOWNERS GROVE

Old Country Buffet
1410 W. 75th St., Grove Shopping Center
Downers Grove, IL 60516 (708) 810-0150
American. This large restaurant with a wide selection of vegetarian items, vegetables, and desserts features an all-you-can-eat buffet. **Cafeteria style, vegan options, $$**

ELGIN

Al's Cafe & Creamery
43 Fountain Square, Elgin, IL 60120 (708) 742-1180
Cafe. Located in a historic building, Al's Cafe and Creamery provides a charming ambiance in which to sample many imaginative soups and sandwiches for vegetarians and non-vegetarians alike. The Creamery features special malts and shakes, and a fountain menu that lets you create your own sundaes. **Closed Sunday. Full service, wine/beer, take-out, VISA/MC/AMX, $$**

Bangkok House
11 N. Grove, Elgin, IL 60120 (708) 742-1460
Thai/Chinese. Here you'll find lots of delicious options for vegans. **Full service, take-out, $$**

Jalapeños
7 Clock Tower Plaza, Elgin, IL 60120 (708) 468-9445
Mexican. The authentic, fresh-cooked Mexican cuisine is mostly vegeterian with a limited vegan selection. **Full service, vegan option, wine/beer/alcohol, take-out, $$**

EVANSTON

• Blind Faith Cafe ⊱
525 Dempster St., Evanston, IL 60201 (708) 328-6875
Vegetarian. This cafe features a bakery, organic produce, and a filtered water system in an environmentally responsible, non-smoking environment. **Full service, vegan/macrobiotic options, fresh juices, wine/beer, catering, take-out, $$**

⊱ Reviewers' choice • Vegetarian restaurant •• Vegan restaurant
$ less than $6 $$ $6–$12 $$$ more than $12
VISA/AMX/MC/DISC/DC—credit cards accepted
Non-alc.--Non-alcoholic Fresh juices—freshly squeezed

Dave's Italian Kitchen
906 Church St., Evanston, IL 60201   **(708) 864-6000**
Italian. Dave's serves homemade pasta and bread, salad, sandwiches, pizza, calzone, and Italian specialties. **Open daily. Full service, vegan options, wine/beer, take-out, no credit cards, $–$$**

GENEVA

Soup to Nuts—The Natural Grocery
425 Hamilton St., Geneva, IL 60134   **(708) 232-6646**
Health-food-store deli. When available, organic ingredients are used to prepare deli items. Allergy-free cooking uses no preservatives or chemicals. Special diets can be accommodated. **Cafeteria style, fresh juices, wine/beer, take-out, VISA/MC, $**

GLEN ELLYN

Prairie Star Cafe & Coffeehouse
538 Crescent, Glen Ellyn, IL 60137   **(708) 790-1993**
Natural foods. This small but attractive cafe serves primarily vegetarian food. **Open for lunch several days a week, and dinner on Friday and Saturday. Live entertainment in evenings. Full service, $–$$**

MOLINE

Le Mekong Restaurant
1606 Fifth Ave., Moline, IL 61265   **(309) 797-3709**
Southeast Asian/French. Traditional curry dishes, tofu, and mock meats are featured in the vegetarian menu section. **Open daily. Full service, vegan options, wine/beer/alcohol, take-out, VISA/MC/AMX, $$**

OAK PARK

Chip & Dale's Natural Market & Deli
109 N. Oak Park, Oak Park, IL 60301   **(708) 524-0406**
Health-food-store deli. Enjoy hot meals daily. **Closed Sundays. Limited service, fresh juices, take-out, VISA/MC/DISC, $$**

PALATINE

Fit Inn Charlie Club
1500 E. Dundee, Palatine, IL 60067   **(708) 934-4900**
Buffet. This twenty-four-hour fitness club offers "health-oriented" food. The buffet features low-fat, low-cholesterol dishes. **Open daily. Buffet, fresh juices, wine/beer/alcohol, take-out, VISA/MC/AMX/DISC, $**

ROCKFORD

Dwaraka India Restaurant
6921 E. State St., Rockford, IL 61108   **(815) 397-2265**
Indian. Authentic Indian food from all parts of India. Boldly displayed on the menu are eleven vegetarian items including traditional curry and paneer (Indian

cheese) dishes plus some more unique items such as Creamed Vegetable Balls and Spiced Eggplant Purée. **Open daily. Full service, vegan options, wine/beer/alcohol, take-out, VISA/MC/AMX, $$**

ROLLING MEADOWS
Old Country Buffet
1400 E. Golf Rd., Rolling Meadows, IL 60008   **(708) 981-8996**
American. See entry under Downers Grove, IL.

SKOKIE
La Salad
3938 W. Dempster, Skokie, IL 60076   **(708) 679-6190**
American. This small restaurant features an all-you-can-eat self-serve buffet including a large variety of fruits, vegetables, and pasta salads. **Cafeteria style, take-out, $$**

Slice of Life
4120 W. Dempster, Skokie, IL 60076   **(708) 674-2021**
Kosher/natural foods. Slice of Life is an Italian/dairy kosher restaurant that serves fish and vegetarian foods. An eclectic menu lists a wide variety of appetizers, salads, soups, pasta, sandwiches, and vegetarian entrees. A children's section is on the menu. Monday is Mexican night. **Open daily. Full service, kosher, fresh juices, espresso/cappuccino, wine/beer/alcohol, take-out, $$**

ST. CHARLES
Al's Cafe & Creamery
105 N. 2nd Ave., St. Charles, IL 60174   **(708) 584-5120**
Cafe. See description under Elgin, IL. **St. Charles location open daily.**

URBANA
• Red Herring Vegetarian Restaurant
1209 W. Oregon, Urbana, IL 61801   **(217) 344-1176**
Vegetarian. The only vegetarian restaurant in Urbana is a nonprofit educational food service. All foods are made from scratch and organic ingredients are used when possible. A primarily vegan menu features international dishes and vegan baked goods. **Closed Sunday. Cafeteria style, vegan options, take-out, $**

VILLA PARK
•• Better Living
100-25 E. Roosevelt, Villa Park, IL 60181   **(708) 782-5433**
Vegan. Several entrees, a salad bar, and sandwiches are offered at this vegan establishment, which has introduced a Sunday brunch by reservation only. **Open Monday through Friday for lunch, Wednesday through Thursday for dinner, Sunday for brunch. Full service, completely vegan, fresh juices, non-alc. beer/wine, take-out, VISA/MC, $**

China Palace

840 W. Main St., W. Dundee, IL 60118 **(708) 428-8888**

Chinese. The management is willing to accommodate vegetarians and will substitute tofu for meat in any dish. **Open seven days. Full service, vegan options, wine/beer/alcohol, take-out, VISA/MC/AMX/DISC, $**

• Shree Vegetarian Restaurant

655 N. Cass Ave., Westmont, IL 60559 **(708) 655-1021**

Vegetarian. A varied and extensive menu of well prepared Indian foods is served in a friendly, clean atmosphere. Incense and Indian music enhance the dining experience. **Open Thursday through Sunday. Reservations required Friday through Sunday. Full service, fresh juices, BYOB, take-out, AMX, $**

INDIANA

Twin Happiness Restaurant

1188 N. Main St., Crown Point, IN 46307 **(219) 663-4433**

Chinese. Twin Happiness offers a large variety of vegetable and tofu dishes. Corn oil is used for cooking, and the restaurant is very willing to accommodate requests for low-salt, low-fat foods, etc. **Open daily. Full service, wine/beer/alcohol, take-out, VISA/MC/AMX, $$**

Anarkali

4213 Lafayette Rd., Indianapolis, IN 46254 **(317) 298-0773**

Indian. Many vegetarian options including appetizers and side dishes are joined by entrees such as paneer and brijani, and many breads. **Open daily for dinner, and lunch on weekends. Full service, wine/beer, take-out, VISA/MC/DISC, $$**

Consulate House

245 S. Meriden St., Indianapolis, IN 46225 **(317) 637-1688**

Chinese. Features a vegetarian menu complete with appetizers, soups, and entrees. **Open daily for lunch and dinner. Full service, non-alc. wine/beer, wine/beer/ alcohol, take-out, VISA/MC/AMX/DC, $$**

Koerys Restaurant

1850 E. 62nd St., Indianapolis, IN 46220 **(317) 253-2252**

Greek. Koerys features Hummus, Baba Ghanouj, Falafel, and Spanakopita. **Open daily for lunch and dinner. Full service, non-alc. beer/wine, wine/beer, take-out, VISA/MC/AMX/DISC/DC, $$**

Mexicana Rose
1850 E. 62nd St., Indianapolis, IN 46220   **(317) 251-1355**
Mexican. At the same location as Koerys Restaurant (see above), this restaurant features enchiladas and burritos, all with vegetarian beans. **Open daily for lunch and dinner. Full service, non-alc. beer/wine, wine/beer, take-out, VISA/MC/ AMX/DISC/DC, $$**

Pesto
303 N. Alabama St., Indianapolis, IN 46204   **(317) 269-0715**
Italian. Pesto features Vegetable Casserole, Fettucine with Four Cheeses, Creamed Spinach, pizza, and salads. **Closed Sunday. Full service, non-alc. beer, wine/beer/ alcohol, VISA/MC/AMX/DC, $$–$$$**

SOUTH BEND

Cornucopia Restaurant
303 S. Michigan St., South Bend, IN 46601   **(219) 288-1911**
Natural foods. Homemade soups and daily specials are served in addition to appetizers, salads, sandwiches, entrees, omelettes, sautéed tofu, and à la carte items. Vegetarian Chili, Spinach Lasagna, and Mexican dishes are included on the menu. **Closed Sunday. Full service, vegan options, fresh juices, wine/beer/alcohol, take-out, VISA/MC, $$**

IOWA

AMES

The Grubstake
2512 Lincoln Way, Ames, IA 50010   **(515) 292-9852**
Natural foods. The Grubstake offers a wide selection of vegetarian dishes, many of which feature Mexican fare and some other ethnic foods. The restaurant is located near Iowa State University. **Full service, $$**

The Pizza Kitchens
120 Hayward Ave., Ames, IA 50010   **(515) 292-1710**
Pizza. Among the gourmet pizza and Italian pasta dishes served here are two vegetarian pizzas and two pastas. Pizza Kitchens is located near Iowa State University. **Full service, espresso/cappuccino, take-out, $$**

DAVENPORT

The Greatest Grains On Earth
1600 Harrison St., Davenport, IA 52803   **(319) 323-7521**
Natural foods. Food, which can be ordered by the piece or by the pound, includes items such as pizza, enchiladas, burritos, Spinach Potato Pie, sandwiches, soups, side dishes, and desserts. **Open daily. Deli style, vegan options, fresh juice, take-out, $**

DES MOINES

A Taste of Thailand
215 E. Walnut St., Des Moines, IA 50309   **(515) 282-0044**
Thai. The authentic Thai cuisine includes an extensive vegetarian menu section. Vegetable soups, spring rolls, Thai salad, and various vegetarian entrees make up the selection at this restaurant. **Closed Sunday. Full service, vegan options, fresh juice, wine/beer, take-out, VISA/MC/AMX, $$**

Campbell's Nutrition Center
4040 University Ave., Des Moines, IA 50311   **(515) 277-6351**
Health-food-store deli. Vegetarian pita sandwiches are featured here. **Closed Sunday. Deli, take-out, $**

El Patio
611 37th, Des Moines, IA 50312   **(515) 274-2303**
Mexican. **Closed Monday. Full service, wine/beer, VISA/MC, $$**

Sheffield's Restaurant
2724 Ingersoll, Des Moines, IA 50312   **(515) 244-7733**

216 6th Ave., Des Moines, IA 50309   **(515) 288-7687**

10201 University, Des Moines, IA 50325   **(515) 224-6774**
Natural foods. Dine on vegetarian soup, sandwich, quesadilla, pizza, and salad. **Open daily. Full service, fresh juice, wine/beer, take-out, $**

FAIRFIELD

Bonnie's China Deli
51 N. Second St., Fairfield, IA 52556   **(515) 472-7587**
Natural foods. The traditional Chinese food includes a good vegetarian selection featuring dishes using tofu, wheat gluten, and veggie tempura. No MSG is used and special diets can be accommodated (no oil, no salt, extra spicy, etc.). There is a wide range of international desserts and beverages. **Open Monday through Saturday for lunch and dinner. Limited service, vegan options, take-out, VISA/ MC, $**

IOWA CITY

Great Midwestern Ice Cream Co.
126 E. Washington St., Iowa City, IA 52240   **(319) 337-7243**
Ice cream/sandwich shop. Some vegetarian soups, sandwiches, and pastries are offered at this ice cream shop. No smoking. **Open daily. Cafeteria style, take-out, $**

URBANDALE

New Delhi Palace
3225 NW 86th St., Urbandale, IA 50322   **(515) 278-2929**
Indian. The palace features a special vegetarian menu section with eight entrees plus appetizers and soup. Fresh Indian breads are baked in clay ovens. **Open daily for lunch and dinner. Full service, vegan options, fresh juice, wine/beer, take-out, VISA/MC/AMX, $$**

KANSAS

Cornucopia Restaurant & Bar

1801 Massachusetts Ave., Lawrence, KS 66044   **(913) 842-9637**

Natural foods. Here you'll find a huge salad bar with homemade soups and breads. Some vegetarian appetizers, salads, stir-fry, pasta dishes, Avocado Sandwich, and Falafel make up the veggie selection. Children's menu has salad bar and veggie lasagna. **Full service, limited vegan options, wine/beer/alcohol, take-out, VISA/MC, $$**

Paradise Cafe

728 Massachusetts St., Lawrence, KS 66044   **(913) 842-5199**

Natural foods. "Good real food" is made from scratch and includes homemade breads and desserts, and entrees based on various ethnic dishes from Italy, India, and Mexico. Breakfast menu includes vegan options. **Open daily for three meals. Full service, vegan options, wine/beer/alcohol, take-out, VISA/MC/DISC, $$**

Mother India Restaurant Inc.

9036 Metcalf, Overland Park, KS 66212   **(913) 341-0415**

Indian. Family-style Indian dining includes many vegetarian specials. Spicewise, dishes are available mild, medium, hot, superhot, and flaming hot!! **Open daily for lunch and dinner. Full service, vegan options, wine/beer/alcohol, take-out, VISA/MC/AMX/DISC, $$**

Manna House Restaurant

5313 W. 94th Terrace, Prairie Village, KS 66207   **(913) 381-9615**

Natural foods. This homey cafe features heart-healthy foods and daily specials. It is located next to a health food store. **Closed Sunday. Limited service, fresh juices, take-out, VISA/MC/AMX, $**

Shawnee Mission Medical Center

9100 W. 74th St., Box 2923, Shawnee Mission, KS 66201   **(913) 676-2496**

Hospital cafeteria. Many vegetarian entrees and side dishes are available every day at this cafeteria. **Open daily. Cafeteria style, take-out, $**

KENTUCKY

Alfalfa

557 S. Limestone, Lexington, KY 40508   **(606) 253-0014**

International. A casual atmosphere surrounds a menu that varies daily, stressing international and regional fare. Vegetarian entrees, salads, home-baked bread and desserts are always offered. **Open daily. Full service, vegan options, wine/beer, take-out, $–$$**

Everybody's Natural Foods & Deli
503 Euclid Ave., Lexington, KY 40502   **(606) 255-4162**
Natural foods. Vegetarian sandwiches, Not Dogs, salads, and daily specials are featured and breakfast is served. Courtyard seating. **Open daily. Limited service, vegan options, fresh juices, take-out, VISA/MC/DISC, $**

LOUISVILLE

• Rainbow Blossom Natural Foods & Deli
106 Fairfax Ave., Louisville, KY 40207   **(502) 893-3626**
Vegetarian deli. Offering many vegan items, this vegetarian deli is take-out only. The foods are made with high quality products using organic ingredients when possible. Rainblow Blossom is dedicated to providing an alternative to those people who seek healthy and convenient gourmet foods to go. **Open daily. Self-service, vegan options, fresh juices, take-out, VISA/MC, $**

LOUISIANA

METAIRIE

Nature Lovers
3014 Cleary Ave., Metairie, LA 70002   **(504) 887-4929**
Natural foods. Nature Lovers provides a deli and salad bar. **Full service, fresh juices, take-out, VISA/MC/AMX/DISC, $**

NEW ORLEANS

The Apple Seed Shoppe
346 Camp St., New Orleans, LA 70130   **(504) 529-3442**
Natural foods. Dig into salads, sandwiches, and specialties. **Open Monday through Friday. Limited service, fresh juices, BYOB, take-out, $**

Old Dog New Trick
307 Exchange Alley, New Orleans, LA 70130   **(504) 511-4569**
Natural foods. Vegetarian burgers, salads, tempeh sandwiches, veggie pizzas, and tofu entrees are offered at this New Orleans restaurant. It often has vegan desserts! **$**

SHREVEPORT

Earthereal Restaurant & Bakery
3309 Line Ave., Shreveport, LA 71104 **(318) 865-8947**
Natural foods/macrobiotic. Salads, many unique sandwiches, and tacos with soymeat or avocado, plus daily specials are offered on the Earthereal menu. **Closed Sunday. Limited service, macrobiotic, fresh juices, take-out, VISA/MC, $**

MAINE

BAR HARBOR

Quiet Earth Restaurant
122 Cottage St., Bar Harbor, ME 04609 **(207) 288-3696**
International. Gourmet international cuisine is provided in a charming European-style atmosphere. Live music is featured regularly. Quiet Earth serves vegetarian, fish, and chicken dishes with non-dairy entrees available on request. **Open for dinner daily in summer, Thursday through Sunday in winter. Full service, wine/beer, take-out, VISA/MC, $$**

BELFAST

Darby's
105 High St., Belfast, ME 04915 **(207) 338-2339**
Natural foods/macrobiotic. Darby's has operated continuously since 1845 with original walls, tin ceiling, and antique bar. Macrobiotic specials are offered daily. **Open daily. Full service, wine/beer/alcohol, take-out, VISA/MC, $$**

Kingsbury House Inn
35 Northport Ave., Belfast, ME 04915 **(207) 338-2419**
Macrobiotic bed-and-breakfast. This small New England bed-and-breakfast serves only macrobiotic fare. **Reservations required. Limited service, BYOB, take-out, $$**

90 Main Street
90 Main St., Belfast, ME 04915 **(207) 338-1106**
Natural foods/macrobiotic. Quality natural foods using organic produce are served when in season. Daily specials and desserts as well as black bean enchiladas, pasta dishes, salads, and vegetarian soups are featured. Outdoor dining in the summer. **Open daily for lunch and dinner. Full service, fresh juices, wine/beer/alcohol, take-out, VISA/MC, $$**

BIDDEFORD

New Morning Natural Food Market and Cafe
230 Main St., Biddeford, ME 04005 **(207) 282-1434**
Natural foods. The cafe offers an ever-changing selection of creative entrees. A wide variety of sandwiches is available on sourdough bread from a local bakery. There are also homemade soups and chili. **Open Monday through Friday. Full service, vegan options, fresh juices, take-out, $**

Basics Natural Foods Store

537 Shore Rd., Cape Elizabeth, ME 04107   **(207) 767-2803**

Natural foods deli. Basics has a deli with sesame noodles, soups, vegetable pot pies, veggie lasagna, sandwiches, and assorted desserts. Many dairy-free and wheat-free items are available. Most entrees are prepared for you to take home and heat. There are a few tables on the premises. **Open daily. Vegan options, wine/beer, mostly take-out, $**

The Corsican Restaurant

9 Mechanic St., Freeport, ME 04032   **(207) 865-9421**

Natural foods. Homemade vegetarian soups, unique whole-wheat pizza, calzones, and fresh baked breads are offered daily. Delicious pies and cakes are also available. No smoking. **Open daily for lunch and dinner. Full service, wine/beer, take-out, $$**

• Geronimo Cafe

Breakneck Hollow Rd., Hulls Cove, ME 04644   **(207) 288-5503**

Vegetarian. Experience whole-foods dining in a peaceful 1840's farm house located on beautiful Mt. Desert Island on the way to Bar Harbor. Choose from a menu of appetizers, soups, grains, greens, and creative specials. Macrobiotic diets can be accommodated with forty-eight hours notice. Five to six entrees are created for each evening. **Open Wednesday through Sunday. Full service, vegan options, fresh juice, BYOB, take-out, no credit cards, $$**

Bagel Works

15 Temple St., Portland, ME 04101   **(207) 879-2425**

Bagel deli. More than sixteen varieties of bagels are offered with various topping options including cream cheeses, tofutti spreads, salads, and vegetarian combinations. Only natural ingredients without preservatives are used. Bagel Works is environmentally conscious and socially active in its community. **Open daily. Counter service, vegan options, fresh juices, take-out, $**

Cafe No

20 Danforth St., Portland, ME 04101   **(207) 772-8114**

International. Cafe No's menu includes many salads, sandwiches, Middle Eastern specialties, fish dishes, and desserts with several vegetarian options. **Open Tuesday through Saturday. Full service, vegan options, wine/beer, take-out, no credit cards, $**

Good Day Market

155 Brackett St., Portland ME 04102   **(207) 772-4937**

Natural foods deli. Good Day Market is a food co-op that has take-out sandwiches, knishes, calzones, soup and chili, muffins, cakes, and tarts. **Deli open Monday through Friday. Take-out only, vegan options, wine/beer, no credit cards, $**

Pepperclub
78 Middle St., Portland, ME 04101 **(207) 772-0531**
Eclectic. The Pepperclub menu is about 50 percent vegetarian and 50 percent fish.
There is always at least one vegan entree as well. **Open daily for dinner. Full service,
wine/beer, take-out, VISA/MC, $$**

Planets
27 Forest Ave., Portland, ME 04101 **(207) 828-0112**
International. Interesting collection of international vegetarian dishes includes
Mexican, Thai, Lebanese, and Italian options. Planets has a unique atmosphere
decorated with stars, planets, and globes. The food is very good. **Closed Sunday
and Monday. Full service, vegan options, take-out, VISA/MC, $-$$**

Raffles Cafe Bookstore
555 Congress St., Portland, ME 04101 **(207) 761-3930**
Natural foods. Raffles focuses on high quality, fresh, and nutritious food. The
offering includes soup, salads, sandwiches, Middle Eastern foods, and daily vegetarian specials and homemade desserts. **Full service, fresh juices, espresso/cap-
puccino, take-out, VISA/MC, $**

Silly's
147 Cumberland Ave., Portland, ME 04102 **(207) 772-0360**
Natural foods. A small restaurant with a colorful and involving atmosphere, Silly's has
delicious and surprising food, with a variety that includes Hummus, Falafel, Sesame
Noodles, pizza, Jamaican Beans and Rice, and sandwiches. Patio for summer dining.
Open daily for lunch and dinner. Full service, vegan options, BYOB, take-out, $

Victory Deli and Bake Shop
1 Monument Way, Portland, ME 04102 **(207) 772-7299**
Deli/cafe. This New York style deli, cafe, and bakery emphasizes preparation of
food items from scratch. Veggie salads, sandwiches, Falafel, and veggie burgers
are offered. There's a whole-grain bakery and organic vegetables in the summer.
**Open for three meals Monday through Friday, for breakfast and lunch on
weekends. Full service, fresh juices, wine/beer, take-out, $**

Walter's Cafe
15 Exchange St., Portland, ME 04101 **(207) 871-9258**
American. Walter's Cafe offers regional cuisine that is prepared fresh daily in the
exhibition-style kitchen. Walter's offers friendly, courteous service in a casual but
professional atmosphere. **Open for lunch and dinner daily. Full service, wine/beer,
take-out, VISA/MC/AMX, $$**

West Side Restaurant
58 Pine St., Portland, ME 04102 **(207) 773-8223**
Gourmet/natural foods. Each entree is prepared to order at the West Side, a
restaurant that prides itself on good quality, healthy food and is willing to
accommodate special diets. Vegetarian dinner options include lasagna, a tofu dish,
fettucine, stir-fry, a Mexican dish, and appetizers. **Open for three meals daily,
Sunday for brunch only. Full service, vegan options, fresh juice, wine/beer,
alcohol, limited take-out, $$-$$$**

The Whole Grocer
118 Congress St., Portland, ME 04101   **(207) 774-7711**
Natural foods deli. Two featured soups daily plus fresh baked muffins, sandwiches, salads, and sometimes desserts are offered here. **Open daily. Self-service, vegan options, wine/beer, take-out, $**

RAYMOND

• Northern Pines Health Resort
559 Route 85, Raymond, ME 04071   **(207) 655-7624**
Vegetarian/natural foods. The menu at Northen Pines is vegetarian but fish is occasionally served. Northern Pines offers a delicious variety of vegetarian dishes for breakfast, lunch, and dinner. Menu changes. **Open mid-June to Labor Day. Buffet, fresh juices, VISA/MC, $$**

SOUTH HARPSWELL

J. Hathaways
Rte. 123, S. Harpswell, ME 04079   **(207) 833-5305**
American. Recommended by a local patron, this restaurant has a terrific vegetarian lasagna and a meatless chili topped with cornbread. The bean soup is also delicious. **Full service, vegan option.**

MARYLAND

BALTIMORE

(For more restaurant listings in the surrounding suburbs, see Cockeysville, Columbia, Ellicott City, Owings Mills, Randallstown, and Timonium.)

Akbar
823 N. Charles St., Baltimore, MD 21201   **(410) 539-0944**
Indian. Akbar features authentic Indian cuisine with a wide variety of vegetarian dishes. The restaurant has consistently given great service. **Open daily. Full service, vegan options, wine/beer/alcohol, catering, take-out, VISA/MC/AMX/DISC, $$**

Al Pacino Cafe
900 Cathedral St., Baltimore, MD 21201   **(410) 962-8859**

609 S. Broadway, Baltimore, MD 21231   **(410) 327-0005**

542 E. Belvedere Ave., (in the Belvedere Market)
Baltimore, MD 21212   **(410) 323-7060**
Middle Eastern/pizza. With a New-York-City-type atmosphere, this bustling cafe has great-tasting Middle Eastern food, steaming hot pita bread, and unique pizza combinations such as the pizza served with curry. All pizza is available without cheese or with soy cheese. **Open daily. Full service, vegan options, take-out, VISA/MC, $$**

Bombay Grill
2 E. Madison St., Baltimore, MD 21202 **(410) 837-2973**
Indian. This cozy Indian restaurant offers Indian breads and many vegetarian entrees including Vegetable Kofta, potato dishes, Okra and Onions, Eggplant Stir-fry, and a grilled vegetable kabab. Dishes are prepared with vegetable or olive oil. **Open daily. Full service, vegan options, wine/beer/alcohol, catering, take-out, VISA/MC/AMX/DISC/DC, $$**

China Palace Restaurant
3333 Greenmount Ave., Baltimore, MD 21218 **(410) 889-0288**
Chinese. China Palace has a simple atmosphere, but a surprisingly interesting homestyle Chinese and Indonesian menu. Enjoy a pickled cabbage appetizer. Your meal will be prepared without salt, MSG, or sugar. **Open daily. Full service, catering, take-out, VISA/MC/AMX, $$**

Ding How
631-637 S. Broadway, Baltimore, MD 21231 **(410) 327-8888**
Chinese. This Fells Point Chinese restaurant offers many vegetarian items including appetizers, soups, tofu, and vegetable entrees. **Full service, vegan options, wine/beer/alcohol, take-out, VISA/MC/AMX/DISC/DC, $–$$**

5 Star Pizza
17 S. Broadway, Baltimore, MD 21231 **(410) 732-1257**
Indian. This all-American meat-based restaurant has an extensive selection of vegetarian Indian take-out food. **Open daily. Catering, take-out, $–$$**

• Golden Temple Cafe
2322 N. Charles St., Baltimore, MD 21218 **(410) 235-1014**
Vegetarian/natural foods. This natural foods store offers counter service and tables at which to sit, and a Mexican Fiesta salad bar. No meat, poultry, fish, or eggs are served. **Cafe open Monday through Saturday for lunch; salad bar available daily until dusk. Counter service, vegan options, fresh juices, catering, take-out, VISA/MC, $**

• Green Earth Natural Food Store & Deli
823 N. Charles St., Baltimore, MD 21201 **(410) 752-1422**
Natural foods/macrobiotic/health-food deli. This take-out-food store features gourmet homestyle cooking using mostly organic ingredients. **Open daily. Vegan/macrobiotic options, fresh juices, take-out only, VISA/MC, $**

Hacienda Mexican Restaurant
4840 Bel Air Rd., Baltimore, MD 21206 **(410) 488-9447**
Mexican. Enjoy vegetarian burritos, tacos, and quiche. **Open for dinner Tuesday through Sunday. Full service, wine/beer/alcohol, limited catering, take-out, VISA/MC/AMX, $$**

Jai Hind Indian Restaurant
5511 York Rd., Baltimore, MD 21212   **(410) 323-8440**
Indian. Jai Hind features formal dining with instrumental Indian music in the background. The restaurant is accommodating to vegetarians, with a nice vegetarian variety included on the menu. **Open Monday through Saturday for lunch, and Monday through Sunday for dinner. Full service, vegan options, wine/beer/alcohol, take-out, VISA/MC/AMX/DISC, $$**

Louie's Bookstore Cafe
518 N. Charles St., Baltimore, MD 21201   **(410) 962-1224**
Cafe/bookstore. Located downtown, Louie's is a fun, crowded, and popular combination of restaurant, bookstore, art gallery, and bakery. It features classical music performances every evening during dinner hours and at Sunday brunch. The menu is eclectic, with both local and international cuisine and a good number of options for vegetarians. **Open daily into night. Full service, vegan options, wine/beer/alcohol, take-out, VISA/MC, $$**

Mencken's Cultured Pearl
1114-16 Hollins St., Baltimore, MD 21223   **(410) 837-1947**
Mexican. Located in a marginal neighborhood that is a hub of the local art scene, Mencken's features monthly art shows and kraft-paper table covers and crayons so you can draw. Fresh-squeezed limes are used in the margaritas, and animal fat is not used to fry the foods. There's a relaxed atmosphere and eclectic music. Weekend evenings, you often have a long wait to be seated. You can wait at the bar. **Open daily. Full service, wine/beer/alcohol, take-out, VISA/MC, $–$$**

Middle East Cafe
3501 St. Paul St., Baltimore, MD 21218   **(410) 235-0444**
Middle Eastern. This is an all-American restaurant with Middle Eastern food. Partake of a unique falafel in rolled up pita bread. Enjoy the friendly service. **Open daily. Full service, vegan options, take-out, $**

Mike's
710 S. Broadway, Fells Point, MD 21231   **(410) 342-6589**
Mexican. Mike's is a small bar and tiny restaurant, but a fun place in the alternative-night-life section of Fells Point. Work by local artists is usually exhibited, and Mike's features guacamole and chips, bean tacos, and very large bean burritos made Mayan style. Refried beans are always made with peanut oil only. **Open daily. Full service, vegan options, wine/beer, take-out, $**

Mr. Chan Schechuan Restaurant ❧
1010 Reistertown Rd., Pikesville, MD 21208   **(410) 484-1100**
Chinese. Savor unique items for vegetarians. The chef is always experimenting to come up with new dishes and will cater to special needs, especially for vegans or macrobiotics. This top Baltimore choice offers great hot and sour soup, tempeh dishes, delicious orange spicy tofu, egg rolls or non-fried dumplings, mustard green treats, and more. **Open daily 10:30 A.M. to 10:30 P.M. Full service, vegan/macrobiotic options, wine/beer/alcohol, catering, take-out, VISA/MC/AMX/DISC, $$**

Puffins Cafe
1000 Reistertown Rd., Pikesville, MD 21208   **(410) 486-8811**
Natural foods. Puffins bakes its own breads and desserts and features salads, pasta, and pizza. All soups and sauces are vegetarian. Vegetarian entrees are generally macrobiotic style. Weekly specials are served in an art-filled atmosphere. No smoking. **Closed Sunday. Full service, non-alc. beer, wine/beer, catering, take-out, VISA/MC, $$$**

Sitar
Pace Plaza
1724 Woodlawn Dr., Baltimore, MD 21207   **(410) 265-5140**
Indian. Inexpensive Indian food is served in an informal atmosphere. **Open daily. Buffet/counter service, vegan options, take-out, $–$$**

Syrumie Cafe
3219 Eastern Ave., Baltimore, MD 21224   **(410) 563-2787**
Middle Eastern. Syrumie offers traditional Egyptian, Lebanese, and Syrian foods. Dinner and show (Egyptian dance) are featured once a month. **Open for dinner only Monday through Friday, lunch and dinner Saturday. Full service, vegan options, wine/beer, catering, take-out, $$–$$$**

The Tell Tale Hearth
1145 Hollins St., Baltimore, MD 21223   **(410) 234-0880**
American/ethnic. Enjoy hearth-baked pizza, Caribbean specialities, and pastas. **Open daily until 2:00 A.M. Full service, wine/beer/alcohol, catering, take-out, VISA/MC, $$**

Thai Restaurant
3316 Greenmount Ave., Baltimore, MD 21218   **(410) 889-7303**
Thai. Although the service and atmosphere are formal, dress is casual. There's a nice selection, and the restaurant will substitute tofu for meat in any of its dishes. Located on a main street, but the neighborhood is somewhat marginal. **Open daily. Full service, wine/beer/alcohol, catering, take-out, VISA/MC/AMX, $$**

Tov Pizza
6313 Reisterstown Rd., Baltimore, MD 21215   **(410) 358-5238**
Kosher/dairy. This popular kosher dairy restaurant in Baltimore is primarily vegetarian with the exception of some fish dishes. Items available include pizzas and Falafel. **Counter service, vegan options, take-out, $**

BEL AIR

Hunan Chef
5 Bel Air South Parkway, Bel Air, MD 21014   **(410) 838-2313**
Chinese. **Monday through Saturday open late afternoon and evening, Sunday open from noon until 10:00 P.M. Full service, vegan options, take-out, VISA/MC/AMX, $$**

BETHESDA

(For more restaurant listings in the surrounding areas, see Washington, D.C.)

Bacchus
7945 Norfolk Ave., Bethesda, MD 20814   **(301) 657-1722**
Lebanese. This Lebanese restaurant offers several vegetarian items including Stuffed Grape Leaves, Hummus, Baba Ghanouj, Stuffed Eggplant, Eggplant Salad, Potato Salad, Cauliflower and Tahini Dip, and Falafel. **Open Daily. Full service, vegan options, wine/beer/alcohol, catering, take-out, VISA/MC/AMX, $$–$$$**

Kabul West
4871 Cardell Ave., Bethesda, MD 20814   **(301) 986-8566**
Afghani. Feast on many vegetarian dishes. **Open weekdays for lunch and dinner, only for dinner on weekends. Full service, wine/beer, take-out, VISA/MC, $$–$$$**

Tako Grill
7756 Wisconsin Ave., Bethesda, MD 20814   **(301) 652-7030**
Japanese. **Closed Sunday. Full service, wine/beer/alcohol, take-out, VISA/MC/ AMX, $**

•• The Vegetable Garden
White Flint Mall (3rd Floor)
11618 Rockville Pike, Bethesda, MD 20852   **(301) 468-9301**
Vegan/Chinese. If you are in the D.C. area and you like Chinese food, this is a must-try restaurant. It has dozens of hard-to-find vegan and vegetarian dishes, expecially seitan and wheat gluten items. It also offers such interesting soups as Sizzling Rice and Asparagus and Corn Soup, and a non-fat menu is available. **Open daily for lunch and dinner. Full service, vegan options, fresh juices, wine/beer/alcohol, take-out, VISA/MC/AMX, $$**

CAPITAL HEIGHTS

Your's Naturally Health Food & Soul Vegetarian Deli
9133 Central Ave., Capital Heights, MD 20799   **(301) 499-0375**
Health foods. Your's Naturally is take-out only, offering sandwiches, soups, and snacks made without dairy or eggs. **Counter service, vegan options, fresh juices, take-out only, VISA/MC $**

COCKEYSVILLE

The Natural Cafe
560 Cranbrook Rd., Cockeysville, MD 21030   **(410) 628-1262**

🍴 Reviewers' choice   • Vegetarian restaurant   •• Vegan restaurant
$ less than $6 $$ $6–$12 $$$ more than $12
VISA/AMX/MC/DISC/DC—credit cards accepted
Non-alc.—Non-alcoholic   Fresh juices—freshly squeezed

Health-food-store juice bar. This self-serve cafe has a chef on duty and offers home-made soup or chili daily. **Open for lunch Monday through Friday. Cafeteria style, vegan options, fresh juices, take-out, VISA/MC/AMX, $**

COLLEGE PARK

(For more restaurant listings in the surrounding areas, see Washington, D.C.)

Berwyn Cafe
5010 Berwyn Rd., College Park, MD 20740   **(301) 345-6655**
Natural Foods. Berwyn Cafe is located in a natural foods store in a college town. It features two to three specials daily, one is usually vegan, and offers pita sand-wiches, veggie burgers and dogs, steamed vegetables, beans and rice, plus much more. **Open daily. Sunday brunch. Counter service, vegan/macrobiotic options, fresh juices, non-alc. beverages, take-out, $**

COLUMBIA

Bombay Peacock Grill
10005 Old Columbia Rd., Columbia, MD 21046   **(410) 381-7111**
Indian. This cozy Indian restaurant offers Indian breads and many vegetarian entrees including Vegetable Kofta, potato dishes, Okra and Onions, Eggplant Stir-Fry, and a Grilled Vegetable Kabab. Dishes are prepared with vegetable or olive oil. **Open daily. Full service, vegan options, wine/beer/alcohol, catering, take-out, VISA/MC/AMX/DIS/DC, $$**

• MELA
6476 Dobbin Center Way, Columbia, MD 21045   **(410) 997-2117**
Vegetarian/Indian. This new small restaurant offers Indian vegetarian food made without eggs. Items may be prepared vegan upon request. Appetizers include samosas and Onion Pakoras. Various lentil soups are offered as well as a wide variety of entrees such as curries, rice-based dishes, and dals. **Open daily for lunch and dinner. Full service, vegan options, wine/beer, catering, take-out, VISA/MC, $–$$.**

CUMBERLAND

Gehauf's
1268 National Hwy., Cumberland, MD 21502   **(301) 729-3300**
American style. In a lovely airy setting, you'll find fresh fruit plates in season, spinach salad, mixed salad with fresh vegetables, and a few vegetarian specials like vegetarian chili. **Open daily. Full service, wine/beer/alcohol, take-out, VISA/MC/AMX, $$**

L'Osteria
Rt 40, Cumberland, MD 21502   **(301) 777-3553**
Italian. The atmosphere is formal, and the food includes Eggplant Parmesan and Pasta Alfredo, imported pastas with vegetables, and a variety of salads and fruits. Some items can be made without cheese. **Open for dinner. Full service, reserva-tions required, wine/beer/alcohol, catering, take-out, VISA/MC/AMX, $$**

The Melting Pot
Winchester Rd., Cumberland, MD 21502   **(301) 729-1960**

Ethnic foods. Various ethnic foods are featured, and the restaurant, which is very accommodating of special needs, will prepare low-fat entrees. There are many lacto-ovo choices. Lunch specials include vegetarian egg rolls. **Open daily. Full service, wine/beer/alcohol, take-out, $$**

Ping's
Country Club Mall, Cumberland, MD 21502   (301) 729-0551
Chinese. This homey restaurant will prepare fat-free stir-fries in woks that are cleaned after each use. It also offers vegetarian egg rolls and vegetarian entrees. **Closed Sunday. Full service, vegan options, take-out, $**

ELLICOTT CITY

Han Sung Restaurant
3570 St. John Ln., Ellicott City, MD 21043   410) 750-3836
Korean/Japanese. Enjoy several vegetarian appetizers, steamed rice, and salads. **Wine/beer, $–$$**

ELDERSBURG

A Touch of Nature
Carrolltowne Mall
6482 Ridge Rd., Eldersburg, MD 21784   (410) 795-8986
Health-food-store deli. This deli's sandwich bar features six sandwiches with either dairy or tofu cheeses, and salad. **Open daily. Limited service, juice, take-out, VISA/MC, $**

FREDERICK

• Common Market (Frederick Co-op)
5813 Buckeystown Pk., Frederick, MD 21701   (301) 663-3416
Vegetarian/health-food-store deli. Enjoy sandwiches made with organically grown foods, and a juice bar. **Lunch hours. Limited service, fresh juices, take-out, $**

Health Express
1540 W. Patrick, Frederick, MD 21701   (301) 662-2293
Health-food-store deli. Sandwiches and homemade soups are the order of the day. **Lunch hours. Limited service, fresh juices, take-out, $**

Lotus Chinese Cuisine
107 Baughman's Ln., Frederick, MD 21702   (301) 694-3388
Chinese. Here's authentic Chinese cuisine in a relaxed atmosphere. There's a vegetarian section on the menu, and Lotus will gladly accommodate vegetarians/vegans. **Open daily. Full service, vegan options, wine/beer, take-out, VISA/MC/DISC, $$**

🐾 Reviewers' choice   • Vegetarian restaurant   •• Vegan restaurant
$ less than $6 $$ $6–$12 $$$ more than $12
VISA/AMX/MC/DISC/DC—credit cards accepted
Non-alc.—Non-alcoholic   Fresh juices—freshly squeezed

The Orchard
48 E. Patrick St., Frederick, MD 21701 (301) 663-4912
Natural foods. This natural foods restaurant serves chicken, seafood, and vegetarian items. It is completely non-smoking and has outdoor dining on the deck from April through October. **Closed Sundays and Mondays. Open Tuesday through Saturday for lunch and dinner. Full service, vegan options, wine/beer, take-out, VISA/MC/AMX/DC, $$**

Sombreros International
490 L. Prospect Blvd., Frederick, MD 21701 (301) 695-8858
Mexican/American/international. In addition to a full American menu, Mexican and international foods are served. The special vegetarian menu includes Falafel, Hummus, boboli bread, Spinach Lasagna, and Mexican entrees. Only vegetable oil is used. **Open daily for lunch and dinner. Full service, wine/beer/alcohol, take-out, VISA/MC/AMX/DISC, $**

Taurasos
4 East St., Frederick, MD 21701 (301) 663-6600
American. This popular restaurant has an elegant formal dining room and a casual pub. A special vegetarian menu is available. **Open for lunch and dinner. $–$$$**

FROSTBURG

Giuseppe's
11 Bowery St., Frostburg, MD 21532 (301) 689-2220
Italian. This unique Italian restaurant in a small town near a ski area offers many lacto-ovo choices and a tasty plain sauce for vegans. Giuseppe's will accommodate special needs. **Open daily late afternoon and evening. Full service, wine/beer/alcohol, take-out, VISA/MC/AMX/DISC, $$**

GAITHERSBURG

Thai Sa-Mai Restaurant
8369 Snouffer School Rd., Gaithersburg, MD 20879 (301) 963-1800
Thai. On the menu are original spicy Thai foods and thirty vegetarian dishes made without MSG. *The Washingtonian* magazine named this restaurant's curry the best four-star. **Open Monday through Saturday. Full service, vegan options, wine/beer, take-out, VISA/MC, $$**

GREENBELT

China Pearl Restaurant
7701 Greenbelt Rd., Greenbelt, MD 20770 (301) 441-8880
Chinese. Enjoy Chinese dishes including vegetarian egg rolls. Tempeh is also available. **Open daily. Full service, alcohol, take-out, VISA/MC/AMX/DISC, $$**

Maharajah
8825 Greenbelt Rd., Greenbelt, MD 20770 (301) 552-1600
Indian. Here you'll find vegetarian appetizers, and main dishes that include

eggplant, curries, and vegetable stir-fry. **Open daily for dinner, lunch served Tuesday through Friday. Full service, vegan options, wine/beer, take-out, VISA/ MC, $$**

LAUREL

Mr. Wang Hunan
675 Main St., Laurel, MD 20707   **(301) 317-8888**
Chinese. A separate vegetarian menu offers a wide selection of mock meats including vegetarian egg rolls and crispy Sesame Chicken. **Open daily for lunch and dinner. Full service, vegan options, wine/beer, catering, take-out, $$**

OLNEY

Olney Ale House
2000 Olney Sandy Spring Rd., Olney, MD 20832   **(301) 774-6708**
Natural foods. This cozy restaurant with a fireplace during winter months offers several vegetarian dishes such as chili, tofu and sunburgers, salads, and home-made breads. It's very crowded on weekends, so expect a long wait. **Closed Monday. Full service, vegan options, wine/beer, take-out, VISA/MC/DISC, $$**

Thai Cafe Restaurant
18050 Georgia Ave., Olney, MD 20832   **(301) 570-0033**
Thai. There's a separate vegetarian menu, and the restaurant will prepare dishes with tofu instead of fish. No MSG is used. **Closed Monday. Full service, vegan options, wine/beer, catering, take-out, VISA/MC/AMX, $–$$**

OWINGS MILLS

Lorraine's
9637 Reistertown Rd., Owings Mills, MD 21117   **(410) 356-1616**
Ethnic/American. A pleasant appetizer bar features international antipasti (mostly vegetarian), whole-grain pizzas that can be made with soy cheese, pastas, and fancy desserts. Entirely non-smoking. **Open Monday through Saturday for lunch and dinner, Sunday for dinner only. Full service, fresh juices, non-alc. wine and beer, catering, VISA/MC/DISC, $–$$**

RANDALLSTOWN

(For more restaurant listings in the surrounding areas, see Baltimore)

Akbar Restaurant 🍴
3541 Brenbrook Dr., Randallstown, MD 21133   **(410) 655-1600**
Indian. See description under Baltimore.

Szechuan Best
8625 Liberty Rd., Randallstown, MD 21133   **(410) 521-0020**
Chinese. This Chinese restaurant has an extensive vegetarian menu. **Full service, take-out, $$**

RIVERDALE

(For more restaurant listings in the surrounding areas, see Washington, D.C.)

• Leland Memorial Hospital Cafeteria
4401 East West Hwy., Riverdale, MD 20737   **(301) 699-2266**
Vegetarian. The cafeteria features Loma Linda and Worthington foods. **Open daily. Cafeteria service, take-out, $**

ROCKVILLE

Hard Times Cafe
1,117 Nelson St., Rockville, MD 20850   **(301) 294-9720**
Ethnic. This old-fashioned Texas chili parlor cooks up vegetarian chili in a variety of ways. **Open daily. Full service, wine/beer, take-out, VISA/MC/AMX, $**

House of Chinese Gourmet
1485 Rockville Pk., Rockville, MD 20852   **(301) 984-9440**
Chinese. Savor the excellent and extensive vegetarian choices, such as Yellow Bird (made with bean curd skins), Crispy Eggplant, and Asparagus and Corn Soup. **Open daily for lunch and dinner. Full service, wine/beer/alcohol, take-out, VISA/MC/AMX, $$**

Natraj Restaurant
1327 F. Rockville Pk., Rockville, MD 20852   **(301) 340-7373**
Indian. No animal fat or MSG is used in cooking, and whole-wheat bread is always available. Natraj has Masala Dosas (large crêpe-like pancake with potato and onions) and a vegetarian all-you-can-eat-buffet. **Open daily. Full service, wine/beer, catering, take-out, VISA/MC/AMX/DISC, $**

SILVER SPRING

• Siddhartha Vegetarian Restaurant
8241 Georgia Ave., Silver Spring, MD 20910   **(301) 585-0550**
Vegetarian/Indian. Savor a wide variety of Indian dishes. **Open daily for lunch and dinner. Cafeteria style, vegan options, fresh juices, take-out, $–$$**

Silver Palace Restaurant
11311 Lockwood Dr., Silver Spring, MD 20904   **(301) 681-9585**
Chinese. The Palace has a large banquet room. **Open daily. Full service, wine/ beer/alcohol, VISA/MC/AMX, $$**

Thai Derm Restaurant
939 Bonifant St., Silver Spring, MD 20910   **(301) 589-5341**
Thai. The noodle specialities and all foods are made without MSG upon request. **Open Sunday. Full service, wine/beer, VISA/MC, $$**

Thai Orchid Restaurant
8519 Fenton St., Silver Spring, MD 20910   **(301) 587-2192**

Thai. MSG is left out upon request. **Open daily for lunch and dinner. Closed afternoons. Full service, wine/beer, take-out, VISA/MC, $$**

SPENCERVILLE

• Edgewood Inn
16101 Oak Hill Rd., Spencerville, MD 20905   **(301) 421-9247**
Vegetarian. Located in a historic house, Edgewood Inn offers a vegetarian buffet including soy products, Nut Loaf, Eggplant Parmesan, Lasagna, Rice Casserole, Potato Salad, homemade breads, Spinach Pie, Pineapple Cream Cake, and fruit. **Buffet, catering, $$$**

TAKOMA PARK

Royal Bengal
6846 New Hampshire, Takoma Park, MD 20912   **(301) 270-6054**
Indian/Pakistani/Bangladeshi. Diners have a choice of fourteen vegetarian dishes served with basmati rice. **Open daily for dinner, open for lunch Monday through Friday. Full service, vegan options, beer, $$**

TIMONIUM

Nature's Gateway
2139 York Rd., Timonium Shopping Center
Timonium, MD 21093   **(410) 628-1760**
Natural foods. This lunch counter and juice bar offers a wide variety of sandwiches, vegetarian burgers, and entrees such as Vegetable Lasagna, Seitan Stew, Chili, and Tacos. **Closed Sunday. Counter Service, vegan options, take-out, $**

WHEATON

China Chef Restaurant
11323 Georgia Ave., Wheaton, MD 20902   **(301) 949-8170**
Chinese. This Chinese restaurant offers several vegetarian entrees. **Open Daily. Full service, wine/beer/alcohol, catering, take-out, VISA/MC/AMX, $$**

Dusit Thai Cuisine
2404 University Blvd. West, Wheaton, MD 20902   **(301) 949-4140**
Thai. Dusit features vegetable and tofu dishes, noodle entrees, and vegetarian soup. **Open daily for lunch and dinner. Full service, wine/beer/alcohol, take-out, VISA/MC/AMX, $$**

• Nut House Pizza
11419 Georgia Ave., Wheaton, MD 20902   **(301) 942-5900**

🏕 Reviewers' choice   • Vegetarian restaurant   •• Vegan restaurant
$ less than $6 $$ $6–$12 $$$ more than $12
VISA/AMX/MC/DISC/DC—credit cards accepted
Non-alc.—Non-alcoholic   Fresh juices—freshly squeezed

Vegetarian (except tuna sometimes)/kosher/pizza. Experience pizza made with soy or kosher cheese, Falafel, vegetarian burgers, and Pita Chips. **Open Sunday through Thursday for lunch and dinner, open Friday until one hour before sundown, Saturday open one hour after sundown to 1:30 A.M. Limited service, catering, take-out, VISA/MC/AMX, $**

Sabang Indonesian Restaurant
2504 Ennali's Ave., Wheaton, MD 20902   **(301) 942-7859**

Indonesian. Sabang features vegetarian reistafel that includes soup, dessert, and about ten different vegetarian dishes. It's fun to go with a few friends. **Open daily for lunch and dinner. Full service, vegan options, wine/beer/alcohol, take-out, VISA/MC/AMX, $$–$$$**

MASSACHUSETTS

AMHERST

(For more restaurant listings in the surrounding areas, see Northampton)

The Raw Carrot
Carriage Shops, 9 E. Pleasant St., Amherst, MA 01002   **(413) 549-4240**

Juice bar. Vegan options are always available at this bright and cheery juice bar that offers a variety of lunch foods including soups, sandwiches, and salads. Organic produce is used when possible. **Limited service, fresh juices, take-out, $**

ARLINGTON

Cafe Barada
161 Massachusetts Ave., Arlington, MA 02174   **(617) 646-9650**

Middle Eastern. Enjoy a wide variety of authentic Middle Eastern vegetarian and non-vegetarian dishes. **Closed Sunday. Full service, take-out, $–$$**

BOSTON

(For more restaurant listings in the Boston area, see Arlington, Braintree, Brookline, Burlington, Cambridge, Concord [about 20 miles away], and Jamaica Plain.)

Acapulco Restaurant
266 Newbury St., Boston, MA 02116   **(617) 247-9126**

Mexican. Beans here are prepared without lard. **Open daily afternoon and evening. Full service, wine/beer/alcohol, take-out, VISA/MC/AMX/DC, $$**

Addis Red Sea Ethiopian Restaurant
544 Tremont St., Boston, MA 02118   **(617) 426-8727**

Ethiopian. Sample authentic Ethiopian cuisine with vegetarian appetizer and entree selections. **Open daily. Full service, vegan options, wine/beer, take-out, VISA/MC/AMX, $**

•• Buddha's Delight ❧

5 Beach St., Boston, MA 02122   **(617) 451-2395**
Vegan/Chinese. The "delight" here is various tofu, vegetable, and mock meat dishes.
Full service, BYOB, take-out, $

Buteco Restaurant

130 Jersey St., Boston, MA 02215   **(617) 247-9508**
Brazilian. The restaurant serves Brazilian cuisine with at least one vegetarian
entree plus a few appetizers and soup. **Open daily. Full service, wine/beer,**
take-out, VISA/MC, $$

•• Country Life Vegetarian Buffet

112 Broad St., Boston, MA 02110   **(617) 350-8625**
Vegan. An all-vegetarian buffet is offered by Seventh-day Adventists. **Open daily**
for lunch except Saturday. Call about dinner. Cafeteria style, vegan options,
fresh juices, take-out, $

India Quality

536 Commonwealth Ave., Boston, MA 02215   **(617) 267-4499**
Indian. Special breads baked freshly in clay ovens accompany an extensive vege-
tarian menu. **Open daily. Full service, vegan options, take-out, VISA/MC/**
AMX/DISC, $$

Joyce Chen Restaurant

115 Stuart St., Boston, MA 02116   **(617) 720-1331**
Chinese. Joyce Chen has been serving the best in Northern Chinese cuisine since
1958. The seasonal menu introduced creative, innovative dishes based on seasonal
foods and Chinese festivals. **Open daily for lunch and dinner. Full service,**
wine/beer/alcohol, take-out, VISA/MC/AMX/DISC, $$

Kebab-N-Kurry

30 Massachusetts Ave., Boston, MA 02115   **(617) 536-9835**
Indian. Savor authentic Indian cuisine with vegetarian specials such as cauliflower
curry, spinach with homemade Indian cheese, nine-vegetable curry, chickpea
curry, and other veggie entrees. **Open daily. Full service, vegan options,**
wine/beer, take-out, VISA/MC/AMX, $$

Milk Street Cafe

50 Milk St., Boston, MA 02109   **(617) 542-2433**

Post Office Square, Boston, MA 02109   **(617) 350-PARK**
Kosher. Features kosher dairy cuisine with daily specials including soups, quiche,
and pizza. The Post Office Square cafe features both indoor and outdoor seating.
Closed weekends. Cafeteria service, take-out, $

Souper Salad

103 State St., Boston, MA 02107   **(617) 227-9151**

102 Water St., Boston, MA 02109	(617) 367-2582
524 Kenmore Sq., Boston, MA 02115	(617) 536-7662
119 Newbury St., Boston, MA 02116	(617) 247-4983
82 Summer St., Boston, MA 02110	(617) 426-6834

Restaurant chain. Salad bar, soups, sandwiches, and entrees are all fresh and homemade with a decent selection of vegetarian options. Mexican dishes are featured. **Open daily. Full service, vegan options, fresh juices, wine/beer, take-out, VISA/MC/AMX, $**

Steve's Restaurants Inc.
316 Newbury St., Boston, MA 02115   (617) 267-1817

Greek. Steve's specializes in authentic Greek cuisine with a variety of vegetarian delights. Examples include Falafel, Grape Leaves, Spinach Pie, Hummus, Tabouleh, Eggplant Salad, Greek salads, etc. **Open daily. Full service, vegan options, take-out, no credit cards, $**

Streets Cafe & Ristorante
226 Newbury Street, Boston, MA 02116   (617) 267-0891

Cafe. Soups, sandwiches, salads, entrees, pasta specials, cakes, and pastries are accompanied by a daily selection of vegetarian dishes and sandwiches. **Open daily. cafeteria style, wine/beer, take-out, $**

BRAINTREE

Souper Salad
South Shore Plaza, 250 Granite Ave., Braintree, MA 02184   (617) 843-4658

Restaurant chain. See entry under Boston for description.

BROOKLINE

Cafe Shalom
404 Harvard St., Brookline, MA 02146   (617) 277-0698

Kosher. Vegetarian and fish items are featured with Middle Eastern and other ethnic foods. The menu lists appetizers, fresh salads, entrees, and desserts. **Open Sunday through Thursday. Full service, vegan options, wine/beer, take-out, VISA/MC/DISC, $$**

Masada
1665 Beacon St., Brookline, MA 02146   (617) 277-3433

Middle Eastern. Soups, appetizers, salads, sandwiches, and entrees all include options for vegetarians. **Open daily. Full service, vegan options, wine/beer/alcohol, take-out, VISA/MC/AMX/DISC, $$**

BURLINGTON

Souper Salad
Burlington Mall, Burlington, MA 01803   (617) 229-2223

Restaurant chain. See entry under Boston for description.

BUZZARDS BAY

Stir Crazy
100 Main St., Buzzards Bay, MA 02532 (508) 759-1781
Southeast Asian. The menu at Stir Crazy features Southeast Asian foods, specifically authentic Cambodian cuisine. It is clear that the restaurant caters to vegetarians and is willing to accommodate special diets. Foods are prepared with 100-percent pure olive oil using no artificial color or MSG. **Closed Mondays. Full service, vegan options, take-out, VISA/MC, $$**

CAMBRIDGE

Averof Restaurant
1924 Massachusetts Ave., Porter Square
Cambridge, MA 02140 (617) 354-4500
Mediterranean. A wide range of Mediterranean cuisine includes many traditional Middle Eastern dishes that are vegetarian. **Open daily. Full service, vegan options, wine/beer/alcohol, take-out, VISA/MC/AMX/DISC, $$**

Bombay Club
57 JFK St., Cambridge, MA 02138 (617) 661-8100
Indian. Authentic Indian cuisine with a vegetarian menu section features various curry dishes, dahl, and vegetable entrees. **Open daily. Full service, vegan options, wine/beer, take-out, VISA/MC/AMX, $$**

Christopher's Restaurant & Bar
1920 Massachusetts Ave., Cambridge, MA 02140 (617) 876-9180
Natural foods. Christopher's has combined mainstream American and Mexican fare with a variety of vegetarian dishes and a dedication to wholesome and healthful foods. (The owner is a long-time vegetarian!) The restaurant uses ingredients that are free of preservatives, artificial colors and flavors. All sauces, dressings, salsa, guacamole, etc., are homemade. Even the brewed decaf is prepared "Swiss water processed" and there are no dioxins in the coffee filters! In addition to quality food, Christopher's aims to be politically correct and supports 1% For Peace and other causes. **Open daily for lunch and dinner. Full service, vegan options, wine/beer/alcohol, take-out, VISA/MC/DISC, $-$$**

Gandhi Restaurant
704 Massachusetts Ave., Cambridge, MA 02139 (617) 491-1104
Indian. Traditional Indian cuisine includes eleven vegetarian entrees plus soups and appetizers. **Open daily. Full service, vegan options, wine/beer, take-out, VISA/MC, $$**

Good Stuff Cafe
1908 Massachusetts Ave., Cambridge, MA 02140 (617) 876-6645

---

❺ Reviewers' choice ● Vegetarian restaurant ●● Vegan restaurant
$ less than $6 $$ $6–$12 $$$ more than $12
VISA/AMX/MC/DISC/DC—credit cards accepted
Non-alc.—Non-alcoholic Fresh juices—freshly squeezed

Natural foods. Family-owned-and-operated restaurant emphasizes Middle Eastern foods. **Closed Sunday. Full service, vegan options, take-out, $–$$**

Joyce Chen Restaurant
390 Rindge Ave., Cambridge, MA 02140 **(617) 492-7373**
Chinese. See entry under Boston for description.

Passage to India
1900 Massachusetts Ave., Cambridge, MA 02140 **(617) 497-6113**
Indian. Authentic Indian cuisine includes a wide variety of vegetarian soups, appetizers, breads, entrees, and rice dishes. No eggs and only vegetable oil are used. **Open daily. Limited service, vegan options, wine/beer, take-out, VISA/MC, $$**

Souper Salad
36 JFK St., Harvard Square, Cambridge, MA 02138 **(617) 497-6689**
Restaurant chain. See entry under Boston for description.

Taha's Natural Foods Restaurant
162 Prospect St., Cambridge, MA 02139 **(617) 864-9368**
Natural foods. Taha's serves natural foods with a Middle Eastern flair. **Open daily. Full service, take-out, VISA/MC/AMX, $**

Tandoor House
991 Massachusetts Ave., Cambridge, MA 02138 **(617) 661-9001**
Indian. Enjoy vegetarian authentic Indian cuisine. **Open daily for lunch and dinner. Full service, wine/beer/alcohol, take-out, VISA/MC/AMX, $$**

CAPE COD

(Restaurants in this area are those listed under Buzzards Bay, Centerville, East Sandwich, Nantucket, Sandwich, and Woods Hole.)

CENTERVILLE

Sprouts Cafe at Cape Cod Natural Foods
Bell Tower Mall, 1600 Route 28, Centerville, MA 02668 **(508) 771-8394**
Natural foods cafe. Lunches feature many vegetarian sandwiches plus soups and salads. **Open daily for lunch. Limited service, vegan options, take-out, VISA/MC, $**

CONCORD

The Natural Gourmet
98 Commonwealth Ave., Concord, MA 01742 **(508) 371-7573**
Natural foods deli. This deli serves everything, from exotic salads such as Quinoa with Pine Nuts and Apricots to soups and entrees such as Wild Rice & Sweet Potato Stew or Potatoes with Russian Walnut Sauce & Colored Peppers. **Open daily. Take-out, fresh juices, $**

EAST SANDWICH

The Beehive Tavern

406 Rte. 6A, E. Sandwich, MA 02537   **(508) 833-1184**

American. The Beehive features salads, sandwiches, dinner entrees, some Middle Eastern foods, and pasta. **Open daily, seasonal hours. Full service, non-alc. beer, wine/beer/alcohol, VISA/MC, $$**

GREAT BARRINGTON

Dos Amigos Mexican Restaurant

250 Stockbridge Rd., Great Barrington, MA 01230   **(413) 528-0084**

Mexican. Vegetarian and vegan diets are easily accommodated at this restaurant serving excellent Mexican fare. Beans are vegetarian. The vegetarian sampler is delicious and can be made vegan. Dos Amigos is located in the Berkshires. **Open daily for lunch and dinner. Full service, vegan options, take-out, $$**

JAMAICA PLAIN

Center Street Cafe

597 Center St., Jamaica Plain, MA 02130   **(617) 524-9217**

American/ethnic. This small, funky neighborhood restaurant serves no red meat but some chicken, fish, and vegetarian options. The eclectic collection of Mexican, Thai, Italian, and American cuisine is made fresh from scratch. **Brunch Wednesday through Sunday, dinner nightly. Full service, vegan options, fresh juices, BYOB, take-out, $$**

LENOX

The Garden Gourmet Deli & Bake Shop

8 Franklin St., Lenox, MA 01240   **(413) 637-4156**

Deli. This deli and bake shop offer a variety of vegetarian dishes with ethnic overtones. Examples include Stuffed Grape Leaves, pierogies, knishes, Falafel, and Chili. Many sandwiches, salads, and sweets are also offered. All soups are prepared with vegetable stock and organic ingredients are used when possible. **Open daily from May through October. Full service, vegan option, fresh juices, take-out, $$**

• Kripalu Center

West St., Lenox, MA 01240   **(413) 637-3280**

Vegetarian. Located in the Berkshire Mountains close to Tanglewood, Kripalu offers wheat-free, dairy-free, and egg-free dishes. **Open daily for lunch and dinner. Cafeteria service, seasonal fresh juices, VISA/MC/AMX, $$**

NANTUCKET

Something Natural

50 Cliff Rd., Nantucket, MA 02554   **(508) 228-0504**

Bakery and sandwich shop. Twenty varieties of breads are baked fresh daily. Large sandwiches and salads are made to order. Garden seating. **Open daily in summer. Counter service, take-out, $**

NORTHAMPTON

Bela
8 Masonic St., Northampton, MA 01060 **(413) 586-8011**
Natural foods. Savor affordable eclectic vegetarian cuisine in a smoke-free environment. The chalkboard menu changes every one to two days and includes dishes from around the world. Many are dairy-free entrees. Desserts include honey- and sugar-sweetened, dairy and dairy-free. Local women's artwork is displayed in the restaurant. Outdoor cafe during nice weather. **Open Tuesday through Saturday. Full service, vegan options, take-out, $**

Paul & Elizabeth's
150 Main St., Northampton, MA 01060 **(413) 584-4832**
Natural foods/macrobiotic. Vegetarian dishes are served at Paul & Elizabeth's, which is conveniently located downtown. Some entrees have dairy, but these are clearly labeled. The menu includes many vegan options. The food is excellent, generously portioned, and reasonably priced. The atmosphere is attractive but somewhat loud. **Full service, vegan/macrobiotic options, take-out, $$**

SANDWICH

Marshland Restaurant
Rte. 6A, Sandwich, MA 02563 **(508) 888-9824**
American. Marshland features salads, sandwiches, dinner entrees, some Middle Eastern foods, and pasta. **Open daily, seasonal hours. Full service, non-alc. beer, wine/beer/alcohol, VISA/MC, $$**

SOUTH ATTLEBORO

Fuller Memorial Hospital
231 Washington St., South Attleboro, MA 02703 **(508) 761-8500**
Cafeteria. This is a not-for-profit hospital owned and operated by the Seventh-day Adventist Church. **Open daily for lunch and dinner. Cafeteria style, vegan options, take-out, no credit cards, $**

SOUTH EASTON

Pizza Haven
135 Belmont St., South Easton, MA 02375 **(508) 230-0095**
Pizza. Enjoy vegetarian pizza options. **Open daily. Counter service, take-out, $**

STOCKBRIDGE

Shogun Restaurant
Stockbridge Railway Station, Depot St.
Stockbridge, MA 01262 **(413) 298-4490**
Japanese/natural foods. Located in old Memorial Train Station, Shogun offers several vegetarian dishes. **Closed Monday. Full service, vegan option, wine/beer, take-out, VISA/MC/AMX/DISC/DC, $–$$**

WEST SPRINGFIELD

- ## Harvest Thyme
  1312 Memorial Ave., West Springfield, MA 01089   (413) 733-7375
  Vegetarian deli. A wide selection of vegetarian soups, stews, salads, sandwiches, and entrees is sold by the pint. Low-cholesterol, yeast- and mold-free, and wheat- and dairy-free items are indicated on the menu. Daily selections rotate. **Open daily. Cafeteria style, vegan option, fresh juices, take-out, VISA/MC, $**

WESTMINSTER

The 1761 Old Mill Restaurant
Rte. 2A East, Westminster, MA 01473   (508) 874-5941
Family dining. Salads and sandwiches are featured, and a children's menu is available. **Open daily. Full service, wine/beer/alcohol, VISA/MC/AMX/DISC, $$**

WOODS HOLE

Dome Restaurant
539 Woods Hole Road, Woods Hole, MA 02543   (508) 548-0800
New England fare. The restaurant is willing to accommodate vegetarians and offers dishes such as Pasta Primavera, Fusilli Pasta, and a steamed vegetable plate. **Open Tuesday through Sunday for dinner and Sunday for brunch as well. Full service, fresh juices, non-alc. beer/wine, wine/beer/alcohol, $$–$$$**

Fishmonger's Cafe
56 Water St., Woods Hole, MA 02543   (508) 540-5376
Natural foods. Along with a full range of vegetarian dishes, fish is served here and home-baked goods, too. **Open daily. Full service, wine/beer, VISA/MC, $$–$$$**

WORCESTER

- ## Annapurna Restaurant
  483 Cambridge St., Worcester, MA 01610   (617) 755-7413
  Vegetarian. Serving and catering vegetarian food of India, Annapurna specializes in Udipi cuisine. The restaurant will accommodate vegan diets upon request. **Full service, catering, $$**

MICHIGAN

ANN ARBOR

The Blue Nile
317 Braun Ct., Ann Arbor, MI 48104   (313) 663-3116
Ethiopian. Authentic Ethiopian cuisine includes many vegetarian options. **Open daily. Full service, vegan options, wine/beer/alcohol, VISA/MC/AMX/DISC, $$–$$$**

Golden Chef
2016 Packard, Ann Arbor, MI 48104   **(313)-741-0778**
Chinese/vegetarian. Golden Chef serves delicious vegetarian pot stickers, spring rolls, and vegetarian entrees. Few dishes contain eggs. Only vegetarian food is served at dinner time. **Open daily for lunch and dinner. Full service, vegan options, take-out, VISA/MC/AMX, $$**

• Seva
314 E. Liberty, Ann Arbor, MI 48104   **(313) 662-1111**
Vegetarian/Mexican. We've been told Seva offers some of the best Mexican food in Michigan. The menu alone is certainly impressive. Vegan options are clearly indicated on the menu. Small Courses, Salads, Soups, Mexican Specialties, Oriental Specialties, Sandwiches, Omelettes, Beverages and Blended Drinks make up the menu headings. There's a blend of traditional and unique foods that sound delicious! **Open daily. Weekend brunch. Full service, vegan options, non-alc. beer, wine/ beer/alcohol, catering, take-out, VISA/MC/DISC, $$**

BERRIEN SPRINGS

• Andrews University
U.S. 31 North, Berrien Springs, MI 49104   **(616) 471-3161**
Vegetarian cafeteria. Cyclical menu changes feature soups, main dishes, hot food selections, plus extensive salad bar and desserts. Soy- and gluten-based meat analogs are utilized in many dishes. **Open daily during school year. Call for summer hours. Cafeteria style, $**

BIRMINGHAM

La Luna Grancafe
183 N. Woodward, Birmingham, MI 48009   **(313) 642-7070**
Italian. Delicious pizza selections include some without cheese. Pasta dishes are also available. **Full service, vegan options, fresh juices, non-alc. beer/wine, take-out, VISA/MC/AMX, $**

DEARBORN

La Shish
12918 Michigan Ave., Dearborn, MI 48126   **(313) 584-4477**
Lebanese. Several vegan dishes are available at La Shish. **Open daily for lunch and dinner. Full service, vegan options, take-out, VISA, $**

DETROIT

The Blue Nile
508 Monroe St., Detroit, MI 48322   **(313) 964-6699**
Ethiopian. See description under Ann Arbor, MI.

Don Pedros
24366 Grand River, Detroit, MI 48219   **(313) 537-1450**
Mexican. Vegetarian dining is easy at Don Pedros as there is no lard in the beans and no chicken broth in the rice. There *is* a nice atmosphere. **Open daily for**

dinner. Lunch weekdays. Full service, vegan options, wine/beer/alcohol, take-out, VISA/MC/AMX/DC, $$

• Govinda's at the Fisher Mansion
383 Lenox Ave., Detroit, MI 48215   **(313) 331-6740**

Vegetarian. Govinda's is located in the formal dining room of the Lawrence Fisher Mansion. The foods are prepared daily using only the freshest ingredients. **Open Friday through Sunday. Full service, vegan options, fresh juices, catering, take-out, VISA/MC/AMX, $$**

Traffic Jam and Snug
511 W. Canfield St., Detroit, MI 48201   **(313) 831-9470**

Natural foods. The menu changes weekly at this natural foods eatery, but there are always vegetarian entrees, usually vegan options as well. Seasonal and local foods are emphasized, and there are homemade breads, brews, and friendly service. **Closed Sunday. Full service, vegan options, fresh juices, wine/beer, take-out, VISA/MC/DISC, $$**

EAST LANSING

Small Planet Food & Spirits
220 Mac Avenue, East Lansing, MI 48823   **(517) 351-6230**

Natural foods. Small Planet specializes in Jamaican, Mexican, vegetarian, and ethnic cuisines. You'll enjoy fine dining in a relaxed and unique atmosphere. **Open daily for lunch and dinner. Full service, fresh juices, non-alc. beer, wine/beer/alcohol, take-out, VISA/MC, $$**

FARMINGTON HILLS

Anita's Kitchen
31005 Orchard Lake, Farmington Hills, MI 48018   **(313) 855-4150**

Middle Eastern/Lebanese. The menu features Falafel and Hummus, as well as Black Bean Soup and Vegetarian Chili. **Open daily for breakfast, lunch, and dinner. Full service, vegan options, take-out, VISA/MC/AMX/DISC, $–$$$**

Shalimar
29200 Orchard Lake Rd., Farmington Hills, MI 48018   **(313) 626-2982**

Indian/Mexican. Vegetarian options are available at this restaurant offering Indian and Mexican foods. **Open for lunch and dinner. Full service, vegan options, non-alc. beer, wine/beer/alcohol, take-out, VISA/MC, $**

FERNDALE

Om Cafe
23136 N. Woodward Ave., Ferndale, MI 48220   **(313) 548-1941**

ᴥ Reviewers' choice   • Vegetarian restaurant   •• Vegan restaurant
$ less than $6 $$ $6–$12 $$$ more than $12
VISA/AMX/MC/DISC/DC—credit cards accepted
Non-alc.—Non-alcoholic   Fresh juices—freshly squeezed

Macrobiotic. Terrific macrobiotic food includes a good range of vegetarian and vegan dishes. **Open for lunch and dinner Monday through Saturday. No smoking. Full service, vegan options, $**

LANSING

Apple Jade
505 Frandor, Lansing, MI 48912 (517) 332-8010

Chinese. This Chinese restaurant offers vegetarian pot stickers as well as many vegetarian entrees. **Open daily for lunch and dinner. Full service, take-out, VISA/ MC, $$**

Clara's
637 E. Michigan, Lansing MI 48912 (517) 372-7120

Italian/Mexican/American. Located in a refurbished train station with beautiful stained glass windows, Clara's offers excellent vegetarian sandwiches, calzones, and Mexican food. **Open daily for lunch and dinner; Sunday for brunch as well. Full service, take-out, VISA/MC/AMX/DISC/DC, $$**

• Hearthstone Bakery & Vegetarian Cafe
2003 E. Michigan, Lansing, MI 48912 (517) 485-8600

Vegetarian. Hearthstone is committed to providing the highest quality breads, baked goods, and ready-to-eat foods made from scratch with all natural ingredients. Organic ingredients are used whenever possible. Daily ethnic dinner and luncheon specials, full salad bar, pizza, egg rolls, deli sandwiches, and more are featured at Hearthstone. At least one of the daily specials is always vegan and there are several vegan options on the menu. **Open for three meals daily, Sunday for brunch and dinner only. Cafeteria style, vegan options, fresh juices, espresso/cappuccino, take-out, $**

MT. CLEMENS

Dimitri's Rendezvous
36247 Gratiot, Mt. Clemens, MI 48043 (313) 792-2200

Greek. A local reader informed us about Dimitri's. It is difficult to find vegetarian food in this area, and Dimitri's has a vegetarian stir-fry and will meet special requests. **Open for lunch and dinner. Full service, vegan option, wine/beer/alcohol, take-out, $–$$**

ROCKFORD

Down To Earth Country Buffet
10025 Belding Rd., NE, Rockford, MI 49341 (616) 691-7288

Natural foods. Everything at this whole-foods restaurant is prepared on the premises. Fresh bread is baked daily. Organic fruits and vegetables are used in summer. **Closed Mondays. Full service, BYOB, take-out, no credit cards, $$**

ROYAL OAK

Cuisine Couriers
508 S. Washington, Royal Oak, MI 48067 (313) 541-2002

Natural foods deli. The slogan for Cuisine Couriers is "good food for people on the go," so that's what's offered on the menu. Various sandwiches, soups, and salads with veggie burgers, "Chic-un" salad sandwich, and chili are some of the vegetarian options. **Closed Sunday. Cafeteria style, vegan options, take-out, $**

• Inn Season Cafe ⟊

500 E. Fourth St., Royal Oak, MI 48067   **(313) 547-7916**

Vegetarian. Inn Season has built its reputation on uncompromising, creative regional cuisine with old-world roots. Vegetarian or not, the clientele come for the dining experience. There's a full menu with pizza, pasta, Mexican, Japanese, and Middle Eastern foods plus daily specials. Sugar-free desserts are also served. **Closed Sunday and Monday. No smoking. Full service, vegan options, fresh juices, non-alc. beer, organic coffee, take-out, VISA/MC/DISC, $$**

Les Auteurs

222 Sherman, Washington Square, Royal Oak, MI 48067   **(313) 544-2887**

American. Vegetarian entrees are served at lunch and dinner in this elegant but expensive establishment. **Full service, wine/beer/alcohol, $$–$$$**

TROY

• Pure'n Simple

2791 Rochester Rd., Troy, MI 48084   **(313) 528-0840**

Vegetarian. There's simply a wide selection of tasty vegetarian and vegan foods for lunch and dinner. Entree examples include Mushroom Cutlets, Nut Roast, Wheat Parmigiana, and a Macro Plate. Non-dairy special desserts are available. **Closed Saturday. Full service, fresh juices, non-alc. beer/wine, take-out, AMX, $$**

UNION CITY

• Creative Health Institute

918 Union City Rd., Union City, MI 49094   **(517) 278-6260**

Living foods. Sample a living foods buffet that includes assorted sprouts, organic indoor greens, seed cheeses, and raw vegetable dishes, soups and salads. **Open Sunday only for open house and buffet. Reservations required for large groups only. Buffet, vegan options, $**

WEST BLOOMFIELD

The Blue Nile

6635 Orchard Lake Rd., West Bloomfield, MI 48322   **(313) 539-1126**

Ethiopian. See entry under Ann Arbor, MI.

MINNESOTA

ANOKA

Anoka Co-op Grocery & Cafe

1917 2nd Ave. S., Anoka, MN 55303   **(612) 427-3552**

Natural foods cafe. Various international vegetarian foods include Veggie Burgers,

Spanakopita, quiche, Wild Rice Stir-fry, soups, salads, sandwiches, pies, cookies, cakes, and more. **Open for lunch weekdays. Cafeteria style, vegan options, fresh juices, take-out, $**

BLOOMINGTON

Sawatdee Thai Restaurant
8501 Lyndale Ave., Bloomington, MN 55420   **(612) 888-7177**
Thai. Vegetarian spring rolls, a noodle dish, and a few vegetable entrees are offered. Tofu can be substituted in most meat dishes as well. **Open daily for lunch and dinner. Full service, vegan options, take-out, VISA/MC/AMX, $–$$**

DULUTH

Taste of Saigon
DeWitt-Seitz Marketplace, 94 Lake Ave. S.
Duluth, MN 55802   **(218) 727-1598**
Vietnamese. The Taste of Saigon offers a selection of vegetarian dishes including tofu and mock meat items. **Closed Sunday. Full service, vegan options, take-out, $–$$**

MINNEAPOLIS

Azur Restaurant
651 Nicollet Ave., S., Minneapolis, MN 55402   **(612) 342-2800**
Fine dining. The Azur Restaurant normally has vegetarian items but is also willing to take special requests. The menu changes frequently. **Reservations required for special meals. Formal, full service, wine/beer/alcohol, VISA/MC/AMX/DISC, $$$**

Cafe Brenda
300 1st Ave., N., Minneapolis, MN 55401   **(612) 342-9270**
Natural foods. Located in a restored warehouse in a historic district of downtown Minneapolis, Cafe Brenda prepares a good selection of vegetarian appetizers, sandwiches, and entrees. There are daily specials plus a full à la carte menu and a children's menu. **Closed Sunday. Full service, vegan options, fresh juice, organic coffee, espresso, non-alc. beer, wine/beer/alcohol, take-out, VISA/MC/AMX/DC/Carte Blanche, $$**

Caper's
2221 W. 50th St., Minneapolis, MN 55419   **(612) 927-4416**
Italian. Gourmet pizza, appetizers, tortellini, salads, and, of course, pasta are offered at Caper's. **Open daily for lunch and dinner, weekend brunch. Full service, vegan options, take-out, VISA/MC/AMX, $$**

• Delites of India 🐾
1123 West Lake St., Minneapolis, MN 55408   **(612) 823-2866**

🐾 Reviewers' choice   • Vegetarian restaurant   •• Vegan restaurant
$ less than $6 $$ $6–$12 $$$ more than $12
VISA/AMX/MC/DISC/DC—credit cards accepted
Non-alc.–Non alcoholic   Fresh juices–freshly squeezed

Vegetarian/Indian. Delites is the only vegetarian Indian restaurant in the Twin Cities. The menu consists of a wide selection of Indian foods plus some Middle Eastern and American dishes such as Hummus and Chili. No MSG or other chemicals are used in the food. Owners and service are "delites," too. Books on Indian philosophy, yoga, and vegetarian cooking line the walls and are for sale along with some Indian food products and tea. Even reading the menu is educational! **Closed Monday. Open daily for lunch and dinner. Full service, vegan options, wine/beer, take-out, VISA/MC/AMX/DC/Carte Blanche, $$**

Diamond Thai Restaurant
1423 Washington Ave., S., Minneapolis, MN 55454   (612) 332-2920
Thai. The restaurant features a vegetarian section on the menu. **Closed Sunday. Full service, BYOB, take-out, VISA/MC/AMX, $–$$**

The Good Earth Restaurant & Bakery
3001 Hennepin Ave. S., Calhoun Square
Minneapolis, MN 55408   (612) 824-8533
Natural foods. The Good Earth is a family-style natural foods chain with four restaurants in the Minneapolis/St. Paul area. The menu features many home-baked goods, soups, salads, sandwiches, and entrees. **Open daily. Full service, fresh juices, non-alc. beer/wine, beer/wine, take-out, MC/VISA/AMX, $–$$**

Loring Cafe
1624 Harmon Place, Minneapolis, MN 55403   (612) 332-1617
Cafe. Salads, appetizers, sandwiches, and vegetarian specials are available at the Loring Cafe. **Open daily. Full service, limited vegan options, wine/beer/alcohol, take-out, VISA/MC, $$–$$$**

The Lotus of Campus
313 Oak St., SE, Minneapolis, MN 55414   (612) 331-1781
Vietnamese. The Lotus has a vegetarian section on its menu. **Full service, beer, take-out, no credit cards, $**

Lotus Uptown
3037 Hennepin Ave. S., Minneapolis, MN 55408   (612) 825-2263
Vietnamese. The vegetarian menu section includes vegetable, tofu, and mock meat dishes. **Open daily. Full service, vegan options, wine/beer, take-out, no credit cards, $**

Lotus to Go Grant Mall
113 W. Grant St., Minnepolis, MN 55403   (612) 870-1218
Vietnamese. Vegetarian options include tofu, vegetable, and mock meat dishes. No eggs are used. **Take-out, vegan options, no credit cards, $**

• Mudpie Vegetarian Restaurant ⤶
2549 Lyndale Ave. S., Minneapolis, MN 55405   (612) 872-9435
Vegetarian. No vegetarian should leave Minneapolis (or even Minnesota!) without visiting the Mudpie. It is certainly a heavenly experience and a trip worth making as often as possible. The menu consists of a variety of creative and traditional international dishes along with some standard vegetarian favorites served in ample portions. There's an extensive breakfast menu on weekends plus salads, soups,

pizza, appetizers, sandwiches, entrees, and wonderful desserts for lunch and dinner. Items that cannot be prepared without dairy are clearly indicated on the menu. There's also an enclosed patio dining area. **Open daily for lunch and dinner, breakfast on weekends only. Full service, vegan options, fresh juices, wine/beer, take-out, VISA/MC/AMX, $–$$**

Nam Restaurant
1005 Nicollet Mall, Minneapolis, MN 55403   (612) 332-3666
Vietnamese. Located in the Nicollet Mall in downtown Minneapolis not too far from the Convention Center, Nam has a large vegetarian section on the menu. Various tofu, vegetable, and mock meat dishes are offered. **Open Monday through Saturday for lunch and dinner. Full service, vegan options, take-out, $**

New French Cafe
128 N. Fourth St., Minneapolis, MN 55401   (612) 338-3790
Ethnic/natural foods. The New French Cafe has a vegetarian lunch plate and is willing to tailor-make vegetarian meals. **Open daily. Full service, wine/beer/alcohol, take-out, VISA/MC/AMX/DC, $$–$$$**

• New Riverside Cafe
329 Cedar Ave., Minneapolis, MN 55454   (612) 333-4814
Vegetarian. This worker-owned-and-managed cafe with its funky, informal coffeehouse atmosphere has been a hub for alternative ideas and a center for community activism since 1970. The cafe is set up cafeteria style with a chalkboard menu that lists daily specials including Mexican dishes, stir-fry, and many vegan options. All of the dishes are made from quality whole foods using local organically grown ingredients and served very inexpensively. There is live music five nights a week. Menu changes monthly. **Open daily (except Sunday) for three meals, Sunday for brunch only. Cafeteria style, vegan options, organic coffee, espresso/cappuccino, take-out, $**

Odaa Restaurant
408 Cedar Ave. S., Minneapolis, MN 55454   (612) 338-4459
Ethiopian. Authentic East African Oromo cuisine is prepared on-site from scratch. African decor and multi-ethnic music provide a soothing atmosphere for diners. Food is served in a traditional communal tray and eaten with bread and fingers. Several vegetarian options are available, and no preservatives are used. **Open daily for lunch and dinner, Sunday for dinner only. Full service, vegan options, espresso, beer, take-out, VISA/MC/AMX, $$**

Organica Deli
400 Central Ave., SE, Minneapolis, MN 55414   (612) 378-7413
Natural foods deli. Located in an educational center, this deli serves organic bean burritos, sandwiches, and special entrees each day. **Closed Sundays. Counter service, fresh juices, take-out, $**

Ping's Szechuan Bar & Grill
1401 Nicollet Ave., Minneapolis, MN 55403   (612) 874-9404
Chinese. Ping's serves Chinese food with a Szechuan emphasis in addition to Cantonese, Hunan, and Mandarin cuisines. Several vegetarian entrees appear on the menu and the restaurant is willing to make substitutions for any dish. Mock

duck is available. Located near the Convention Center. **Open daily for lunch and dinner. Full service, vegan options, wine/beer/alcohol, take-out, VISA/MC/ AMX/DISC/DC/CB, $$**

Seward Community Cafe
2129 E. Franklin Ave., Minneapolis, MN 5540   **(612) 332-1011**
Natural foods cafe. The Seward Cafe is located on the corner across from the Seward Co-op and offers sandwiches, soups, salads, and desserts in a cafeteria/cafe atmosphere. Seward Co-op just recently celebrated its twentieth anniversary. Patio dining. **Cafeteria style, vegan options, take-out, $**

St. Martin's Table
2001 Riverside Ave., Minneapolis, MN 55454   **(612) 339-3920**
Natural foods. St. Martin's Table is a nonprofit restaurant/bookstore with various political titles and resources on peace. The chalkboard menu has two soups daily, three sandwiches, and special salads. Fresh baked goods made from scratch are also featured. Bring your own container for take-out. **Closed Sunday. Full service, take-out (you provide container), no credit cards, $**

Tao Natural Foods and Books
2200 Hennepin Ave., S., Minneapolis, MN 55405   **(612) 377-4630**
Juice bar/deli. The Tao has a small juice bar and deli in the front of its natural foods store. Daily sandwich and soup specials are offered along with a great selection of books. Tao is located next to an eco-store. **Closed Sunday. Limited service, fresh juices, take-out, $**

Wedge Community Co-op Deli
2105 Lyndale Ave. S., Minneapolis, MN 55405   **(612) 871-3993**
Natural foods deli. The Wedge Co-op has a deli counter in the back with a wide selection of salads, sandwiches, and some soups. **Counter service, take-out only, $**

MINNETONKA

The Marsh Restaurant
15000 Minnetonka Blvd., Minnetonka, MN 55345   **(612) 935-2202**
Health club restaurant. The Marsh Restaurant serves some vegetarian foods. All muffins and breads are baked on site from scratch using the freshest ingredients possible with a minimum of processed foods. **Open daily. Cafeteria style, fresh juice, wine/beer, take-out, VISA/MC, $$**

NEW BRIGHTON

Los Banditos
2321 Palmer Dr., New Brighton, MN 55112   **(612) 636-5858**
Mexican. Los Banditos offers authentic Mexican food with vegetable or guacamole as fillings. Beware—beans contain ham soup base. **Open daily for lunch and dinner, Sunday for dinner only. Full service, wine/beer/alcohol, take-out, VISA/MC/AMX, $**

ST. PAUL

Lotus Victoria Crossing
867 Grand Ave., St. Paul, MN 55105   **(612) 228-9156**
Chinese. See Lotus to Go entry under Minneapolis, MN, for description.

The Old City Cafe
1571 Grand Ave., St. Paul, MN 55105   **(612) 699-5347**
Kosher. The only kosher restaurant in the Twin Cities, this cafe offers various Middle Eastern foods in addition to pizza, salads, veggie burgers, knishes, stuffed peppers, mock meats, and other items. **Closed Saturdays. Limited service, vegan options, take-out, DISC, $**

ST. PETER

St. Peter Food Co-op Sandwich Shop
100 S. Front St., St. Peter, MN 56082   **(507) 931-4880**
Natural-food-store deli. The shop offers self-serve soups and entrees, plus a cooler stocked with pre-made sandwiches and salads. Fresh baked goods are also available. Here you will find low prices in a relaxed atmosphere. **Open daily. Cafeteria style, vegan options, take-out, $**

MISSISSIPPI

JACKSON

•• High Noon Cafe
4147 Northview Dr., Jackson, MS 39206   **(601) 366-1602**
Primarily vegan. The High Noon Cafe serves only vegan food every day except Saturday, which is a vegetarian day. The menu changes daily. **Open Monday through Saturday for lunch. Vegan, take-out, $–$$**

MISSOURI

CLAYTON

Candicci's
7910 Bonhomme, Clayton, MO 63105   **(314) 725-3350**
Italian. Candicci's has a good selection of vegetarian pasta dishes and appetizers. **Open daily. Full service, vegan option, fresh juice, wine/beer/alcohol, take-out, VISA/MC/AMX, $$**

ᘎ Reviewers' choice   • Vegetarian restaurant   •• Vegan restaurant
$ less than $6 $$ $6–$12 $$$ more than $12
VISA/AMX/MC/DISC/DC—credit cards accepted
Non-alc.—Non alcoholic   Fresh juices—freshly squeezed

Lettuce Leaf Restaurants
7823 Forsyth, Clayton, MO 63105   **(314) 727-5439**
Natural foods. Entrees, salads, gourmet sandwiches, pizza, homemade soups, and quiche. The menu is changed four times a year with the season in order to have the freshest ingredients available. **Open daily. Full service, wine/beer, take-out, VISA/MC/AMX/DISC, $$**

COLUMBIA

International Cafe
209 Hitt St., Columbia, MO 65201   **(314) 449-4560**
International, primarily Middle Eastern. One local patron recommends the appetizer combo as the best-bet dish. Patio dining. **Limited service, $**

Mixed Company
1025 E. Walnut, Columbia, MO 65201   **(314) 449-1141**
Coffeehouse. This coffeehouse has a limited but expanding vegetarian menu. **Full service, vegan options, $**

KANSAS CITY

Amber Waves
4305 Main St., Kansas City, MO 64111   **(816) 931-8191**
Macrobiotic. Amber Waves has a limited menu, but the Grainburger Platter is excellent. Specials are offered. **Open Tuesday and Thursday for dinner, Saturday for lunch. Full service, vegan options, take-out, $$**

Daily Bread
4501 Genessee, Kansas City, MO 64111   **(816) 531-1452**
Natural foods. This restaurant's menu changes daily; however, it always offers some vegetarian soups, salads, entrees, sandwiches, and desserts. Every meal includes a daily special bread. No smoking is allowed. **Open for breakfast and lunch Tuesday through Saturday, also for dinner on Friday. Closed Sundays. Take-out dinners available Tuesday through Thursday. Limited service, vegan options, espresso/cappuccino, take-out, $-$$.**

Zo's Cafe
614 W. 26 St., Kansas City, MO 64108   **(816) 221-5373**
Natural foods. Zo's Cafe overlooks a park and has an informally elegant atmosphere that features classical music and fresh flowers. Organic ingredients are used whenever possible. The menu changes daily; however, two vegetarian entrees are always offered, including many which are vegan. Fresh sourdough bread is baked every Tuesday. Smoking is not permitted. **Open for lunch Monday through Friday and dinner Friday through Saturday. Closed Sundays. Full service, vegan options, non-alc. beer, VISA/MC/DISC, $-$$**

ST. LOUIS

Al Baker's
8101 Clayton Rd., St. Louis, MO 63117   **(314) 863-8878**
Italian. There is a "Heart Smart" menu section at Al Baker's with a Vegetarian

Plate, Linguini, and Pasta Primavera. Other vegetarian pasta dishes are also on the menu. Enjoy elegant dining with live entertainment and dancing. **Open Monday through Saturday for dinner. Formal, full service, vegan options, wine/beer/alcohol, VISA/MC/AMX/DISC, $$$**

Bombay Coffee House
4249 S. Kings Hwy., St. Louis, MO 63109   (314) 353-1594
Indian. Enjoy authentic Indian cuisine with seven vegetarian entrees. Appetizers and bread are also on the menu. **Closed Monday. Full service, vegan options, take-out, VISA/MC, $$**

California Pizza Kitchen
1493 St. Louis Galleria, St. Louis, MO 63117   (314) 863-4500
Pizza. In the Galleria, a large up-scale shopping center, you'll find good cheeseless pizzas, vegetarian pastas, and salads. **Full service, $$**

• The Golden Grocer Cafe
335 N. Euclid, St. Louis, MO 63108   (314) 367-0405
Vegetarian. The Golden Grocer features a fresh salad bar with mostly organic produce. There's also Hummus, Curried Tofu, Rice Salad, veggie pizza, and vegan burritos, and a deli case full of vegetarian items, and eggless baked goods, most of which are vegan. **Open Monday through Saturday. Limited service, vegan options, fresh juices, take-out, VISA/MC/DISC, $**

• Govinda's
3926 Lindell Blvd., St. Louis, MO 63108   (314) 535-8085
Vegetarian. Govinda's features a wide variety of vegetarian foods. **Closed Saturday. Buffet, vegan options, fresh juices, take-out, $**

Koh-i-noor
608 Eastgate Ave., St. Louis, MO 63130   (314) 721-3796
Pakistani. Vegetarian appetizers and main dishes are served here. **Full service, $–$$**

La Patisserie
6269 Delmar Blvd., St. Louis, MO 63130   (314) 725-4902
Ethnic. La Patisserie has a vegetarian sausage for breakfast plus soups, sandwiches, and barbecued tofu. **Full service, $–$$**

Lettuce Leaf Restaurants
620 Westport Plaza, St. Louis, MO 63146   (314) 576-7677
Natural foods. See Clayton, MO, entry for description. **Closed Sunday.**

Lettuce Leaf Restaurants
107 N. 6th St., St. Louis, MO 63101   (314) 241-7773
Natural foods. See Clayton, MO, entry for description. **Open on weekends in spring and summer only.**

Red Sea
6511 Delmar Blvd., St. Loius, MO 63130   (314) 863-0099

Ethiopian. Many vegetarian dishes are served in the traditional style with injera bread. **Full service, vegan options, $–$$**

Saleem's Restaurant
6501 Delmar, St. Louis, MO 63130   **(314) 721-7947**
Lebanese. Vegetarian appetizers, platter, and eggplant dish are offered. **Closed Sunday. Full service, wine/beer/alcohol, take-out, VISA/MC/DISC, $$**

Shalimar Gardens
4569 LaClede Ave., St. Louis, MO 63108   **(314) 361-6911**
Indian. Many vegetarian options are made without salt, sugar, or MSG. **Open daily. Full service, vegan options, beer, take-out, VISA/MC/AMX, $$**

Sunshine Inn ಊ
8¹/₂ S. Euclid, St. Louis, MO 63108   **(314) 367-1413**
Natural foods. Vegetarian options include veggie burgers, soy foods, dairy-free dishes, and homemade soups. Sunday brunch offers an à la carte menu featuring omelettes, multi-grain pancakes, potato pancakes, fresh fruit and juices. **Closed Monday. Full service, vegan options, fresh juices, non-alc. wine/beer, take-out, VISA/MC/AMX/DISC, $$**

UNIVERSITY CITY

Brandt's Market & Cafe
6525 Delmar, University City, MO 63130   **(314) 727-3663**
Natural foods. Eggplant Parmagiana, Veggie Burger, Black Bean Chili, spring rolls, pizza, and other options are available. There is live music nightly. **Open daily. Full service, vegan options, fresh juice, wine/beer/alcohol, VISA/MC/AMX/DISC, $$**

Red Sea
6511 Delmar, University City, MO 63112   **(314) 863-0099**
Ethiopian. Red Sea offers several vegetarian Ethiopian dishes. **Open daily for dinner, Wednesday through Saturday for lunch. Full service, non-alc. wine/beer, wine/beer/alcohol, catering, take-out, VISA/MC/AMX/DISC, $$**

WEBSTER GROVES

The Webster Grill and Cafe
8127 Big Bend Blvd., Webster Groves, MO 63119   **(314) 962-0564**
New American. Vegetarian Stir-Fry, Falafel, salads, and sandwiches are offered here. **Open daily for lunch and dinner, breakfast on weekends. Full service, vegan options, non-alc. beer, wine/beer/alcohol, take-out, VISA/MC/AMX/DISC/DC, $$**

ಊ Reviewers' choice   • Vegetarian restaurant   •• Vegan restaurant
$ less than $6 $$ $6–$12 $$$ more than $12
VISA/AMX/MC/DISC/DC—credit cards accepted
Non-alc.–Non-alcoholic   Fresh juices—freshly squeezed

MONTANA

CORWIN SPRINGS

The Ranch Kitchen
Hwy. 89, Corwin Springs, MT 59021 **(406) 848-7891**
Natural foods/American. Offers miso soups, seitan dishes, soy burgers, Mexican vegetarian dishes, and fruit-sweetened desserts. Features a weekend buffet and a dinner theater behind the restaurant. **Open May through mid-September for breakfast, lunch, and dinner. Full service, non-alc. wine/beer, take-out, VISA/MC/AMX, $$–$$$**

MISSOULA

• The Black Dog
138 W. Broadway St., Missoula, MT 59802 **(406) 542-1138**
Vegetarian. The Black Dog features a menu that changes daily, and includes organic ingredients whenever possible. Two or three soups, at least three entrees, sandwiches such as tempeh or lentil burgers, many vegan options, and desserts are offered. **Closed Sunday, open for lunch during the week, for dinner only on Saturday. Full service, vegan options, catering, no credit cards, $$**

China Garden
2100 Stephens Ave., Missoula, MT 59801 **(406) 721-1795**
Chinese. This restaurant uses no MSG. Vegetarian options include vegetable sautées, soups, vegetable and noodle dishes, Vegetarian Foo Young, and Vegetable Fried Rice. **Open for lunch and dinner, closed Monday. Full service, take-out, VISA/MC/AMX, $$**

Mammyth
131 W. Main St., Missoula, MT 59802 **(406) 549-5542**
Natural foods cafe. This comfortable cafe features a great salad bar *and* the work of local artists and live music during lunches. The menu reflects many options in sandwiches, soups, and entree specials that change daily. **Closed Sunday. Cafeteria style, fresh juices, take-out, VISA/MC/AMX, $**

The Mustard Seed
419 W. Front St., Missoula, MT 59802 **(406) 728-7825**
Contemporary Oriental. The Mustard Seed offers a separate vegetarian menu that includes sushi, spring rolls, wok dishes, and tofu and vegetable dishes with various sauces. Smoking is not allowed. **Open daily for lunch and dinner. Full service, non-alc. wine/beer, wine/beer/alcohol, take-out, VISA/MC/AMX/DISC, $**

NEBRASKA

LINCOLN

Asian Palace
3031 "O" St., Lincoln, NE 68510   **(402) 435-8884**
Chinese. Partake of a good selection of Chinese vegetarian fast food. **Open daily. Limited service, take-out, $**

Open Harvest Natural Foods Grocery
1618 South St., Lincoln, NE 68502   **(402) 475-9069**
Natural-foods-store deli. This natural foods deli has a good selection of vegetarian items and a whole-grain bakery. **Open daily. Deli, take-out, $**

Taste of India
1320 "O" St., Lincoln, NE 68508   **(402) 475-1642**
Indian. Enjoy authentic Northern Indian cuisine from family recipes handed down for generations. Taste of India offers a wide variety of vegetarian entrees, fresh baked breads, desserts, and beverages. **Open daily. Full service, vegan options, wine/beer/alcohol, take-out, VISA/MC/AMX/DISC, $$**

The Oven
201 N. 8th, Ste. 117, Lincoln, NE 68508   **(402) 475-6118**
Indian. Enjoy fine dining and Indian food with a very good selection for vegetarians. **Open daily. Full service, vegan options, wine/beer/alcohol, VISA/MC/ AMX, $$**

OMAHA

The Food Gallery
312 S. 72nd St., Omaha, NE 68114   **(402) 393-4168**
Middle Eastern. This is a deli featuring Middle Eastern/Lebanese foods with several vegetarian selections. **Closed Sundays. Cafeteria style, vegan options, take-out, $–$$**

Indian Oven
1010 Howard St., Omaha, NE 68102   **(402) 342-4856**
Indian. The hallmark of Indian Oven's cuisine is its "Tandoori Cuisine," cooking in its clay oven. Included on the menu are stuffed and plain tandoor breads, pakoras, papadums, and samosas as well as various other vegetarian options. **Open daily. Full service, fresh juices, wine/beer/alcohol, take-out, VISA/MC/ AMX, $$**

NEVADA

LAS VEGAS

Lotus of Siam
953 E. Sahara #A5, Las Vegas, NV 89104   **(702) 735-4477**

Thai. Enjoy an extensive menu for vegetarians with many delectable appetizers, salads, entrees, and noodle dishes. Spiciness is adjusted to your taste. **Open daily. Full service, vegan options, wine/beer/alcohol, take-out, VISA/MC/AMX, $$**

• Rainbow's End Vegetarian Restaurant

1120 E. Sahara Ave., Las Vegas, NV 89104 **(702) 737-0323**

Vegetarian. Rainbow's End features cooking without sugar, hydrogenated oil, white flour, artificial ingredients, or preservatives. Sunday buffet. **Open daily. Full service, vegan/macrobiotic options, fresh juices, take-out, VISA/MC/AMX, $$**

RENO

• Blue Heron Natural Foods Restaurant & Bakery

1091 S. Virginia, Reno, NV 89502 **(702) 786-4110**

Vegetarian. Partake of sandwiches, salads, soup specials, side orders, and numerous vegetarian entrees; 75 percent of all soups and meals are vegan. There's a bookstore at the same location. **Open daily for lunch and dinner. Full service, vegan/macrobiotic options, fresh juices, wine/beer, take-out, no credit cards, $$**

Sapna Indian Restaurant

3374 Kietzke Center, Reno, NV 89502 **(702) 829-1537**

Indian. Sapna specializes in the cooking of North and South India. Various vegetable soups, appetizers, side orders, and curry entrees are offered. **Open Monday through Saturday for lunch and dinner. Full service, vegan options, wine/beer, take-out, VISA/MC/AMX, $$**

NEW HAMPSHIRE

KEENE

Bagel Works Inc.

120 Main St., Keene, NH 03431 **(603) 357-7751**

Bagel deli. Sample more than sixteen varieties of bagels with various topping options, including cream cheeses, tofutti spreads, salads, and vegetarian combinations. Foods are prepared with all-natural ingredients without preservatives. Bagel Works is environmentally conscious and socially active in its community. **Open daily. Counter service, vegan options, fresh juices, take-out, $**

MEREDITH

For Every Season

67 Main St., Meredith, NH 03253 **(603) 279-8875**

Whole-foods deli. This restaurant located in the beautiful Lakes Region of New Hampshire offers homemade soups and salads in a casual, kid-friendly environment. Breakfast is served all day. Garden deck. **Open daily for breakfast and lunch during summer. Open Tuesday through Saturday during winter. Limited service, vegan options, BYOB, take-out, $**

NORTH CONWAY

Cafe Chimes
Norcross Pl., Main St., North Conway, NH 03860   (603) 356-5500
Natural foods. "Homemade" and "natural" are the passwords at Cafe Chimes, which features soups, salads, quiche, pizza, grain dishes, and specials. The cafe's wheat mill grinds wheat berries daily to create unique whole-wheat bread.

NEW JERSEY

CLEMENTON

New Japan
Blackwood-Clementon Rd., Laurel Plaza
Clementon, NJ 08021   (609) 435-5630
Japanese. New Japan features Vegetable Sushi and Vegetable Tempura. **Open daily for lunch and dinner. Closed for dinner Monday. Full service, take-out, VISA/ MC/AMX/DISC/DC, $$**

COLONIAL

• Siddhartha Authentic Indian Vegetarian Restaurant
1133 St. Georges Ave., Colonial, NJ 07067   (201) 750-0231
Vegetarian/Indian. Closed Tuesday. **Full service, vegan options, fresh juice, take-out, $**

DEPTFORD

Shaan-E-Tandoor
5 Point Plaza, Deptford, NJ 08096   (609) 232-8388
Indian. A reader of *Vegetarian Journal* mentioned that this restaurant is very accommodating and willing to prepare special foods or omit dairy products or other items from dishes. **Open daily for lunch and dinner. Full service, vegan options, take-out, VISA/MC/AMX, $$**

EAST RUTHERFORD

Park and Orchard Restaurant ❧
240 Hackensack St., East Rutherford, N.J. 07073   (201) 939-9292
Extensively vegetarian. Park and Orchard was voted best restaurant in Northern New Jersey by readers of *New Jersey Magazine.* There's an award-winning wine list, and an excellent eclectic menu. **Full service, fresh juice, wine/beer/alcohol, take-out, VISA/MC/AMX/DISC, $$$**

HAINESPORT

Hainesport Health Haven
Rt. 38 and Lumberton Rd., Hainesport NJ, 08036   (609) 267-7744

Lunch bar. Enjoy the pleasant atmosphere in this fully stocked natural foods store. The lunch bar is very willing to accommodate special diets, and there are many vegetarian options. **Lunch only. Limited service, take-out, VISA/MC, $**

HOBOKEN

Hoboken Farm Boy
229 Washington St., Hoboken, NJ 07030   **(201) 656-0581**
Primarily vegetarian deli. Farm Boy offers deli-style service with an extensive vegetarian menu—sandwiches, burgers, Baked Tofu, soups, Black Bean Chili, plus more. Seating is very limited. **Open daily for lunch and dinner. Fresh juice, catering, take-out, VISA/MC/AMX, $**

ISELIN

• Udupi Authentic Indian Vegetarian Cuisine
1380 Oak Tree Rd., Iselin, NJ 08830   **(908) 283-0343**
Vegetarian/Indian. Udupi offers vegetarian Indian specialities. **Full service. $–$$**

LAWRENCEVILLE

The Great Impasta
2021 Brunswick Ave., Lawrenceville, NJ 08648   **(609) 393-4664**
Italian. Classic Italian food, including many pasta dishes, is served in a warm, comfortable atmosphere. **Closed Mondays. Full service, vegetarian options, BYOB, take-out, VISA/MC/AMX, $–$$**

MARLTON

Mexican Food Factory
State Hwy. 70 and Cropwell Rd., Marlton, NJ 08053   **(609) 983-9222**
Mexican. The refried beans are made without lard or animal products. **Full service, vegan options, take-out, VISA/MC/AMX, $$**

TGI Friday's
970 Route 73 N., Marlton, NJ 08053   **(609) 596-9117**
Restaurant chain. A few vegetarian entrees are offered, and a no-smoking section is available. **Open daily for lunch and dinner. Full service, vegetarian options, beer/wine/alcohol, $$**

MONTCLAIR

Clairmont Health Food Centre
15 Bloomfield Ave., Montclair, NJ 07042   **(201) 744-7122**

ᨇ Reviewers' choice   • Vegetarian restaurant   •• Vegan restaurant
$ less than $6 $$ $6–$12 $$$ more than $12
VISA/AMX/MC/DISC/DC—credit cards accepted
Non-alc.—Non-alcoholic   Fresh juices—freshly squeezed

Health-food-store deli. Clairmont offers Hummus, Brown Rice with Steamed Vegetables, Veggie Burgers, sandwiches to go, and daily specials. **Open daily for lunch. Counter service, vegan/macrobiotic options, fresh juices, take-out, VISA/MC, $**

■ MOORESTOWN ■

Homestyle Family Buffet
Moorestown Shopping Center
Route 38 and Lenola Road, Moorestown, NJ 08057   (609) 234-7542
American. Four or five vegetarian options are available at every meal, and there's a salad bar. **Cafeteria Style. Vegetarian options, $–$$.**

■ MOUNT LAUREL ■

Garden of Eden Natural Foods & Country Kitchen
1155 N. Route 73, Ramblewood Center
Mt. Laurel, NJ 08054   (609) 778-1971
Natural foods/deli. This deli-style restaurant has an extensive vegetarian menu, a daily vegetarian entree, and soup du jour. Organic foods are used as much as possible. Enjoy the friendly atmosphere, natural groceries, juice bar, and cooking classes in this recently expanded establishment. **Lunch and dinner Monday through Saturday, brunch on Sunday. Limited service/deli style, fresh juices, catering, take-out, VISA/MC, $–$$**

■ NEWARK ■

• Magic Lotus Catering
87 Tiffany Blvd., Newark, NJ 07104   (201) 484-1087
Vegetarian/caterer. Although not a restaurant, Magic Lotus caters vegetarian food only. Menu items include a choice of over twenty salads, ten appetizers, ten soups, chutneys and sauces, and entrees such as Spinach Lasagna, Eggplant Moussaka, Chili Con Tofu, Hungarian Potato Goulash, Philippine Vegetable Stew, Stuffed Peppers, Middle Eastern Potato and Chick Peas, plus more. You also can choose from a wide variety of rice dishes, breads, and desserts. **Catering. Full service or delivery only. Price varies according to number in party.**

■ OCEAN CITY ■

Bashful Banana Cafe & Bakery
944 Ocean City Boardwalk—Colony Walk
Ocean City, NJ 08226   (609) 398-9677
Natural foods/extensively vegetarian. Offering a contemporary full-service menu using only healthy, fresh ingredients, the cafe focuses on low-fat, sugar-free, low-calorie, and some dairy-free items. Grams of fat, calories, and cholesterol are listed on the menu for each item. This restaurant and bakery offers outdoor dining with an ocean view. **Open daily Memorial day through Labor Day; open weekends in April, May, September, and October. Full service restaurant and bakery, vegan options, fresh juice, catering, VISA/MC, $**

PENNSAUKEN

Jade Panda Chinese Restaurant
5201 Route 38, Pennsuaken, NJ 08109   **(609) 662-7711**
Chinese. This is a traditional Chinese restaurant with an extensive vegetarian menu. **Open daily for lunch and dinner. Full service, vegetarian options, BYOB, take-out, VISA/MC/AMX/DISC, $$**

PRINCETON

Mykonos Greek Restaurant
22 Witherspoon St., Princeton NJ 08542   **(609) 921-2200**
Greek. Mykonos is a Greek restaurant with an extensive vegetarian menu. **Open for lunch and dinner daily except Sunday. Full service, vegan options, take-out, $–$$**

RED BANK

The Eurasian Eatery
110 Monmouth St., Red Bank, NJ 07701   **(908) 741-7071**
European/Asian. Along with eclectic European and Asian offerings, there's an extensive vegetarian menu. **Closed Monday, open Tuesday through Saturday for lunch and dinner, Sunday for dinner only. Full service, vegan options, BYOB, take-out, AMX, $$**

• Garden Vegetarian Restaurant
7 E. Front St., Red Bank, NJ 07701   **(908) 530-8681**
Vegetarian. Garden proudly serves vegetarian foods, including unique and original combinations of the finest fresh vegetables. All food on the extensive lunch and dinner menus is cooked to order and will be tailored to special dietary needs. **Open Monday through Saturday for lunch and dinner. Full service, vegan options, fresh juice, BYOB, catering, take-out, $$**

RUNNEMEDE

Li's Peking Chinese Restaurant
**Runnemede Plaza, 835 E. Clements Bridge Rd.,
Runnemede, NJ 8078**   **(609) 939-4440**
Chinese. Li's has a vegetarian menu with appetizers, many soups, and entrees featuring vegetable, tofu, and mock-meat dishes. There's an excellent vegetarian selection, and foods are low in salt and prepared without MSG. **Open daily. Full service, vegan options, BYOB, take-out, VISA/MC/AMX, $$**

SEA GIRT

Everybody's American Bistro
Sea Girt Mall, Route 35, Sea Girt, NJ 08750   **(908) 223-0235**
American/ethnic. This "Cafe with a difference" offers international foods, many vegetarian selections, freshly baked breads, European desserts, specialty coffees and teas. **Open Monday through Saturday for lunch and dinner, Sunday for dinner only. Full service, vegan options, BYOB, catering, take-out, AMX, $$**

STONE HARBOR

Green Cuisine
302 96th St., Stone Harbor, NJ 08247   **(609) 368-1616**
Natural foods. This restaurant has been serving delicious healthy food for over ten years. Menu selections include gourmet sandwiches, exotic salads, and beautiful fresh fruit selections. Vegetarian items such as Hummus Pita, Tabouli Salad, and Veggie Burgers are very popular. **Open daily for lunch and dinner. Full service, vegetarian options, fresh juice, BYOB, take-out, no credit cards, $$**

VORHEES

Richard's Natural Foods Restaurant
10 White Horse Rd., Vorhees, NJ 08043   **(609) 627-5057**
Primarily vegetarian/natural foods. Richard's is a restaurant with a natural foods store. It offers many pasta dishes and other vegetarian entrees. The menu is almost entirely vegetarian. Cooking classes are available. **Open Monday through Friday for lunch, and Wednesday through Saturday for dinner. Full service, vegan options, fresh juice, BYOB, take-out, $$**

WOODBURY

•• Veggie Express
830 N. Broad St., Woodbury, NJ 08096   **(609) 384-2775**
Vegan. This small, smoke-free restaurant serves only vegan foods, is combined with a health food store, and offers a fresh juice bar. Try Carrot "Tuna," Tempeh Salad, Brown Rice Salad, or Veggie Steak made from seitan. Vegan muffins, cookies, cakes, and pies are available, cooking classes, too. **Open Monday through Friday for lunch. Deli service, completely vegan, fresh juice, party platters, take-out, $$**

NEW MEXICO

ALBUQUERQUE

•• Adam's Table
3619 Copper NE, Albuquerque, NM 87108   **(505) 266-4214**
Vegan. This is Albuquerque's only vegan restaurant serving Southwestern food. You'll find a big salad bar, fresh soups daily, hot buffet lunch, and sugarless desserts. The only non-vegan food is the soy cheese, which contains casein, a milk protein. **Closed Saturday in summer. Full service, fresh juices, catering, take-out, VISA/MC, $**

🏵 Reviewers' choice   • Vegetarian restaurant   •• Vegan restaurant
$ less than $6 $$ $6–$12 $$$ more than $12
VISA/AMX/MC/DISC/DC—credit cards accepted
Non-alc.—Non-alcoholic   Fresh juices—freshly squeezed

Alejandro's New Mexican Restaurant
6416 Zuni SE, Albuquerque, NM 87108   **(505) 265-9555**

5801 Wyoming NE, Albuquerque, NM 87109   **(505) 821-3481**
New Mexican. Whether you prefer patio dining at the Zuni location or fireplaces at the Wyoming site, you'll find a vegetarian plate, chili, and other veggie options. Items that can be prepared to meet the dietary standards of the American Heart Association are indicated on the menu. Live guitar music is played on Friday and Saturday nights. **Open daily. Full service, wine/beer, take-out, VISA/MC/AMX/ DISC, $–$$**

Artichoke Cafe
424 Central SE, Albuquerque, NM 87106   **(505) 243-0200**
International. Stark modern decor, rotating art exhibits, and a dedication to fine food, wine, and service have made the Artichoke Cafe one of Albuquerque's popular dining spots. The food is a mix of French, Italian, and creative American cuisine, and there are limited veggie options. It's pricey. **Closed Sunday. Full service, fresh juices, wine/beer, take-out, VISA/MC/AMX, $$$**

Bangkok Cafe
5901 Central NE, Albuquerque, NM 87108   **(505) 255-5036**
Thai. An entire vegetarian menu section that includes appetizers, soups, curry dishes, wok fried dishes, rice and noodles, and desserts is included on the Bangkok Cafe menu. All of the foods may be ordered from mild to spicy. Patio dining. **Open daily. Full service, vegan options, wine/beer, take-out, VISA/MC/AMX/ DISC, $$**

Bodhi Tree Restaurant
127 Harvard Dr., SE, Albuquerque, NM 87106   **(505) 260-0919**
Indian. Vegetarian items are about one-third of the menu, and only vegetable oil is used. There's patio dining with lots of shade. **Open daily. Full service, fresh juices, take-out, $$**

EJ's Cafe
2201 Silver SE, Albuquerque, NM 87106   **(505) 268-2233**
American/international. Located near the University, EJ's has a menu that includes various vegetarian and non-vegetarian foods for breakfast, lunch, and dinner. Pasta, Veggie Burgers, stir-fry, and Mexican dishes are offered as is a wide variety of coffees. **Open daily. Full service, vegan options, take-out, VISA/MC, $**

• Health Hunters Deli
355 Nara Visa NW, Albuquerque, NM 87107   **(505) 344-8866**
Vegetarian. Salads, sandwiches, hot entrees, specials and desserts make up the menu at Health Hunters. Some examples include Nori Rolls, Chili, and Mexican dishes. There are fresh homemade soups, and selections are mostly dairy-free. Enjoy sunlit atrium dining with local art for sale. **Closed Sunday. Full service, vegan options, fresh juices, limited catering, take-out, VISA/MC, $**

Imperial Wok Oriental Cuisine
601 Juan Tabo NE, Albuquerque, NM 87123   **(505) 294-1555**
Chinese. Vegetables, tofu, and mock meats make up the vegetarian selections at

this restaurant. The large selection is distinguished by wonderful and unusual sauces. **Open daily for lunch and dinner. Full service, vegan options, wine/beer/ alcohol, take-out, VISA/MC/DISC, $$**

India Kitchen Restaurant

6910 Montgomery NE, Albuquerque, NM 87109 **(505) 884-2333**

Indian. Eleven vegetarian entrees plus soup and appetizers are on the India Kitchen menu. Everything is prepared fresh to order. **Open daily. Full service, vegan options, wine/beer, VISA/MC/AMX/DISC, $**

La Montanita Co-op Supermarket

3500 Central Ave. SE, Albuquerque, NM 87106 **(505) 265-4631**

Health-food-store deli. La Montanita's deli features a wide variety of healthy salads and entrees. Hot soups and sandwiches and vegetarian and vegan foods are also featured. **Open daily. Deli, vegan options, fresh juices, take-out, $**

Oasis Restaurant & Lounge

5400 San Mateo NE, Albuquerque, NM 87109 **(505) 884-2324**

Mediterranean. Oasis features the foods of France, Italy, Greece, and Spain. Vegetarian entrees include Hummus, Falafel, Tabouleh, Moussaka, and pasta dishes. Desserts are homemade. There's live entertainment Wednesday through Saturday evenings. **Open daily for lunch and dinner, Sunday for dinner only. Reservations encouraged. Full service, vegan options, wine/beer/alcohol, take-out, VISA/ MC/AMX/DC, $$-$$**

El Patio Restaurant

142 Harvard SE, Albuquerque, NM 87106 **(505) 268-4245**

Mexican. Located near the University, this restaurant has vegetarian green and red chili and usually a veggie special. Savor a vegetarian burrito with fresh avocados, tomatoes, and vegetarian beans. **Open daily. Full service, vegan options, wine/beer, take-out, VISA/MC, $**

Shalimar Indian Cuisine

84-5 Montgomery NE, Albuquerque, NM 87111 **(505) 275-7949**

Indian. Vegetarian and non-vegetarian options are available. **Open daily. Full service, wine/beer, take-out, VISA/MC, $$**

BERNALILLO

Thyme to Savor

2000 Camino del Pueblo, Bernalillo, NM 87004 **(505) 867-5444**

Cafe. This small lunch cafe serves vegetarian and some vegan foods. **Dinner is carryout only. Counter service, take-out, $**

RIO RANCHO

Fortune Cookie

1011 Rio Rancho Blvd., Rio Rancho, NM 87124 **(505) 892-4500**

Chinese. **Full service, wine/beer, take-out, VISA/MC/AMX/DISC, $$**

SANTA FE

Baja Tacos
2621 Cerrillos Rd., Santa Fe, NM 87501   **(505) 988-5258**
Mexican. Enjoy fast, healthy and fresh Mexican food with no preservatives or additives. There's a vegetarian menu. **Open for three meals daily. Counter service, vegan options, BYOB, take-out, $**

Cafe Pasqual's
121 Don Gaspar, Santa Fe, NM 87501   **(505) 983-9340**
Natural foods. A Santa Fe classic, Cafe Pasqual's is known for its breakfasts and delicious Southwestern fare that pays particular attention to quality and authenticity. The menu is based on simple ingredients such as red and green chiles, pinto beans, garlic, onions, blue and yellow cornmeal, and white cheese. A lot of the menu items include fish or free-range chicken, but there is a decent selection for vegetarians, and specials are offered. Pasqual's is a place for locals and travelers alike who want innovative meals based on traditional fare. **Open for three meals daily but closed for Wednesday dinner. Full service, fresh juices, wine/beer, take-out, VISA/MC, $$–$$$**

Cloud Cliff Bakery & Restaurant
1805 Second St., Santa Fe, NM 87501   **(505) 983-6254**
Natural foods. Cloud Cliff integrates contemporary arts with fresh foods. The management works closely with local farmers and uses organically grown grains in the European breads and alternative pastries. **Open daily. Full service, fresh juice, wine/beer, take-out, VISA/MC, $$**

Delhi Palace Cuisine of India
142 Lincoln Ave., Santa Fe, NM 87501   **(505) 982-6680**
Indian. Vegetarian foods are available. **Open daily for lunch and dinner. Full service, wine/beer, take-out, VISA/MC/AMX, $$**

• Healthy David's Cafe
418 Cerrillos Rd., Santa Fe, NM 87501   **(505) 982-4147**
Vegetarian. Healthy David's is a Santa Fe classic with a variety of delicious vegetarian entrees, sandwiches, salads, and Middle Eastern foods. **Open daily for lunch and dinner. Full service, vegan options, fresh juices, organic coffee, take-out, $**

Hunan Chinese Restaurant
2440 Cerrillos Rd., Santa Fe, NM 87501   **(505) 471-6688**
Chinese. If you need a break from Southwestern cuisine, you can find a wide variety of vegetarian Hunan- and Peking-style Chinese foods at this restaurant. Appetizers, soups, and sixteen vegetarian entrees are offered to delight your taste buds. **Open daily for lunch and dinner. Full service, vegan options, wine/beer, take-out, VISA/MC/AMX, $$**

Natural Cafe
1494 Cerrillos Rd., Santa Fe, NM 87501   **(505) 983-1411**
International. Innovative international cuisine features vegetarian and non-vegetarian

dishes. Entrees include East India Tempeh Curry, Szechuan Vegetables, and Black Bean Enchilada. Whole-wheat French bread and delicous desserts are prepared daily. Local art decorates the dining room. Garden patio. **Closed Monday. Full service, vegan options, wine/beer, limited take-out, VISA/MC, $$**

Szechwan Restaurant
1965 Cerrillos Rd., Santa Fe, NM 87501   (505) 983-1558
Chinese. Ten vegetable and tofu entrees such as Broccoli with Hot Garlic Sauce and Sizzling Bean Curd are included on the menu. Appetizers, soup, and daily vegetarian specials are also offered. **Open daily for lunch and dinner. Full service, vegan options, wine/beer, take-out, VISA/MC, $$**

Tecolote Cafe
1203 Cerrillos Rd., Santa Fe, NM 87501   (505) 988-1362
Mexican/New Mexican. Known for its breakfasts, Tecolote features fresh baked goods and original atole/pinon hot cakes made with blue cornmeal and roasted pine nuts. The cafe is also open for lunch and serves various Mexican classics with a New Mexican twist. Beans and chili sauces are made with pure soy oil and no lard. The work of local artists is featured on the walls. **Open Tuesday through Sunday for breakfast and lunch. Full service, fresh juices, wine/beer, take-out, VISA/MC/AMX/DC, $**

Tomasita's Santa Fe Station
500 S. Guadalupe, Santa Fe, NM 87501   (505) 983-5721
New Mexican. Located in a historic red-brick station house, Tomasita's is a distinctive Northern New Mexican restaurant using recipes that have been handed down for generations. Vegetarian options are clearly indicated on the menu. Beware, the red and green chiles do contain beef. **Open Monday through Saturday for lunch and dinner. Full service, vegan options, take-out, VISA/MC, $$**

Wild Oats Market
1090 St. Francis Dr., Santa Fe, NM 87501   (505) 983-5333
Natural foods deli. This deli has vegetarian options and a large selection of breads and pastries. **Open daily. Deli, fresh juices, take-out, VISA/MC, $**

TAOS

Apple Tree Restaurant
123 Bent St., Taos, NM 87571   (505) 758-1900
Natural foods. Salads, soups, appetizers, and specials all include options for vegetarians. The red and green chile and the beans are vegetarian. Foods are prepared using the freshest ingredients available and reflecting a variety of ethnic persuasions. **Open daily, Sunday brunch. Full service, vegan options, espresso/cappuccino, wine/beer, take-out, VISA/AMX/MC, $–$$$**

The Caffe Tazza
122 Kit Carson Rd., Taos, NM 87571   (505) 758-8706
Cafe. An espresso bar with locally made ethnic vegetarian tamales, vegetarian chili plus daily soup specials, and, of course, espresso. There are great magazines and courtyard seating in summer. **Open daily. Limited service, take-out, no credit cards, $**

The Outback
712 Paseo del Pueblo Norte, Taos, NM 87571 **(505) 758-3112**
Pizza. Gourmet pizza with toppings such as dried tomatoes, spinach, artichoke, and pineapple. Pasta and salads also appear on the menu. **Open Monday through Saturday for lunch and dinner, closed Sunday. Full service, espresso/cappuccino, wine/beer, take-out, VISA/MC, $$**

• Wild & Natural Cafe
812 Paseo del Pueblo Norte, Taos, NM 87571 **(505) 751-0480**
Vegetarian. Wild & Natural has a Southwestern-style low-fat, heart-healthy menu. There are non-dairy daily specials, blue corn guacamole enchiladas, tempeh burgers, and veggie burritos. **Open for lunch and dinner Monday through Saturday. Full service, vegan options, fresh juices, espresso/cappuccino, wine/beer, take-out, VISA/MC, $–$$**

NEW YORK

ALBANY

• Dahlia's Vegetarian Bistro
858 Madison Ave., Albany, NY 12208 **(518) 482-0931**
Vegetarian. Dahlia's features international vegetarian cuisine. Every item on the menu is made from scratch. Dinners include Spinach Lasagna, Black Bean Chili, Angel Hair Pasta, and Jamaica Jerk Tempeh. The ice cream bar offers sorbet. **Open for lunch and dinner Sunday through Thursday. Closed November 15 to January 31. Full service, vegan/macrobiotic options, fresh vegetable juice, sorbet-with-7-Up coolers, catering, take-out, VISA/MC, lunch $, dinner $$**

El Loco Mexican Cafe
465 Madison Ave., Albany, NY 12210 **(518) 426-1855**
Mexican. Sample no-lard refried beans, veggie brown Mexican rice, veggie chili and soups, blue cornbread, etc. Most items can be prepared vegetarian, and there are soy cheese options. Here you'll find a funky atmosphere, outdoor patio, interesting t-shirts. **Tuesday through Saturday open afternoon and evening, Sunday open later afternoon and evening; may begin a Sunday brunch. Full service, wine/beer/alcohol, catering, take-out, VISA/MC/AMX, $$**

Nature's Way Cafe
227 Washington Ave., Albany, NY 12206 **(518) 462-0222**

Ꝝ Reviewers' choice • Vegetarian restaurant •• Vegan restaurant
$ less than $6 $$ $6–$12 $$$ more than $12
VISA/AMX/MC/DISC/DC—credit cards accepted
Non-alc.—Non-alcoholic Fresh juices—freshly squeezed

Natural foods. Vegetarian foods, poultry, and fish are served. Emphasis is on a healthy menu—low-salt, etc. The menu includes homemade soups and desserts, Veggie Burger, Burrito, Tofu Tortellini Marinara, Tofu Stir-Fry, and other choices. **Closed Sunday. Full service, vegan options, wine/beer/alcohol, VISA/MC/ AMX, $$.**

AMHERST

Pizza Plant
3085 Sheridan Dr., Amherst, NY 14226   **(716) 833-0882**
American with natural food choices. This restaurant offers veggie burgers (vegan), vegetarian chili, burritos, pasta with Pizza Plant's own marinara sauce, vegetarian stew in winter, homemade soups, a large variety of pizzas including soy cheese pizza, and a selection of fresh salads. Over sixty domestic and imported beers are featured. **Open daily. Full service, vegan options, wine/beer, catering, take-out, VISA/MC/AMX/DISC, $$**

AMITYVILLE

• Santosha Vegetarian Dining
40 Merrick Rd, Amityville, NY 11701
(Mailing address: 40 Forrest Place)   **(516) 598-1787**
Vegetarian. Created and owned by an Ashram, Santosha's food is cooked and served by Ashram members. The atmosphere is pleasant and relaxed. Entrees include Tortillas, Tempeh Fillets, Scallops of Tofu, Saffron Couscous African, and more. Desserts include vegan Chocolate Blackout Cake, Banana Berry Parfait, Vegan Berry Pie, and Precious Peach Cake. The in-store bakery will make a carrot wedding cake. **Open for dinner every night except Monday, open for lunch Tuesday through Friday. Full service, vegan options, dairy and non-dairy cappucino, non-alc. beer, catering, take-out, $$$**

BINGHAMTON

Whole in the Wall
43 S. Washington St., Binghamton, NY 13903   **(607) 722-0006**
Natural foods. At Whole in the Wall, bread and bagels are baked fresh every day. Soups are made from scratch; pies are made with fresh fruit and whole-wheat crust. All non-vegetarian items are cooked separately, and the restaurant can accommodate special diets. Tofu, tempeh, and Middle Eastern dishes are served, and live music is featured on Saturday night. **Open Tuesday through Saturday for lunch and dinner. Full service, vegan/macrobiotic options, fresh carrot or grape juices, $$**

BROOKLYN

(For more restaurant listings in the surrounding areas, see New York City.)

The Gourmet Cafe
1622 Coney Island Ave., Brooklyn, NY 11230   **(718) 338-5825**
Kosher/vegetarian (except for some fish)/macrobiotic/ethnic. The fare includes hearty soups such as split pea and mushroom barley, Chopped Vegetarian Liver, Stuffed Cabbage, Veggie Burger, chickenlike schnitzel, Zucchini Muffins, Carrot Cake, and ice cream desserts. Gourmet Cafe retails frozen entrees. **Open Sunday through**

Thursday for lunch and dinner. Full service, vegan options, catering, take-out, VISA/MC/AMX/DISC, $$

Healthy Henrietta's
60 Henry St., Brooklyn, NY 11201   **(718) 858-8478**

Mexican/natural foods. Henrietta's has an artsy atmosphere and features great brunches and desserts. Mexican items are offered with tofu sour cream. **Vegan/ macrobiotic options, take-out, $–$$.**

Kar
428 5th Ave., Brooklyn, NY 11215   **(718) 965-1010**

Chinese. Savor sautéed string beans with pickled cabbage, tangy and spicy tofu, spinach sautéed with Fu-U sauce. Brown rice is available. **Open daily to 10:30 P.M., wine/beer, take-out, VISA/MC/AMX, $$**

Kar Too Restaurant
5908 Ave. N, Brooklyn, NY 11234   **(718) 531-8811**

Chinese. See description in preceding entry.

• King Vegetarian Restaurant
4705 Church Ave., Brooklyn, NY 11203   **(718) 284-4533**

Vegetarian. This is an East Flatbush restaurant. **Open Monday through Saturday for lunch and dinner. Full service, catering, $**

The Leaf & Bean Cafe
136 Montague St., Brooklyn, NY 11214   **(718) 855-7978**

Natural foods. Located on the parlor floor of a brownstone, the Leaf & Bean Cafe offers a continental menu of salads, omelettes, and items such as Vegetable Lasagna, sandwiches, and desserts. Cakes, tarts, pies, and scones can be ordered to accompany your gourmet coffee or tea selection. Brunch and lunch only. **Open daily. Limited service, gourmet coffee, take-out, VISA/MC/AMX, $$**

Moustache Pizza
405 Atlantic Ave., Brooklyn, NY 11217   **(718) 852-5555**

Middle Eastern. Behind this small neighborhood restaurant is a garden setting with tables and umbrellas. Bread is baked when ordered. **Open daily. Limited service, Turkish coffee, Mideastern citrus drink, mint tea, $**

Mr. Falafel Restaurant
226 Seventh Ave., Brooklyn, NY 11215   **(718) 768-4961**

Egyptian. **Open daily. Full service, Turkish coffee, cappucino, carrot juice, take-out, AMX, $**

Steve and Sons Bakery and Caterers, Inc.
9305 Church Ave., Brooklyn, NY 11212   **(718) 498-5800**

Ethnic/American. This is the home of the vegetarian patties or turnovers. You'll also find vegetarian stew, vegetarian barbecue ribs, vegetable steaks, and gluten in wine sauce. **Open for three meals Sunday through Thursday. Full service, fresh juices, beer, $$**

Taam Eden Restaurant
5001 13th Ave., Brooklyn, NY 11219   **(718) 972-1692**
Kosher. Features French service and a nice dining room. **Open daily for breakfast, lunch, and dinner. Full service and cafeteria style, wine, take-out, $$**

Weiss's Restaurant
1146 Coney Island Ave., Brooklyn, NY 11230   **(718) 421-0164**
Kosher. Kosher dairy cuisine with added vegetarian dishes such as Tofu Primavera, Vegetables & Linguine, and Vegetarian Chopped Liver. **Open Sunday through Thursday from 12 P.M. to 9:30 P.M.; in winter, open Saturday 90 minutes after sundown (after the Sabbath ends). Full service, egg cream, wine/beer/alcohol, catering, take-out, $$**

Who's on Seventh
183 Seventh Ave. (at Second Street), Brooklyn, NY 11215   **(718) 765-0597**
Natural foods. Enjoy natural sandwiches, soups, entrees, and juices. The restaurant, which also serves fish, is near the Seventh Avenue C/D/Q/F subway stops. **Full service, $$**

BUFFALO

Amy's Place
3234 Main St., Buffalo, NY 14214   **(716) 832-6666**
Natural foods/American/Middle Eastern. About one-half of the menu is vegetarian. **Open daily for three meals. Full service, take-out, $**

El Charro Mexican Restaurant
3447 Bailey Ave., Buffalo, NY 14215   **(716) 837-5300**
Mexican. El Charro serves tamales, empanadas, burritos, tacos, tostados. **Open daily. Full service, wine/beer/alcohol, catering, VISA/MC/AMX/DISC, $$$**

CANTON

• Willow Island
1 West Main, Canton, NY 13617   **(315) 386-8822**
Vegetarian/ethnic. Enjoy eating complete vegetarian cuisine on open or screened decks that overlook the Levasse River. Occasionally, there's live music. All desserts and breads are made on the premises with organic whole-wheat flour and maple syrup or honey. **Open Tuesday through Saturday for lunch and dinner. Closed Thanksgiving week and Christmas week. Full service, vegan options, wine/beer, catering, take-out, VISA/MC/AMX, $$**

CEDARHURST

La Pasta
530 Central Ave., Cedarhurst, NY 11516   **(516) 374-9232**
Kosher. Offers a completely kosher and mostly vegetarian (except for fish) menu including Three Cheese Penne and Potato Pirogen, which are all freshly prepared. Also features a brunch menu and daily lunch specials. **Open Sunday through Thursday from noon to 10 P.M. Closed Friday. Open Saturday 90 minutes after sundown (after the Sabbath ends). Full service, catering, take-out, AMX, $$–$$$**

GARDEN CITY

Akbar
One Ring Rd. West, Garden City, NY 11530
(On grounds of Roosevelt Field) **(516) 248-5700**
Indian. Akbar has a good vegetarian selection with at least four vegan entrees; three others have some dairy. Spicy food is available. **Full service, vegan options, $$**

GREAT NECK

Earth's Harvest
5 Great Neck Rd., Great Neck, NY 11021 **(516) 829-8605**
Health-food-store counter. **Open daily. Limited service, macrobiotic options, take-out, VISA/MC/AMX, $**

Garden of Plenty
4 Wellwyn Rd., Great Neck, NY 11021 **(516) 482-8868**
Ethnic/Chinese. Offers unique vegetarian dishes like Sautéed Chinese Spinach, Snow White Chow Fun Rolls, Fish Fantasy (made out of bean curd), and Enoki Mushrooms. **$$**

HUNTINGTON

Jholla
36 Gerard St., Huntington, NY 1174 **(516) 385-7956**
Indian take-out. Jholla features Northwestern Indian cuisine with the emphasis on vegetarian food. **Open daily. Take-out only, $$**

ITHACA

ABC Cafe
308 Stewart Ave., Ithaca, NY 14850 **(607) 277-4770**
Natural foods. This was previously the Apple Blossom Cafe. It features free music Tuesday night, Sunday brunch, monthly art shows, seasonal menus. Vegetarian favorites include ABC Burger, Tempeh Reuben, Cashew Jambalaya. **Closed Mondays and between Christmas and New Year's. Table service at dinner and brunch only. Counter service other times. Vegan/macrobiotic options, wide selection of coffee and espresso drinks, smoothies, wine/beer, take-out, $–$$**

• Cabbagetown Cafe
404 Eddy St., Ithaca, NY 14850 **(607) 273-2847**
Vegetarian. This cafe is an often-recommended vegetarian restaurant. It was founded in 1973 by Cornell students who wanted to serve wholesome foods close to campus. By a stroke of fate, the cafe became vegetarian when the first head cook hired by the founders said she wouldn't cook meat. Though you can't find meat here, you can find Cabbagetown Tostada, Cashew Chili, and Steve's Tofu Dressing. **Open daily for three meals. Full service, fresh juices, non-alc. wine/beer, wine/beer/alcohol, catering, take-out, VISA/MC, $–$$**

Moosewood Restaurant ⧫

DeWitt Building, Ithaca, NY 14850   **(607) 273-9610**
Natural foods. Moosewood serves gourmet and natural foods cuisine with ethnic specialties on Sunday nights. The cooperatively owned and managed restaurant offers homemade desserts, Bully Hill 100% New York State Grape Juice, and Yuengling beer, ale, and porter. **Call for hours, which change seasonally. Full service, wine/beer, limited catering and take-out, $$**

LOCUST VALLEY

Charlies Restaurant

324 Forest Ave., Locust Valley, NY 11560   **(516) 676-6229**
American. Charlies offers pasta dishes, personalized pizzas, and calzones made with a whole-wheat crust, vegetarian sandwiches, and tofu dishes. **Open daily 4 P.M. to midnight. Full service, wine/beer/alcohol, take-out, VISA/MC/AMX/ DISC, $$**

LONG ISLAND

For restaurants in this area, see Amityville, Cedarhurst, Garden City, Great Neck, Huntington, Locust Valley, Montauk, Oceanside, Sag Harbor, Seaford, West Hempstead, and Woodmere. For restaurant listings in the surrounding area, see New York City.

MANHATTAN

(For more restaurant listings in the surrounding areas, see New York City.)

Abyssinia Ethiopian Restaurant

35 Grand St., New York, NY 10013   **(212) 226-5959**
Ethiopian. The Abyssinia Restaurant has the beguiling air of Ethiopia's 4000-year-old-culture. Its arched vaults and grass-cloth walls are adorned with artifacts from another time, with top African background music and wines. There are no utensils! Vegetarian dishes are eaten with a spongy bread as you sit on hand- carved wooden stools around colorful woven-basket-tables called mesobs. All natural ingredients are used in cooking. **Open Monday through Friday for dinner, Saturday and Sunday for lunch and dinner. Full service, vegan options, wine/beer, catering, take-out, AMX, $$**

•• Angelica's Kitchen ⧫

300 E. 12th St., New York, NY 10003   **(212) 228-2909**
Vegan/macrobiotic. This vegan restaurant uses 95 percent organic ingredients. Daily specials are offered along with excellent homemade cornbread and tahini dressing. Angelica's has been rated highly by many New Yorkers. **Open daily. Full service, vegan/macrobiotic options, fresh juices, smoothies, $$**

⧫ Reviewers' choice   • Vegetarian restaurant   •• Vegan restaurant
$ less than $6 $$ $6–$12 $$$ more than $12
VISA/AMX/MC/DISC/DC—credit cards accepted
Non-alc.—Non-alcoholic   Fresh juices—freshly squeezed

Apple Restaurant
17 Waverly Pl., New York, NY 10003   **(212) 473-8888**
Ethnic. Lunch, dinner, and brunch are served. This restaurant uses separate cooking equipment when preparing vegetarian foods and features Karaoke sing-a-long. Though Apple serves plenty of meat dishes, there are many interesting natural food choices including Yam Tempura, Watercress Salad, Tempeh Burger, Stir-Fried Cabbage with Soba Noodles, BBQ Seitan, and more. **Open daily for lunch and dinner. Full service, wine/beer/alcohol, catering, take-out, VISA/ MC/AMX, $$**

B & H Dairy Restaurant
127 Second Ave., New York, NY 10003   **(212) 505-8065**
Kosher. This vegetarian restaurant does serve fish. Home cooking includes omelettes, baked goods, sandwiches, salads, soups, and hot entrees such as Vegetarian Stuffed Cabbage and Vegetarian Chili. Sandwiches, salads, and desserts round out the menu at B & H, which offers daily soup and sandwich specials. **Open daily. Limited service, vegan options, fresh juices, take-out, no credit cards, $**

•• Bachue
36 W. 21st St., New York, NY 10010   **(212) 229-0870**
Vegan/natural foods. New York City is fortunate to have a new vegan restaurant. Diners can enjoy vegan breakfasts with items such as waffles, scrambled tofu, and a juice bar including tropical shakes. Entrees during the day include many international items such as Chickpea Crêpes, enchiladas, and empanadas. Organic grains and beans as well as organic produce, when available, are used at this restaurant. Flour is ground on the premises to make fresh bread. This new restaurant offers a breakfast and lunch menu that is available until 6 P.M. Future plans include adding on an expanded dinner menu. **Open Monday through Saturday for breakfast and lunch. Full service, vegan options, catering, take-out, $$**

Benny's Burritos
93 Avenue A, New York, NY 10009   **(212) 254-3286**

113 Greenwich Ave., New York, NY 10014   **(212) 727-0584**
Mexican. Benny's serves Cal-Mex style cuisine emphasizing fresh vegetarian foods in a fifties atmosphere. The food contains no preservatives, no lard, and no MSG. Benny's uses non-dairy tofu sour cream, whole-wheat tortillas, and brown rice. **Open daily for lunch and dinner. Full service, vegan options, wine/beer/alcohol, catering, take-out, $-$$**

The Blue Nile Restaurant
103 W. 77th St., New York, NY 10024   **(212) 580-3232**
Ethiopian. This traditional Ethiopian restaurant offers vegetarian entrees and appetizers. Enjoy its distinct decor of woven-basket-tables and hand-carved stools. **Open daily for dinner, lunch Friday through Sunday. Full service, vegan options, wine/beer, catering, take-out, AMX/DISC/DC, $$**

Boostan
85 MacDougal St., New York, NY 10012   **(212) 533-9561**
Natural foods. This restaurant is vegetarian with the exception of one fish dish.

Located in the heart of Greenwich Village, it offers an extensive menu, including appetizers, soups, salads, sandwiches, pasta dishes, various entrees, and desserts. **Open daily for lunch and dinner. Full service, vegan options, catering, take-out, $$**

Brownie's
101 Second Ave., New York, NY 10003   **(212) 254-5004**
American. Near the Second Avenue F subway stop, Brownie's offers an extensive vegetarian menu featuring baked goods and ice cream. Outdoor seating is also provided. **Open Sunday through Thursday from 8 A.M to midnight, Friday and Saturday from 8 A.M. to 2 A.M. Cafeteria style, fresh juices, take-out, $**

• Caravan of Dreams
405 E. 6th St., New York, NY 10009
(between First Avenue and Avenue A)   **(212) 254-1613**
Vegetarian/natural foods. This smoke-free restaurant is committed to using only organically grown ingredients whenever available, and to designing balanced dishes for healthful eating. Almost all foods are dairy-free, many are wheat-free, and the water is osmosis-filtered. Caravan offers completely vegetarian foods such as Black Bean Chili, Corn Polenta with Sweet Potato and Leek Sauce, and Grilled Marinated Tofu. It features live music nightly, art gallery, lectures, and various classes. **Open daily to midnight or later. Full service, vegan options, fresh juices, cappuccino/espresso, $–$$**

• The Friday Night Dinner Club
48 W. 21st St., Second Floor, New York, NY 1001   **(212) 645-5170**
Vegetarian/natural foods. Enjoy a vegetarian meal (including seasonal vegetables) that has been carefully balanced so that it is sugar- and dairy- free, high in fiber and complex carbohydrates, low in fat, and cholesterol-free. **Open Fridays only. Reservations required. Closed major holidays. Full service, BYOB, catering, take-out, VISA/MC, $$$**

Ganges Restaurant
344 E. 6th St., New York, NY 10003   **(212) 228-3767**
Indian. Various exotic Indian rice, curry, and vegetable entrees, plus appetizers and soups are available. Entrees include Vegetable Biryani, Seasonal Mixed Vegetable Curry, and Coconut Soup. **Open daily for lunch and dinner. Full service, fresh juices, catering, take-out, VISA/MC/DISC , $$**

Gindi
935 Broadway, New York, NY 10010   **(212) 505-5502**
Natural foods. This tiny bakery with tables and outdoor dining in season is near the Twenty-third Street N/R subway stops. It offers a salad/sandwich menu. **Full service, take-out, $**

Good Food Cafe
401 Fifth Ave., New York, NY 10016   **(212) 686-3546**
Natural foods store/cafe and juice bar. This cafe serves healthful foods like Vegetarian Chili, Spinach Pie, Macrobiotic Plate, and Special Brown Rice and Veggies. **Open Monday through Saturday. Limited service, vegan/macrobiotic options, fresh juices, catering, take-out, VISA/MC/AMX, $**

Good Health Cafe
324 E. 86th St., New York, NY 10028   **(212) 439-9680**
Natural foods/ethnic. Foods are mostly dairy-free; some items are made with eggs.
Middle Eastern, Mexican, Italian, and Japanese dishes are featured. **Open weekdays for lunch and dinner, weekends for brunch. Full service, fresh juices,
non-alc. beer, delivery, take-out, VISA/MC/AMX/DC, $$**

The Great American Health Bar
55 John St., New York, NY   **(212) 227-6100**

76 Beaver St., New York, NY   **(212) 344-7522**

2 Park Ave., New York, NY   **(212) 685-7117**

821 Third Ave., New York, NY   **(212) 758-0883**

10 E. 44 St., New York, NY   **(212) 661-3430**

35 W. 57th St., New York, NY   **(212) 355-5177**
Natural foods/kosher. The Health Bar offers a wide variety of vegetarian entrees
such as Eggplant Parmesan, Pizza of the Day, and Pasta of the Day and is know for
its fresh-squeezed juices and homemade soups. Sandwiches include Hummus,
Falafel, The Garden Patch, and Avocado. **Open daily. Full service, vegan options,
fresh juices, catering, take-out, $**

Hana Restaurant
675 Ninth Ave., New York, NY 10036   **(212) 582-9742**
Korean/Japanese. Hana offers a separate vegetarian menu that includes Korean and
Japanese specialties. The menu features Jap Cahe (vegetables with rice noodles),
Hana Noodle (stir-fried noodles), Woo Dong (soup with noodles and vegetables),
and four types of vegetarian sushi. **Open for lunch and dinner Monday through
Saturday. Full service, vegan options, carrot juice, sake/plum wine/wine/beer,
VISA/MC/AMX, $$**

•• The Health Nuts
1208 Second Ave., New York, NY 10021   **(212) 593-0116**

835 Second Ave., New York, NY 10017   **(212) 490-2979**

2611 Broadway, New York, NY 10025   **(212) 678-0054**
Vegan. A natural deli and juice bar are situated inside a large health food store.
Freshly prepared gourmet vegetarian salads, pasta, grains, hot foods, pizza, soups,
pastries, cakes, and snacks are available. Foods are cholesterol-free, low in calories,
and made without sugar, eggs, milk, butter, or other animal products. Sometimes
a vegan cheese cake is offered! **Open daily. Counter service, completely vegan,
fresh juices, take-out, VISA/MC/AMX, $**

The Health Pub
371 Second Ave., New York, NY 10010   **(212) 529-9200**
Natural foods. A spacious dining area and leisurely pace are the hallmarks of this
exceptional restaurant. Food is vegan, except for some salmon. Menu items
include Marinated Grilled Tofu with Horseradish Dressing, Black Bean Chili with
Cilantro and Tofu Sour Cream, Marinated Lima Beans with Fennel and Shallots,

delicious desserts such as Lemon Pecan Tart, Hazelnut Carob Torte with Raspberry Sauce, and organic wines. **Open daily. Full service, vegan options, non-alc. beer, organic wine/beer, take-out, AMX, $$–$$$**

• Healthy Candle, Inc.

972 Lexington Ave., New York, NY 10021   (212) 472-0970
Vegetarian/macrobiotic/take-out juice bar. Limited space allows only for take-out, but parks are nearby. You'll find Tofu Salad, watercress, Hummus, Tofu Burger, Spinach Tofu Roll, Broccoli Tofu Knish, daily specials such as Pasta with Peanut Sauce or Tempeh Stew and Stuffed Yam, and a variety of desserts and handmade breads. Sugar-free and dairy-free desserts are available. **Open for three meals Monday through Saturday. Limited service/take-out, vegan/macrobiotic options, VISA/MC, $$**

• House of Vegetarian

68 Mott St., New York, NY 10013   (212) 226-6572
Vegetarian/Chinese/macrobiotic. House of Vegetarian offers health food and brown rice. There's no meat, chicken, seafood, or MSG. The restaurant serves more than 200 dishes with many different meat imitations. There are assorted mock chicken dishes using pineapple, lemon, mango in season, yams, etc; mock iron steak, imitation fish, vegetarian egg rolls, and more. **Open daily. Full service, vegan/macrobiotic options, take-out, $–$$**

Indian Delhi

392 Columbus Ave., New York, NY 10024   (212) 570-0962
Indian. Many items are dairy-free; only canola oil is used in cooking. Space is limited. **Open daily. Full service, vegan options, fresh carrot juice, take-out, $–$$**

Life Cafe

343 E. 10th St., New York, NY 10009   (212) 477-9001
Natural foods/primarily vegetarian. Possibly the hippest near- vegetarian restaurant around, Life Cafe has plenty of local color and great food. It's tiny and fills up fast, but the food is worth the crowd. Most offerings are vegetarian or vegan. **Open daily for lunch and dinner, brunch on weekends. Full service, vegan options, fresh juice, wine/beer/alcohol, take-out, VISA/MC, $$**

•• Living Springs Restaurant

116 E. 60th St., New York, NY 10022   (212) 319-7850
Vegan. Vegans, it's worth going out of your way! The special is changed daily. Dishes include Oat Burgers, Pasta with Tofu Balls, Beans and Franks, Vegetable Pot Pie, Cream of Black Bean, Oat Waffles, Baked Yams, or similar items. Food is priced by weight. Desserts are made without sugar or honey. Living Springs is happy to have children as customers. **Open Monday through Friday for breakfast and lunch; open for dinner Sunday, and Tuesday through Thursday; closed Saturday; open for Sunday brunch. To find out the daily menu call (212) 751-0631. Cafeteria style, completely vegan, $$**

Luma

200 Ninth Ave., New York, NY 10011   (212) 633-8033
Natural foods/macrobiotic. Luma has an extensive vegetarian menu that uses many

organic ingredients. **Open daily for dinner. Full service, catering, take-out, VISA/MC, $$$**

• Madras Palace
104 Lexington Ave., New York, NY 10016   **(212) 532-3314**
Vegetarian/Indian/kosher. Madras Palace features South Indian kosher vegetarian cooking near Manhattan's Little India section. Dairy products are used but no eggs. **Open daily for lunch and dinner. Full service, vegan options, non-alc. beer, catering, take-out, VISA/MC/AMX/DC, $$**

Mana Restaurant
2444 Broadway, New York, NY 10024
(between 90th and 91st Sts.)   **(212) 787-1110**
Japanese. Mana is vegetarian except for fish and offers Japanese natural and macrobiotic cooking with no sugar, chemicals, preservatives, or dairy products. Filtered water and organic ingredients are used. **Open for lunch and dinner Monday through Saturday. Full service, vegan options, BYOB, take-out, no credit cards, $$**

Mizrachi Kosher Dairy Restaurant
105 Chambers St., New York, NY 10007   **(212) 964-2280**
Kosher/natural foods. Mizrachi provides a fresh salad bar, full breakfast menu, Middle Eastern and vegetarian dishes, different types of pizzas, plus many kinds of sandwiches and homemade soups. **Open for three meals Monday through Thursday, Friday for breakfast and lunch. Cafeteria style, fresh juices, catering, no credit cards, $**

The Natural Food Bar
166 West 72nd St., New York, NY 10023   **(212) 874-1213**
Kosher/natural foods. Vegetarian except for fish, the Natural Food Bar has an extensive vegetarian offering, including Tabouleh Salad, Baba Ghanouj, Veggie-Nut Burgers, and fresh-squeezed juices. It has a small sit-down bar and other limited seating. **Open Monday through Saturday from 8 A.M. to midnight, Sunday from 11 A.M. to 10 P.M. Limited/take-out service, fresh juices, $**

Naturworks
200 A West 44th St., New York, NY 10036   **(212) 869-8335**
Natural foods. A wide variety of natural food is offered with an emphasis on vegetarian sandwiches, vegetarian soups, and quiche. Baked desserts, frozen yogurt, and non-dairy frozen desserts are available at reasonable prices, and there's a large selection of herbal teas. **Closed Sunday. Cafeteria style, vegan options, fruit juices, take-out, $**

Nawab Restaurant
256 E. 49th St., New York, NY 10017   **(212) 755-9100**

Indian. Serving Northern Indian cuisine, Nawab is open for lunch and dinner and offers a buffet. There's a vegetarian section on the menu and some vegetarian appetizers, soup, salads, and rice items. **Open daily. Full service, vegan options, wine/beer/alcohol, take-out, VISA/MC/AMX, $$–$$$**

Nirvana
30 Central Park South, New York, NY 10019   **(212) 486-5700**
Indian. Near the Fifty-seventh Street N/R and B/Q subway stops, Nirvana has a terrific view north into Central Park. **Formal, full service, $$$**

Nosmo King
54 Varick St., New York, NY 10013   **(212) 966-1239**
Contemporary American. Organically grown food is used, although there are many non-vegetarian dishes. The restaurant uses litttle or no dairy and features such gourmet items as Napolean of Asparagus with Wild Mushrooms. **Open for lunch Monday through Friday, dinner daily. Full service, reservations recommended, fresh juices, wine/beer/alcohol, VISA/MC/AMX, lunch—$$, dinner—$$$**

Nutrisserie
142 W. 72nd St., New York, NY 10023   **(212) 721-3039**
Natural foods. This health food deli and store has an organic juice bar with an extensive vegetarian menu. **Open daily for three meals. Cafeteria style, fresh juices, catering, take-out, VISA/MC/AMX, $**

Ozu Restaurant
566 Amsterdam Ave., New York, NY 10024   **(212) 787-8316**
Macrobiotic. A primarily Japanese menu includes soups, breads, salads, and entrees featuring tofu, grains, noodles, tempura, and vegetables. Fish is also served here as are daily entree and dessert specials. **Open daily. Full service, vegan/macrobiotic options, beer/organic wine, take-out, VISA/MC, $$**

• Plum Tree Vegetarian Restaurant
1501 First Ave., New York, NY 10021   **(212) 535-0442**
Vegetarian/natural foods/macrobiotic. Plum Tree has served vegetarian, macrobiotic, and vegan cuisine since 1981. The menu includes items such as Azuki and Black Bean Soup, Fire Dragon Chili, Macro-Ratatouille, and Vegetable Crêpes. **Open for lunch and dinner Tuesday through Sunday, closed Mondays. Full service, vegan/macrobiotic options, fresh juices, take-out, no credit cards, $$**

Pumpkin Eater
2452 Broadway, New York, NY 10024   **(212) 877-0132**
Natural foods/juice bar. Located not too far from Columbia University, Pumpkin Eater is usually busy. **Open daily for lunch and dinner. Full service, wine/beer, catering, take-out, AMX, $$**

Quantum Leap
88 W. Third St., New York, NY 10012   **(212) 677-8050**
Natural foods. Many tasty vegan and vegetarian dishes are served in this relaxed and homey atmosphere, natural pies and house dressing, too. **Full service, $$**

Ratner's
138 Delancey St., New York, NY 10002 **(212) 677-5588**
Dairy restaurant. This eatery is near Delancey Street F subway stop and Essex Street J/M subway stop. **Full service, $$**

St. Mark's Pizza
23 Third Ave., New York, NY 10003 **(212) 420-9531**
Pizza. In the heart of the East Village, this local corner pizza place has a wide variety of vegetarian pizzas. **Limited service, take-out, $**

The Salad Bowl
566 Seventh Ave., New York, NY 10018 **(212) 472-9318**

A and S Plaza, Floor 7
901 Sixth Ave., New York, NY 10001 **(212) 594-6512**

721 Lexington Ave., New York, NY 10022 **(212) 752-7201**

906 Third Ave., New York, NY 10022 **(212) 644-6767**

South Street Seaport Pier 17, New York, NY 10022 **(212) 693-0590**
Natural foods. Vegetarian sandwiches, soups, and salads are offered at this cafe. All foods are home-cooked. **Open daily. Cafeteria style, fresh juices, catering, take-out, $$**

• The Sanctuary
33 St. Mark's Pl., New York, NY 10003 **(212) 505-8234**
Vegetarian/mixed ethnic. This dinner club offers a unique menu that features different ethnic foods each night. Tuesday features foods from India; Thursday, America; and Saturday, the Middle East. Call for details. **Open Tuesday through Saturday from noon to 8:30 P.M. Cafeteria style, vegan options, catering, take-out, $**

Scallions
48 Trinity Pl., New York, NY 10006 **(212) 480-9135**
Natural foods/juice bar. Scallions is a health food restaurant specializing in dishes that are low in fat, cholesterol, and sodium. **Open for three meals Monday through Friday from 7:30 A.M. to 7 P.M. Fresh juices, catering, take-out, $**

Shaagureka
94 Second Ave., New York, NY 10003 **(212) 979-7448**
Indian. A small and friendly Indian restaurant, Shaagureka will serve brown rice on request. **Full service, take-out, $$.**

•• Shojin
23 Commerce St., New York, NY 10014 **(212) 989-3530**
Vegan/Japanese. Known for Tofu Pie, this restaurant serves entrees such as Sweet & Sour Tofu, Tempura, Gluten Cutlet, and Okara Burgers. Absolutely no animal products are used. Malt is used as a sweetener. **Open for dinner Monday through Saturday, closed Sundays. Full service, take-out, $$**

Souen Restaurant
28 E. 13th St., New York, NY 10003   **(212) 627-7150**
Macrobiotic/natural foods. Sample various seitan, tofu, and tempeh entrees, plus appetizers, soups, salads, tempura, and noodle dishes with option of udon or soba noodles. Fish is also served here, and there are indoor and outdoor gardens. **Open daily. Full service, vegan/macrobiotic options, fresh juices, organic coffee, organic wine/beer, take-out, VISA/MC/AMX, $$–$$$**

Spring Street Natural
62 Spring St., New York, NY 10012
(Corner of Lafayette)   **(212) 966-0290**
Natural foods. Enjoy vegetarian soups, salads, entrees, and even some sugar-free and dairy-free desserts. **Open daily. Full service, fresh juices, cappuccino/espresso, catering, take-out, VISA/MC/AMX, $$**

Temple in the Village Restaurant
74 W. Third St., New York, NY 10012   **(212) 475-5670**
Natural foods/macrobiotic. This small buffet-style health food restaurant for macrobiotics and vegetarians serves vegetables, noodles, five–seven grain rice, and teas. All foods are prepared on the premises. Seating is limited. **Open for lunch and dinner Monday through Saturday. Cafeteria style, BYOB, catering, take-out, $**

• Vegetarian Heaven
304 W. 58th St., New York, NY 10019
(4 Columbus Circle)   **(212) 956-4678**
Vegetarian/kosher/Chinese. Enjoy vegetarian dishes such as Shredded Beef with Basil, Chicken with Sesame Sauce, or Sweet and Sour Pork, all made from soybean protein, all completely vegetarian. Other dishes include Eggplant in Spicy Sauce, Vegetable Tempura, and Bean Noodle Slice with Vegetables. This restaurant serves numerous vegan dishes as well. It's near the Columbus Circle stop of the A/B/C/D/1/9 subways. **Open daily for lunch and dinner. Reservations required. Full service, fresh juice, BYOB, catering, take-out, VISA/MC, $$**

• Vegetarian Paradise 3
33–35 Mott St., New York, NY 10013   **(212) 406-6988**
Vegetarian. Located in the heart of Chinatown, this restaurant is kin to VP2 (see that entry for description).

Village East
2 Saint Marks Place, New York, NY 10003   **(212) 533-9898**
Natural foods. In this brightly lit, roomy restaurant, you'll find whole grains and steamed, sautéed, and fried foods that are well-seasoned. **Full service, take-out, $$**

Village Natural Food Corp.
46 Greenwich Ave., New York, NY 10011   **(212) 727-0968**
Natural foods. This spacious Greenwich Village restaurant offers whole grains only, and has daily specials. **Full service, take-out, $$**

•• VP2 ❧

144 W. 4th St., New York, NY 10012 **(212) 260-7141**

Vegan. Extensive menu features exquisite Chinese vegetarian cuisine. The menu includes hot and cold appetizers, salads, desserts, and many entree categories such as bean curd, greens, mock meat, mushroom, wheat gluten, noodle, and rice. Hot clay pots and house specials such as Taro Whole Fish (vegetarian), Stuffed Lotus Leaf, and Spinach Dumpling are featured. It's not to be missed!! You'll find it near the West Fourth Street subway stop on the A/B/C/D/E/F trains. **Open for lunch and dinner daily. Full service, vegan options, fresh juices, catering, take-out, VISA/MC/AMX, $$**

•• VP-2-GO

140 W. 4th St., New York, NY 10012 **(212) 260-7049**

Vegan take-out. Enjoy outstanding vegetarian fare at excellent prices. The take-out menu lists thirty-five items from Fried Taro Dumplings to Stuffed Lotus Leaf to Lemon Tofu Pudding plus 100-percent vegetarian authentic Dim Sum "like nowhere else in NYC." Wholesale and retail foods are available at this location. **Open daily. Cafeteria style, vegan options, catering, take-out, VISA/MC/AMX, $**

• Whole Earth Bakery and Kitchen

70 Spring St., New York, NY 10012 **(212) 226-8280**

Vegetarian bakery. Enjoy fresh baked goods that are predominately vegan. Menu includes muffins, cookies, brownies, and much more. Some sandwiches are also offered. **Open daily. Vegan options, take-out, $**

Whole Foods in SoHo

117 Prince St., New York, NY 10012 **(212) 673-5388**

Health food store and deli. Whole Foods features gourmet natural take-out, deli, and a salad bar. **Open daily. Take-out, VISA/MC/AMX/DISC, $**

Whole Wheat 'N Wild Berrys

57 W. Tenth St., New York, NY 10011 **(212) 677-3410**

Natural foods. Enjoy items such as Nutburgers, Manicotti, Black Bean Sauté, and Vegetarian Chili. This small restaurant located near the IND West Fourth Street station (A/B/C/D/E/F trains) recently celebrated its seventeenth anniversary. **Open daily for lunch and dinner. Full service, wine/beer/alcohol, catering, AMX, $$**

Yaffa Cafe

97 Saint Marks Place, New York, NY 10009 **(212) 674-9302**

Natural foods. In this bohemian atmosphere, vegetarian dishes include crêpes, stir fry, tofu, Baba Ghanouj, salads, and Hummus. There's garden seating during the summer, as well as a sidewalk cafe. **Open 24 hours daily. Full service, vegan options, fresh juices, wine/beer, take-out, AMX, $$**

❧ Reviewers' choice • Vegetarian restaurant •• Vegan restaurant
$ less than $6 $$ $6–$12 $$$ more than $12
VISA/AMX/MC/DISC/DC—credit cards accepted
Non-alc.—Non-alcoholic Fresh juices—freshly squeezed

• Zen Palate 🍃

663 Ninth Ave., New York, NY 10036 (at 46th street)   (212) 582-1669
Vegetarian/Chinese. Zen Palate offers dishes like Stuffed Chinese Cabbage Deluxe, Vegetarian Squid, and Steam-fried Brown Rice with Vegetables. **Open daily for lunch and dinner. Full service and cafeteria, vegan options, fresh juices, take-out, VISA/MC/AMX, $–$$**

Zucchini

1336 First Ave., New York, NY 10021   (212) 249-0559
Natural foods. The restaurant will cook to order any special dietary requests. Only olive oil is used in cooking and salads. Items include Baked Stuffed Zucchini, Four-Bean Vegetarian Chili, and Four-Cheese Zucchini-Spinach Lasagna. **Open daily for lunch and dinner except in July and August for dinner only. Full service, catering, take-out, VISA/MC/AMX, $$**

MANLIUS

• Incredible Edibles

209 E. Seneca St., Manlius, NY 13104   (315) 682-6684
Vegetarian/natural foods store. This natural-foods-store deli sells all-vegetarian lunches. Spanikopita, Hummus, hot soups, pasta salad, Tofu Lasagna, egg rolls, and more are on the menu. There are also cooking classes, massage, and poetry readings. **Open Tuesday through Saturday. Limited service, vegan options, macrobiotic options, fresh juices, limited catering, take-out, $**

MIDDLETOWN

Canal Street Kosher Cafe

5 Canal Street, Middletown, NY 10940   (914) 344-1230
Kosher. This cafe uses tofu cream cheese on breakfast items and offers many vegetarian dishes such as eggplant, vegetarian liver, pasta salads, and falafel. **Full service, catering, take-out, $–$$**

MONTAUK

Naturally Good Foods & Cafe

S. Essex St., Montauk, NY 11954   (516) 668-9030
Natural-foods-store cafe. Breakfast, lunch, and dinner are available at this cafe where you'll also find a deli case, take-out, fresh baked goods daily, fruit smoothies, and a natural foods store. **Open daily. Limited service, vegan/macrobiotic options, fresh juices, take-out, AMX, $**

NEW PALTZ

• Wildflower Cafe

18 Church St., New Paltz, NY 12561   (914) 255-0020
Vegetarian. Enjoy a nice inside/outside atmosphere with occasional live classical guitar music while sampling a wide variety of dishes and specials. **Call for hours. Closed Wednesday. Full service, wine/beer/alcohol, take-out, no credit cards, $$**

NEW YORK CITY

New York City actually consists of the five boroughs of Manhattan, Queens, Brooklyn, Bronx, and Staten Island. Most tourists tend to go to Manhattan, which is generally referred to as New York City. There are many, many restaurants in Manhattan. If you visit New York, it is easiest to explore the large variety of restaurants in Manhattan rather than go off to other areas. You actually can have a fun walk across the Brooklyn Bridge to Brooklyn, and with a tour guide map find Brooklyn Heights where there are numerous natural foods restaurants. You can also travel to other boroughs–except Staten Island–relatively easily by subway. If you choose to visit other places using mass transit, we would recommend that you start with Queens and Brooklyn. (Though part of New York City politically and via mass transit, these boroughs are geographically on Long Island.)

If you have a car, you can visit restaurants on Long Island. This can end up being a one- to three-hour drive, depending on traffic and how far out on Long Island you are going. If you are willing to make the trip, see entries under Amityville, Cedarhurst, Garden City, Great Neck, Huntington, Locust Valley, Montauk, Oceanside, Sag Harbor, Seaford, West Hempstead, and Woodmere.

Some New Jersey cities are also within the vicinity of Manhattan. See entries under Colonia, East Rutherford, Hoboken, Montclair, and Newark. Hoboken and Newark can be reached by "PATH" trains from Manhattan. Buses also go from Manhattan to New Jersey cities.

For detailed listings of restaurants in New York City or the surrounding areas, refer to the individual boroughs or the areas listed above.

OCEANSIDE

Prima Pasta
3450 Long Beach Rd, Oceanside, NY 11572   **(516) 536-7660**
Pasta restaurant. This small, cozy pasta restaurant features nineteen entrees, at least six are vegan. Calories, protein, and fat content are listed for Pasta Delites. **Full service, take-out, $$**

OLIREREA

Mountain Gate Indian Restaurant
212 Mc Kinky Hollow Road, Olirerea, NY 12410   **(914) 254-6000**
Ethnic/Indian. Mountain Gate offers a vegetarian buffet and features outdoor dining and hiking trails. **Open daily for lunch and dinner. Full service, wine/ beer/alcohol, take-out, VISA/MC/AMX/DISC/DC, $$**

ONEONTA

The Autumn Cafe
244 Main St., Oneonta, NY 13820   **(607) 432-6845**
Natural foods. This American bistro offers daily specials and uses whole foods. All items are prepared on the premises. **Open daily Tuesday through Saturday from 11 A.M. to 9 P.M.; Sunday brunch, 11 A.M. to 3 P.M. Full service, wine/beer, catering, take-out, VISA/MC/AMX, $—lunch $$—dinner**

QUEENS

(For more restaurant listings in the surrounding areas, see New York City.)

• Annam Brahma Restaurant
84-43 164 St., Jamaica Hills, NY 11432   **(718) 523-2600**
Ethnic/Indian. This completely vegetarian restaurant offers dishes such as Vegetable Kabob, Vegetarian Casserole, and samosas. **Open daily for lunch and dinner. Full service, vegan options, fresh juices, catering, take-out, $–$$**

• Bamboo Garden
41-28 Main St., Flushing, NY 11355   **(718) 463-9240**
Vegetarian/kosher/Chinese. In the Golden Shopping Mall, Bamboo Garden offers 116 choices served with brown or white rice. Food contains no MSG or dairy. **Open daily. Full service, vegan options, VISA/MC, $–$$**

Hunan Dynasty
271-01 Union Turnpike, New Hyde Park, NY 11040   **(718) 962-6868**
Ethnic/Hunan. Enjoy such vegetarian options as Moo Shu Vegetables, Eggplant with Garlic Sauce, Bean Curd with Brown Sauce. **Open daily for lunch and dinner. Full service, catering, take-out, VISA/MC/AMX, $$**

India Corner
178-19 Union Turnpike, Flushing, NY 11366   **(718) 523-9682**
Indian. This restaurant specializes in Northern Indian cuisine. **Open daily except Tuesday. Full service, catering, take-out, VISA/MC/AMX/DISC, $$**

Quantum Leap
65-64 Fresh Meadows Lane, Fresh Meadow, NY 11365   **(718) 461-1307**
Natural foods/health foods store. See description under Manhattan.

The Salad Bowl
24-20 Jackson Ave., Long Island City, NY 11101   **(718) 786-1002**
Natural foods. See The Salad Bowl listing under Manhattan.

• Smile of the Beyond
86-14 Parsons Blvd., Jamaica, NY 11432   **(718) 739-7453**
Vegetarian. Smile of the Beyond started as an ice cream parlor and now sells predominantly traditional American breakfast items plus bown rice veggie salad, mock meats, rice, and salads. **Open daily 7 A.M. to 4 P.M., closed Sundays. Counter service, fresh juices, take-out, $**

• Blessed Thistle Bakery

146 University Ave., Rochester, NY 14605 **(716) 454-1156**

Vegetarian/natural foods. This vegetarian cafe and whole-grain bakery offers many vegan options including soups, Banana Cashew French Toast without eggs or dairy, and Hummus. Organically grown foods are used whenever possible. Foods are displayed with an ingredient list to help those on various diets. **Open Monday through Saturday. Limited service, vegan options, fresh organic carrot juice, organic coffees, catering, take-out, $**

Provisions of Sag Harbor, Ltd.

Main St., P.O. Box 67, Sag Harbor, NY 11963 **(516) 725-2666**

Natural foods/health-food-store deli. In this homey atomosphere, you'll find a salad bar with organic lettuce, and such natural meals as Scrambled Tofu, Organic Vegetable Pot Pie, and Tempeh Rueben. **Open daily for breakfast, lunch, and early dinner. Full service, vegan options, organic carrot juice, fresh juices, VISA/MC/AMX, $–$$**

• Mrs. Green's Natural Market

365 Central Park Ave., Scarsdale, NY 10583 **(914) 472-9675**

Vegetarian/health food store/juice bar. **Open daily. Vegan options.**

• Earth's Harvest Natural Market

1244 Hicksville Rd., Seaford, NY 11783 **(516) 797-0700**

Vegetarian/health food store. See Earth's Harvest under Great Neck.

Oneg Pizza and Dairy Restaurant

33 Maple Ave., Spring Valley, NY 10977 **(914) 356-3560**

Pizza and dairy restaurant. Sample Whole-Wheat Pizza, Kugel, Cholent (bean and potato stew). **Cafeteria style, $**

(For more restaurant listings in the surrounding areas, see New York City.)

Dairy Palace

2210 Victory Blvd., Staten Island, NY 10314 **(718) 761-5200**

ᴥ Reviewers' choice • Vegetarian restaurant •• Vegan restaurant
$ less than $6 $$ $6–$12 $$$ more than $12
VISA/AMX/MC/DISC/DC—credit cards accepted
Non-alc.—Non-alcoholic Fresh juices—freshly squeezed

Kosher/dairy restaurant. This pizza and dairy restaurant features a Chinese menu, mock-meat dishes, and ice cream bar. **Open Sunday through Thursday for lunch and dinner, open Friday from 11 A.M. until sunset, open after sundown Saturday night until 12:30 A.M. Cafeteria style, vegan options, $$**

Taste of India Restaurant
287 New Dorp Lane, Staten Island, NY 10306   (718) 987-4700
Indian. Taste of India features Saturday and Sunday buffet with at least two vegetarian options. There are nine vegetarian specials, and coconut soup flavored with almond and pistachio is vegetarian. **Open daily. Full service, wine/beer/alcohol, take-out, VISA/MC/AMX, $$**

SUFFERN

Natura Whole Food Market
41 Lafayette Ave., Rte 59, Suffern, NY 10901
(five miles west of Tappan Zee Bridge)   (914) 357-9200
Health food store/juice bar. Fresh organic wheat grass juice is made to order, and the baked goods are homemade. **Open Monday through Saturday morning and afternoon. Counter service, fresh juices, VISA/MC, $**

SYRACUSE

• Cafe Margaux
317 W. Fayette St., Syracuse, NY 13212   (315) 472-5498
Vegetarian/macrobiotic. Home-baked organic breads including a wheat-free spelt bread are featured in this old-style natural foods restaurant. There is entertainment after 9:30 P.M. on weekends and Tuesdays. It's worth visiting for the wide selection of good natural foods including tofu, tempeh, and seitan dishes, and vegan frozen desserts. **Open daily until 10 P.M. Full service, many vegan/macrobiotic options, fresh juices, wine/beer/alcohol, catering, take-out, VISA/MC, $$**

King David Restaurant
129 Marshall St., Syracuse, NY 13210   (315) 471-5000
Middle Eastern. This Middle Eastern style restaurant is in the heart of the Syracuse University area. **Open daily for lunch and dinner, closed one day a week. Full service, wine/beer, VISA/MC/AMX, $$**

TRUMANSBURG

• The Network Cafe
49 E. Main St., P.O. Box 227, Trumansburg, NY 14886   (607) 387-5588
Vegetarian. Enjoy a serene atmosphere and a unique variety of tofu, tempeh, and bean dishes. The cafe features Zelmos' Spinach Cheese Roll, and there's live folk, blues, and jazz on weekend nights. **Open Monday through Saturday for lunch and dinner, Sunday for brunch. Full service, vegan options, fresh juices, wine/beer, take-out, $$**

UTICA

The Phoenician Restaurant
623 French, Utica, NY 13413   (315) 733-2709

Middle Eastern. Vegetarian platters include Falafel, Fattoush, Tabouleh, and other Middle Eastern items. **Closed Sundays. Full service, wine/beer, VISA/MC, take-out, $**

- ## West St. Whole Foods, Ltd.
7 West St., Warwick, NY 10990 (914) 986-3669
Vegetarian/health-food-store deli. You'll find sandwiches and fresh baked goods every day, and fresh bread on Saturday. **Open Monday through Saturday. Limited service, fresh juices, take-out, $**

Taj Mahal Restaurant
221 Hempstead Turnpike, W. Hempstead, NY 11552 (516) 565-4607
Ethnic. **Open daily for dinner, lunch Monday through Saturday. Full service, wine/beer/alcohol, VISA/MC/AMX, $$**

Pizza Plant
8020 Transit Rd., Williamsville, NY 14221 (716) 632-0800
Pizza/ethnic. Vegetarian items on the menu are indicated by a carrot. Choices include Nachos, Chili, Bread Bowl Stew, and a wide variety of pizzas. Whole-wheat dough and sesame, spinach, or garlic doughs are available. **Open daily. Full service, wine/beer, take-out, VISA/MC/AMX/DISC, $$**

Earth's Harvest
1002 Broadway, Woodmere, NY 11598 (516) 295-1505
Health-food-store counter. See entry under Great Neck.

NORTH CAROLINA

Pyewacket Restaurant 🐾
The Courtyard, 431 W. Franklin St.
Chapel Hill, NC 27516 (919) 929-0297
Natural foods. Vegetarian options are available. **Open daily. Full service, fresh juices, wine/beer/alcohol, take-out, VISA/MC/AMX/DC, $$**

Berrybrook Farm
1257 East Blvd., Charlotte, NC 28203 (704) 334-6528

Natural foods take-out. Homemade soups, salads, sandwiches, and spreads are made fresh daily at this natural food grocery and deli. The menu at Berrybrook changes monthly and is primarily vegetarian. There's a tasting fair once a month. **Closed Sundays. Take-out only, vegan options, fresh juices, VISA/MC, $**

Cafe Flavors
540-B Brandywine Rd., Charlotte, NC 28205   **(704) 527-6392**
Ethnic. Vegetarian items or items that can be made vegetarian are indicated on the menu. Foods from around the world include Spuds on a Stick, Broccoli Cheese Strata, Griddled Cajun Polenta, Singapore Noodle Cakes, Navajo Taco Salad, and others. **Open Monday through Friday for lunch, dinner daily. Full service, fresh juices, wine/beer/alcohol, catering, take-out, VISA/MC/AMX, $$**

Cafe Verde at Talley's Green Grocery
1408-C East Blvd., Charlotte, NC 28203   **(704) 334-9200**
Natural foods. Ethnic, low-fat vegetarian, vegan, and non-vegetarian dishes are offered in addition to daily soups, a wonderful salad bar, sandwiches, and desserts made without refined sugars. Enjoy the best selection of beers in town. **Open daily. Cafeteria style, vegan options, fresh juices, wine/beer/alcohol, take-out, VISA/MC, $**

Casablanca Restaurant
212 E. Independence Blvd., Charlotte, NC 28204   **(704) 375-6893**
Middle Eastern. Falafel, Spinach Filo, Hummus, Baba Ghanouj, Tabouleh, and salads make up the vegetarian options at this Middle Eastern restaurant. **Open daily for lunch and dinner. Full service, vegan options, fresh juices, take-out, VISA/MC/DISC, $$**

Chicken Delight
4113 Monroe Rd., Charlotte, NC 28205   **(704) 333-1818**
Indian. Extensive menu of Indian and American foods includes over thirty-four vegetarian options ranging from dumplings and curry dishes to vegetarian chili and stir-fry. Incredibly inexpensive. **Closed Sunday. Full service, vegan options, fresh juices, take-out, $**

Dragon Inn Chinese Restaurant
204A W. Woodlawn Rd., Charlotte, NC 28217   **(704) 503-3900**
Chinese. Dragon Inn features Cantonese-, Hunan-, and Szechuan-style vegetarian options. MSG is omitted upon request. **Open daily. Full service, vegan options, wine/beer, take-out, VISA/MC/AMX/DISC, $$**

House of Chinese Gourmet
5608 Independence Blvd., Charlotte, NC 28212   **(704) 563-8989**
Chinese. Here's a deliciously inviting menu with over twenty vegetarian entrees, plus soups and appetizers. Many tofu dishes are available, and MSG is omitted upon request. **Open daily. Full service, vegan options, wine/beer/alcohol, take-out, VISA/MC/AMX, $$**

India Palace
6140 E. Independence Blvd., Charlotte, NC 28212   **(704) 568-7176**

Indian. Authentic Indian cuisine is offered, and great care is taken in the preparation and use of spices. Nine vegetable entrees are on the menu. **Open daily for dinner. Full service, vegan options, take-out, VISA/MC/AMX, $$**

Pewter Rose
1820 South Blvd. #109, Charlotte, NC 28203   **(704) 332-8149**
Seasonal. Fresh, electic cuisine is served in an airy but cozy atmosphere. There are limited vegetarian options, primarily appetizers. **Open daily for lunch and dinner. Full service, wine/beer/alcohol, take-out, VISA/MC/AMX, $$**

Thai Cuisine Restaurant
4800 Central Ave., Charlotte, NC 2820   **(704) 532-7511**
Thai. Tofu is substituted for the meat in any dish to create delicious vegetarian options. There are some vegetarian appetizers, salads, and soup. No MSG or salt is used in the preparation of food. **Open daily. Full service, vegan options, wine/beer/alcohol, take-out, VISA/MC/AMX, $$**

DURHAM

Anotherthyme
109 N. Gregson St., Durham, NC 27701   **(919) 682-5225**
Seasonal. Enjoy gourmet seasonal cuisine with pasta, vegetarian, and non-vegetarian dishes. No red meat is served. **Open daily. Full service, fresh juices, wine/beer/alcohol, take-out, VISA/MC/AMX, $$–$$$**

Seventh Street Restaurant
1104 Broad St., Durham, NC 27705   **(919) 286-1019**
Ethnic. Here's new American cuisine with an emphasis on healthful, vegetarian entrees. **Open daily for lunch and dinner. Full service, wine/beer/alcohol, take-out, VISA/MC/AMX, $$**

GREENSBORO

Sunset Cafe
4608 W. Market St., Greensboro, NC 27407   **(919) 855-0349**
Natural foods. A blackboard menu changes daily. At least four of the sixteen entrees are vegetarian and some are vegan. Examples include Russian Cheese Dumplings, Vegetarian Cheese Nut Loaf, Rice and Cheese Croquettes, Grilled Vegetable Kabobs, Vegetarian Lasagna, Spinach Manicotti, and more. **Open daily. Full service, vegan options, wine/beer/alcohol, take-out, VISA/MC, $$**

HILLSBOROUGH

The Regulator Cafe
108 S. Churton St., Hillsborough, NC 27278   **(919) 732-5600**

🐾 Reviewers' choice   ● Vegetarian restaurant   ●● Vegan restaurant
$ less than $6 $$ $6–$12 $$$ more than $12
VISA/AMX/MC/DISC/DC—credit cards accepted
Non-alc.–Non-alcoholic   Fresh juices—freshly squeezed

New American. A quaint, historical setting with romantic overtones of candlelight and light music sets the atmosphere for sampling Regulator's combination of vegetarian and other health-conscious foods. Pasta, tempeh dishes, salads, and appetizers make up the vegetarian selection. **Open daily. Full service, vegan options, wine/beer, take-out, VISA/MC/DISC, $$**

RALEIGH

Bombay Grille
6026 Falls of Neuse Rd., Raleigh, NC 27609   **(919) 872-3148**
Indian. Sample eleven vegetarian specialties plus soup, appetizers, and bread. **Open daily for lunch and dinner. Full service, vegan options, wine/beer/alcohol, take-out, VISA/MC/AMX/DISC, $–$$**

Irregardless Cafe
901 W. Morgan St., Raleigh, NC 27603   **(919) 833-8898**
Natural foods. A new menu each night features vegetarian, vegan, and non-vegetarian entrees. Fresh baked breads, cookies, and desserts are also available in this totally non-smoking environment. **Open daily, Sunday brunch. Full service, vegan options, espresso/cappuccino, wine/beer/alcohol, take-out, VISA/MC/AMX, $–$$**

WINSTON-SALEM

Rainbow News & Cafe
712 Brookstown Ave., Winston-Salem, NC 27101   **(919) 723-0858**
Cafe. This European-style cafe offers homemade soups, salads, sandwiches, and desserts. **Open for three meals daily. Full service, wine/beer, VISA/MC, $$**

The Rose and Thistle
107 Lockland Ave., Winston-Salem, NC 27103   **(919) 725-6444**
American. The Rose and Thistle features such vegetarian entrees as pizza, Vegetable Medley, eggplant subs, and five salads. **Open daily, dinner served only on Saturday. Full service, fresh juices, non-alc. beer, beer/wine, take-out, $–$$**

NORTH DAKOTA

BISMARCK

Green Earth Cafe
208 E. Broadway, Bismarck, ND 58501   **(701) 223-8646**
Natural foods. Green Earth features daily specials with vegetarian and ethnic options. Co-located with One World Coffeehouse. **Open for coffee and lunch Monday through Saturday, dinner Friday through Saturday. Limited service, catering, take-out, $**

OHIO

Mustard Seed Market Cafe
3885 W. Market Street, Akron, OH 44333 **(216) 666-7333**
Natural foods/macrobiotic. Mustard Seed Market is one of the largest natural foods stores in the Midwest. The restaurant located in the store offers great natural foods dishes. There is a strong emphasis on vegetarian dishes including macrobiotic and vegan meals. Some seafood and poultry are also served. The Mustard Seed Market emphasizes organic foods and has the best produce department in town. **Open daily for lunch, Tuesday through Saturday for dinner. Full service, vegan options, fresh juice, beer/wine to go only, catering, take-out, VISA/MC, $$**

Alpha Restaurant
204 W. McMillan St., Cincinnati, OH 45219 **(513) 381-6559**
American. This restaurant features a relaxed and friendly atmosphere. Vegetarian selections are offered for breakfast, lunch, and dinner, and Alpha is willing to accommodate special dietary needs. **Open daily. Full service, vegetarian options, fresh juice, beer/wine/alcohol, take-out, VISA/MC/AMX/DISC, $$**

Arnold's Bar & Grill
210 E. 8th St., Cincinnati, OH 45202 **(513) 421-6234**
American tavern. Arnold's is a unique turn-of-the-century tavern with good food, fresh ingredients, and a strong selection of vegetarian specials and soups. **Open Monday through Friday for lunch and dinner. Full service, vegetarian options, fresh juice, beer/wine/alcohol, take-out, $$**

Bacchus Restaurant
1401 Elm St., Cincinnati, OH 45210 **(513) 421-8314**
American. Bacchus is an intimate dining spot with old-world charm and peaceful surroundings. Enjoy eclectic gourmet American cuisine, including some vegetarian offerings. **Open Thursday and Friday for lunch, Wednesday through Sunday for dinner. Full service, vegetarian options, catering, take-out, VISA/MC/AMX, $$$**

Cheng-I Cuisine
203 W. McMillan St., Cincinnati, OH 45219 **(513) 723-1999**
Chinese. Cheng-I is a traditional Chinese restaurant with an extensive vegetarian menu. The vegetarian spring rolls were voted best vegetarian appetizer by *Cincinnati Magazine*. **Open Monday through Saturday for lunch and dinner, Sunday for dinner. Full service, vegetarian options, beer/wine/alcohol, catering, take-out, VISA/MC/AMX/DISC/DC, $$**

Chin Dynasty
4609 Vine St., Cincinnati, OH 45217 **(513) 641-2888**
Traditional Chinese. A vegetarian menu is available, with extra vegetarian specials

offered Tuesday through Thursday. Vegetarian Seitan Spring Rolls are also offered. **Full service, vegetarian options, $$**

Floyd's of Cincinnati, Inc.
129 Calhoun St., Cincinnati, OH 45219　　　　　　　　**(513) 221-2434**
Middle Eastern. Various vegetarian Middle Eastern dishes including Tabouleh, Baba Ghanouj, Hummus, Falafel Sandwich, and salads are offered. **Open daily for lunch and dinner but closed Sunday. Vegan options, take-out, $**

Jerusalem Cafe
235 W. McMillan St., Cincinnati, OH 45219　　　　　　**(513) 241-2323**
Ethnic. Enjoy an authentic Middle Eastern dining experience reflective of Mediterranean traditions and culture. All dishes are available without meat, and there is an extensive vegetarian menu. **Open daily for lunch and dinner. Full service, vegan options, BYOB, catering, take-out, VISA/MC, $$**

Mayura Restaurant
3201 Jefferson Ave., Cincinnati, OH 45220　　　　　　**(513) 221-7125**
East Indian. This Indian restaurant with its attached bar offers many vegetarian dishes. **Open for lunch and dinner Tuesday through Saturday. Full service, beer/wine/alcohol, catering, take-out, VISA/MC/AMX/DISC, $$**

Myra's Dionysus
121 Calhoun St., Cincinnati, OH 45219　　　　　　　　**(513) 961-1578**
International. An extensive international menu includes Middle Eastern, Chinese, Greek, Brazilian, Mexican, Turkish, Indian, and Italian dishes and features an incredible variety of excellent soups and many vegan selections. Outdoor seating is available. **Open daily for lunch and dinner. Full service, vegan options, wine/ beer, catering, take-out, no credit cards accepted, $**

•• Ulysses Whole World Foods
350 Ludlow Ave., Cincinnati, OH 45220　　　　　　　　**(513) 281-5050**
Vegan/international. Ulysses offers the finest in vegetarian cuisine, including an array of fresh, homemade soups, sandwiches, salads, chili, entrees, and desserts. All food is prepared without milk, butter, cheese, eggs, meat, chicken, or fish. **Open Tuesday through Saturday for lunch and dinner. Full service, vegan options, limited catering, take-out, VISA/MC, $-$$**

CLEVELAND

(For more restaurant listings in the surrounding areas, see Cleveland Heights.)

Ali Baba Restaurant
12021 Lorain Rd., Cleveland, OH 44111　　　　　　　　**(216) 251-2040**
Middle Eastern. Ali Baba has delicious Middle Eastern specialities and a vegetarian section on the menu. The recipes used are those of the owner's grandmother. Falafel, Hummus, and Baba Ghanouj are outstanding. Brown rice, whole-wheat pita, and all other foods are prepared without MSG, artificial flavorings, or preservatives. The hosts are friendly, cheerful, and accommodating. **Open Tues-**

day through Friday for lunch and dinner, dinner only on Saturday. **Full service, catering, take-out, $$**

Parma Pierogies
5580 Ridge Rd., Cleveland, OH 44129 (216) 888-1200
Polish/ethnic. This no-smoking restaurant offers fifteen varieties of vegetarian pierogies. The dough has no preservatives. **Limited service. Open daily, vegan options, non-alc. beer, take-out, $**

CLEVELAND HEIGHTS

Taj Mahal Restaurant
1763 Coventry Rd. at Mayfield Road
Cleveland Heights, OH 44118 (216) 321-0511
Indian. Savor very good vegetarian curry selections. Meals include pure vegetarian lentil/pea soup and basmati rice pilaf with raisins and nuts. Many vegetarian appetizers and main entrees are available. **Open daily for dinner, Sunday brunch. Full service, vegan options, beer/wine/alcohol, catering, take-out, VISA/MC/ AMX, $$**

Tommy's
1820 Coventry Rd., Cleveland Heights, OH 44118 (216) 321-7757
Greek. Cleveland Heights natives have told us this is the place to go. Taped music is played, and Falafel, Hummus, Spinach Pies, Tempeh Burgers, and fruit freezes are offered. **Open daily. Full service and counter service, vegan options, fresh juices, take-out, $$**

Yaakov's Kosher Restaurant
13969 Cedar Rd., Cleveland Heights, OH 44118 (216) 932-8848
Kosher. Excellent pizza, Falafel, and Eggplant Parmesan. **Cafeteria style, vegan options, take-out, $**

CLIFTON

(For more restaurant listings in the surrounding areas, see Dayton.)

• Clifton Natural Foods Deli & Juice Bar
207 W. McMillan St., Clifton, OH 45316 (513) 651-5288
Vegetarian/natural foods. Clifton has an extensive menu of vegetarian salads, entrees, sandwiches, soups, drinks, and desserts. **Open daily. Deli service, vegan options, fresh juice, take-out, $**

COLUMBUS

Estrada's Restaurant
240 King Ave., Columbus, OH 43201 (614) 294-0808
Mexican. Very inexpensive, fresh, and good Mexican food—the best Mexican food in town—is featured. There are many vegetarian and a few vegan options. Lard is not used in the preparation of the food. **Open Monday through Saturday for lunch and dinner. Full service, vegan options, catering, take-out, DISC, $**

• King Avenue Coffeehouse
247 King Ave., Columbus, OH 43201   **(614) 294-8287**
Vegetarian/ethnic. The coffeehouse features daily menu additions, vegan options, and organic ingredients whenever possible. A non-smoking environment and art exhibits are also featured. Made-to-order brunch is available on Sundays. **Open Tuesday through Sunday for lunch and dinner. Full service, vegan options, fresh juice, take-out, VISA/MC/AMX/DISC, $–$$**

Nong's Hunan Express
1634 Northwest Blvd., Columbus, OH 43212   **(614) 486-6630**
Thai/Oriental. Nong's offers a huge variety of vegetarian dishes, including soups and egg rolls. The atmosphere is casual. **Full service, vegetarian options, take-out, $$**

Rigsby's Cuisine Volatile
698 North High St., Columbus, OH 43215   **(614) 461-7888**
American. This formal restaurant offers several vegetarian and a few vegan selections. **Full service, vegan options, $$**

• Whole World Bakery
3269 N. High St., Columbus, OH 43202   **(614) 268-5751**
Vegetarian/American. Whole World offers baked goods made without sugar, wholewheat pizza, tofu sloppy Joes, veggie burgers, and great vegetarian soups. A wide variety of entrees is offered. **Closed Monday. Full service, vegan options, BYOB, catering, take-out, $–$$**

DAYTON

(For restaurant listings in the surrounding areas, see Clifton, Fairborn, Kettering, and Yellow Springs.)

FAIRBORN

Euro Bistro
1328 Kauffman Ave., Fairborn, OH 45324   **(513) 878-1989**
Natural foods/bistro. This smoke-free bistro offers freshly baked breads, specialty sandwiches, homemade salads, soups and quiche, incredible cookies and cheesecakes. Outdoor seating available. **Closed Sunday. Limited service, beer, catering, take-out, $**

KENT

The Zephyr
106 W. Main, Kent, OH 44240   **(216) 678-4848**

🕏 Reviewers' choice   • Vegetarian restaurant   •• Vegan restaurant
$ less than $6 $$ $6–$12 $$$ more than $12
VISA/AMX/MC/DISC/DC—credit cards accepted
Non-alc.—Non-alcoholic   Fresh juices—freshly squeezed

Natural foods. This restaurant is vegetarian with the exception of some fish dishes. The menu features Middle Eastern appetizers, salads, veggie stir fry, Potato Pancakes, Veggie Burger, Falafel, plus much more. Desserts are baked fresh daily. **Open Tuesday through Sunday for breakfast, lunch, and dinner. Full service, catering, take-out, $**

KETTERING

• Kettering Medical Center Cafeteria
3533 Southern Blvd., Kettering, OH 45429   **(513) 296-7262**
Vegetarian. The menu has a twenty-eight-day cycle. Most items have dairy and eggs. **Open daily for three meals. Cafeteria style.**

TOLEDO

Jalmers Health Foods
1488 Sylvania Ave., Toledo, OH 43612   **(419) 476-7918**

Health-food-store deli/juice bar. **Open Monday through Saturday. Limited service/deli, fresh juice, take-out, VISA/MC, $**

YELLOW SPRINGS

Carol's Kitchen
101 Corry St., Yellow Springs, OH 45387   **(513) 767-7959**
American. This smoke-free establishment offers a sandwich, soup, and fruit bar. Other options include fresh breads, croissants, muffins, and pastries, and there are many vegetarian selections. **Cafeteria service, $$**

Ha Ha Pizza
108 Xenia Ave., Yellow Springs, OH 45387   **(513) 767-1261**
Pizza. Ha Ha features homemade white or whole-wheat dough, sauce, and fresh vegetables. Several meat alternatives are offered. Soy cheese is available for the pizzas. **Lunch and dinner daily, dinner only on Sunday. Full service, catering, take-out, $**

• Organic Grocery
225 Xenia Ave., Yellow Springs, OH 45387   **(513) 767-7215**
Vegetarian deli. This smoke-free deli offers vegetarian chili, sandwiches, thick fruit drinks, Hummus, and more. **Full counter, vegan options, fresh juice, $**

Sunrise Cafe
259 Xenia Ave., Yellow Springs, OH 45387   **(513) 767-1065 or -7211**
Natural/ethnic foods. This charming restored 1940's diner uses fresh ingredients, and everything is made from scratch. The smoke-free diner continues to expand its vegetarian offerings. **Open daily, but no dinner served on Sunday. Full service, vegan options, catering, take-out, VISA/MC, $**

Winds Cafe And Bakery
215 Xenia Ave., Yellow Springs, OH 45387   **(513) 767-1144**
Natural foods. Specialities include fresh baked breads and pastries, scrambled tofu,

and a constantly changing menu that always includes several vegetarian selections. **Open Monday through Saturday for lunch and dinner, brunch on Sunday. Full service, vegan options, fresh juice, beer/wine/alcohol, take-out, VISA/MC/ AMX/DISC, $$–$$$**

OKLAHOMA

NORMAN

The Earth Natural Foods & Deli
309 S. Flood St., Norman, OK 73069   **(405) 364-3551**
Natural foods store/deli. This deli offers sandwiches, salads, and drinks to go. Seating is not available. **Open daily. Deli/counter service only, vegetarian options, fresh juice, catering, take-out, VISA/MC/AMX, $**

Love Light Restaurant
529 Buchanan St., Norman, OK 73069   **(405) 364-2073**
American/ethnic. In a bright airy atmosphere with patio dining, you'll find a "sandwich factory" where you choose your own ingredients for sandwiches and salads. Homemade whole-grain bread and bakery items are also offered. Love Light offers the best vegetarian selection in Norman. **Open daily. Counter service, vegan options, fresh juice, beer, take-out, VISA/MC, $**

OKLAHOMA CITY

The Earth Natural Foods & Deli
1101 NW 49th St., Oklahoma City, OK 73118   **(405) 840-0502**
Natural foods. This natural foods restaurant and store offers a menu with many vegetarian selections. Limited service is available only in the evenings. **Open daily. Limited deli service, fresh juice, catering, take-out, VISA/MC/AMX, $**

OREGON

ASHLAND

Ashland Bakery & Cafe
38 E. Main St., Ashland, OR 97520   **(503) 482-9463**
Cafe/bakery. This restaurant offers an extensive vegetarian menu, including vegetarian chili and soups, and fresh baked goods. **Open daily. Full service, wine/ beer, take-out, VISA/MC, $–$$**

Geppetto's
345 E. Main St., Ashland, OR 97520   **(503) 482-1138**
Italian. Enjoy a wide selection of vegetarian meals, including great Eggplant

Burgers. **Open daily. Full service, vegetarian options, fresh juice, beer/wine/alcohol, take-out, VISA/MC, $–$$$**

House Of Thai Cuisine
1667 Siskiyou Blvd., Ashland, OR 97520 **(503) 488-2583**
Thai. This family-owned-and-operated restaurant offers a separate vegetarian menu. It was voted best Oriental restaurant in Ashland in 1992. **Open for lunch Monday through Saturday, open daily for dinner. Full service, beer/wine, catering, take-out, VISA/MC, $$**

• North Light Vegetarian Restaurant
120 E. Main St., Ashland, OR 97520 **(503) 482-9463**
Vegetarian. North Light is a cooperatively managed restaurant with a great regular menu and daily specials. Organic ingredients are used whenever possible. **Open daily. Full service with buffet, vegan options, fresh juice, beer/wine/alcohol, catering, take-out, VISA/MC, $$**

ASTORIA

The Columbia Cafe
1114 Marine Dr., Astoria, OR 97103 **(503) 325-2233**
Natural foods. Here you'll find lots of delicious vegetarian and vegan options including rice and veggie dishes, bean burritos, homemade pasta, and other international options. The owner is the cook and is very hospitable. Salsas are made out of all types of fruits and vegetables. Crêpes are a speciality. **Open daily. Full service, vegan options, fresh juices, non-alc. beer, wine/beer, $$**

BEAVERTON

McMenamins Pub
2927 SW Cedar Hills Blvd., Beaverton, OR 97005 **(503) 641-0151**
Tavern. Enjoy a pub atmosphere featuring an extensive vegetarian menu. **Open daily for lunch and dinner. Full service, vegetarian options, beer/wine, catering, take-out, VISA/MC, $**

BEND

Cafe Sante
718 NW Franklin St., Bend, OR 97701 **(503) 383-3530**
American. This cafe-style restaurant has an almost exclusively vegetarian menu and is a local favorite. Organic produce is used whenever possible. **Open daily for breakfast and lunch. Full service, vegan options, fresh juice, take-out, $**

CORVALLIS

The Beanery
500 SW 2nd St., Corvallis, OR 97333 **(503) 753-7442**

2541 NW Monroe St., Corvallis, OR 97330 **(503) 757-0828**
Coffeehouse. The Beanery features Vegetarian Lasagna, burritos, soups, salads, espresso, cappuccino, and desserts. **Open late daily. Counter service, espresso/cappuccino, take-out, VISA/MC/DISC, $$**

Bob's Burger Express
360 NW 5th, Corvallis, OR 97330   **(503) 754-1583**
Fast food. A mainstream, fast food joint, Bob's also sells an inexpensive vegetarian burger, yogurt, and soups. **Open daily. Counter service, take-out, $**

China Blue
2307 NW 9th St., Corvallis, OR 97330   **(503) 757-8088**
Chinese. China Blue has a large vegetarian selection including sweet and sour tofu and other tofu dishes. **Full service, vegan options, take-out, $–$$**

• Nearly Normal's Gonzo Cuisine
109 NW 15 St., Corvallis, OR 97330   **(503) 753-0791**
Vegetarian. This very local, finely crafted restaurant has an extensive and diverse vegetarian menu. Great salads with seasoned tofu and homemade dressings and homemade vegan desserts are featured. There are farm-fresh specials from the family farm in the summertime. Run by OSU college students, Nearly Normal's is closed during Christmas break. All visitors should have a Nearly Normal's experience while in the area! **Open Monday through Saturday, Sunday brunch in the spring and summer. Limited service, vegan options, fresh juice, beer/wine/ alcohol, catering, take-out, $–$$**

EUGENE

(For more restaurant listings in the surrounding areas, see Springfield.)

Anitolio's
992 Willamette, Eugene, OR 97401   **(503) 343-9661**
Natural foods/Mediterranean. This restaurant offers a wide variety of Mediterranean vegetarian dishes including an eggplant and chickpea stew, several curries, soups, and salads. **Open Monday through Saturday for lunch and dinner; Sunday, dinner only. Full service, non-alc. beer, wine/beer, take-out, VISA/MC, $$**

The Beanery
152 W. 5th St., Eugene, OR 97401   **(503) 342-3378**

2465 Hilyard St., Eugene, OR 97405   **(503) 344-0221**
Coffeehouse. See entry under Corvallis, OR.

Bob's Burger Express
620 West 6th St., Eugene, OR 97402   **(503) 342-3121**

296 Coburg Road, Eugene, OR 97401   **(503) 485-4332**

1990 West 11th St., Eugene, OR 97405   **(503) 686-9313**
Fast food. See listing under Corvallis, OR.

Casablanca
Fifth St. Market, Eugene, OR 97401   **(503) 342-3885**
Middle Eastern. Enjoy a good selection of vegetarian foods. **Cafeteria style, vegan options, take-out, $**

• Fast-N-Healthy
1030 River Rd., Eugene, OR 97404   **(503) 689-8324**
Vegetarian. Fast-N-Healthy believes in meatless food for fitness, energy, and health. No sugar or salt is used in the cooking. Wheat- and dairy-free foods are also available. **Open Monday through Saturday for three meals. Full or limited service, vegan option, fresh juice, catering, take-out, $**

The Glenwood Restaurants
1346 Alder St., Eugene, OR 97401   **(503) 343-8303**

2588 Willamette St., Eugene, OR 97405   **(503) 687-8201**
American/Californian. Enjoy a wide variety of vegetarian options—quiche, Tofu Burrito, Spicy Tofu Stir-Fry, Cabbage Rolls, Fried Rice Mandarin, Kima, and others. **Alder Street location open 24 hours daily; Willamette open daily 6:30 A.M. to 9 P.M. Vegan options, wine/beer, take-out, VISA/MC/AMX/DISC, $**

• Govinda's Vegetarian Buffet
270 W. 8th Street, Eugene, OR 97401   **(503) 686-3531**
Vegetarian/natural foods. Self-serve buffet offers all-you-can-eat salad bar and ten hot entrees including such items as curried vegetables, lasagna, enchiladas, and tofu dishes. Other options are also available. **Open Monday through Friday for lunch and dinner. Limited buffet-style service, vegan options, take-out, $–$$**

Kestral Cafe
454 Willamette, Eugene, OR 97401   **(503) 344-0943**
American/international. The Kestral Cafe cooks vegetarian and meat dishes in separate pots and serves Mexican foods, homemade soups, and salads. The beans have no lard. **Open Tuesday through Saturday for three meals. Closed for dinner Sunday through Monday. Full service, vegan options, fresh juice, take-out, $$**

Keystone Cafe
395 W. 5th Ave., Eugene, OR 97401   **(503) 342-2075**
American. Breakfast is served all day. Plate-sized pancakes are a specialty, including oatmeal/sesame, whole-wheat, corn/rice, and buckwheat barley varieties. **Open daily 7 A.M. to 3 P.M. Full service, vegan options, fresh juice, very limited catering, take-out, $**

Mekala's Thai Restaurant
296 E. 5th Ave., Eugene, OR 97401   **(503) 342-4872**
Thai/ethnic. Experience outstanding Thai vegetarian dishes containing no MSG. Only canola oil is used. Located in the Fifth Street Public Market, the restaurant has a very nice atmosphere. **Open daily for lunch and dinner. Full service, vegan options, fresh juice, beer/wine, catering, take-out, VISA/MC, $–$$**

Zahara
Station Square, Eugene, OR 97401   **(503) 342-5159**
Middle Eastern. Zahara offers an outstanding vegetarian selection. **Vegan options, take-out, $$**

GRANTS PASS

Sunshine Natural Food Cafe
128 SW H St., Grants Pass, OR 97526   **(503) 474-5044**
Natural foods. Enjoy Sunshine's organic salad bar, and a buffet Tuesday thru Friday. **Closed Sunday. Full service and buffet, vegan options, fresh juice, beer/wine, take-out, $**

JUNCTION CITY

Bob's Burger Express
890 Ivy St., Junction City, OR 97448   **(503) 998-3264**
Fast food. See listing under Corvallis.

PORTLAND

(For more restaurant listings in the surrounding areas, see Beaverton and Troutdale.)

• The Daily Grind Restaurant
4026 SE Hawthorne Blvd., Portland, OR 97214   **(503) 233-5521**
Vegetarian. This eatery offers a steam table that is dairy- and egg-free with soup, three entrees, vegetables, mashed potatoes, and gravy. There's also a large salad bar. Menu items include vegetarian sandwiches and burgers, and other items. **Open Monday through Thursday for lunch and early dinner. Lunch only on Friday. Limited service/cafeteria, vegan options, fresh juice, take-out, VISA/MC, $**

• Garden Cafe
Portland Adventist Medical Center
10123 SE Market St., Portland, OR 97216   **(503) 251-6125**
Vegetarian/natural foods. This is a full-service cafeteria offering vegetarian entrees, salad bar, fresh fruit bar, and a fast-food grill featuring fifteen vegetarian sandwiches. Over 1000 meals are served daily. Vegetarian meals have been served here for over 100 years. Enjoy a wide variety of foods in a comfortable dining area with indoor and outdoor seating just six blocks off Interstate 205. **Closed Saturday and Sunday. Cafeteria-style service, vegan options, catering, take-out, $**

• Happy Harvest Grocers
2348 SE Ankeny, Portland, OR 97214   **(503) 235-5358**
Vegetarian. This restaurant features Curried Tofu and Braised Tempeh, and serves full vegetarian and vegan breakfasts on weekends. **Open daily. Counter service, vegan options, take-out, $**

Healthway Food Center
524 SW 5th, Portland, OR 97204   **(503) 226-2941**

Health-food-store deli. The Healthway deli features fresh juice, soups, and salads. **Open weekdays for lunch. Counter service, take-out, $**

Old Wives Tales
1300 E. Burnside, Portland, OR 97214　　　　　　　**(503) 238-0470**
Ethnic. Enjoy a soup and salad bar, soy products, rice noodles, black bean stew, Mexican dishes, an Egyptian loaf, plus much more. **Open daily for three meals. Full service, fresh juices, non-alc. beer/wine, wine/beer, take-out, VISA/MC/ DISC, $$**

Plainfield Mayur ๒ฺ
852 SW 21st St., Portland, OR 97205　　　　　　　**(503) 223-2995**
Indian. Probably one of the most elegant Indian restaurants you'll find, Plainfield Mayur is located in one of Portland's landmark homes with table settings of fine European crystal, china, and full silver service. The menu includes a vegetarian section with delicious, original entrees, appetizers, and soup. The Tandoor Show Kitchen is the only one in Oregon, and private dining rooms are available for business meetings or private gatherings. **Reservations recommended. Full service, vegan options, wine/beer/alcohol, take-out, VISA/MC/AMX/DISC, $$**

Thanh Thao Restaurant
4005 SE Hawthorne, Portland, OR 97214　　　　　　　**(503) 238-6232**
Ethnic. Thanh Thao has recently expanded its vegetarian options and now offers a wide selection of tofu, vegetable, eggplant, and mock-meat entrees. Appetizers, soup, and noodle dishes are also available. **Open for lunch and dinner every day except Tuesday. Full service, vegan options, take-out, $–$$**

REDMOND

Bob's Burger Express
433 W. Antler St., Redmond, OR 97756　　　　　　　**(503) 548-1405**
Fast food. See entry under Corvallis, OR.

SALEM

Bob's Burger Express
1415 Capitol St., NE, Salem, OR 97303　　　　　　　**(503) 363-8983**

3999 Commercial St., Southeast Salem, OR 97302　　　　　**(503) 364-5798**

5130 River Rd., North Salem, OR 97303　　　　　　　**(503) 393-1072**

890 Lancester Dr., Northeast Salem, OR 97301　　　　　**(503) 399-8383**

831 Lancaster Dr., Northeast Salem, OR 97301　　　　　**(503) 399-7710**

710 Wallace Rd., Northwest, Salem, OR 97304　　　　　**(503) 399-7933**
Fast food. See entry under Corvallis, OR.

SPRINGFIELD

Bob's Burger Express
5803 Main Street, Springfield, OR 97477　　　　　　　**(503) 747-5544**

720 South 8th St., Springfield, OR 97477   (503) 747-3421
Fast food. See listing under Corvallis, OR.

Kuraya's Thai Cuisine
1410 Mohawk Blvd., Springfield, OR 97477   (503) 746-2951
Thai/ethnic. Kuraya's is a full-service traditional Thai restaurant offering many wonderful vegetarian selections. **Open daily. Dinner only on Sunday. Full service, vegan options, beer/wine, catering, take-out, VISA/MC, $**

TROUTDALE

Multnomah Falls Lodge Restaurant
Hwy. 30 at Multnomah Falls, Troutdale, OR 97060   (503) 695-2376
American. This is a standard American restaurant that has a Garden Burger on the menu. **Open daily. Full service, non-alc. beer, wine/beer/alcohol, VISA/MC/ AMX, $$**

PENNSYLVANIA

ARDMORE

Saladalley
Suburban Square, Coulter Ave. and Saint James St.
Ardmore, PA 19003   (215) 642-0453
American. This is the main office for a chain of franchised restaurants around Philadelphia. Call for the location near you. Saladalley features an extensive salad bar with a wide variety of vegetarian salads, soups, and entrees. Every unit has non-smoking sections and easy access for the handicapped. Some units have live entertainment, happy hour specials, and displays of local artists' work. **Full service, non-alc. beer, wine/beer/alcohol, take-out, $$**

BALA CYNWYD

The Carrot Bunch
51 E. City Line Ave, Bala Cynwyd, PA 19004   (215) 664-5231
Natural foods. **Open Monday through Saturday for lunch and dinner. Full service. Fresh juices, take-out, VISA/MC, $**

EAST STROUDSBURG

Chang's Garden
Pocono Plaza, Lincoln Ave., K Mart Shopping Center
E. Stroudsburg, PA 18301   (717) 424-8655

🐾 Reviewers' choice   • Vegetarian restaurant   •• Vegan restaurant
$ less than $6 $$ $6–$12 $$$ more than $12
VISA/AMX/MC/DISC/DC—credit cards accepted
Non-alc.—Non-alcoholic   Fresh juices—freshly squeezed

Chinese. The menu's vegetable section includes tofu and vegetable dishes, an eggplant dish, and Vegetable Egg Foo Young. **Open daily. Full service, VISA/ MC/AMX/DC, $$**

HONESDALE

Nature's Grace Health Foods and Deli
947 Main St., Honesdale, PA 18431 **(717) 253-3469**
Health-food-store deli. Soft-serve frozen yogurt is available seasonally. Homemade soups, enchiladas, salads, baked goods, hoagies, and other entrees are available daily. **Open Monday through Saturday, 10 A.M. to 5 P.M. Counter service, fresh juices, take-out, $**

JENKINTOWN

Orient Jade Palace Restaurant
501-515 Old York Rd., Jenkintown, PA 19046 **(215) 886-4709**
Chinese/Vietnamese. This Chinese and Vietnamese restaurant has a larger-than-average vegetarian menu. **Open daily. Full service, alcohol, take-out, VISA/MC/ AMX/DISC, $$**

LANCASTER

Akbar Indian Restaurant
2080 Bennet Ave., Hechinger Plaza, Lancaster, PA 17603 **(717) 299-1810**
Indian. Akbar offers several vegetarian dishes. **Open Monday through Saturday for lunch and dinner, Sunday for lunch only. Buffet lunch Friday through Sunday. Take-out, VISA/MC, $$**

Asian Restaurant
553 North Pine St., Lancaster, PA 17603 **(717) 397-7095**
International. The Asian Restaurant has eight options in the vegetable section of the menu plus chow mein and lo mein dishes. **Closed Monday. Open Tuesday through Sunday for lunch and dinner. Full service, vegan options, VISA/MC/ DC, $–$$**

Lanvina Vietnamese Restaurant
1762 Columbia Ave., Lancaster, PA 17603 **(717) 393-7748**
Ethnic. Lanvina has an excellent vegetarian selection featuring mock duck, tofu, rice dishes, and soups. **Open daily. Full service, take-out, $**

LITITZ

• It's Only Natural
10 E. Front St., Lititz, PA 17543 **(717) 626-7374**
Vegetarian/macrobiotic. **Open Monday through Wednesday at 5 P.M. for take-out, Friday at 6 P.M. for eat-in or take-out. Reservations required by noon, $$**

MARSHALL'S CREEK

Naturally Rite Restaurant and Natural Foods Market
Route 209 N., Marshall's Creek, PA 18335 **(717) 223-1133**

Natural foods. It's a pleasure to find this restaurant among the Pocono vacation spots. Among the wide variety of menu selections are Garden Burgers, Millet Croquettes, Pasta and Broccoli, and Fettucini Pomadora. Vegetarian and non-dairy soy products are available. Desserts can be served with non-dairy ice cream. A health-food store and clinic are connected to the restaurant; however, you do not feel as if you are in a store as the restaurant has its own atmosphere. Informal, outdoor patio. **Open daily except Tuesday. Breakfast is available on weekends. Full service, fresh juices, take-out, VISA/MC, $$**

Sitar Cuisine of India
Route 209, Jay Park, Marshall's Creek, PA 18335   (717) 223-1670
Indian. This Pocono Mountains area restaurant offers a wide variety of vegetarian dishes including Indian breads, curries, and samosas. **Full service, take-out, $$**

Garden of Eatin'
231 Haverford Ave., Narberth, PA 19072   (215) 667-7634
Natural foods. This restaurant is in the rear of Narberth Natural Foods. **Open Monday through Saturday for lunch. Full service, fresh juices, take-out, VISA/ MC, $**

• Avatar's Golden Nectar
321 Bridge St., New Cumberland, PA 17070   (717) 774-7215
Vegetarian. Daily specials and smoothies are available. **Open daily except Sunday. Full service, fresh juices, take-out, VISA/MC, $**

• White Cloud
RD 1, Box 215, Newfoundland, PA 18445   (717) 676-3162
Vegetarian. Nestled in the Pocono Mountains, White Cloud is a casual vegetarian and natural foods restaurant and inn. A good selection of vegetarian foods is offered, and organic foods are served when available. **Open for three meals daily during the summer, only on weekends the rest of the year. Reservations are required. Full service, fresh juices, take-out, VISA/MC/DISC, $$**

Taco Shell's
15 N. Third St., Oxford, PA 19363   (215) 932-9445
Mexican. Restaurants are limited as it is in this area of southeastern PA so finding Taco Shell's, which has excellent homemade Mexican food in a small-town restaurant atmosphere, is a real treat. Ask about the beans and guacamole as they sometimes contain lard or sour cream, respectively. However, the rice and home-made salsa are delicious, and you can always get a filling vegetarian burrito or enchilada. **Open Tuesday through Friday for lunch and dinner. Full service, limited vegan options, BYOB, take-out, $**

PENNS CREEK

Walnut Acres Organic Farm
Walnut Acres Rd., Penns Creek, PA 17862 **(717) 837-5095**
Natural foods. Walnut Acres is an organic farm with a lunch counter. **Open Monday through Saturday for lunch. Limited service, VISA/MC/DISC, $**

PHILADELPHIA

(For more restaurant listings in the surrounding areas, see Ardmore, Bala Cynwyd, Jenkintown, and Narberth. Springfield and Willow Grove are farther away.)

•• A-free-ya's
6108 Germantown Ave., Philadelphia, PA 19144 **(215) 848-5554**
Vegan. A-free-ya's offers an exciting new concept in healthy foods with its extensive menu of interesting and creative raw foods dishes. Some stir-fries and soups are available during the winter. **Open Tuesday through Friday, 11 A.M. to 2 P.M. for take-out only. Open at other times Tuesday through Saturday for sit-down. Full service, fresh juices, fresh-pressed solar wines, catering, take-out, VISA/MC, $$**

• The Basic Four Vegetarian Juice Bar
Reading Terminal Market, 12th and Filbert Sts.
Philadelphia, PA 19107 **(215) 440-0991**
Vegetarian. Located in the heart of center city Philadelphia, this is a food-stand in Reading Terminal. Savor fast-food vegetarian style, including sandwiches, salads, veggie steaks, veggie burgers, mock chicken and tuna salad. **Open Monday through Saturday, 11:30 A.M. to 4:30 P.M. Cafeteria style, fresh juices, take-out, $**

Ben's Restaurant
The Franklin Institute, 20th and the Parkway
Philadelphia, PA 19103 **(215) 448-1355**
American. Ben's claims "An All-American menu with a nutritional twist." **Open daily for breakfast and lunch. Cafeteria style, take-out, $**

Boccie Pizzeria Bar and Restaurant
The Warehouse, 4040 Locust St.
Philadelphia, PA 19104 **(215) 386-5500**
Pizza. Owned by Saladelley Restaurants, this pizzeria offers a wide variety of pizza—even a pizza without cheese—and Angel Hair Primavera. **Open daily. Cappuccino, $$**

• Center Foods Natural Grocer
337 S. Broad St., Philadelphia, PA 19107 **(215) 735-5673**
Vegetarian. Center Foods features a completely organic take-out counter with macrobiotic options. **Open Monday through Saturday. Take-out only, macrobiotic options, $**

•• Cherry Street Chinese Vegetarian Restaurant ᨑ
1010 Cherry St., Philadelphia, PA 19107   **(215) 923-3663**
Vegan/Chinese. This smoke-free Chinese restaurant has an extensive menu, featuring vegetable, tofu, and mock-meat dishes. Sample Sesame Lemon Beef, Watercress with Tofu Soup, Eggplant in Black Bean Sauce, and more. An upstairs banquet room is available. **Open for lunch and dinner daily. Full service, vegan/macrobiotic options, take-out, VISA/MC/AMX/DISC, $$**

The Dining Car
8826 Frankford Ave., Philadelphia, PA 19136   **(215) 338-5113**
American. This diner offers some vegetarian meals. **Open 24 hours daily. Full service, alcohol, take-out, $**

Eden Restaurant
3701 Chestnut St., Philadelphia, PA 19104   **(215) 387-2471**
Cafeteria. Eden features soups, salads, stir-fries, pasta, and bakery items. **Open daily. Cafeteria style, take-out, VISA/MC/AMX/DISC, $**

European Dairy
20th and Sansom Sts., Philadelphia, PA 19103   **(215) 568-1298**
Kosher. **Open Sunday through Thursday, 11 A.M. to 9 P.M.; Friday, 11 A.M. to 3 P.M. Full service, take-out, VISA/MC/AMX/DISC, $**

Gina's Delight
1929 Chestnut St., Philadelphia, PA 19103   **(215) 561-5575**
Middle Eastern. Enjoy delicious vegetarian Middle Eastern dishes including Tabouli, Hummus, Baba Ghanouj, Stuffed Grape Leaves, Spinach Pie, and Falafel. **Open daily for lunch and dinner. Counter service, vegan options, catering, take-out, $**

Golden Empress Garden
610 S. 5th St., Philadelphia, PA 19147   **(215) 627-7666**
Chinese. A separate menu lists vegetarian options. No MSG is used. **Open daily. Full service, vegan options, take-out, $–$$.**

Golden Pond Chinese Restaurant
1006 Race St., Philadelphia, PA 19107   **(215) 923-0303**
Chinese. Golden Pond has an extensive vegetarian menu. **Open daily for lunch and dinner. Full service, take-out, VISA/MC, $$**

•• Harmony Vegetarian Restaurant ᨑ
135 N. 9th St., Philadelphia, PA 19107   **(215) 627-4520**
Vegan/Chinese. Any vegetarian who visits Philadelphia will undoubtedly hear "make sure you visit Harmony!" from friends familiar with this Philadelphia treasure. Harmony is a highly rated, completely vegan Chinese restaurant with a very extensive menu. Many delicious soups, appetizers, and countless vegetable, tofu, and mock-meat dishes are featured. The service is friendly and the atmosphere is pleasant. Weekends are usually very busy. Non-smoking. **Open Monday through Saturday for lunch and dinner. Full service, completely vegan, BYOB, take-out, VISA/MC, $$**

Jumby Bay Juice Bar Cafe
250 South St., Philadelphia, PA 19148   **(215) 625-2596**
Juice Bar. A wide variety of fresh juices are available. **Open daily. Counter service, take-out, $**

Kawabata
110 Chestnut St., Philadelphia, PA 19106   **(215) 928-9564**

2455 Grant Ave., Philadelphia, PA 19114   **(215) 969-8225**
Japanese. Dishes include vegetarian sushi and sukiyaki. **Open daily. Full service, vegetarian/macrobiotic options, take-out, VISA/MC/AMX, $$$**

Keyflower Dining Room
20 South St., Philadelphia, PA 19104   **(215) 386-2207**
Natural foods. **Open Monday through Friday for lunch and dinner. Non-smoking, cafeteria style, take-out, $**

Lemon Grass Thai Restaurant
3626-30 Lancaster Ave., Philadelphia, PA 19104   **(215) 222-8042**
Thai. On request, any entree can be prepared without meat. **Open for lunch and dinner Monday through Thursday, for dinner only on Friday and Saturday. Closed Sunday. Full service, take-out, VISA/MC/AMX/DISC, $$**

Mary's Restaurant
400 Roxborough Ave., Philadelphia, PA 19128   **(215) 487-2249**
Natural foods. This mostly vegan restaurant offers freshly baked breads and desserts. **Open for dinner Tuesday through Sunday. Sunday Brunch. Full service, vegan/macrobiotic options, take-out, VISA/MC/AMX/DISC, $$**

Middle East Restaurant
126 Chestnut St., Philadelphia, PA 19106   **(215) 922-1003**
Middle Eastern. This restaurant offers several vegetarian dishes. **Open 5 P.M. to midnight. Full service, vegan options, wine/beer/alcohol, take-out, VISA/MC/ AMX/DISC, $**

Saladalley
1720 Sansom St., Philadelphia, PA 19103   **(215) 564-0767**

The Bourse Building, 21 S. 5th St.
Philadelphia, PA 19106   **(215) 627-2406**

4040 Locust St., Philadelphia, PA 19104   **(215) 349-7644**

Temple University Campus, 1926 Park Mall
Philadelphia, PA 19122   **(215) 787-5151**
American. See entry under Ardmore, PA, for description.

🕭 Reviewers' choice   ● Vegetarian restaurant   ●● Vegan restaurant
$ less than $6 $$ $6–$12 $$$ more than $12
VISA/AMX/MC/DISC/DC—credit cards accepted
Non-alc.–Non-alcoholic   Fresh juices—freshly squeezed

•• Singapore Vegetarian Restaurant 🍃
1029 Race St., Philadelphia, PA 19107   **(215) 922-3288**
Vegan/Chinese. This new vegan restaurant is located in Philadelphia's Chinatown. Both the food and service are outstanding. **Open daily for lunch and dinner. Full service, vegan options, fresh juices, take-out, VISA/MC, $$**

South East Restaurant
1000 Arch St., Philadelphia, PA 19107   **(215) 629-1888**
Chinese. South East has a good selection of vegetarian dishes. **Open daily for lunch and dinner. Full service, vegan/macrobiotic/Pritikin options, take-out, VISA/MC/AMX/DISC, $$**

Szechuan Empire
1699 Grant Ave., Philadelphia, PA 19115   **(215) 676-6220**
Chinese. Szechuan Empire features an extensive vegan menu. **Open daily, only for dinner on Sunday. Full service, alcohol, take-out, VISA/MC/AMX, $$**

Tang Yean
220 N. 10th St., Philadelphia, PA 19107   **(215) 925-3993**
Chinese. Here you'll find a great vegetarian menu with vegan options. **Open daily 3 P.M. to midnight. Full service, vegan options, take-out, VISA/MC/AMX, $$**

Taste of India
4015 Chestnut St., Philadelphia, PA 19104   **(215) 662-1777**
Indian. Savor vegetarian options and a buffet lunch daily. **Open daily for lunch and dinner. Full service, take-out, VISA/MC/AMX/DISC, $$**

Tel Aviva Restaurant and Pizzaria
6724 Castor Ave., Philadelphia, PA 19149   **(215) 722-7877**
Middle Eastern/pizzas. Vegetarian Middle Eastern dishes and veggie pizzas are featured here. **Open daily for lunch and dinner. Full service, vegan options, wine/beer/alcohol, take-out, $$**

Thai Royal
123 S. 23rd St., Philadelphia, PA 19103   **(215) 567-2542**
Thai. Several vegetarian dishes are offered. **Open daily, only for dinner on weekends. Full service, take-out, wine/beer/alcohol, VISA/MC/AMX, $**

•• Uhuru's Place
4900 Chestnut St., Philadelphia, PA 19139   **(215) 474-0226**
Vegan. The menu changes daily and includes homemade desserts. **Open Monday through Saturday for lunch and dinner. Full service, vegan options, take-out, $**

Ziggy's
1210 Walnut St., Philadelphia, PA 19107   **(215) 985-1838**
Japanese. Ziggy's offers some vegetarian dishes. **Open daily for dinner. Full service, take-out, VISA/MC/AMX, $$**

PHOENIXVILLE

Taste of India
450 W. Bridge St., Phoenixville, PA 19460 (215) 935-3663
Indian. Taste of India offers a buffet lunch daily. Menu items include pakoras, samosas, and entrees such as eggplant, chickpea, spinach, and potato dishes. **Open daily 11:30 A.M. to 2:30 P.M. and 4:30 P.M. to 10:00 P.M. Full service, take-out, VISA/MC/AMX/DISC, $$**

PINE FORGE

Gracie's New Age Eatery and 21st Century Cafe
Manatawny Rd., Pine Forge, PA 19548 (215) 323-4004
Natural foods. The atmosphere has a Southwestern flavor with an outdoor dining terrace. Gracie's goal is to provide a place where both vegetarians and non-vegetarians can be comfortable and share a delicious meal. Foods served include Black Bean Chili, Middle Eastern Sampler, Saffron Curry, and Broccoli with Ravioli. **Open Wednesday through Saturday for dinner, Friday for lunch also. Reservations appreciated. Full service, fresh juices, non-alc. beer, wine/beer/alcohol, take-out, AMX, $$$**

PITTSBURGH

Ali Baba Restaurant
404 S. Craig St., Pittsburgh, PA 15213 (412) 682-2829
Middle Eastern. Located in the Oakland section, Ali Baba offers a variety of vegetarian Middle Eastern dishes including a noteworthy couscous dish. **Open Monday through Friday for lunch and daily from 4 P.M. to 10 P.M. Full service, vegan options, beer, take-out, VISA/MC/AMX/DISC, $$**

Star of India
412 S. Craig St., Pittsburgh, PA 15213 (412) 681-5700
Indian. There are several vegan dishes plus many other selections using dairy. **Open Monday through Friday for lunch, daily for dinner. Full service, vegan options, dairy or non-dairy mango shake, non-alc. beverages, VISA/MC/AMX, $$**

PORT TREVERTON

• Somewhere in Time
Routes 11 and 15, RD 1, Box 901
Port Treverton, PA 17864 (717) 374-2202
Vegetarian. Homemade baked goods are available. **Open Monday through Saturday for three meals. Full service, take-out, VISA/MC, $**

READING

A Comfy Chair Coffeehouse
253 N. Fifth St., Reading, PA 19601 (215) 376-8950
Coffeehouse. This coffeehouse displays handmade jewelry and artwork. Entertainment is offered several nights per week. The menu lists numerous vegetarian

dishes such as Black Bean Soup, Winterbean Soup, California Pasta Salad, Mushroom and Spinach Quiche, and Spinach Lasagna. **Open Monday through Friday for lunch, Wednesday through Saturday for dinner. Full service, espresso/cappuccino, take-out, VISA/MC/DISC, $**

Nature's Garden Natural Foods
Reading Mall, Reading, PA 19606   **(215) 779-3000**
Natural-foods-store deli. Sample Tofu Hogi (tofu, sprouts, and more in whole-wheat pita), Brown Rice Burgers, and Banana Whirl Blender Treat. **Open Monday through Saturday. Limited service, fresh juices, macrobiotic options, take-out, VISA/MC, $**

Someplace Special
1401 Lancaster Ave., Reading, PA 19607   **(215) 777-2516**
Natural foods/American/herbal store. This store sells herbal plants and herbal seasonings, and uses herbs from its own garden in its prepared foods. You can try Vegetarian Chili with Tempeh over Basmati Rice, Hot Seitan Mock Beef on Pita, and other interesting dishes. The owners prefer that you call ahead for the vegetarian options. There is in-store seating, but it's 99 percent take-out. Cooking classes are offered. **Open Thursday through Sunday for lunch, Tuesday through Sunday for dinner. Take-out, vegan options, usually macrobiotic options, $**

• Yours Naturally
1407 Lancaster Ave., Reading, PA 19607   **(215) 777-0336**
Vegetarian/natural foods store. The food is not made on the premises, and you need to order one day in advance. Featured dishes include Cucumber Soup, Rice Tofu Loaf, Couscous Loaf, and bean soups. **Open Monday through Saturday for lunch. Take-out only, vegan options, macrobiotic options, $**

SPRINGFIELD

Saladalley
1001 Baltimore Pike, Springfield Square
Springfield, PA 19064   **(215) 328-5880**
American. See entry under Ardmore, PA, for description.

STROUDSBURG

• Earthlight Supply
Quaker Plaza, Stroudsburg, PA 18360   **(717) 424-6760**
Vegetarian/health-food-store deli. Snack-bar lunches, soups, casseroles, and sandwiches are served. **Open Monday through Saturday for lunch. Counter service, fresh juices, take-out, $**

&❧ Reviewers' choice   • Vegetarian restaurant   •• Vegan restaurant
$ less than $6 $$ $6–$12 $$$ more than $12
VISA/AMX/MC/DISC/DC—credit cards accepted
Non-alc.—Non-alcoholic   Fresh juices—freshly squeezed

Everybody's Cafe
905 Main St., Stroudsburg, PA 18360 **(717) 424-0896**
Natural foods/European. Polish and Italian dishes and other European-style fare
include such dishes as Mushroom Picata and many creative entrees. **Open daily
for lunch and dinner. Full service, take-out, AMX, $**

WAYNE

Only Natural
500 Chesterbrook Blvd., Chesterbrook Shopping Center
Wayne, PA 19087 **(215) 296-0700**
Natural foods. This small restaurant is connected to a natural foods store. Sandwiches, hot platters, homemade soups, entrees, and desserts are available. No red
meat is served. **Open Monday through Saturday for lunch, and Thursday through
Saturday for dinner. Full service, vegan/macrobiotic options, fresh juices,
non-alc. beer, take-out, VISA/MC, lunch—$, dinner—$$**

WEST CHESTER

Great Pumpkin Market and Deli
607 E. Market St., Market St. Plaza
West Chester, PA 19380 **(215) 696-0741**
Natural foods deli. The deli moved in 1992 and expanded significantly, adding an
organic produce section and nice deli counter. Vegetarian Chili, Tofu Meatball
Sandwich, Falafel, a mini salad bar and daily macro platter, daily specials such as
lasagna, baked goods, and two soups are served. **Open daily. Deli, vegan/macro-
biotic options, non-alc. beer, take-out, VISA/MC, $**

Hunan Chinese Restaurant
1103 West Chester Pike,
Town and Country Shopping Center
West Chester, PA 19382 **(215) 429-9999**
Chinese. Hunan added a very extensive vegetarian menu in 1992 with numerous
appetizers, soups, and entrees, including a large selection of tofu dishes and
mock meats. The food is excellent and the staff is very friendly. This is a real
treasure for vegetarians, especially for those living in southeastern PA! **Open daily
for lunch and dinner. Full service, take-out, VISA/MC/AMX/DISC, $–$$**

Star of India
155 W. Gay St., West Chester, PA 19380 **(215) 429-0125**
Indian. Star of India opened in 1992 and is West Chester's only Indian restaurant.
It is located in quaint downtown West Chester and has many vegetarian options.
Full service, take-out, $$

WILLOW GROVE

Nature's Harvest Cafe and Natural Foods Market
101 C E. Moreland Rd., Willow Grove, PA 19090 **(215) 659-7705**

Natural foods. Sandwiches, salads, hot entrees, and Middle Eastern selections are available. **Open Monday through Saturday, 10 A.M. to 8 P.M., Sunday from noon to 4 P.M. Limited service, fresh juices, take-out, VISA/MC/AMX/DISC, $**

PUERTO RICO

HUMACAO

Nutrilife
Calle Miguels Casillas #9
Humacao, Puerto Rico 00791   **(809) 852-5068**
Natural foods. This health food store and vegetarian restaurant offers fruit shakes. **Closed Sundays. Cafeteria style, fresh juices, beer, take-out, catering, $**

RHODE ISLAND

NEWPORT

Harvest Natural Foods & Catering
1 Casino Terr., Newport, RI 02840   **(401) 846-8137**
Health-food-store deli. This deli offers a veggie-pocket bar, fresh salad bar, homemade muffins, hearty soups and stews, sandwiches, oriental stir-fries, and pastas. **Closed Sunday. Limited service, vegan options, take-out, VISA/MC/AMX, $**

PROVIDENCE

Extra Sensory
388 Wickendon St., Providence, RI 02903   **(401) 454-3920**
Natural foods. Located amidst several other alternative businesses on Wickendon St., Extra Sensory offers an excellent selection of high quality natural foods in an upbeat environment. Various sandwiches, soups, salads, and entrees are available, and home-baked goods and delicious desserts are served. **Closed Sunday. Full service, vegan options, fresh juices, espresso/cappuccino, take-out, VISA/MC/AMX/DISC, $$**

Taj Mahal Restaurant
230 Wickendon St., Providence, RI 02903   **(401) 331-2442**
Indian. Nine options are included on the vegetarian menu, plus some appetizers and soups. **Open Monday through Saturday for lunch and dinner, Sunday for dinner only. Full service, vegan options, take-out, VISA/MC/AMX/DISC, $$**

🍲 Reviewers' choice   • Vegetarian restaurant   •• Vegan restaurant
$ less than $6 $$ $6–$12 $$$ more than $12
VISA/AMX/MC/DISC/DC—credit cards accepted
Non-alc.—Non-alcoholic   Fresh juices—freshly squeezed

Taste of India
221 Wickendon St., Providence, RI 02903 **(401) 421-4355**
Indian. A vegetarian section on the menu lists several options. **Full service, vegan options, take-out, $$**

SOUTH CAROLINA

CHARLESTON

Angel Fish
520 Folly Rd., Merchant Village Center
Charleston, SC 29412 **(803) 762-4722**
Natural foods. Everything is fresh at Angel Fish, and there are daily specials in addition to the regular menu, which lists soups, salads, and pasta dishes with vegetarian options. No meat base is used in soups. **Closed Monday. Full service, vegan options, fresh juices, wine/beer/alcohol, take-out, VISA/MC/AMX, $$**

Doe's Pita Plus
334 E. Bay St., Charleston, SC 29401 **(803) 577-3179**
Middle Eastern. Sandwiches are made with freshly baked pita bread and a variety of fillings. Salads, Stuffed Grape Leaves, Hummus, and other Middle Eastern foods are served. Everything is made on the premises with only the freshest ingredients. **Open daily. Counter service, vegan options, beer, take-out, $**

Nosh With Josh
217 Meeting St., Charleston, SC 29401 **(803) 577-6674**
Kosher/natural foods. Nosh With Josh, South Carolina's only kosher restaurant, is a restaurant with integrity that doesn't believe in taking shortcuts. Various Middle Eastern and health foods are prepared from scratch including Falafel, Tabouleh, Hummus, Burritos, and Mock Chicken Salad. **Limited service, vegan options, take-out, $**

COLUMBIA

Annabelle's of Columbia
Dutch Square Mall, Columbia, SC 29210 **(803) 772-5586**
Family restaurant. This is a regular family restaurant, but a local vegetarian recommends the Stir-Fry Vegetable Platter, and says the chef is willing to create various veggie dishes. **Open daily. Full service, vegan option, wine/beer/alcohol, take-out, VISA/MC/AMX, $$**

The Basil Pot
928 Main St., Columbia, SC 29201-3964 **(803) 799-0928**
Natural foods/macrobiotic. This is the home of the kitchen of the original Southern Vegetarian Hunting Lodge. Here you will find the elusive pinto bean and the more common but equally succulent tofu loaf. Soups and salads, Chili, Tofu Burger, Pizza, sandwiches, daily specials, and a breakfast menu are featured. Primarily vegetarian, Basil Pot serves chicken, turkey, and tuna. **No dinner served on Sunday.**

Full service, vegan options, fresh juices, non-alc. beer/wine, beer/wine, take-out, VISA/MC, $–$$

Nice-N-Natural
1217 College St., Columbia, SC 29201   **(803) 799-3471**
Natural foods. Nice-N-Natural specializes in sandwiches and salads, with soups and some side orders to round out the menu. Numerous fresh fruit salads are available. **Open Monday through Friday. Limited service, vegan options, fresh juices, take-out, no credit cards, $**

GREENVILLE

Annie's Cafe
121 S. Main St., Greenville, SC 29601   **(803) 271-4872**
Natural foods. This natural foods restaurant offers some Mexican and other ethnic options. Vegetarian, low-sugar, and low-salt dishes are available. No preservatives are used. Bread is baked fresh daily. **Open daily. Full service, wine/beer, take-out, VISA/MC/AMX, $$**

SOUTH DAKOTA

YANKTON

Body Guard
2101 Broadway Mall, Yankton, SD 57078   **(605) 665-3482**
Natural foods. Experience a natural foods bakery with a lot of specialty and non-allergenic baked goods. **Open daily. Limited service, take-out, $**

TENNESSEE

CHATTANOOGA

•• Country Life Buffet
3748 Ringgold Rd., Chattanooga, TN 37412   **(615) 622-2451**
Vegan. Enjoy an all-you-can-eat vegan buffet with different entrees each day, brown rice, beans, cornmeal rolls, and a salad bar. **Open Sunday through Thursday for lunch only. Buffet, take-out, VISA/MC, $–$$**

•• Foods for Life
3220 Brainerd Rd., Chattanooga, TN 37411   **(615) 624-2829**
Vegan. Foods for Life offers vegan entrees made of grains, wheat gluten, tofu, and legumes. Whole-grain breads and a salad bar are also available. **Open Monday through Friday for lunch and dinner. Self service, fresh juices, limited catering, take-out, VISA/MC/DISC, $**

KNOXVILLE

El Charro

6701 Kingston Pike, Knoxville, TN 37919 **(615) 584-9807**

Mexican. The veggie burritos, enchiladas, tacos, and rice and beans are prepared without lard. **Open daily. Full service, non alc. beer/wine, wine/beer/alcohol, take-out, VISA/MC/AMX, $-$$**

Falafel Hut

601 15th St., Knoxville, TN 37916 **(615) 522-4963**

Middle Eastern. Falafel Hut offers Hummus, Tabouleh, lentil soups, and salads. **Open daily for breakfast, lunch, and dinner. Full service, non-alc. beer, take-out, VISA/MC/AMX, $-$$**

Hawkeye's Corner

1717 White Ave., Knoxville, TN 37916 **(615) 524-5326**

American/continental. You'll find a wide range of homemade foods with some vegetarian options, and the management is willing to accommodate special requests. Try the Vegetarian Alfredo, Vegetarian Pita, and the salads. There are live concerts Wednesday through Saturday and no cover charge. **Open Monday through Saturday until midnight. Full service, non-alc. beer, wine/beer/alcohol, take-out, VISA/MC/AMX/DISC/DC, $$**

House of Chan

3701 Chapman Highway, Knoxville, TN 37920 **(615) 577-3255**

Chinese. This fast-food style restaurant offers Buddha's Delight and Tofu Cantonese and will leave meat out of any dish. **Open daily. Limited service, $**

Mexicali Rose

6500 Kingston Pike, Knoxville, TN 37919 **(615) 588-9191**

Mexican. Beans are made without lard, and there are three types of enchiladas and burritos. **Open Tuesday through Saturday. Full service, non-alc. beverages, beer, $$**

La Paz

8025 Kingston Pike, Knoxville, TN 37919 **(615) 670-5250**

Mexican. This restaurant and bar combo serves no meat or meat stock in beans or sauces. You can get Vegetarian Chili, and Mexican dishes with spinach fillings. Inquire about the rice as it contained chicken stock at the time of this writing. **Open Tuesday through Sunday for dinner. Full service, non-alc. beer, wine/ beer/alcohol, VISA/MC/AMX, $$**

Silver Spoon Cafe

7250 Kingston Pike, Knoxville, TN 37919 **(615) 584-1066**

American cafe. The cafe offers Italian specialties with vegetarian options, including three to four strict vegetarian entrees. Pasta salads and whole-wheat breads are available. **Open daily. Full service, non-alc. beer/wine, wine/beer/alcohol, take-out, VISA/MC/AMX/DISC/DC, $-$$**

Wang's Place

4009 Chapman Hwy., Knoxville, TN 37920 **(615) 573-4580**

Chinese. The menu lists five vegetarian entrees, a vegetables and tofu dish, and two vegetarian soups. Wang's Place will accommodate vegetarians. **Open daily. Full service, non-alc. beer, wine/beer/alcohol, take-out, VISA/MC/AMX/ DISC/DC, $**

MADISON

• Tennessee Christian Medical Center Cafeteria
500 Hospital Dr., Madison, TN 37115   **(615) 865-37115**
Vegetarian. This Seventh-day Adventist run cafeteria serves only vegetarian food including options such as Cheese Manicotti, Burritos, Cashew Casserole, and Quiche. There's also a great salad bar. **Open daily. No breakfast on weekends. Cafeteria style, limited take-out, $**

NASHVILLE

• Country Life
1917 Division St., Nashville, TN 37203   **(615) 327-3695**
Vegetarian. Country Life features fresh fruit and fresh vegetable salad bars, soups, and hot entrees. **Closed Saturday and Sunday. Cafeteria/buffet style, vegan options, take-out, $**

Slice of Life Restaurant and Bakery 🐝
1811 Division St., Nashville, TN 37203   **(615) 329-2525**
Natural foods. The emphasis here is on healthy and delicious entrees including Spinach Lasagna, and Black Bean Cakes with Artichoke Stuffing. All items are free of sugar and preservatives. **Open daily. Full service, vegan/macrobiotic options, wine/beer, take-out, VISA/MC/AMX/DISC, $$**

Windows on the Cumberland
112 2nd Ave. North, Nashville, TN 37201   **(615) 244-7944**
Natural foods. This almost completely vegetarian restaurant offers "lunch and dinner with a view," and live entertainment. **Cafeteria service for lunch, full service for dinner, $**

SAVANNAH

• Gina's Country Health and Vegan Shoppe
1315 Wayne Rd., Savannah, TN 38372   **(901) 925-7220**
Vegetarian. The food served here is vegan. There is honey in some dishes. **Open weekdays. Limited service, vegan options, take-out, $**

TEXAS

AMARILLO

Back to Eden Snack Bar and Deli
2425 I-40 W., Amarillo, TX 79109   **(806) 353-7476**

Natural foods. Described as the healthiest place to eat in Amarillo, this restaurant features fresh baked goods and salads, homemade salad dressings, and fresh soups made without MSG. **Closed Sunday. Limited service, catering, take-out, VISA/ MC/AMX/DISC, $–$$**

AUSTIN

Martin Bros. Cafe
914 N. Lamar, Austin, TX 78703   **(512) 476-7601**
Natural foods. Located in the original Whole Foods Market near downtown, Martin Bros. is a good place to people-watch—artists, musicians, professionals, and politicians. Enjoy Chalupas with Beans and Cheese, soft whole-wheat tacos with black beans or hummus, Nachos, Vegetarian Tamale and Brown Rice Dinner. Frozen desserts include ice cream, yogurt, and sorbet. **Open daily for three meals. Counter service, vegan options, fresh juices, smoothies, take-out, $**

El Mercado
1302 South 1, Austin, TX 78724   **(512) 447-7445**
Mexican. You'll find some vegetarian and some vegan items here. **Full service, take-out, $$**

• Mother's Cafe and Garden
4215 Duval, Austin, TX 78751   **(512) 451-3994**
Vegetarian. International vegetarian food includes Enchiladas, Stir-Fry, Veggie Burger, Lasagna, soups, salads, and desserts. **Open daily for lunch and dinner. Full service, vegan options, fresh juices, wine/beer, take-out, VISA/MC/DC $$**

• Mr. Natural
1901 E. First St., Austin, TX 78702   **(512) 477-5228**
Vegetarian. Mr. Natural features Mexican vegetarian food—Vegetarian Fajitas, Veggie Burgers, Veggie Ceviche, Veggie Tamales, Breakfast Tacos with Veggie Chorizo (sausage)— a whole-wheat bakery, and a juice bar. **Open daily 7 A.M. to 8 P.M. Cafeteria style, fresh juices, take-out, $**

• West Lynn Cafe
1110 W. Lynn, Austin, TX 78703   **(512) 482-0950**
Vegetarian. Enjoy a delicious selection of various vegetarian foods from a variety of countries. Soups, sandwiches, light fare, pasta, Southwestern, Mexican, Indian and other international specialties are offered in an eclectic, historic neighborhood close to downtown. **Open daily for lunch and dinner. Weekend brunch. Full service, vegan options, fresh juices, espresso/cappuccino, wine/beer, take-out, VISA/MC/AMX, $–$$**

DALLAS

(For more restaurant listings in the surrounding areas, see Denton, Irving, Richardson, and Waxahachie.)

Francis Simun's
1507 N. Garret Ave., Dallas, TX 75206   **(214) 824-4910**

Vegetarian. This vegetarian establishment serves international cuisine including Mexican and Italian food. **Open daily for lunch and dinner. Full service, fresh juices, wine/beer, catering, take-out, AMX/DISC/DC, $-$$$**

H and M Natural Foods Grocery
9191 Forest Lane, Dallas, TX 75243   (214) 231-6083
Natural foods. Enjoy the salad bar and entrees such as vegetable burger, vegetarian soup, Tabouleh, Hummus, Avocado Sandwich, Nachos. **Open Monday through Saturday in the afternoon. Limited service, vegan options, fresh juices, VISA/MC/AMX, $**

• Kalachandji's Restaurant and Palace
5430 Gurley Ave., Dallas, TX 75223   (214) 821-1048
Vegetarian/natural foods. No preservatives or refined sweeteners are used. A House Tamarind Tea and fresh homemade breads are served. There's an Indian gift shop and indoor or outdoor dining. **Open Tuesday through Sunday. Self-service buffet, VISA, $$**

Macro Gourmet
850 S. Greenville Ave., Suite 110, Dallas, TX 75081   (214) 669-8328
Macrobiotic. Soups, entrees, desserts, and sandwiches feature organic whole-cereal grains and vegetables. Foods are prepared without dairy, sugar, or preservatives. **Open Monday through Saturday for breakfast and lunch. Dinner is served Thursday through Saturday. Limited service, vegan/macrobiotic options, catering, VISA/MC, $$**

Roy's Nutrition Center
130 Preston Shopping, Dallas, TX 75230   (214) 987-0213
Health-food-store deli/juice bar. Roy's is a deli, bakery, and juice bar cafe offering salads, sandwiches, and entrees such as Lasagna, Brown Rice and Stir-Fry Vegetables, and calzones. **Open Sunday through Friday morning and afternoon. Closes early on Friday in the winter. Juice bar, fresh juices, take-out, VISA/MC/AMX/DISC, $**

Sala Thai
4503 Greenville (at Yale), Dallas, TX 75206   (214) 350-8945

2415 W. Northwest Hwy. (at Harry Hines)
Dallas, TX 75220   (214) 350-8945
Thai. The management is willing to substitute items and accommodate vegetarians. Tofu dishes are available. **Open Monday through Friday for lunch and on weekends for dinner. Full service, wine/beer, take-out, VISA/MC/DC, $$**

La Suprema Tortilleria
7630 Military Pkwy., Dallas, TX 75227   (214) 388-1244

🏵 Reviewers' choice   • Vegetarian restaurant   •• Vegan restaurant
$ less than $6 $$ $6–$12 $$$ more than $12
VISA/AMX/MC/DISC/DC—credit cards accepted
Non-alc.—Non-alcoholic   Fresh juices—freshly squeezed

Tex-Mex. La Suprema offers organically grown grains and produce, and many dairy-free entrees. It is adjacent to a greenhouse and gardens. **Closed Monday. Full service, vegan/macrobiotic options, take-out, VISA/MC/AMX, $$**

Thai Lotus Kitchen
3851 D Cedar Springs, Dallas, TX 75219 **(214) 520-9385**
Thai. Thai cooking classes are offered in this smoke-free restaurant. **Open Friday and Saturday for lunch and dinner. Full service, take-out, VISA/MC/AMX, $–$$**

DENTON

Mr. Chopsticks
1120 W. Hickory, Denton, TX 76201 **(817) 382-5437**
Thai. The Denton Area Vegetarian Organization said Mr. Chopsticks' owner has been wonderful about accommodating vegetarians and will make special items. **Open daily. Limited service, take-out, VISA/MC, $**

FORT WORTH

(For more restaurant listings in the surrounding area, see Waxahachie.)

The Back Porch
3400-B Camp Bowie, Ft. Worth, TX 76107 **(817) 332-1422**
Sandwich and salad shop. Located across the street from the museums and Omni theater, The Back Porch offers a salad bar (items sold by weight), vegetarian sandwiches and burgers, and low-fat ice cream. **$**

HOUSTON

A Moveable Feast
2202 West Alabama, Houston, TX 77098 **(713) 528-3585**
Natural foods. Several people recommended this restaurant, which offers blackboard specials and at least one macrobiotic plate daily. The wide selection of vegetarian food includes Chili Tempeh Burgers, Blue Corn Enchiladas with Black Beans, Cheeseless Florentine Lasagna, Vegetarian Barbecue (made with seitan), Vegan Spinach Enchiladas, Vegetarian Chicken Fried Steak with Roasted Potato Sticks, Meatless Happy Burgers, Vegetarian Fajitas, Pita Pizzas, and more. Breakfast is served on weekends. **Open daily 9 A.M. to 10 P.M. Limited service, vegan/macrobiotic options, fresh juices, organic coffee, take-out, catering, VISA/MC/AMX/DISC, $–$$**

Asian Restaurant
3701 Weslayan, Houston, TX 77027 **(713) 850-0450**
Chinese/Vietnamese. A separate vegetarian menu includes such items as Mongolian Vegetable Clay Pot, Charlie's Sizzling Plate, Lemon Grass Tofu, and more. Management claims to have the best macrobiotic food in town. **Open Monday through Saturday. Full service, vegan/macrobiotic options, wine/beer, catering, take-out, VISA/MC/AMX/DISC/DC, $**

Bombay Palace
3901 Westheimer, Houston, TX 77027 **(713) 960-8472**

Indian. Bombay Palace is a member of a worldwide chain of Indian restaurants. The daily luncheon buffet includes vegetarian options. **Open daily for lunch and dinner. Full service, wine/beer/alcohol, catering, take-out, VISA/MC/AMX, $$**

Guilin Chinese Cafe
4005 H Bellaire, Houston, TX 77025   **(713) 661-1963**
Chinese. Some vegan entrees are available. **Counter service, $**

Health Food Express
4400 Memorial Dr. (at the Bayou Park Club)
Houston, TX 77007   **(713) 861-2800**
Natural foods/macrobiotic. Health Food Express is a food delivery business, supplying the client with a week's worth of food, split into two deliveries. Lunches are also available in a cafe; vegetarian, macrobiotic, and Mexican/American foods contain no eggs, dairy, or white sugar. Pasta dishes, whole grains, land and sea vegetables, salads, fruit-juice-sweetened desserts, and more are served. **Open for lunch Monday through Friday. Limited service, macrobiotic options, delivery, wine/beer/alcohol, take-out, VISA/MC/DISC, $$**

On the Border
9705 Westheimer, Houston, TX 77042   **(713) 977-9955**

4608 Westheimer, Houston, TX 77027   **(713) 961-4494**
Mexican. A *Vegetarian Journal* reader wrote to tell us that this is "Not a vegetarian restaurant, but the only Mexican restaurant in town that I know of that serves Grilled Vegetable Fajitas. Great!!" **Full service, $$**

Red Pepper Restaurant
5626 Westheimer, Houston, TX 77056 (713) 622-7800
Chinese. Savor such unique selections as Vegetarian Peking Duck, Vegetable Dumplings, Spinach Bean Curd Soup, Shredded Dry Bean Curd, Vegetarian Fish (made from black mushrooms wrapped in bean curd skin), Spinach in Light Fresh Garlic Sauce, Red Pepper's Bean Curd, and much more. The restaurant is somewhat formal, but you can dress casually. **Open daily. Full service, wine/beer/alcohol, catering, take-out, VISA/MC/AMX/DC, $$**

Seekers Natural Foods and Vitamins
4004 Bellaire, Houston, TX 77025   **(713) 665-2595**
Natural foods. This restaurant inside a health food store uses no salt or white sugar. As much organic produce as possible is served at the ninety-item salad bar. Menu includes Rice-N-Veggies, Whole-Wheat Noodle Lasagna, Tofu Spring Rolls, Veggie Cheese Burger, and other items. **Open daily. Full service, vegan/macrobiotic options, fresh juices, smoothies, wine/beer, take-out, VISA/MC/AMX, $**

Thai Pepper
2049 W. Alabama, Houston, TX 77098   **(713) 520-8225**
Thai. We've been told that the staff is accommodating, the cooks are willing to turn meat entrees into veggie entrees, and it's the best Thai food in Houston. **Full service, $$**

•• Wonderful Vegetarian Restaurant
7549 Westheimer, Houston, TX 77063   **(713) 977-3137**

Vegan/Chinese/kosher. More than 100 dishes are vegan, and there's a special "all-you-can-eat" buffet lunch. You'll find seven wheat-gluten dishes, ten soybean gluten platters, eight marinated mushroom plates, nine types of imitation seafood, and other selections. **Open Tuesday through Sunday. Full service, vegan options, wine/beer, VISA/MC/AMX/DC, $**

IRVING

La Suprema Tortilleria
6311 N. O'Connor #104, Irving, TX 75039 **(214) 506-0988**
Tex-Mex. La Suprema offers organically grown grains and produce, eleven organic wines, and many dairy-free entrees. Live music is featured Tuesday through Saturday nights. **Closed Monday. Full service, vegan/macrobiotic options, organic wines, take-out, VISA/MC/AMX, $$**

RICHARDSON

Macro Gourmet Natural Foods Restaurant
850 S. Greenville, #110, Richardson, TX 75081 **(214) 669-8328**
Natural foods/macrobiotic. Fresh organic meals are served daily. Only fresh vegetables, grains, beans, nuts, seeds, unrefined oils, and sea vegetables are used. **Open daily for lunch, Thursday night for dinner. Limited service, vegan options, take-out, $–$$**

SAN ANTONIO

Fiesta Patio Cafe
1421 Pat Booker, San Antonio, TX 78148 **(512) 658-5110**
Mexican/natural foods. Whole-grain brown rice is prepared Spanish style. No lard is used; foods are made with peanut oil. Foods are prepared without preservatives, MSG, or other artificial ingredients. Alfalfa sprouts and natural cheese are available. **Open daily except Monday. Full service, wine/beer, VISA/MC/AMX, $**

Gini's Home Cooking and Bakery
7214 Blanco, San Antonio, TX 78216 **(512) 342-2768**
American/natural foods. Good old-fashioned foods are prepared a healthy way and served in a totally smoke-free atmosphere. A *Vegetarian Journal* reader called the fresh baked breads, pies, and cookies "scrumpdilliicious!!" Pritikin-style meals and baked goods are available. Menu choices for vegetarians include seasonal fresh fruit and whole-wheat pancakes. **Open daily. Full service, fresh juices, wine/ beer, VISA/MC/AMX, $$**

Thai Kitchen
445 McCarty, San Antonio, TX 78216 **(512) 344-8366**
Thai/Chinese. Enjoy nine vegetarian entrees plus soups and appetizers including Spring Rolls, Hot and Sour Soup, Bean Curd with Hot Pepper, and Noodles with Vegetable Gravy. **Open Monday through Saturday for lunch and dinner. Full service, wine/beer, VISA/MC/AMX/DISC/DC, $$**

Reviewers' choice   • Vegetarian restaurant   •• Vegan restaurant
$ less than $6 $$ $6–$12 $$$ more than $12
VISA/AMX/MC/DISC/DC—credit cards accepted
Non-alc.–Non-alcoholic   Fresh juices—freshly squeezed

Twin Sisters Bakery and Cafe
6322 N. New Braunfels, San Antonio, TX 78209   (512) 822-0761
Natural foods/American/Mexican. The owners call this an "herbally influenced restaurant." Whole-wheat Chalupas and Quesadillas are samples of the natural choices. Oatmeal Special and Tacos are included on the breakfast menu. **Open for breakfast daily. Lunch and dinner served Tuesday through Saturday. Closed Sunday. Full service, vegan/macrobiotic options, fresh juice, wine/beer, $–$$**

Zuni Grill
511 Riverwalk, San Antonio, TX 78205   (512) 227-0864
Southwestern. This relatively new restaurant is located one block from the San Antonio Convention Center. In the heart of the Riverwalk tourist district, it has both indoor and outdoor seating. Zuni Grill offers vegetarian and vegan soups and three vegetarian entrees. Vegans may request that dishes be prepared without cheese. **Open daily for breakfast, lunch, and dinner. Full service, vegan options, catering, take-out, VISA/MC/AMX/DISC/DC, $$**

WACO

Joe's Sandwich Shop
1900 S. 12th St., Waco, TX 76706   (817) 756-5151
International/American. Close to Baylor University, this shop features Veggie Sandwich (pita stuffed with vegetables), Falafel, Thyme Pizza, Labneh Sandwich (Middle Eastern cheese spread with tomatoes and dried mint), and Tabouleh. **Open daily except Sunday; in the summer, lunch hours only. Cafeteria style, catering, take-out, $**

Waco Natural Foods
1424 Lake Air Dr., Waco, TX 76710   (817) 772-5743
Natural foods. You'll find a vegetarian menu; vegan food is available. **Hours vary. Full service, vegan options, take-out, $**

WAXAHACHIE

Kirkpatrick's Natural Foods
207 S. College, Waxahachie, TX 75165   (214) 937-0010
Natural foods. Lunches include homemade soups, soy burgers, and homemade pastas. Dinner is new-American-cuisine style served by candlelight. **Open for lunch Monday through Friday. Open for dinner Thursday through Saturday. Full service, catering, take-out, VISA/MC/AMX, $–$$$**

WESLACO

Pelly Health Ranch
1616 S. Bridge Ave., Weslaco, TX 78596   (512) 968-5343
Natural foods. Pelly specializes in raw food dishes. **Open daily. Full service, take-out, $**

UTAH

- ## Chumley's Cafe
130 S. Main , Hurricane, UT 84737   **(801) 635-9825**

Vegetarian. Outdoor seating is available next to a garden—a wonderful setting for a meal. Fresh dessert specials and cappuccino are featured. **Closed Sunday. Self-serve counter, espresso/cappuccino, $**

Honest Ozzie's Cafe and Desert Oasis
60 N. 100 W., Moab, UT 84532   **(801) 259-8442**

Natural foods. Moab's only natural foods restaurant, bakery, and deli, Honest Ozzie's features garden seating and displays of local artwork. This nearly vegetarian restaurant serves whole grains for breakfast, and tempting appetizers and entrees for dinner. **Open daily. Closed in December and January. Full service/counter service only for lunch, vegan options, wine/beer, $–$$**

Bright Day Natural Lunches
952 28th St., Ogden, UT 84403   **(801) 394-7503**

Natural foods. Bright Day features soups made from fresh vegetables, sandwiches on seven-grain bread, fruit shakes, and baked goods. **Closed Sunday, open for lunch Monday through Saturday. Counter service, vegan options, fresh juices, take-out, $**

The Mexican Place - Senior Frogs
455 25th St., Ogden, UT 84405   **(801) 394-2323**

Mexican. Only vegetable oil is used, and many entrees can be made without cheese. **Open daily. Full service, vegan options, wine/beer/alcohol, take-out, VISA/ MC, $–$$**

- ## Govinda's Buffet
260 N. University Ave., Provo, UT 84601   **(801) 375-0404**

Vegetarian. This restaurant uses no eggs, and breads and salad dressings are homemade. Buffet includes fresh salads, soups, curried vegetables, and main entrees such as Lasagna, and Eggless Vegetable Quiche. **Open for lunch and dinner Monday through Saturday, closed Sunday. Full service, vegan options, catering, VISA/MC/AMX/DISC, $**

Deloretto's
2939 E. 3300 So., Salt Lake City, UT 84109   **(801) 485-4534**

Italian. Some vegetarian options are available here. **Open daily. Full service, beer, take-out, $**

New Frontiers Natural Foods
2454 S. 700 East, Salt Lake City, UT 84106   **(801) 359-7913**

812 E. 200 South, Salt Lake City, UT 84102   **(801) 355-7401**
Natural foods. This natural bakery and deli features items made to order from scratch and excellent desserts. **Open daily. Counter service, fresh juices, catering, VISA/MC/AMX/DISC, $**

• Sun Bun Cafe
878 S. 900 West, Salt Lake City, UT 84102   **(801) 328-1313**
Vegetarian. This restaurant views vegetarianism as "a global ecological neccessity," and works towards educating its patrons. Specialties include freshly baked breads, "Save the Chicken" Salad, and homemade soups. Dinner specials change nightly. **Closed Sunday. Limited service, vegan options, catering, VISA/MC, $$**

VERMONT

BRATTLEBORO

Common Ground
25 Elliot St., Brattleboro, VT 05301   **(802) 257-0855**
Natural foods. A community-based worker-owned cooperative, Common Ground emphasizes the use of local and organic foods. The restaurant strives to maintain a balance between business needs and social and environmental concerns. Fish is served on weekends only, and stir-fry and seitan dishes are always served. **Closed Tuesday. Vegan options, take-out, fresh juices, wine/beer, no credit cards, $**

BURLINGTON

• Freddy's
171 Church St., Burlington, VT 05401   **(802) 863-7171**
Vegetarian. You'll find a bright, cheery atmosphere with a menu offering vegetarian fast food such as burgers, sandwiches, subs, side dishes, and desserts. No eggs are used and dairy items are indicated on the menu. Opened in 1992, Freddy's is a good place for the whole family. **Open daily. Limited service, vegan options, non-alc. beer, take-out, $**

• Origanum Natural Foods Cafe
227 Main St., Burlington, VT 05401   **(802) 863-6103**
Vegetarian deli. This deli offers an excellent selection of hot dishes, soups, veggie burgers, sandwiches, salads, beverages, and an extensive salad bar with many organic ingredients. Various ethnic foods are featured as well. Eggs are not used. **Open daily. Cafeteria style, vegan options, fresh juices, take-out, VISA/MC, $**

MANCHESTER CENTER

Bagel Works
Routes 11 & 30, Manchester Center, VT 05255   **(802) 362-5082**

Bagel deli. More than sixteen varieties of bagels are available with various topping options including cream cheeses, tofutti spreads, salads, and vegetarian combinations. Ingredients are all natural and prepared without preservatives. Bagel Works is environmentally conscious and socially active in the community. **Open daily. Counter service, vegan options, fresh juices, take-out, $**

MONTPELIER

• Horn of the Moon Cafe
8 Langdon St., Montpelier, VT 05602   **(802) 223-2895**

Vegetarian. Established in 1977, the Horn of the Moon is the oldest vegetarian restaurant in New England. The menu lists salads, sandwiches, soups, homemade breads, and daily specials. Vegan and heart-healthy dishes are clearly indicated on the menu, and local organic produce and ingredients are used when possible. The walls of the cafe are decorated with the work of local artists in a rotating exhibit. **Open Tuesday through Sunday for three meals; Monday for breakfast and lunch. Full service, vegan options, fresh juices, wine/beer, catering, take-out, no credit cards, $**

State Street Market Grocery and Deli
20 State St., Montpelier, VT 05602   **(802) 229-9353**

Natural foods. Homemade natural foods include soups, sandwiches, deli salads, and hot entrees. **Closed Sunday. Cafeteria style, take-out, $**

NEWPORT

• Newport Natural Foods/Dana's Bakery
66 Main St., Newport, VT 05855   **(802) 334-2626**

Vegetarian. Several hot soups and entrees are offered daily plus sandwiches, salads, desserts, and fresh baked goods. A chalkboard menu changes daily. **Closed Sunday. Cafeteria style, take-out, $**

VIRGINIA

ALEXANDRIA

Mediterranean Bakery and Cafe
352 S. Pickett St., Alexandria, VA 22304   **(703) 751-1702**

Natural foods/Middle Eastern. Mediterranean decor— including arches, columns, and a terra cotta canopy—is found in this wonderful cafe. Dine on Middle Eastern vegetarian delicacies including Falafel, Hummus, Baba Ghanouj, Stuffed Grape Leaves, various salads, spinach pies, and casseroles. All baked goods are prepared fresh on the premises. A grocery store offering Middle Eastern, Italian, and Greek items is also located here. **Open daily for breakfast, lunch, and dinner. Limited service, take-out, $-$$**

ARLINGTON

Adulis Restaurant
2325 Eads St., Arlington, VA 22202   **(703) 920-3188**
Ethiopian. Eight vegetarian specials plus appetizers are available at Adulis. **Full service, vegan options, espresso/cappuccino, wine/beer, $-$$**

Bardo Rodeo
2000 Wilson Blvd., Arlington, VA 22201   **(703) 527-9399**
Pub. This pub, seating 600 indoors and 400 on the outdoor patio, serves no red meat and offers many vegetarian dishes (some of which require your specifying that the chicken or fish be omitted) including Indonesian Sauté, Hummus, an Indian platter, Salsa, Guacamole, Grilled Vegetable Lasagna, tostadas, burritos, salads, and sandwiches. The menu changes regularly. **Open daily. Full service, vegan options, wine/beer, VISA/MC, $-$$**

Bombay Curry House
2529 Wilson Blvd., Arlington, VA 22201   **(703) 528-0849**
Indian. Bombay Curry House has several options for vegetarians. **Open daily. Full service, wine/beer, take-out, VISA/MC/AMX, $-$$**

Chesapeake Seafood & Crab House
3607 Wilson Blvd., Arlington, VA 22201   **(703) 528-8888**
International. A pleasant surprise for any vegetarian who might find himself here, the Chesapeake House has a wide selection of unique and creative vegetarian appetizers, soups, and gourmet specialties. Examples include Lemon Grass Tofu, Mongolian Vegetable Clay Pot, and Cantonese Chow Mein. **Open daily. Full service, vegan options, wine/beer, take-out, VISA/MC/AMX/DISC, $-$$**

China Gourmet Cafe
2154 Crystal Plaza Arcade, Arlington, VA 22202   **(703) 415-0300**
Chinese. Located underground in Crystal City, China Gourmet offers low-priced lunch and dinner combination specials featuring many meatless dishes. China Gourmet is willing to accommodate special requests. **Closed Sunday. Limited service, vegan options, wine/beer, take-out, $**

Kabul Caravan Restaurant
1725 Wilson Blvd., Arlington, VA 22209   **(703) 522-8394**
International. Authentic international foods are prepared fresh daily. There is a vegetarian menu section with four options plus side dishes. **Open daily. Full service, vegan options, wine/beer/alcohol, take-out, VISA/MC/AMX, $$**

Pamir Afghan Restaurant
561 S. 23rd St., Arlington, VA 22204 **(703) 979-0777**
Afghan. Three vegetarian entrees plus appetizers make up the veggie selections at Pamir. **Closed Sunday. Full service, vegan options, wine/beer/alcohol, take-out, VISA/MC/AMX, $$**

BLACKSBURG

South Main Cafe
117 S. Main St., Blacksburg, VA 24060 **(703) 552-3622**
Ethnic foods. A variety of delicious-sounding, international vegetarian entrees includes Lemon Grilled Tempeh Filet, Thai Eggplant, and Tofu and Pad Thai. Chicken and fish are also served. **Open for lunch and dinner. Closed Sunday. Full service, vegan options, fresh juice, wine/beer/alcohol, take-out, $-$$**

CENTREVILLE

• Herb Garden Express
5705 Regimental Court, Centreville, VA 22020 **(703) 818-8477**
Vegetarian. Herb Garden Express is a catering service that offers vegetarian, vegan, and macrobiotic meals with an international flavor. Herb Garden caters weddings and other parties, and also delivers to homes. **Catering, $$**

CHARLOTTESVILLE

• Ming Dynasty Restaurant
1417 Emmet Street, Charlottesville, VA 22901 **(804) 979-0909**
Vegetarian/Chinese. This completely vegetarian Chinese restaurant features an all-you-can-eat lunch buffet and Sunday brunch. **Open daily. Full service, vegan options, take-out, VISA/MC/AMX/DISC/DC, $-$$**

• Integral Yoga
923 Preston Ave., Charlottesville, VA 22901 **(804) 293-4111**
Vegetarian. This self-serve restaurant offers deli food by the pound, sandwiches, baked goods, knishes, Lasagna, Hummus, pasta dishes, and Mexican foods. **Open daily. Self-serve, vegan options, non-alc. beer/wine, take-out, VISA/MC, $**

FALLS CHURCH

Panjshir Restaurant
924 West Broad St., Falls Church, VA 22046 **(703) 536-4566**
Afghan. Panjshir features vegetarian eggplant, pumpkin, and spinach dishes. **Open daily. Full service, wine/beer/alcohol, take-out, VISA/MC/AMX, $$**

FREDERICKSBURG

Sammy T's Light Food and Ale
801 Caroline St., Fredericksburg, VA 22401 **(703) 371-2008**
Natural foods. Foods are made fresh to order with vegan and vegetarian options, some Middle Eastern and Mexican dishes, and a wide selection of beer. **Open for**

three meals daily. **Full service, vegan options, wine/beer, take-out, VISA/MC/ DISC, $–$$**

A Little Place Called Siam
328 Elden St., Herndon, VA 22070   **(703) 742-8881**
Asian. An extensive vegetarian selection distinguishes the Thai and Southeast Asian cuisine here. Many tofu, eggplant, and vegetable entrees are available as are appetizers and soup. **Full service, vegan options, wine/beer/alcohol, take-out, VISA/MC/AMX, $$**

Ariana Afghan Restaurant
283 Sunset Park Dr., Herndon, VA 22070   **(703) 435-0151**
International. One of the few restaurants offering Afghan cuisine, Ariana specializes in kabobs, low-cholesterol, low-fat, and vegetarian dishes. Indian and Middle Eastern specialities are also offered. The vegetable dishes include eggplant, spinach, pumpkin, leek, cauliflower, and lentils. No MSG is used. **Closed Sunday. Full service, vegan options, non-alc. beer, wine/beer, take-out, VISA/MC, $$**

Andy's Pizza & Subs
9F Catoctin Circle SW, Leesburg, VA 22075   **(703) 771-0277**
Deli. Many Middle Eastern favorites such as Falafel, Hummus, Baba Ghanouj, and Stuffed Grape Leaves are offered. Andy will make Lemon-Tahini Sauce for the Falafel for vegans. **Full service, vegan options, $**

City Deli & Market
5604 Patterson Ave., Richmond, VA 23226   **(804) 288-7668**
Natural foods. City Deli is located inside of the City Market, Richmond's natural foods grocery. The deli features many fresh baked goods made without eggs, wheat, or sugar. The store has a large organic produce section. **Open daily. Cafeteria style, fresh juices, take-out, VISA/MC, $**

• Grace Place
826 W. Grace St., Richmond, VA 23220   **(804) 353-3680**
Vegetarian. This twenty-year-old vegetarian restaurant specializes in international cuisine. Grace Place, with its rotating art show on the walls, is a sanctuary to artists, musicians, the sensitive, and well-informed. **Closed Sunday. Full service, vegan options, fresh juices, organic coffee, wine/beer/alcohol, take-out, VISA/MC $$**

•• The Eden Way Place
307 Market St., SE, Roanoke, VA 24011   **(703) 344-3336**
Vegan. Located in the historic market district of downtown Roanoke, Eden Way offers a low-fat vegan menu with entrees, soups, burgers, and Falafel. Whole-grain breads and desserts are baked fresh in the restaurant's bakery, and there's a

natural foods store in the same location. **Closed Saturday. Full service, vegan, take-out, $**

VIENNA

Naturally Yours Cafe
330 W. Maple Ave., Vienna, VA 22180   **(703) 938-4485**
Natural foods. Daily specials, sandwiches, and salads are made with the freshest ingredients possible. Located in the rear of a natural foods store, Naturally Yours is very willing to cater to special diets. Soy cheese is available. **Closed Sunday. No smoking. Counter service, vegan/macrobiotic options, fresh juices, take-out, VISA/MC/AMX, $**

Panjshir II Restaurant
224 W. Maple Ave., Vienna, VA 22180   **(703) 281-4183**
Afghan. See listing under Falls Church.

VIRGINIA BEACH

Fresh Market Deli, Inc.
550 First Colonial Rd., 309 Hilltop Square
Virginia Beach, VA 23451   **(804) 425-5383**
Natural foods. Open daily, only for take-out on Sunday. **Full service, wine/beer/alcohol, take-out, $**

WILLIAMSBURG

Baja Bean Co.
120-G Waller Mill Rd., Williamsburg, VA 23185   **(804) 220-4848**
Mexican. All the beans are prepared in vegetable oil. Vegetarian options include enchiladas, tacos, burritos, tostadas, and much more. **Open daily for lunch and dinner. Full service, take-out, no credit cards, $**

Chez Trinh
Williamsburg Shopping Center
Monticello Ave. at Richmond Rd.
Williamsburg, VA 23185   **(804) 253-1888**
Vietnamese. All dishes are prepared fresh and cooked to order; service can, therefore, be slow at times. Vegetarian dishes include Bean Curd with Vegetables, Vegetarian Noodles, Tofu Cutlets and Peanut Sauce served with Rice Paper, and Sauteéd String Beans. **Open daily for lunch and dinner. Full service, take-out, $$**

WASHINGTON

BAINBRIDGE ISLAND

Natural Gourmet
Harold's Square, Bainbridge Island, WA 98110   **(206) 842-2759**

Natural foods. Vegetarian dishes include fresh salads, entrees, soups, and sandwiches. **Closed Sunday. Limited service, vegan options, fresh juices, espresso, take-out, VISA/MC, $**

BELLEVUE

Thai Chef
1645 140th Ave., NE, Bellevue, WA 98005   **(206) 562-7955**
Thai. A wide selection of Thai foods includes vegetarian appetizer, soup, and entree specialties. **Open daily. Full service, vegan options, wine/beer, take-out, VISA/MC/AMX, $$**

Twelve Baskets Restaurant & Catering
825-116th Ave., Bellevue, WA 98004   **(206) 455-3684**
Natural foods. All seating is non-smoking in this country cottage atmosphere. Enjoy vegetarian entrees, excellent homemade soups, sandwiches, salads, pasta, and desserts. Christian music, drama, and entertainment are featured on weekends. **Closed Sunday. Full service, vegan options, fresh juices, espresso, take-out, VISA/MC/AMX/DISC, $$**

BELLINGHAM

Bangkok House Restaurant
2500 Meridan, Bellingham, WA 98225   **(206) 733-3322**
Thai. Many tofu dishes are offered. **Closed Sunday. Full service, vegan options, non-alc. beer, wine/beer, take-out, VISA/MC, $$**

Old Town Cafe
316 W. Holly St., Bellingham, WA 98225   **(206) 671-4431**
Natural foods. The Old Town Cafe has a special philosophy regarding its staff: "The people who work here are a team. All jobs are equally important and all tips are shared equally by the cooks, dishwashers, and waitpersons." This social consciousness extends to recycling everything possible, reducing use of non-recyclables, and supporting local food suppliers. Sandwiches, salads, soups, and vegetarian specials are offered. **Open daily for breakfast and lunch. No smoking. Full service, vegan options, fresh juices, espresso, $**

Taste of India
3930 Meridan St., #J, Bellingham, WA 98226   **(206) 647-1589**
Indian. Many vegetarian specialties are prepared to order. The breads are delicious. **Open daily for lunch and dinner. Full service, vegan options, wine/beer, $$**

Thai House
3930 Meridan St., Bellingham, WA 98226   **(206) 734-5111**
Thai. Vegetarian offerings include rice and noodle dishes, and spring rolls. **Take-out, $–$$**

🐾 Reviewers' choice   ● Vegetarian restaurant   ●● Vegan restaurant
$ less than $6 $$ $6–$12 $$$ more than $12
VISA/AMX/MC/DISC/DC—credit cards accepted
Non-alc.—Non-alcoholic   Fresh juices—freshly squeezed

COLLEGE PLACE

• Walla Walla College Cafeteria

32 SE Ash, College Place, WA 99324 **(509) 527-2732**

Vegetarian. Sample meat analogues, Mexican food bar, and "Nature's Inn" bar without eggs or dairy. Desserts are sweetened with dates. **Open daily during school year. Limited hours in summer. Cafeteria service, vegan options, take-out, $**

ELLENSBURG

Valley Cafe & Takeout

105 W. 3rd, Ellensburg, WA 98926 **(509) 925-3050**

Northwest cuisine. Pacific Northwest cuisine is featured in an original art deco facility. There are some vegetarian options, and all dishes are prepared fresh using only the best ingredients. **Open 11 A.M. to 9 P.M. Monday through Friday, 7:30 A.M. to 10 P.M. Saturday and Sunday. MC/VISA/AMX/DISC**

FEDERAL WAY

Marlene's Market & Deli

31839 Gateway Center Blvd., S.
Federal Way, WA 98003 **(206) 839-0937**

Natural foods. This clean and inviting deli/restaurant has an adjoining espresso bar serving only organically grown coffee. There's easy access next to Interstate 5. **Open daily. Limited service, fresh juices, take-out, VISA/MC, $**

MT. VERNON

The Deli Next Door

202 S. First St., Mt. Vernon, WA 98723 **(206) 336-3886**

Natural foods. Enjoy wholesome sandwiches, salads, specialties, hot entrees, deli salads, and kids' plates. **Open daily. Limited service, fresh juices, espresso, $**

OLGA

Doe Bay Cafe

Star Route 86, Olga, WA 98279 **(206) 376-2291**

Natural foods. Doe Bay Cafe is situated in a turn-of-the-century building overlooking Otter Cove at the historic Doe Bay Village Resort and Retreat on Orcas Island. Serving dishes with an international flavor, Doe Bay has a casual and social setting. Mineral spring, hot tubs, cedar sauna, massage, and a daily guided-kayak-trip help build appetites worthy of the meals at Doe Bay Cafe. Indoor and outdoor seating. **Open daily in summer, only weekends after September. Full service, wine/beer, $$**

OLYMPIA

Red Apple Natural Foods

400 Cooper Point Rd., Olympia, WA 98502 **(206) 357-8779**

Health-food-store deli. This deli offers soups, Veggie Burgers, sandwiches, Chili, and vegan espresso in case you need a little boost! **Closed Sunday. Counter service, vegan options, fresh juices, organic coffee, espresso, take-out, VISA/MC, $**

The Urban Onion
116 Legion Way, Olympia, WA 98501   **(206) 943-9242**
Health-conscious cuisine. The Urban Onion is located in the Hotel Olympian across from Sylvester Park. Vegetarian health-conscious cuisine is featured along with espresso and delicious desserts. **Open daily. Full service, fresh juices, espresso, wine/beer, take-out, VISA/MC/AMX, $$**

PORT ANGELES

Cafe Garden
1506 E. First St., Port Angeles, WA 98362   **(206) 457-4611**
Ethnic. Breakfast items are served all day, and there are creative salads, pasta, and Szechuan stir-fries. **Open daily. Vegan options, wine/beer, $$**

ROCKPORT

Cascadian Farm Organic Market
5375 Hwy 20, Rockport, WA 98283   **(206) 853-8629**
Juice bar. This organic farm offers juices, espresso, freshly baked goods, and sorbet. There's a picnic area, and self-guided tours are permitted. **Open until dusk from May until October. Counter service, fresh juices, espresso, VISA/MC, $**

SAN JUAN ISLAND

Springtree Cafe
310 Spring St., Friday Harbor
San Juan Island, WA 98250   **(206) 378-4848**
Cafe. Innovative and tasty vegetarian entrees are served every night. **$$**

SEATTLE

(For additional restaurant listings, see Bellevue.)

Bagel Express
205 1st Ave., So., Seattle, WA 98104   **(206) 682-7202**
Sandwich shop. "Handcrafted" soups are the specialty here; 80 percent of them are vegetarian. Lunch special is a bagel sandwich with a cup of soup. Vegetarian sandwiches are also on the menu. **Open daily in summer. Closed Sundays the rest of the year. Counter service, vegan options, fresh juices, take-out, $**

Bahn Thai Restaurant
409 Roy St., Seattle, WA 98109   **(206) 283-0444**
Thai. Thirteen vegetarian entrees, appetizers, and rice and noodle dishes are included on this Thai menu. **Open daily. Full service, vegan options, wine/beer, take-out, VISA/MC/AMX/DISC, $**

•• Bamboo Garden
364 Roy St., Seattle, WA 98109   **(206) 282-6616**
Vegan/Chinese. The extensive vegetarian menu features delicious vegan Chinese cuisine. Don't be confused when you see turkey and chicken; they're all made from

vegetable protein. No eggs or dairy products are used. **Open for lunch and dinner daily. Reservations accepted. Full service, completely vegan, wine/beer/alcohol, take-out, VISA/MC/AMX, $$**

Bangkok Hut
2126-3rd Ave. & Blanchard, Seattle, WA 98121   (206) 441-4425
Thai. Eleven vegetarian options, appetizers, and salad are offered. **Open daily. Full service, vegan options, wine/beer, take-out, VISA/MC/AMX, $–$$**

• The Blue Planet Cafe
2208 N. 45th St., Seattle, WA 98103   (206) 632-0750
Vegetarian. Almost everthing served at this cafe is organically grown. Tofu Nut Burgers, Lasagna, pasta, salads, and vegan pastries are featured. **Open daily. Full service, vegan options, fresh juices, organic coffee, take-out (in your own container), VISA/MC, $$**

Cafe Counter Intelligence
94 Pike Suite 32, Seattle, WA 98101   (206) 622-6979
Natural foods. Egg dishes, soups, and salads are served here. **Open Monday through Wednesday for breakfast and lunch. Full service, wine/beer, take-out, $**

• Cafe Flora
2901 E. Madison, Seattle, WA 98112   (206) 325-9100
International vegetarian. Savor fine international vegetarian food featuring the flavors of Mexico, Japan, and India. The many creative dishes include Wild Mushroom Stroganoff, Grilled Nutburger, Curried Eggplant with Mangoes and Tomato, and several unique pizzas. **Closed Monday. Full service, vegan options, fresh juices, non-alc. wine/beer, take-out, VISA/MC, $$**

Cafe Loc
407 Broad St., Seattle, WA 98109   (206) 441-6883
Cafe. Cafe Loc offers family-style cooking with vegetarian options. **Open daily. Full service, beer, take-out, $**

Cause Celeb
524 15th Ave. E., Seattle, WA 98112   (206) 323-1888
Natural Foods. Enjoy Spinach Nut Burgers, and stir-fries. **Open daily. Full service, catering, wine/beer, take-out, $**

Cyclops Cafe
2416 Western Ave., Seattle, WA 98121   (206) 441-1677
Cafe. Vegetarian fare is offered in a fun eclectic setting. **Open daily. Full service, espresso, wine/beer, take-out, $$**

Elliot Bay Cafe
101 S. Main St., Seattle, WA 98104   (206) 686-6664
Cafe. In a cozy cafe under a bookstore in a historic area of Seattle, a chalkboard menu features some vegetarian options. **Open daily. Cafeteria style, wine/beer, take-out, no credit cards, $**

•• Five Loaves Deli & Bakery
2719 E. Madison, Seattle, WA 98112   **(206) 726-7989**
Vegan. The bakery and deli feature freshly baked whole-grain bread and muffins made without refined oils, sugars, or animal products. Sandwiches, burgers, soups, salads, desserts, and fruit shakes are offered for lunch. **Open for breakfast and lunch every day except Saturday. Limited service, vegan options, fresh juices, take-out, no credit cards, $**

•• The Globe Cafe & Bakery
1531 14th Ave., Seattle, WA 98122   **(206) 324-8815**
Vegan. This funky coffeehouse has monthly art shows, occasional acoustic music, poetry readings, good food and baked goods, breakfast and brunch menu. **Closed Monday. Limited service, completely vegan, fresh juices, espresso, soy latte, take-out, no credit cards, $**

• Grand Illusion Vegetarian Cafe
1405 NE 50th, Seattle, WA 98105   **(206) 525-9573**
Vegetarian. Sample granola, baked goods, soups, salads, and quiches. **Open daily, counter service, take-out, $**

Gravity Bar
113 Virginia, Seattle, WA 98101   **(206) 448-8826**

415 Broadway E., Seattle, WA 98102   **(206) 325-7186**
Natural foods. Modern food is offered in a high tech but very human atmosphere. The extensive menu (with raw to macrobiotic choices and a breakfast menu) and the decor are creative and out of this world! **Open for three meals daily. Full/limited service, vegan/macrobiotic options, fresh juices, take-out, no credit cards, $–$$**

The Hi Spot Cafe
1410 34th Ave., Seattle, WA 98122   **(206) 325-7905**
Natural foods. Situated in a Victorian house, Hi Spot Cafe has a bakery featuring low-salt, low-sugar, and whole-grain pastries. Sweets and decadent desserts are also offered. The menu includes various sandwiches, soups, salads, and beverages for vegetarians and non-vegetarians alike. No smoking and no cellular phones are allowed inside! **Open daily except Tuesday for breakfast and lunch. Full service, vegan options, fresh juices, wine/beer, take-out, VISA/MC as a last resort, $**

• Honey Bear Bakery
2106 N. 55th, Seattle, WA 98103   **(206) 545-7296**
Vegetarian. A Seattle institution, Honey Bear specializes in whole, organic baked goods and pastries, and offers Black Bean Chili, soups, salads, and more in a homey and fun atmosphere. **Open daily 6 A.M. to 11 P.M. Self service, vegan options, fresh juices, espresso, no credit cards, $**

India House
4737 Roosevelt Way, NE, Seattle, WA 98105   **(206) 632-5072**
Indian. Authentic Indian cuisine includes an extensive vegetarian menu. The

Indian decor is elegant with many paintings and artifacts. **Open daily. Full service, vegan options, wine/beer/alcohol, take-out, VISA/MC/AMX, $$**

Kokeb Restaurant
926 12th Ave., Seattle, WA 98122   **(206) 322-0485**

Ethiopian. Eight to ten vegetarian options are offered. **Open daily. Full service, wine/beer/alcohol, take-out, VISA/MC/AMX/DISC, $–$$**

• Mid City Cafe Co.
401-A Yale Ave. North, Seattle, WA 98109   **(206) 623-7979**

Vegetarian. American-style vegetarian food with some ethnic dinner plates includes Veggie Burgers, Veggie Hot Dogs, Chili, Stir-Fry, and Mexican dishes, plus soups salads, and delightful desserts! Organic ingredients are used when possible. No eggs are used. **Open daily. Saturday and Sunday brunch. Full service, vegan options, fresh juices, take-out, $–$$**

• Morningtown
4110 Roosevelt Way, Seattle, WA 98105   **(206) 632-6317**

Vegetarian. Nearly vegan, this restaurant uses no eggs and offers such dishes as Tofu Rancheros and Blue Corn Pancakes for brunch. Soups, salads, and sandwiches are also available. **Open daily. Full service, catering, vegan options, take-out, $**

New Orleans Creole Restaurant
114 First Ave. S., Seattle, WA 98104   **(206) 622-2563**

Creole/Cajun. The menu features a vegetarian section. Very little salt, animal fats, or stocks are used. Located in historic Pioneer Square, this restaurant offers live jazz and blues every evening. **Open daily for lunch and dinner. Full service, vegan options, wine/beer/alcohol, take-out, VISA/MC/AMX/DC, $$**

Ranee Thai Restaurant
121 Prefontaine Pl. S., Seattle, WA 98104   **(206) 223-9456**

Thai. Several vegetarian options include Tofu Hot and Sour Soup, curries, Vegetable Pot Pie, and other vegetable dishes. **Open for lunch. Closed Sunday. Full service, vegan options, beer, take-out, $–$$**

• Silence-Heart-Nest Restaurant
5247 University NE, Seattle, WA 98105   **(206) 524-4008**

Vegetarian/Indian. Sample Western-style Indian cooking with a menu to please vegans and vegetarians alike—from burgers and "Neatloaf" to curries, samosas, and finger-licking chutneys to fresh salads! Prices are affordable and the atmosphere is peaceful, enlightening, and uplifting. **Closed Sunday. Full service, vegan options, take-out, $**

Sound View Cafe
1501 Pike Place #501, Seattle, WA 98101   **(206) 623-5700**

🐾 Reviewers' choice   • Vegetarian restaurant   •• Vegan restaurant
$ less than $6 $$ $6–$12 $$$ more than $12
VISA/AMX/MC/DISC/DC—credit cards accepted
Non-alc.—Non-alcoholic   Fresh juices—freshly squeezed

Natural foods. This health-minded restaurant has an unusual variety of vegetarian specialties. **Open daily. Cafeteria style, wine/beer, take-out, $**

• Sunlight Cafe
6403 Roosevelt Way, NE, Seattle, WA 98115   **(206) 522-9060**
Vegetarian. Known for its eggless waffles and pastries, Sunlight offers many vegan options including desserts, sautéed vegetables, and much more. **Open daily for three meals. Full service, vegan options, fresh juices, organic espresso, wine/ beer, take-out, $$**

Thai Palace
2224 8th Ave. and Blanchard, Seattle, WA 98121   **(206) 343-7846**
Thai. No MSG is used in the preparation of foods, and vegetarian options are available. **Open daily. Full service, vegan options, wine/beer/alcohol, take-out, VISA/MC/AMX, $**

Viet My
129 Prefontaine Pl. S., Seattle, WA 98104   **(206) 382-9923**
Vietnamese. Viet My offers lots of vegetarian dishes including appetizers, veggie rolls, curry, Tofu Peanut Sauce, and other tofu dishes. **Open Monday through Friday. Full service, vegan options, take-out, $**

Wanza Ethiopian Cuisine
6409 Roosevelt Way, NE, Seattle, WA 98115   **(206) 525-3950**
Ethiopian. Eight vegetarian options are served with Ethiopian injera bread. No dairy, eggs, or animal products are used in vegetarian foods. **Open daily. Full service, wine/beer, take-out, VISA/MC/AMX, $$**

SPOKANE

China Best
West 223 Riverside, Spokane, WA 99201   **(509) 455-9042**
Chinese. In addition to twenty-two vegetarian menu items with excellent tofu dishes, China Best is willing to accommodate special diets. Every dish is freshly prepared to order. **Open daily. Full service, vegan options, wine/beer/alcohol, take-out, VISA/MC/AMX/DISC, $$**

• Eat Rite Vegetarian Restaurant
W. 314 Sprague, Spokane, WA 99204   **(509) 838-0382**
Vegetarian. The menu is free of saturated fats, cholesterol, and sugar. Main entrees change daily and feature various ethnic dishes. There's also a fourteen-foot-long salad bar, bread, soups, and desserts. **Closed Saturday. Cafeteria style, vegan options, fresh juices, take-out, VISA/MC, $**

Niko's
W. 725 Riverside, Spokane, WA 99201   **(509) 624-7444**

S. 321 Dishman Mica Rd., Spokane, WA 99206   **(509) 928-9590**
Greek/Middle Eastern. Niko's offers many vegetarian items and an all-you-can-eat lunch bar. **Full service, $$**

The Spice Corner
N. 6010 Division, Spokane, WA 99207　　　　**(509) 483-3710**
Thai. The Spice Corner has a special vegetarian menu with vegan spring rolls! **Full service, vegan options, $$**

Cookie Mill
9808 SR 532, Stanwood, WA 98292　　　　**(206) 629-2362**
Natural foods. This deli offers baked goods, a gift shop, and a blackboard menu. **Open daily. Cafeteria style, take-out, no credit cards, $**

Dog Days Cafe
17530 Vashon Highway, SW, Vashon, WA 98070　　**(206) 463-6404**
Juice bar. Daily vegetarian specials are fresh, and homemade desserts are complemented by a full juice bar and extensive coffee menu. **Open daily except Sunday. Full service, fresh juices, beer/wine, $**

Sound Food
20312 Vashon Highway, SW, Vashon, WA 98070　　**(206) 463-3565**
Natural foods. Enjoy tofu and vegetable dishes, fresh baked breads, organic produce when available, sandwiches, and salads. **Open daily. Full service, non-alc. beer, beer/wine, VISA/MC/AMX, $$–$$$**

WEST VIRGINIA

• Mountain People's Kitchen
1400 University Ave., Morgantown, WV, 26505　　**(304) 291-6131**
Vegetarian. This vegetarian restaurant attached to a natural foods co-op offers non-dairy entrees and Sunday brunch. The casual and funky atmosphere is conducive to finding out what is going on in town, music, etc. **Closed Saturday. Cafeteria style, take-out, no credit cards, $**

• Palace of Gold Restaurant
RD 1 NBU #24, Moundsville, WV 26041　　　　**(304) 843-1812**
Vegetarian/Indian. Authentic Indian cuisine includes vegetarian options. **Open daily. Full service, take-out, VISA/MC, $$**

WISCONSIN

Los Banditos
2335 W. Mason St., Green Bay, WI 54303   **(414) 494-4505**

1258 Main St., Green Bay, WI 54302   **(414) 432-9462**
Mexican. Authentic Mexican food features vegetable or quacamole fillings. Beans contain a ham-soup base. **Open daily for lunch and dinner, Sunday for dinner only. Full service, wine/beer/alcohol, take-out, VISA/MC/AMX, $–$$**

Zimmani's
333 Main St., Green Bay, WI 54301   **(414) 436-2340**
Italian. Fresh pasta specials and homemade pasta salads are highlighted at this up-scale restaurant with a full bar and complete deli/bakery. At least one vegetarian special is offered each day, and the staff is willing to accommodate special orders. **Closed Sunday. Full service, wine/beer/alcohol, take-out, VISA/MC/ AMX, $–$$**

• Country Life
2465 Perry St., Madison, WI 53713   **(608) 257-3286**
Vegetarian. The primarily vegan menu is complemented by a great salad bar and many imitation meat products. **Closed Saturdays. Full service, vegan/macrobiotic options, $–$$**

Himal Chuli
318 State St., Madison, WI 53705   **(608) 251-9225**
Nepalese. Authentic Nepalese cuisine is featured on a menu divided into vegetarian and non-vegetarian dishes. Seven vegetarian entrees feature various vegetable stews and dumplings. **Open daily. Limited service, beer, take-out, $–$$**

Husnu's
547 State St., Madison, WI 53703   **(608) 256-0900**
Turkish/Italian. Sample Hummus, Falafel, eggplant, and vegetable couscous. **Open daily for breakfast, lunch, and dinner. Full service, non-alc. beer, take-out, VISA/MC, $$**

Mt. Everest Restaurant
1851 Monroe St., Madison, WI 53711   **(608) 255-1704**
Indian. Mt. Everest offers exotic vegetarian and non-vegetarian Indian cuisine. **Closed Sundays. Reservations recommended Friday through Saturday. Full service, wine/beer/alcohol, take-out, VISA/MC/AMX, $$**

Ovens of Brittany
305 State St., Madison, WI 53703   **(608) 257-7000**

3244 University Ave., Madison, WI 53705   **(608) 233-7710**

1831 Monroe St., Madison, WI 53711   (608) 251-2119

1718 Fordem Ave., Madison, WI 53704   (608) 241-7779

American. On a menu that ranges from simple to fancy, there's stir-fry and occasional vegetarian specials such as Quiche with Goat Cheese, and Spinach Gateau. An excellent bakery and desserts are also available. **Open daily. Full service, non-alc. beer, beer/wine/alcohol, take-out, $$**

Rocky Rocco
Main Office   (608) 271-6411

1618 W. Beltline Hwy., Madison, WI 53713   (608) 251-0304

411 W. Gilman St., Madison, WI 53703   (608) 256-0600

3001 N. Sherman Ave., Madison, WI 53704   (608) 241-4423

651 State St., Madison, WI 53703   (608) 255-6888

3730 University Ave., Madison, WI 53705   (608) 238-3558

4002 E. Washington Ave., Madison, WI 53704   (608) 241-8001

4 West Towne Mall, Madison, WI 53562   (608) 829-2901

694 S. Whitney Way, Madison, WI 53711   (608) 273-1223

Pizza chain. Enjoy whole-wheat-crust pizza by the slice, an excellent salad bar, and pasta dishes in a family atmosphere. **Open daily for lunch and dinner. Counter service, vegan options, non-alc. beer, beer, take-out, VISA/MC, $**

Sunprint Cafe & Gallery
638 State St., Madison, WI 53703   (608) 255-1555

Ethnic. Several international vegetarian dishes and gourmet desserts are available at this European-style cafe and art gallery on the university campus. **Open daily. Full service, fresh juices, espresso/cappuccino, wine/beer/alcohol, take-out, VISA/MC, $$**

MIDDLETON
Rocky Rocco
2620 Allen Blvd., Middleton, WI 53562   (608) 836-5444

Pizza chain. See entry under Madison, WI. **Delivery only.**

MILWAUKEE
Abu's Restaurant
1978 N. Farwell Ave., Milwaukee, WI 53202   (414) 277-0485

Middle Eastern. Sample spinach pies, Hummus, Eggplant Casserole, lentils, eggplant, Baba Ghanouj, Egyptian Chili, and many more interesting dishes. **Open daily. Full service, take-out, $**

≈ Reviewers' choice   • Vegetarian restaurant   •• Vegan restaurant
$ less than $6 $$ $6–$12 $$$ more than $12
VISA/AMX/MC/DISC/DC—credit cards accepted
Non-alc.—Non-alcoholic   Fresh juices—freshly squeezed

Beans & Barley
1901 E. North Ave., Milwaukee, WI 53202   **(414) 278-7878**
Natural foods. Vegetarian, Mexican, and Middle Eastern specialties include home-made soups, salads, sandwiches, burritos, and stir-fry. All foods are prepared using the freshest ingredients possible. **Open daily for lunch and dinner. Full service, vegan options, fresh juices, wine/beer, take-out, VISA/MC, $$**

RACINE

Old Country Buffet
Westgate Mall, 4901 Washington Ave., Racine, WI 53406   (414) 634-5122
American. This large restaurant with a wide selection of vegetarian items, vegetables, and desserts features an all-you-can-eat buffet. **Cafeteria style, vegan options, $$**

WYOMING

CASPER

Mei Ling
232 E. 2nd, Casper, WY 82601   **(307) 237-1109**
Chinese. A Chinese vegetarian soup is among the vegetarian options offered. **Open daily. Full service, wine/beer/alcohol, take-out, VISA/MC/AMX, $**

Peking Chinese Restaurant
333 E. A, Casper, WY 82601   **(307) 266-2207**
Chinese. Vegetarian menu includes six entrees as well as soups. **Open daily for lunch and dinner. Full service, wine/beer, take-out, VISA/MC, $**

CHEYENNE

Twin Dragons
1809 Carey Ave., Cheyenne, WY 82007   **(307) 637-6622**
Chinese. This Mandarin Chinese restaurant offers ten vegetarian entrees including tofu dishes, Broccoli and Garlic Sauce, Vegetable Lo Mein, Chow Mein, and Veggie Egg Rolls. **Open daily for lunch and dinner. Full service, wine/beer/alcohol, take-out, VISA/MC/AMX, $**

CODY

The Hong Kong Restaurant
1244 Sheridan Ave., Cody, WY 82414   **(307) 527-6420**
Chinese. Enjoy vegetable and bean curd dishes. **Open for lunch and dinner daily during the summer, Tuesday through Sunday during the winter. Full service, wine/beer/alcohol, take-out, VISA/MC, $–$$**

LANDER

China Garden
140 N. 7th St., Lander, WY 82520   **(307) 332-7666**

Chinese. Several vegetarian dishes including Tofu and Mixed Vegetables, Noodles and Vegetables, and Stir-Fry Broccoli are offered at this Chinese establishment. **Open daily. Full service, BYOB, take-out, $$**

RIVERTON

The Golden Coral
400 N. Federal, Riverton, WY 82501 **(307) 856-1152**

Steak house. Although this is a family-style steak house, there is a huge salad bar with baked potatoes. **Open daily. Sunday breakfast buffet. Full service, VISA/ MC, $–$$**

CANADA

ALBERTA

BANFF

Michael's Cafe
415 Banff Ave., Banff, AB T0L 0C0   **(403) 762-9339**
Natural foods. Vegetarian dishes include Hearty Lentil Soup, Hummus, Curried Tofu Veggie Crêpe, Whole-Wheat Spaghetti, Totini with Pesto, and Tamari Ginger Tofu Stir-Fry. Menu items do not contain MSG or refined sugar. Organically grown short-grain brown rice is used and, when available, organically grown produce. The restaurant does serve non-vegetarian items. **Open for three meals daily. Full service, vegan options, non-alc. beer, take-out, wine/beer/alcohol, VISA/MC/ AMX, $$**

CALGARY

Cedars Restaurant
1009A 1st St., SW, Calgary, AB T2R 0T8   **(403) 264-2532**
Lebanese. Vegetarian and vegan options are available. The owner is the author of several cookbooks. **Open Monday through Saturday. Full service, vegan options, wine/beer, take-out, VISA/MC/AMX, $$**

The King and I Thai Cuisine
822 11th Ave., SW, Calgary, AB T2R 0E5   **(403) 264-7241**
Thai. Enjoy the contemporary decor with soft jazz background music. Vegetarian selections include Chili Club Tofu made with Japanese eggplant. **Open daily. Full service, wine/beer/alcohol, take-out, VISA/MC/AMX, $$**

Meelen Restaurant, Ltd.
118 32nd Ave., NE, Calgary, AB T2E 7C8   **(403) 291-3188**
East Indian. This restaurant features traditional family recipes. **Open daily for lunch and dinner. Full service, reservations required, wine/beer/alcohol, take-out, VISA/MC/AMX/DISC, $$**

Thai sa-on
351 10th Ave., SW, Calgary, AB T2R 0A5   **(403) 264-3526**
Thai. Authentic Thai cuisine is featured here, including homemade curries, sauces, and desserts. **Open for lunch and dinner Monday through Friday, and only for dinner on Sunday. Full service, catering, beer/wine/alcohol, $$**

EDMONTON

ABC Health Shoppe
10550 82nd Ave., Edmonton, AB T6E 1Z9   **(403) 432-7885**

Natural foods. Soups, burgers, and salads are joined by a daily vegetarian special. **Open daily except Sunday. Counter service, fresh juices, non-alc. beer, take-out, $**

High Level Diner
10912 88 Ave., Edmonton, AB T6B 0V6 (403) 433-0993
Natural Foods. The High Level Diner is an environmentally responsible natural foods eatery furnished with antiques and decorated with local artwork. **Open 9 A.M. to midnight Tuesday through Saturday, to 11 P.M. Sunday and Monday. Full service, wine/beer/alcohol, take-out, VISA/MC/AMX, $$**

• High Level Natural Foods and Cafe
10313 82 Ave., N.W., Edmonton, AB T6E 1Z9 (403) 433-6807
Vegetarian. You'll enjoy great veggie burgers and wheat-free baked foods in a casual atmosphere. **Open daily until 5:30 P.M. Full service, vegan options, fresh juices, catering, take-out, VISA/AMX, $**

The King and I Thai Cuisine
10160 82nd Ave., Edmonton, AB T6E 1Z4 (403) 433-2222
Thai. The owners emphasize healthy cooking, and special requests will be cooked to order. The Vegetarian Bird's Nest is a must! **Open for lunch Monday through Friday, and dinner Monday through Saturday. Full service, wine/beer/alcohol, take-out, VISA/MC/AMX, $$**

New Asian Village Restaurant
7908 104 Street, NW, Edmonton, AB T6E 4C8 (403) 433-3804
Indian. In an atmosphere of Indian decor and music, vegetarian options are provided by a friendly staff. **Open daily. Full service, wine/beer/alcoholic/non-alc. beverages, take-out, catering, VISA/MC/AMX, $$**

Sidney's Deli and Pizza
10416 118 Ave., Edmonton, AB T5X 0P7 (403) 471-1560
Ethnic/mixed. Enjoy homemade foods at this family restaurant offering fifteen vegetarian dishes. **Open daily. Full service, wine/beer/alcohol, take-out, VISA/MC/AMX**

• Veggies
10331 82nd Ave., Edmonton, AB T6E 1Z9 (403) 432-7560
Vegetarian. Enjoy many vegetarian dishes such as veggie burgers, whole-wheat pizza, and various ethnic entrees in a homey and smoke-free atmosphere. **Open daily except Monday. Full service, vegan options, wine/beer, catering, take-out, VISA/MC/AMX, $$**

BRITISH COLUMBIA

BURNABY

• Govinda's
5462 SE Marine Dr., Burnaby, B.C. V5J 3G8 (604) 433-2454
Vegetarian. Enjoy dining in a relaxed atmosphere with a spiritual theme where you

can take a stroll before or after diner in the park-like grounds. **Open daily except Sunday. Cafeteria style, take-out, catering, $$**

COQUITLAM

•• Nature's Bakery & Restaurant
105 1120 Westwood St. (at Lincoln)
Coquitlam, B.C. V3B 4S4   **(604) 942-2206**
Vegan. Dairy-free and egg-free cakes, muffins, turnovers, pies, and cookies are featured as are pastries from Copenhagen and other European capitals. Baked goods are made with raw sugar, maple and corn syrup, and brown sugar (no honey!). Homemade soups, veggie burgers, and other hot meals are available. **Open daily except Sunday. Cafeteria style, espresso/cappuccino.**

COURTENAY

• Bar None Cafe
244 4th St., Box 3093, Courtenay, B.C. V9N 5N3   **(604) 334-3112**
Vegetarian. A vegetarian buffet features fresh juices and an espresso bar. **Open daily except Sunday. Cafeteria style, fresh juices, espresso, take-out, catering, $–$$**

NELSON

• The Alleyway Cafe'
620 Herridge Lane, Nelson, B.C. V1L 6A7   **(604) 352-5200**
Vegetarian. Enjoy a variety of vegetarian Mexican, American, and Italian dishes. **Open daily except Sunday. Full service, vegan options, take-out, catering, MC, $–$$**

NORTH VANCOUVER

• Woodlands Natural Food Restaurant
93 Lonsdale Ave., N. Vancouver, B.C. V7M 2E5   **(604) 985-9328**
Vegetarian. Menu includes sandwiches, burgers, salads, soups, and breakfast items. **Open daily except Sunday. Cafeteria style, take-out, catering, VISA, $**

VANCOUVER

(For additional restaurants in the surrounding areas, see Burnaby, Coquitlam, North Vancouver, and West Vancouver.)

Afghan Horsemen Restaurant
445 W. Broadway, Vancouver, B.C. V5Y 1R4   **(604) 873-5923**
Afghani. Enjoy Afghan soups, salads, and entrees such as Hummus, Badenjan Borani (baked eggplant), and Dahl (lentil stew). **Open daily except Sunday. Full service, wine/beer/alcohol, take-out, VISA/MC/AMX, $$**

🍴 Reviewers' choice   • Vegetarian restaurant   •• Vegan restaurant
$ less than $6 $$ $6–$12 $$$ more than $12
VISA/AMX/MC/DISC/DC—credit cards accepted
Non-alc.—Non-alcoholic   Fresh juices—freshly squeezed

- ## Aspects Restaurant International Vegetarian Cuisine
  530 Hornby St., Vancouver, B.C. V6C 2E7 **(604) 685-4377**
  Vegetarian. Be enticed by homemade dishes such as Mexican Chili, Vegetable Curry, and Three-Cheese Lasagna. **Open Monday through Friday. Cafeteria style, catering, take-out, $**

- ## Bodai Vegetarian Restaurant
  337 E. Hastings St., Vancouver, B.C. V6A 1P3 **(604) 682-2666**
  Vegetarian/ethnic. Pure vegetarian food is provided in a smoke-free environment. Entrees include Colorful Bamboo Shoots, Celery with Mushrooms, and Chili Bean Curd with Sesame Seed Oil. **Open daily. Full service, take-out, VISA/MC, $$**

- ## Bo-Jik Vegetarian Restaurant
  820 W. Broadway, Vancouver, B.C. V5Z 1J8 **(604) 872-5556**
  Vegetarian/Asian. Enjoy pure Buddhist vegetarian cuisine. **Open daily. Full service, take-out, VISA/MC, $$**

- ## Buddhist Vegetarian Restaurant
  363 E. Hastings St., Vancouver, B.C. V5K 2L9 **(604) 687-5231**
  Vegetarian/Chinese. Bean curd, vegetarian (all-simulated) gluten meats, and deluxe clear vegetarian soups are the types of food you will find at this authentic Chinese vegetarian restaurant. **Open daily. Full service, vegan options, take-out, VISA, $$**

- ## •• Circling Dawn
  1045 Commercial Dr., Vancouver, B.C. V5L 3X1 **(604) 255-2326**
  Vegan/organic food store. This vegan restaurant serves French toast, pancakes, tofu scrambles, hot cereals, sandwiches, salads, tofu burger, lasagna. **Open daily for breakfast, lunch, and dinner. Counter service, vegan options, fresh juices, catering, $**

- ## Evergreen
  4166 Main St., Vancouver, B.C. V5V 3P7 **(604) 879-3380**
  Vegetarian/Chinese. The menu is completely vegetarian, and all foods are prepared without preservatives. Choose from Sweet Tofu Cake, Lo-Hon Mixed Vegetables, and other dishes. **Open daily. Vegan options, take-out, $**

- ## Greens and Gourmet
  2681 W. Broadway, Vancouver, B.C. V6K 2G2 **(604) 737-7373**
  Vegetarian/macrobiotic/natural foods. Items included on the extensive vegetarian menu are cooked with purified water, which is also served for drinking. At the self-service hot and cold buffet, food is sold by weight. **Open daily. Full service, macrobiotic, vegan options, fruit juices, take-out, catering, VISA/MC, $–$$**

- ## The Naam Restaurant ❧
  2724 W. 4th Ave., Vancouver, B.C. V6K 1R1 **(604) 738-7151**
  Vegetarian/Ethnic. A completely vegetarian menu offers a wide assortment of dishes, from Mexican to East Indian. All foods are made on the premises. Live

music is provided at lunch and dinner. **Open daily. Full service, vegan/macrobiotic options, fruit juices, wine/beer, take-out, VISA/MC, $–$$**

The Noodle Maker Restaurant
122 Powell St., Vancouver, B.C. V6A 1G1   **(604) 683-9196**
Chinese. This gourmet Chinese restaurant offers nine vegetarian entrees. Appetizers and soup are also available. **Open Monday through Friday. Full service, vegan options, wine/beer/alcohol, VISA /MC/AMX, $$$**

Noor-Mahal Restaurant
4354 Fraser St., Vancouver, B.C. V5V 4G3   **(604) 873-9263**
South Indian. A choice of dosas and other vegetable dishes as well as several vegetarian appetizers. **Open daily. Full service, take-out, VISA/MC, $–$$**

Nyala African Restaurant
2930 W. 4th Ave., Vancouver, B.C. V6K 1R2   **(604) 731-7899**
Ethiopian. Choose from six vegan options including Shuro Watt and Yeshebera Asa. Nyala also offers a couple of salads. **Open daily. Full service, vegan options, wine/beer/alcohol, catering, take-out, VISA/MC/AMX, $$**

• Surat Sweets
6665 Fraser St., Vancouver, B.C. V5X 3T6   **(604) 322-9544**
Vegetarian/Indian. Serves a variety of pure vegetarian Gujarati foods. **Open daily. Limited service, vegan options, take-out, $$**

• Woodlands Restaurant ⫘
2582 W. Broadway, Vancouver, B.C. V6J 2V1   **(604) 733-5411**
Vegetarian/North American. The menu contains numerous vegetarian dishes. None of the food contains meat, fish, fowl or eggs. Desserts are prepared in Woodlands' own bakery. **Open daily. Full service and buffet style, vegan options, fruit juices, wine/beer, catering, take-out, VISA/MC, $$**

VERNON

• Sunseed Vegetarian Cafe
2919 30th Ave., Vernon, B.C. V1T 2B8   **(604) 542-7892**
Vegetarian. In addition to two soups daily, including one special vegan soup, Sunseed offers Vegetable Lasagna, Shepherd's Pie, and international dishes. **Open morning and afternoon. Closed Sunday. Cafeteria style, vegan options, fresh juice, espresso/non-dairy cappuccino, non-alc. beer, take-out, MC/VISA, $**

VICTORIA

Eugene's Greek Restaurant
1280 Broad St., Victoria, B.C. V8W 2A5   **(604) 381-5456**
Greek. Eugene's specializes in traditional Greek food. The menu includes Vegetarian Soullaki. **Open Monday through Saturday. Self-service, $**

•• Green Cuisine
560 Johnson, Victoria, B.C., V8W 3C6   **(604) 385-1809**

Vegan. In the Market Square area, this totally vegan restaurant offers a hot buffet and a salad buffet that changes daily. Desserts made without white sugar are available as are bean and grain dishes. Organic items are used whenever possible. **Open daily. Self service, vegan options, fresh juices, espresso/cappuccino, non-alc. beer, catering, take-out, VISA/MC, $**

India Curry House
2561 Government St., Victoria, B.C V8T 4P6   (604) 384-5622
Indian. No MSG or preservatives are used in the preparation of ten vegetarian main courses. Free parking is available. **Open daily for lunch and dinner. Full service, reservations recommended, formal, non-alc. beer, wine/beer/alcohol, take-out, VISA/MC/AMX/DISC, $$-$$$**

Jack Lee's Chinese Village
755 Finlayson St., Victoria, B.C. V8T 4W4   (604) 384-8151
Chinese. Jack Lee's offers vegetarian options, and meals can be prepared to satisfy any dietary preferences. **Open daily. Full service, wine/beer/alcohol, catering, take-out, VISA/MC/AMX, $$**

Re-Bar
50 Bastian Sq., Victoria, B.C. V8W 1J2   (604) 361-9223
Natural foods. Re-Bar is mostly vegetarian, with fish served once a week. All baked goods are made in Re-Bar's kitchen daily, with minimum use of refined sugars and flours. Organic produce is used when available in the summer. Soups are made with 100-percent vegetable stock, and the tortillas do not contain animal fats. Re-Bar uses filtered water. Typical breakfasts include bagels, cinnamon raisin toast, scrambled eggs, and muffins. Lunch options include Miso Soup, Szechuan Noodle Salad, Almond Burger, and Enchilada. **Open daily for breakfast, lunch, and dinner. Full service, fresh juices, non-alc. beer, wine/beer, take-out, VISA/MC, $-$$**

Taj Mahal Restaurant
679 Herald St., Victoria, B.C. V8W 1S8   (604) 383-4662
Indian. Taj Mahal serves vegetarian dishes from all regions of India and also has various kinds of leavened and unleavened breads. All foods are prepared without MSG or preservatives. **Open Monday through Saturday for lunch and dinner, Sunday for dinner only. Full service, wine/beer/alcohol, catering, take-out, VISA/MC/AMX, $$**

• The Veggie Cafe
1219 Wharf St., Victoria, B.C. V8W 1T9   (604) 389-1289
Vegetarian. This primarily vegan cafe serves vegetarian pizza and lots of soups. There's live music in the evening. **Open daily. Limited service, vegan options, fresh juices, organic beer, take-out, $**

ᏚᏰ Reviewers' choice   • Vegetarian restaurant   •• Vegan restaurant
$ less than $6 $$ $6-$12 $$$ more than $12
VISA/AMX/MC/DISC/DC—credit cards accepted
Non-alc.—Non-alcoholic   Fresh juices—freshly squeezed

• Viteway
1019 Blanshard St., Victoria, B.C. V8W 2H4   **(604) 384-5677**
Vegetarian/natural foods. Enjoy terrific chili, a large bakery selection, and music in a relaxing environment. **Open daily. Limited service, take-out, VISA/MC, $**

WEST VANCOUVER

Capers
2496 Marine Dr., West Vancouver, B.C. V7V 1L1   **(604) 925-3316**
Natural foods/health-food store. A wide variety of vegetarian foods such as Caper's Falafel, assorted salads, and an organic stir-fry are offered. **Open daily. Full service, fruit juices, wine/beer, catering, take-out (deli only), VISA/MC, $$**

MANITOBA

WINNIPEG

Desserts Plus
1595 Main St., Winnipeg, MB R2V 1Y2   **(204) 339-1957**
Dairy. All food in this smoke-free restaurant is homemade without additives. Pastries, vegetable soups, blintzes, knishes of all types, and vegetarian egg rolls are typical vegetarian selections. Catering is the main business. **Open Monday through Friday for lunch and Thursday for dinner. Full service, reservations recommended, catering, take-out, VISA/MC, $$**

Falafel Place and Deli
612 Academy Road, Winnipeg, MB R3N 0E6   **(204) 489-5811**
Middle Eastern. The owner claims that customers say his is the best apple strudel and baklava in town. You can also try the Hummus, Veggie Burgers, Couscous, Potato Pancakes, meatless soups, and foul (fava beans). **Open daily. Counter service, vegan options, fresh juices, non-alc. beer/wine, catering, take-out, $**

Moti-Mahal Curry Place
998 St. Mary's Road, Winnipeg, MB R2M 3S3   **(204) 257-8218**
Indian. Large selection of vegetarian curries. **Open daily for dinner. Full service, reservations recommended, vegan options, Indian beer/wine/alcohol, VISA/MC, $$**

Mrs. Lipton's
Ardjuna
962 Westminster Ave., Winnipeg, MB R3G 1B8   **(204) 775-6743**
Natural foods/Indonesian/international. At the same location, using the same tables, are two different restaurants, run by totally different owners who share space. In the daytime, Mrs. Lipton's serves lunch items such as veggie burgers, Falafel, curries, salads, and vegetarian soups. Table service is provided. In the evening, the restaurant is Ardjuna, which serves Indonesian dishes. Vegetarian selections include Steamed Vegetables with Peanut Sauce and Tofu, Bean Cake in Hot

Tomato Sauce, and Peanut Wafers. **Mrs. Lipton's is open Tuesday through Saturday for lunch. Full service, alcohol, VISA, $. Ardjuna is open Tuesday through Sunday for dinner. Full service, reservations recommended on weekends. Vegan options, beer/wine, catering, take-out, VISA/MC/AMX, $$**

• Wheat Song Cafe and Bakery
578 Broadway (at Balmoral), Winnipeg, MB R3C 0W5   (204) 775-0031
Vegetarian/natural foods. The bakery uses 100-percent stone-ground flour in its whole-wheat, multi-grain, and sandwich buns. It also offers cinnamon buns, cookies, date squares, muffins, cakes, logs, and apple pie slices prepared without white sugar. The cafe serves homemade soups, sandwiches such as Sunflower Lentil Burger, spinach pie, and vegetarian pizza. **Open Tuesday through Saturday. Counter service, take-out, limited catering, $**

NOVA SCOTIA

ANTIGONISH

Sunshine Cafe
194 Main St., Antigonish, N.S. B2G 2R6   (902) 863-1194
Natural foods. Located in the Sunflower Natural Foods Store, Sunshine Cafe offers simple breakfasts such as coffee and bran muffins. For lunch, the cafe features hearty whole-wheat sandwiches and Chili as well as salads—including Tabouleh. Desserts in this smoke-free cafe are made with local maple syrup. **Open Monday through Saturday. Full service, catering, take-out, VISA/MC, $$**

HALIFAX

• Satisfaction Feast Vegetarian Restaurant
1581 Grafton St., Halifax, N.S. B3J 2C3   (902) 422-3540
Vegetarian. The menu includes a large selection of appetizers, soups, sandwiches, salads, and entrees that are all vegetarian. **Open daily. Full service, vegan options, fruit juices, VISA/MC/AMX, $–$$**

ONTARIO

CONCORD

East Moon Restaurant
2150 Steeles Ave. W., Concord, ON L4K 2T5   (905) 738-1428
Chinese. The menu lists approximately ten vegetarian entrees plus vegetarian egg and spring rolls. **Open daily. Full service, catering, take-out, wine/beer/alcohol, VISA/MC/AMX, $$**

KINGSTON

Darbar Restaurant

479 Princess St., Kingston, ON K7L 1C3   **(613) 548-7053**

Indian. Darbar offers more than ten vegetarian dishes. **Open daily. Darbar Coffee, lassi, $**

• Sunflower Restaurant ✿

20 Montreal St., Kingston, ON K7L 3G6   **(613) 542-4566**

Vegetarian. The all-vegetarian international menu includes vegan entrees, soups, salads, a soy burger, and wheat-free items. There are daily specials, and organic produce is used when possible. **Open Tuesday through Saturday. Full service, vegan options, fresh juice, natural beer/wine, MC/VISA, $$**

MISSISSAUGA

Champion House Restaurant

25 Watline Ave., 2nd Fl., Mississauga, ON L4Z 2Z1   **(905) 890-8988**

Chinese. The menu has a vegetarian section with vegetable and tofu dishes. **Open daily. Full service, vegan options, wine/beer, take-out, VISA/MC/AMX/DC, $$**

NORTH YORK

Haifa Restaurant

3022-3024 Bathurst St., North York, ON M6B 3B6   **(416) 783-6406**

Ethnic. This restaurant offers BBQ Eggplant, Stuffed Grape Leaves, Fried Chick Peas, and more. **Open daily. Full service, wine/beer/alcohol, catering, VISA, $**

La Mexicana Restaurant

3337 Bathurst St., North York, ON M6A 2B7   **(416) 783-9452**

Mexican. This Mexican restaurant features authentic Mexican cuisine, Latin American music, and an open outdoor patio. Choose from several vegetarian dishes including Vegetable Enchiladas, Chilaquiles (Mexican lasagna), a chili dish, and an eggplant casserole. **Open daily. Full service, wine/beer/alcohol, catering, take-out, VISA/MC/AMX, $$**

OTTAWA

Domus Cafe

269 Dalhousie St., Ottawa, ON K1N 7E3   **(613) 241-6410**

Natural foods. Eclectic gourmet foods are prepared with fresh produce from local farmers. There's a daily change in the menu. The restaurant is connected to a kitchen/housewares store. **Open daily for breakfast and lunch. Full service, wine/beer, take-out, VISA/MC/AMX, $$**

• The Green Door

198 Main St., Ottawa, ON K1S 1C6   **(613) 234-9597**

Vegetarian/natural foods. Open the door and find organic grains, beans, salads, and sea vegetables. Organic flours are used in sourdough baking, yeast-free baked goods, wheat-free breads, and sugar-free baked goods (no honey is used.) The Green Door specializes in macrobiotic foods and organic foods; very few dairy products or eggs are used, and food is sold by the pound. **Open daily except Monday. Self service, vegan/macrobiotic options, fresh juices, wine/beer, catering, take-out, VISA/MC, $**

Rosie Lee Cafe

167 Laurier Ave. E, Ottawa, ON K1N 6N8   **(613) 234-7299**

French. Enjoy French-style quiches, sandwiches, entrees, and soups. **Open daily. Full service, wine/beer/alcohol, take-out, $$**

Silk Roads Restaurant

300 Sparks St., Mall, Ottawa ON K2C 2E9   **(613) 236-4340**

Afghan. The Afghan cuisine includes vegetarian options. **Open daily. Full service, wine/beer/alcohol, VISA/MC/AMX, $$–$$$**

THORNHILL

Sonny Langer's Vegetarian Dairy Restaurant

180 Steeles Ave. W., Thornhill, ON L4J 2L1   **(905) 881-4356**

Kosher. Sonny Langer's is vegetarian except for fish and is famous for pierogies. Everything is made from scratch with no preservatives or food colorings. **Open daily. Full service, vegan options, take-out, catering, VISA/MC, $$**

United Bakers Dairy Restaurant

390 Steeles Ave. W., Thornhill, ON L4J 6X2   **(905) 764-1149**

Ethnic/Jewish dairy. This dairy restaurant features European-style dishes including blintzes, kreplach, quiche, Cabbage Rolls, Stuffed Green Peppers, Vegetarian Lasagna, Vegetarian Chopped Liver, bagels, soups, and salads. **Open daily. Full service, vegan options, take-out, catering, VISA/MC, $$**

TORONTO

(For additional restaurants in the surrounding area, see Thornhill.)

• Annapurna

1085 Bathurst St., Toronto, ON M5R 3G8   **(416) 537-8513**

Macrobiotic/Indian. Macrobiotic foods and southern Indian cuisine are served. **Open daily. Full service, macrobiotic options, catering, take-out, $**

Champion House Restaurant

480 Dundas St. W., Toronto, ON M5T 1G9   **(416) 977-8282**

Chinese. Enjoy Northern Chinese cuisine, a separate vegetarian menu, and a full Chinese tea menu. **Open daily. Full service, vegan options, wine/beer/alcohol, take-out, catering, $$**

Charmers Cafe

1384 Bathurst St., Toronto, ON M5R 3J1   **(416) 657-1225**

Tex/Mex. Charmers offers vegetarian tostadas, burritos, enchiladas, sauces, Baba Ghanouj, soups, salads, and desserts. **Open daily. Limited service, wine/beer, take-out, catering, VISA/MC, $$**

- # Chinese Vegetarian House 🍃
39 Baldwin St., Toronto, ON M5T 1L1   **(416) 599-6855**
Vegetarian/Chinese. The Chinese vegetarian cuisine is based on contemporary and 1000-year-old recipes. Some wheat-gluten dishes are available. No MSG is used. **Closed Monday. Full service, vegan options, organic wine/beer, catering, take-out, $$**

- # Earth Tones Whole Food Emporium and Vegetarian Restaurant
357 Queen St. W., Toronto, ON M5V 2A4   **(416) 599-9054**
Vegetarian. Enjoy the restaurant's wide selection of vegetarian foods, and visit the health food store and deli at the same location. **Open daily. Cafeteria style, wine/beer, take-out, catering, VISA/MC, $**

Epicure Cafe
512 Queen St. W., Toronto, ON M5V 2B2   **(416) 363-8942**
Natural foods. Enjoy items from the traditional Italian and French bistro blackboard menu, which changes daily and is seasonal. **Open daily. Full service, wine/beer/alcohol, take-out, catering, VISA/MC/AMX, $$**

Grainfield's Bakery
1464 Kingston Rd., Toronto, ON M1N 1R6   **(416) 691-6061**
Natural foods. This alternative bakery specializes in sourdough and yeast-free breads and pasteries. Organic flours are used, and most products are dairy- and egg-free. **Open 9 A.M. to 5 P.M. Tuesday through Friday, to 4:30 P.M. Saturday. Take-out only.**

The Groaning Board
287 King St. West, Toronto, ON M5V 1JS   **(416) 595-7232**
North American style/natural foods. The Groaning Board appropriately features a self-serve soup, salad, and make-your-own-sundae bar. There is also waiter service for such items as Vegetarian Lasagna, Spanakopita, Brown Rice Pilaf, and Mushroom-Spinach Quiche. **Open daily. Limited service, wine/beer, take-out, VISA/MC/AMX/DISC, $$**

- # Hare Krishna Center
243 Avenue Rd., Dupont, Toronto, ON M5R 2J6   **(416) 922-5415**
Vegetarian. In downtown Toronto, you'll find this all-you-can-eat buffet. Foods are egg-free, and different dishes are featured daily—usually rice, dahl, and soups. **Open Monday through Saturday, Sunday evening feast. Cafeteria style, limited catering, take-out, $**

- # Hey Good Cooking
238 Dupont St., Toronto, ON M5R 1V7   **(416) 929-9140**

🍃 Reviewers' choice   • Vegetarian restaurant   •• Vegan restaurant
$ less than $6 $$ $6–$12 $$$ more than $12
VISA/AMX/MC/DISC/DC—credit cards accepted
Non-alc.—Non-alcoholic   Fresh juices—freshly squeezed

Vegetarian. Daily specials include Chickpea and Vegetable Curry, Texan Chili, Mushroom Nut Loaf, and Southern Spiced Tofu, as well as homemade Veggie Burgers, soups, and salads. **Open daily. Cafeteria style, vegan options, take-out, $**

•• Juice for Life
238 Queen St. W., Toronto, ON M5V 1Z1   **(416) 408-3581**
Vegan. You'll find vegan dishes and an extensive juice bar. **Open daily. Cafeteria style, vegan options, fresh juices, take-out, catering.**

Le Kashmire
605 Bloor St. W., Toronto, ON M6G 1K5   **(416) 533-5955**
Indian/Pakistani. Indian/Pakistani cusine here includes a special luncheon buffet and Saturday and Sunday brunch. **Closed Monday. Buffet lunch, full service dinner, vegan options, wine/beer/alcohol, take-out, catering, $$**

• Lennies Whole Foods
489 Parliament St., Toronto, ON M5A 3A3   **(416) 967-5196**
Vegetarian/natural foods. There are a few seats in this take-out restaurant that offers gourmet pizzas, "the best guacamole this side of Mexico," falafel sandwiches, soups, and salads. **Open daily. Counter service, vegan options, take-out, VISA/AMX, $**

La Mexicana Restaurant
229 Carlton St., Toronto, ON M5A 2L2   **(416) 929-6284**
Mexican. This Mexican restaurant features authentic Mexican cuisine, Latin American music, and an open outdoor patio. Choose from several vegetarian dishes including vegetable enchiladas, chilaquiles (Mexican lasagna), a chili dish, and an eggplant casserole. **Open daily. Full service, wine/beer/alcohol, catering, take-out, VISA/MC/AMX, $$**

Mickey's Hideaway
352 Pape Ave., Toronto, ON M4M 2X1   **(416) 461-2035**
Mexican. This cozy restaurant offers California/Mexican dishes prepared from scratch and baked or sautéed instead of fried. A live blues duo performs on Friday and Saturday nights. **Closed Monday. Full service, wine/beer/alcohol, take-out, VISA/MC, $$**

Motimahal Restaurant
1422 Gerrard St. East, Toronto, ON M4L 1Z6   **(416) 461-3111**
Indian. This Northern Indian restaurant offers a wide variety of curries. **Closed Tuesday. Cafeteria style and full service, wine/beer/alcohol, take-out, catering, VISA/MC/AMX, $**

Le Papillon
16 Church St., Toronto, ON M5E 1M1   **(416) 363-0838**
French. Savor the crêpes in a comfortable French atmosphere. Children are welcome. **Closed Monday. Full service, wine/beer/alcohol, take-out, catering, VISA/MC/AMX, $$**

Queen Mother Café
208 Queen St. W., Toronto, ON M5V 1Z2   **(416) 598-4719**

Laotian/Thai. Queen Mother has been serving Lao-Thai food and vegetarian burgers since 1978. In spring and summer, you can eat on the garden patio. **Closed Sunday. Full service, wine/beer/alcohol, take-out, catering, VISA/MC/AMX, $$**

The Queen of Sheba
1198 Bloor St. W., Toronto, ON M6H 1N2   **(416) 536-4162**
Ethiopian. Some vegetarian dishes are featured and are served with injera, Ethiopian bread. There's also a six-dish vegetarian sampler. **Open daily. Full service, wine/beer/alcohol, take-out, catering, VISA/MC, $$**

• Renaissance Cafe
509 Bloor St. W., Toronto, ON M5S 1Y2   **(416) 968-6639**
Vegetarian. West Indian and Indonesian dishes are just a sample of the type of vegetarian food served here. Renaissance Cafe is open late into the evening every day. Outdoor patio. **Open daily for lunch and dinner. Full service, vegan options, catering, take-out, VISA/MC/AMX, $$**

The Rivoli
332 Queen St. W., Toronto, ON M5V 2A2   **(416) 596-1908**
Oriental. In the summertime, a sidewalk cafe affords additional seating. Live entertainment is sometimes offered. **Open daily. Full service, wine/beer/alcohol, catering, take-out, VISA/MC, $$**

United Bakers Dairy Restaurant
506 Lawrence Ave. W., Toronto, ON M6A 1A1   **(416) 789-0519**
Ethnic/Jewish dairy. Toronto's oldest dairy restaurant features European-style dishes including blintzes, kreplach, quiche, Cabbage Rolls, Stuffed Green Peppers, Vegetarian Lasagna, Vegetarian Chopped Liver, bagels, soups, and salads. **Open daily. Full service, vegan options, take-out, catering, VISA/MC, $$**

• The Vegetarian Restaurant
4 Dundonald St., Toronto, ON M4Y 1K2   **(416) 961-9522**
Vegetarian/natural foods. This restaurant avoids frying and uses filtered water. Organic food is used when possible, and the menu lists ingredients for all items—an international selection, salad bar, prepared salads, burritos, Lasagna, bean dishes, Nut Loaf, and vegan desserts. Live music is featured on Wednesday. **Open daily, Sunday for dinner only. Cafeteria style, vegan options, fresh juices, non-alc. beer/wine, take-out, VISA/MC/DC**

• The West End Vegetarian Restaurant
2849 Dundas St. W., Toronto, ON M6P 1Y6   **(416) 762-1204**
Vegetarian/natural foods. This vegetarian restaurant has been open for more than eighteen years. Dishes, which vary seasonally, are listed on a chalkboard menu. Organic products are used when available. **Open daily. Cafeteria style, vegan options, take-out, VISA/MC, $$**

Willow Restaurant
193 Danforth Ave., Toronto, ON M4K 1N2   **(416) 469-5315**
Mexican. The Mexican fare includes vegetarian burritos, chimichangas, enchilladas, quesadillas, and fajitas. **Open daily. Full service, wine/beer/alcohol, take-out, VISA/MC/AMX, $$**

Yofi's Restaurant and Patio
19 Baldwin St., Toronto, ON M5T 1L1   **(416) 977-1145**
Primarily vegetarian/ethnic. This restaurant is vegetarian with the exception of one tuna entree. A wide variety of different ethnic dishes includes Middle Eastern Hummus, Baba Ghanouj, and Tabouli; Mexican Nachos; Greek Salad; and many different vegetarian burgers. **Patio dining. Closed Sunday. Full service, vegan options, take-out, catering, VISA/MC, $–$$**

WILLOWDALE

Yonge Garden Restaurant and Tavern
5186 Yonge St., Willowdale, ON M2N 5P6   **(416) 225-2383**
Chinese. This Chinese restaurant offers more than a dozen different vegetarian dishes including Mixed Greens and Tofu, Vegetable Balls (made out of wheat gluten), Chow Mein, Vegetable Fried Rice, and Mixed Vegetables. **Open daily. Full service, wine/beer/alcohol, take-out, catering, VISA/MC/AMX, $$**

QUEBEC

LAFEBVRE

• Vegies Story Land
169 St. Jean D'Arc, Lafebvre, P.Q. J0H 2C0   **(514) 738-9062**
Vegetarian. Visit this vegetarian restaurant by appointment—mostly during the summertime. Vegies also has a bed-and-breakfast arrangement. **Open weekends during summer. Cafeteria style, $**

MONTREAL

• Le Commensal
2115 St-Denis, Montreal, P.Q. H2X 3K8   **(514) 845-0248**

680 Ste-Catherine West, Montreal, P.Q. H3D 1C2   **(514) 871-1480**

3715 Queen Mary, Montreal, P.Q. H3T 1X8   **(514) 733-9755**
Vegetarian. Voted best vegetarian restaurant by the *Montreal Monitor* in 1992, Le Commensal has been in business for more than fifteen years and offers various ethnic dishes. **Open daily. Buffet, take-out, catering, VISA/MC/AMX, $$**

Cuillere D'or (Golden Spoon)
5217 De Carie, Montreal, P.Q. H3W 3C2   **(514) 481-3431**
Kosher. Vegetarian with the exception of a few dishes, this kosher dairy restaurant serves Stuffed Grape Leaves, blintzes, vegetarian burgers, Lasagna, pizza, and Middle Eastern platters. **Full service, vegan options, take-out, catering, VISA, $$**

Foxy's Kosher Pizza
5987 Victoria, Montreal, P.Q. H3W 2R9   **(514) 739-8777**

Kosher/natural foods. Foxy's features kosher pizza. **Closed Saturday. Cafeteria style, beer, take-out, $**

• Pushap Restaurant and Sweets
5195 Pare, Montreal, P.Q. H4P 1P4   **(514) 737-4527**

11999 Boul. Goulin W., Pierrefonds, P.Q. H8Z 1V8   **(514) 683-0556**
Vegetarian/Indian. Pushap is a family-run restaurant offering Indian vegetarian food. **Open daily. Full service, Indian spice tea, $$**

QUEBEC CITY

The Cafe Millefeuille
32 Rue Ste.-Angele, Quebec City, Quebec G1R 4G4   **(418) 692-2147**
Natural foods. Situated in an old historic house with a fireplace, the cafe offers outdoor dining in the summer. In addition to dining, you can also enjoy an art exhibition. The primarily vegetarian menu features Chili (without meat), Cauliflower with Mushroom and Cheese in Tomato Sauce, Millet Pie, quiche, bread with cheese, salads, and Spanakopita. **Open daily for breakfast, lunch, and dinner in the summer. Open Wednesday through Sunday other times of the year. Full service, reservations recommended, espresso/cappuccino, non-alc. beer and wine, beer/wine/alcohol, catering, take-out, VISA/MC , $$**

SASKATCHEWAN

REGINA

Alfredo's
1801 Scarth St., Regina, Saskatchewan S4P 2G9   **(306) 522-3366**
Italian. Appealing to vegetarians are Baked Zucchini Parmesan, Spinach Tortelini, and Eggplant Parmesan. Homemade pasta (with eggs) is prepared fresh daily. **Open Monday through Saturday. Full service and cafeteria options, reservations recommended, espresso/cappuccino, beer/wine/alcohol, catering, take-out, VISA/MC/AMX/DC, $–$$$**

VEGETARIAN VACATION SPOTS

"From Atlantic to Pacific, gee, the traffic is terrific!"—it must be vacation time. Whether you choose to vacation on one of the coasts or any place in between, you'll find that vegetarians now have a multitude of options. Choose one of the following spots and combine rafting, yoga, or what have you with tastes galore.

ALABAMA

Yuchi Pines Institute
Route 1, Box 443, Seale, AL 36875   **(205) 855-4781**
A health-conditioning center for ambulatory people who have health problems, the institute operates within the framework of Seventh-day Adventist beliefs and is supervised by two M.D.'s. All meals are vegan.

ARKANSAS

The Garden of Eve Health Spa
1 Washington Street, Eureka Springs, AR 72632   **(501) 253-7777**
Located in the Ozarks, this spa serves vegetarian cuisine from a variety of ethnic cultures.

The Oasis
HC 33, Box 10, Tilly, AR 72679   **(501) 496-2364**
A health retreat located in the Boston Range of the Ozark Mountains, The Oasis specializes in organically grown foods as a mainstay of its vegetarian meals. Nearby is Buffalo River National Park.

CALIFORNIA

Ananda
14618 Tyler Foote Road, Nevada City, CA 95959   **(800) 346-5350**
The beauty of the Sierra Nevadas has been the setting of Ananda's meditative and yoga retreats for more than twenty-five years. It is a strictly vegetarian establishment, and almost always serves a vegan option.

EarthSave
706 Frederick Street, Santa Cruz, CA 95062   **(408) 423-4069**
Wilderness retreats and river-rafting trips are conducted in California, and there are environmental youth camps nationwide. All are "pure vegetarian."

La Maida House and Bungalows
11159 La Maida Street, North Hollywood, CA 91601   **(818) 769-3857**
For ethical reasons, this "romantic city-hideaway executive retreat" no longer serves animal products.

Land of Medicine Buddha
5800 Prescott Road, Soquel, CA 95073   **(408) 462-8383**
Health retreats here include organic, vegetarian meals.

Mendocino Summer Retreat
21109 Costanso St., Woodland Hills, CA 91364   **(818) 716-6332**
Programs here integrate macrobiotic living and Waldorf education. The retreat is vegan.

Mount Madonna Center
445 Summit Road, Watsonville, CA 95076   **(408) 847-0406**
The center is a community for the creative arts and health sciences within a context of spiritual growth. Campgrounds in redwood groves are located on the site. The center is strictly lacto-vegetarian but can accommodate vegans.

The Oaks at Ojai
122 E. Ojai Ave., Ojai, CA 93023   **(805) 646-5573**
This resident health spa located in the Ojai Valley serves vegetarian meals on an "alternative" basis, but is looking into a more extensive veggie cuisine.

The Palms
572 North Indian Canyon Drive, Palm Springs, CA 92262 (619) 325-1111
The Palms calls itself one of the top ten health spas in the country. It offers vegetarian options at every meal.

Rancho La Puerta
P.O. Box 2548, Escondido, CA 92033   **(619) 744-6677**
The ranch prides itself on being the world's first fitness spa. Largely vegetarian since its opening fifty years ago, it does serve fish.

Royal Gorge Cross Country Ski Resort
P.O. Box 1100, Soda Springs, CA 95728   **(800) 634-3086**
The resort serves vegetarian food to its guests.

Sivananda Yoga Vedanta Center
Sivananda Ashram Yoga Farm,
14651 Ballantree Lane, Grass Valley, CA 95949   **(916) 272-9322**
The center offers a lacto-vegetarian menu at all of its yoga retreats. It also conducts weekend workshops on vegetarian lifestyles.

Stony Brook Inn
309 W. Colombero, P.O. Box 1860
McCloud, CA 96057-1860   **(916) 964-2300**
or (800) 369-6118

This Shasta Mountain bed-and-breakfast retreat offers "diverse international vegetarian cuisine with vegan alternatives."

Vega Study Center's Summer Camp
1511 Robinson Street, Oroville, CA 95965   **(916) 533-7702**

An annual affair in Tahoe National Forest, the program centers around macrobiotic living.

We Care Health Center
18000 Long Canyon Rd., Desert Hot Springs, CA, 92240   **(619) 251-2261**
or (800) 888-2523

The center is run by a wholistic health group devoted to physical and mental wellness. It offers a wide variety of raw vegetable juices as part of its vegetarian regimen.

Weimar Institute
P.O. Box 486, 20601 W. Paoli Lane
Weimar, CA 95736-0486   **(916) 637-4111**

A strictly vegan health resort, Weimar also offers a variety of health-related seminars.

COLORADO

Mind and Body River Adventures
P.O. Box 863, Hotchkiss, CO 81419   **(303) 527-3365**

This organization specializes in "river adventures to self-awareness." Yoga and tai chi are part of its program. The adventures are primarily organically vegan, but other diets will be catered to upon request.

CONNECTICUT

Butterbrooke Bed and Breakfast
78 Barry Road, Oxford, CT 06483   **(203) 888-2000**

This restored 1711 colonial house is located on a small organic farm, and serves a vegetarian breakfast.

DELAWARE

Savannah Inn
330 Savannah Road, Lewes, DE 19958   **(302) 645-5592**

Located near the Atlantic Ocean, this vegetarian bed-and-breakfast serves food only in the summer months.

FLORIDA

Abundant Health Lifestyle Center
Rt. 2 Box 451A, Webster, FL 33597   **(904) 568-1119**

A Christian health resort specializing in a vegan diet, the center offers twenty-six-day lifestyle sessions.

Club Hygiene
105 Bruce Court, Marathon, FL 33050-2915   **(305) 743-3168**
Located in the Keyes area, Club Hygiene offers "comprehensive hygienic vacations" including 100-percent raw, vegan meals.

Crystal Springs Wilderness Retreat
1932 Deer Lane, Zephyrhills, FL 33540   **(813) 782-4226**
Various outdoor activities are available on the retreat's grounds, and it is close to many Florida resorts. Management told us that many dietary preferences can be accommodated.

The Great Outdoors Inn
65 N. Main Street, P.O. Box 387, High Springs, FL 32643   **(904) 454-2900**
This bed-and-breakfast inn is located on forty acres near a state park, and serves vegetarian food. The inn can accommodate up to twenty-four people for conferences. Nearby is the Great Outdoors Cafe offering vegetarian entrees.

Hippocrates Health Institute
1443 Palmdale Court, West Palm Beach, FL 33411   **(407) 471-8876**
A strictly vegan health resort, the institute now offers a singles program.

Hygeia Center
P.O. Box 845, Estero, FL 33928   **(813) 489-3337**
This is a wholistic preventive health-care retreat serving gourmet vegetarian cuisine. A vegan option is offered. Vegetarian trips to places such as Paros, Greece, are sometimes offered.

Indigo Inn
Drayton Island, Box 5, Georgetown, FL 32139   **(904) 467-2446**
A bed-and-breakfast open all year, the inn is located on a twelve-acre working farm on an island. The proprietor, a vegetarian/vegan cook for eighteen years, completed macrobiotic studies at the Kushi Institute.

Palm-Aire Spa Resort
2601 Palm-Aire Drive North, Pompano Beach, FL 33069   **(305) 968-2750**
Vegetarian options are offered every day.

Regency Health Resort and Spa
2000 S. Ocean Drive, Hallandale, FL 33009   **(305) 454-2220**
This is a luxury class beach resort offering gourmet vegetarian cuisine.

Russell House of Key West
611 Truman Avenue, Key West, FL 33040   **(305) 294-8787**
Russell House, which bills itself as a tropical wellness retreat, serves a vegetarian diet with a vegan option.

Safety Harbor Spa and Fitness
105 N. Bayshore Dr., Safety Harbor, FL 34695 (800) 237-0155
Calling itself the "ultimate spa vacation," Safety Harbor offers a few vegetarian/vegan options on its regular menu.

HAWAII

Hana Plantation Houses
P.O. Box 489, Hana Maui, HI 96713 (808) 248-7248
This beach resort is operated by a vegetarian who was a founder of the Ecologically Conscious Host Network and operates two Environmental Information Centers.

Hawaiian Fitness Holiday
P.O. Box 279, Koloa, Kauai, HI 96756 (808) 332-9244
Focus on total health and fitness in a tropical paradise. Vegetarian cuisine (fish is also served) with a vegan option is offered.

Kalani Honua
RR2 Box 4500, Pahoa, HI 96778 (808) 965-7828
This conference and retreat center specializes in vegetarian cuisine although fish and fowl entrees are offered. The center also conducts a wide variety of workshops and festivals.

The Plantation Spa
51-550 Kam Hwy., Ka'a'awa, Oahu, HI 96730 (800) 422-0307
This Swedish Polynesian retreat bills itself as a "spa resort for body and mind," and offers lacto-vegetarian cuisine with a vegan option.

IDAHO

Idaho Afloat
P.O. Box 542, Grangeville, ID 83530 (208) 983-2414
A white-water rafting organization in the Pacific Northwest, Idaho Afloat can accommodate vegetarians, and would be happy to bring in a local vegan cook for a group of more than twelve.

ILLINOIS

The Heartland
20 E. Jackson Blvd., Chicago, IL 60604 (312) 427-6465
Located eighty miles south of Chicago, this health and fitness retreat is situated on thirty-one acres of woods and farmland. The cuisine is "basically vegetarian supplemented with fish."

KENTUCKY

Bluegrass Spa
901 Galloway Rd., Stamping Ground, KY 40379 (502) 535-6261
A "wholistic" fitness resort in the rolling horse-country of central Kentucky, Bluegrass is primarily vegetarian/vegan but does serve fish and chicken. The spa also offers a raw foods and juices regimen.

Bouldaire

Blue Hill Falls, ME 04615   **(207) 359-4692**

Located on the shorefront, Bouldaire is a newly renovated older home. It is close to Acadia National Park, and offers yoga and cooking classes. The cuisine is macrobiotic.

Kingsbury House

35 Northport Avenue, Belfast, ME 04915   **(207) 338-2419**

A macrobiotic bed-and-breakfast, Kingsbury House regularly serves miso soup and tofu French toast.

Northern Pines

559 Rt. 85, Raymond, ME 04071- 6248   **(207) 655-7624**

A lakeside resort in southern Maine, Northern Pines is largely vegetarian, serving fish once a week and offering soy substitutes for dairy. The resort can provide kosher foods, and accommodate diabetics and vegans.

Poland Spring Health Institute

Summit Spring Road, RFD 1, Box 4300
Poland Spring, ME 04274   **(207) 998-2894**

This institute offers a lifestyle improvement program including a vegan regimen.

The Roaring Lion

995 Main Street, P.O. Box 756, Waldoboro, ME 04572   **(207) 832-4038**

Open all year, this bed-and-breakfast caters to vegetarian and macrobiotic diets.

West of Eden

Rt. 102 and Kelleytown Rd., P.O. Box 114
Seal Cove, ME 04674   **(207) 244-9695**

You'll find this small bed-and-breakfast on Mt. Desert Island, just outside of Acadia National Park. It is macrobiotic with a very strong vegan emphasis.

Gramercy Bed & Breakfast

1440 Greenspring Valley Rd., Box 119
Stevenson, MD 21153   **(410) 486-2405**

Located outside of Baltimore on fifty-four acres of forest, organic flower and herb gardens, Gramercy's facilities include a pool, tennis court, and hiking trails. Breakfast items include omelettes, French toast, pancakes, cereals, and fresh fruit.

Insight Meditation Society

1230 Pleasant St., Barre, MA 01005   **(508) 355-4378**

Eighty wooded acres is the perfect setting for vipassana (insight meditation). Meals are vegetarian.

The Kushi Institute
P.O. Box 7, Becket, MA 01223 **(413) 623-5741**
The Institute is a nonprofit educational resort located in the Berkshire Mountains. It is macrobiotic with a vegan emphasis.

Rowe Camp and Conference Center
Kings Highway Rd., Box 273, Rowe, MA 01367 **(413) 339-4216**
The center offers all types of programs to aid in the revitalization of mind and body for all ages. It is surrounded by 1,400 acres of protected forest, and the cuisine is "gourmet vegetarian."

The Turning Point Inn
RD2 Box 140, Great Barrington, MA 01230 **(413) 528-4777**
A year-round bed-and-breakfast, The Turning Point is a 200-year-old inn in the heart of the Berkshires. The inn serves lacto-ovo vegetarian meals and can accommodate vegans.

Whispering Maples
P.O. Box 382, Surriner Road, Becket, MA 01223 **(413) 623-2392**
This bed-and-breakfast specializes in natural and macrobiotic foods.

MICHIGAN

Circle Center Pines
8650 Mullen Road, Delton, MI 49046 **(616) 623-5555**
This cooperative recreation and education center provides vegetarian meals in a campground setting.

MONTANA

Feathered Pipe Foundation
Box 1682, Helena, MT 59624 **(406) 442-8196**
Located in the Rockies, the foundation offers programs for those seeking a healthier mind and body. It also organizes international tours. The cuisine is primarily vegetarian, but fish and chicken are occasionally served.

NEW HAMPSHIRE

Star Island Corporation
110 Arlington St., Boston, MA 02116 **(617) 426-7988**
Summer conferences covering a wide-range of topics are offered on Star Island off the coast of New Hampshire. Meals are vegetarian.

NEW JERSEY

Appel Farms
P.O. Box 770, Elmer, NJ 08318-2472 **(609) 358-2472**
This dormitory-style conference center specializes in home-style vegetarian and kosher vegetarian cuisine. Some of the produce is organically grown on the grounds.

Mayer's Manor
57 Dupont Avenue, P.O. Box 85
Seaside Heights, NJ 08751   (908) 793-6606
Located close to many places of interest in New Jersey, Mayer's bills itself as a vegetarian guest house.

Serendipity Bed and Brunch
712 9th Street, Ocean City, NJ 08226-3554   (609) 399-1554
Vegetarian and macrobiotic entrees are served buffet style.

NEW YORK

Farm Sanctuary
P.O. Box 150, Watkins Glen, NY 14891   (607) 583-2225
This shelter for abused farm animals also has a bed-and-breakfast serving a continental vegetarian breakfast. The shelter is open year round.

Highland House
Airport Road, Yulan, NY 12792   (914) 557-8391
Located on the Delaware River in the Shawangunk Mountains, this hotel follows a philosophy of "Supernutrition." It is strictly lacto-vegetarian, buffet style, and caters to vegans and those with food allergies. Camping inquiries are welcome.

Living Springs Lifestyle Center
136 Bryant Lifestyle Center, Putnam Valley, NY 10579   (800) SAY-WELL
In cooperation with Seventh-day Adventists, the center offers seminars on health issues. Vegan meals are a mainstay of the program.

New Age Health Spa
Neversink, NY 12765   (800) 682-4348
This spa is located on 155 acres in the Catskill Mountains. It offers three types of dietary regimens: non-vegetarian with a vegetarian option; vegan; and juice fast.

Omega Institute
RD 2, Box 377, Rhinebeck, NY 12572   (914) 266-4301
This conference and workshop resort "exists to encourage and promote a hopeful response to personal and cultural challenges . . . based on the belief that a sane world starts with healthy people." The institute also offers outdoor journeys and kids' camps. It is primarily lacto-ovo vegetarian but serves fish.

The Open Space
HCR 1 Box 171, Livingston Manor, NY 12758   (914) 439-3119
Located in the Catskill Mountains, this conference center is committed to Zen practice and offers vegetarian meals.

VATRA Vegetarian Lodge
P.O. Box F, Rte. 214, Hunter, NY 12442   (518) 263-4919
The name says it all.

NORTH CAROLINA

North Carolina Macrobiotic Oceanside Retreat
P.O. Box 262, Corolla, NC 27927 **(919) 453-3553**
The retreat is located one block from the ocean.

OHIO

Sans Souci
3745 Rte. 725, Bellbrook, OH 45305 **(513) 848-4851**
A spa resort located on an eighty-acre private estate, Sans Souci offers a highly individualized program including vegetarian meals. The spa grows its own vegetables.

PENNSYLVANIA

Himalayan Institute
RR 1, Box 400, Honesdale, PA 18431 **(717) 253-5551**
The institute, devoted to teaching yoga and meditation, serves vegetarian meals and offers workshops on vegetarianism.

The Peetham: A Center for Well-Being
RD 8, Box 8116, Stroudsburg, PA 18360 **(717) 629-0481**
This retreat nestled in the heart of the Poconos has conference facilities and serves vegetarian meals.

Quest Center
RR 1, Box 1366, Hop Bottom, PA 18824 **(717) 289-4021**
At a rustic log cabin in the Pocono Mountains, you'll find three dormitory-style bedrooms, vegetarian meals, and yoga and meditation workshops.

White Cloud
RD 1, Box 215, Newfoundland, PA 18445 **(717) 676-3162**
Meals at this country inn located in the Poconos are strictly lacto-ovo vegetarian, and vegans can be accommodated.

PUERTO RICO

Instituto de Vida Natural
222 Park Avenue South, #6D
New York, NY 10003 **(212) 260-5823**
This is "the only spa with both a rain forest and an ocean at its doorstep." The spa is primarily vegan, but will cater to lacto-ovo vegetarians and macrobiotics. Organic food is grown on the premises, and there is an open-kitchen policy.

Grateful Bed & Breakfast
Box 568 - CO, Luquillo, PR 00773 **(809) 889-4919**
Enjoy vegetarian meals and the nearby snorkeling and scuba diving.

SOUTH DAKOTA

Black Hills Health and Education Center
Box 19, Hermosa, SD 57744 **(605) 255-4101**
This strictly vegan health resort is situated in the famous Black Hills.

TEXAS

Church of the White Eagle Lodge
P.O. Box 930, Montgomery, TX 77356 **(409) 597-5757**
This spiritual retreat center is dedicated to following and teaching White Eagle's philosophy. It is strictly lacto-ovo vegetarian and will accommodate vegans.

UTAH

Snowbird Ski and Summer Resort
Snowbird, UT 84092 **(801) 742-2222**
The resort offers 11,000-foot peaks for your enjoyment all year round, and is also a conference facility. The menu contains a few vegetarian entrees.

VERMONT

Greenhope Farm
RFD, Box 2260, E. Harwick, VT 05836 **(802) 533-7772**
At this women-only vacation farm in a tiny hamlet in northeast Vermont, the cooking is vegetarian/vegan.

VIRGINIA

Hartland Health Center
P.O. Box 1, Rapiden, VA 22733 **(703) 672-3100**
Located on 500 acres of gently rolling hills, Hartland is just two hours from Washington, D.C. With a Seventh-day Adventist orientation, the Center is determinedly vegetarian.

Satchidananda Ashram-Yogaville
Buckingham, VA 23921 **(804) 969-3121**
This spiritual center offers a strictly lacto-vegetarian menu and has an annual summer camp.

WASHINGTON

Towerhouse Bed and Breakfast
San Juan Island, 1230 Little Road
Friday Harbor, WA 98250 **(206) 378-5464**
Located on ten acres, Towerhouse offers vegetarian (vegan upon request) breakfasts.

Annapurna Inn
538 Adams at Clay Street, Port Townsend, WA 98368 **(206) 385-2909**

A relatively new vegetarian bed-and-breakfast, the Inn is smoke-free and located in an historic district.

WEST VIRGINIA

Kanawha Farm
RR 1, Box N79, Newville, WV 26601   **(304) 765-7922**

The only vegetarian establishment in the county, Kanawha is located in the heart of West Virginia. It is an organic family farm that welcomes visitors. Camping and bath facilities are available; indoor space is limited. Workshops and a work-exchange program are also offered.

The Woods
P.O. Box 5, Hedgeville, WV 25427   **(800) 248-2222**

This 18,000-acre resort and conference center, located close to the Baltimore-Washington area, offers a few vegetarian entrees.

WISCONSIN

Ralph and Jan's Roadside Attraction
703 Railroad Street, Blanchardville, WI 53516   **(608) 523-2001**

Ralph and Jan run a vegetarian bed-and-breakfast.

CANADA

BRITISH COLUMBIA

Hollyhock Farm
Box 127, Manson's Landing
Cortes Island, BC Canada VOP IKO   **(604) 935-6465**
Wholistic-living workshops and retreats are offered, and camping is available. There is also a "Journeys Program." Fresh vegetarian and seafood fare is served buffet-style.

Strathcona Park Lodge
Box 2160S, Campbell River
British Columbia, Canada V9W 5C9   **(604) 286-2008**
Located in the center of Vancouver Island in a wilderness area, the lodge offers outdoor expeditions that are mostly vegetarian. Special trips are offered for young students.

NOVA SCOTIA

Nada Hermitage
Box 119, Crestone, CO 81131   **(719) 256-4778**
The Hermitage is a monastic spiritual institute in the wilderness of the Sangre de Cristo mountains. People may eat as they choose, but the institute is primarily vegetarian. A sister institute, **Nova Nada,** is in Kemptville, Nova Scotia, Canada BOW 1Y0.

ONTARIO

Hidden Valley Farm
RR 2, Chatsworth, Ontario, Canada, NOH 1G0   **(519) 794-3727**
Most of the food served on this farm is home-cooked and home-grown on 120 acres of organic farmland located close to many points of interest. Meals are vegan but dairy and eggs are available for those in transition.

Philoxia
P.O. Box 56, Marlbank
Toronto, Ontario, Canada KOK 2L0   **(613) 478-6070**
This vacation resort serves macrobiotic and vegetarian foods with an international flavor.

QUEBEC

Vegetarian Story Village
Box 136, S. Durham, P.Q. Canada, JOH 2CO   **(514) 738-9062**
The strictly vegan village bills itself as a "vegetarian mini-resort for nature's lovers and for relaxation."

WHISTLER

• Golden Dreams B and B

6412 Easy St., Whistler, B.C. V0N 1B6   **(604) 932-2667**

At this vegetarian bed-and-breakfast, rooms are tastefully decorated in Victorian, Oriental, and Aztec themes and feature sherry decanters, moccasins, and duvets. Relax in the private jacuzzi bath and awake to a nutritious, hearty breakfast including homemade jams and fresh herbs served in a country kitchen.

AMERICAN VEGETARIAN TRAVEL TOURS & SERVICES

When you're smitten by wanderlust, peruse this alphabetical listing of organizations; you're sure to find an American expedition that will satisfy your needs.

Always Travel
6304 Walhonding Road, Bethesda, MD 20816   (800) 783-8990
Ask for or write to Donna Zeigfinger who specializes in arranging travel plans for vegetarians.

Ancient Forest Adventures
800 NW 6th Avenue, Suite 201, Portland, OR 97209   (503) 248-0492
Interpretive tours of the Pacific Northwest are conducted on foot, snowshoe, or cross-country skis. Vegetarian meals are served; on some tours, vegan is standard. The organization donates 5 percent of the proceeds to conservation efforts.

AZI Guide Service
CVSR Box 2207, Moab, UT 84532   (801) 259-7620
This service wants to assist those wishing to approach zero impact on an outdoor expedition in the Southwest. The service offers an organic vegetarian menu.

The Biking Expedition
Box 547V, Henniker, NH 03242   (800) 245-4649
Bike tours in New Hampshire feature vegetarian meals as an option at every meal; vegan meals are available upon request. Vegetarian dishes include Pasta Primavera, Chili, Lentil Stew, and Curried Rice and Vegetables. The emphasis is on healthy meals.

Celebrity Cruises
5200 Blue Lagoon Drive, Miami, FL 33126   (800) 437-6111
With twenty-four hours' notice, vegetarian or vegan meals will be arranged on cruises.

Country Walkers, Inc.
P.O. Box 180, Waterbury, VT 05676-0180   **(802) 244-1387**

Specializing in fine walking and hiking vacations around the country with an emphasis on natural history, Country Walkers donates some of its proceeds to conservation groups. The inns and hotels used by the group usually offer a vegetarian option. Upon request, vegans will be accommodated gladly.

The Crash Network
519 Castro St., #7, San Francisco, CA 94114

Billing itself as "the new guide to traveling through the underground," the network publishes a directory of folks to home-exchange with as you travel.

Desert Journeys
P.O. Box 241, Bodega, CA 94922   **(707) 874-3342**

Small groups are organized for trips into the deserts of California and Arizona. Journeys take place four times a year, one every season. Lacto-vegetarian food is offered (the dairy products are kept separate and vegans can be accommodated).

Environmental Travel
P.O. Box 253, Kew Gardens, NY 11415   **(800) 929-3005**

This is a new travel service run by vegetarians.

Figaro Cruises
P.O. Box 1336, Camden, ME 04843   **(800) 473-6169**

Figaro offers sailing cruises along the Maine coast for health-minded folks. The menu is lacto-ovo vegetarian although macrobiotic and vegan preferences can be accommodated. Figaro makes most of the foods from scratch, and offers a seafood side option.

4 Adventure
P.O. Box 8857, Jackson Hole, WY 83001   **(800) 654-2577**

This organization arranges personalized outdoor expeditions throughout the Rocky Mountains, and can easily accommodate any type of dietary preference for both summer and winter travel.

Hatch River Expeditions
P.O. Box 1150, Vernal, UT 84078   **(800) 342-8243**

You can take a white-water rafting trip down the Colorado River; request vegetarian/vegan meals in advance.

Hawk, I'm Your Sister
P.O. Box 9109, Santa Fe, NM 87504-2268   **(505) 984-2268**

Women's wilderness canoe trips feature primarily vegetarian meals. A few co-ed trips are also offered.

Her Wild Song
P.O. Box 6793, Portland, ME 04101   **(207) 773-4969**

Specializing in wilderness journeys for women, Her Wild Song serves vegetarian fare.

Kaibab Mountain Bike Tours
37 S. First West, Moab, UT 84532   **(800) 451-1133**
Kaibab easily outfits vegetarians and vegans for tours in Utah.

Laughing Heart Adventures
P.O. Box 669, Willow Creek, CA 95573   **(916) 629-3516**
Laughing Heart specializes in "consciousness-raising canoe outings on wild and scenic rivers throughout the West and Mexico." The meals are mostly vegetarian, and vegans can be accommodated. All staff members are vegetarian.

Michigan Bicycle Touring
3512 Red School Road, Kingsley, MI 49649   **(616) 263-5885**
"Glen Lake Veggie Amble" tours feature food prepared by a chef who "creates magic with her non-dairy, international cuisine."

Mind Body River Adventures
P.O. Box 863, Hotchkiss, CO 81419   **(303) 527-4466**
This service specializes in wilderness river-retreats in Colorado and Utah. Vegetarian meals are served.

New Routes Inc.
RR2 Box 2030, Brunswick, ME 04011   **(207) 729-6062**
New Routes conducts river expedition trips for women. Vegetarian fare is prepared communally; dietary restrictions can be accommodated.

Resources
Box 1067 Harvard Square Station
Cambridge, MA 02238   **(617) 825-8895**
This is a directory of more than 12,000 alternative groups and organizations. A travel guide is also available.

River Travel Center
Box 6, Pt. Arena, CA 95468   **(800) 882-RAFT**
River Travel specializes in rafting and kayaking in the American West. Most of its outfitters can accommodate vegetarians.

Sierra Club
730 Polk Street, San Francisco, CA 94109   **(415) 776-2211**
The club offers a wide range of outdoor expeditions. A trip to New Mexico (#92226) features vegetarian food.

Uncle John's Foods
500 Hathaway, P.O. Box 489, Fairplay, CO 80440   **(719) 836-2710**
                                                     or (800) 530-8733
Supplies nutritious, air-dried, vegan food suitable for camping and backpacking.

Vermont Bicycle Touring
Box 711, Bristol, VT 05443   **(802) 453-4811**

On biking tours in Vermont as well as elsewhere, this group serves vegetarian meals upon request.

Woodswomen Adventure Travel for Women of All Ages
25 West Diamond Lake Road, Minneapolis, MN 55419   (800) 279-0555
Woodswomen's trips are primarily vegetarian.

Working Assets Travel Service
701 Montgomery Street #400, San Francisco, CA 94111   (415) 788-0777
This service donates 2 percent of the proceeds from travel purchases to some nonprofit organizations working for peace, human rights, economic justice, or the environment.

INTERNATIONAL VEGETARIAN TRAVEL TOURS & VACATION SPOTS

The many ethnic foods described in this book may well give you a taste for a foreign adventure. If so, contact one of the following groups for assistance in finding just the right trip.

Adventure Associates
P.O. Box 16304, Seattle, WA 98116   **(206) 932-8352**
Offers co-ed and women-only expeditions around the world. The Associates serve primarily vegetarian meals in the field; they can accommodate special requests but may ask the guest to supply some food.

Amazonia Expeditions
163 Russell Street, Brooklyn, NY 11222   **(212) 642-5405**
Amazonia offers trips to the South American rain forests. All meals are vegan, with eggs and canned milk an option. Much of the fruit is native to the area.

Animal Amnesty
Galleria Passarella 1, 20122 Milano, Italy   **02-4224620 or 02- 4224506**
Vegetarian holidays are available to members.

Carnival Cruise Lines
327 E. 49th Street, Hialeah, FL 33013   **(800) 232-4666**
A vegetarian menu is offered to guests.

Crackington Manor
Crackington Haven
North Cornwall, England EX23 OJG   **(08403) 397 or 536**
A beach hotel owned by vegetarians, Crackington was voted "Vegetarian Restaurant of the Year" by *Vegetarian Living* magazine. Token meat and fish dishes are offered, but the manor is primarily ovo-vegetarian.

D'Astros Le Pin
82 340 Auvillar, France   **63-95-95-20**
This bed-and-breakfast offers vegetarian meals.

Delicious Diamond
P.O. Box 202, Soufriere, St. Lucia, West Indies **(809) 454-7007**
This cottage and guest house situated in a tropical paradise serves creole and vegetarian cuisine.

Forum Travel International
91 Gregory Lane, #21, Pleasant Hill, CA 94523 **(510) 671-2900**
Specializing in "classic and unusual travel" all over the world, Forum employees told us that most of its European biking trips can accommodate vegetarians very easily.

Greg Johnson Associates
60 E. 42nd Street, Ste. 1111, NY, NY 10165 **(212) 599-0300**
This organization arranges trips throughout the world. The service accommodates vegetarians and can easily arrange a tour for a large group of vegetarians.

Hi-Lo Travel
459 Route 79, PO Box 27, Morganville, NJ 07751 **(908) 591-9292**
Worldwide travelers themselves, staff members have had experience arranging trips for both diabetics and vegetarians. Ask for or write to Tema.

Hippocrates Health Center
Elaine Avenue, Mudgeeraba 4213, Gold Coast
Queensland, Australia **(075) 302860**
A guest described the center as a national park with luxuries. It offers raw vegan foods on Ann Wigmore's Wheatgrass Program.

The Invented City
41 Sutter Street, #1090, San Francisco, CA 94104 **(415) 673- 0347**
or (800) 788-CITY
This international home-exchange service offers travelers a way to swap lodgings. The service does not designate kitchens as vegetarian or not, although we were told that many members are vegetarians.

Inverdene
11 Bridge Square, Ballater, Scotland AB35 5QJ **(03397) 55759**
This vegan guest house is nestled in the mountains near the river Dee.

Kesher Worldwide Jewish Home Link
75 Solvent Road, West Hampstead,
London, England NW6 1TY **071-794-0073**
An exchange and rental organization servicing the world, Kesher works only with vegetarian, kosher, and other Jewish families.

Miranda's Veranda
Umaran 122, San Miguel de Allende
Guanajuato 37700, Mexico **011-52-465-22659**
Miranda's is a smoke-free, vegetarian bed-and-breakfast that has a water treatment system.

Moshav Amirim
Bikat Beit Hakarem, Carmel, Israel 20115   **06-980946**
Billing itself as a vegetarian/naturalist village, Moshav Amirim is located in the beautiful upper Galilee overlooking the Kinnert. Most of the foods and herbs are organically grown on the premises.

O'Reilly's Guest House
Via Canungra, QLD 4275, Australia   **(075) 440-644**
Located in Lamington National Park, O'Reilly's offers lacto-ovo vegetarian meals.

Rio Caliente
c/o Barbara Dane Associates, 480 California Terrace
Pasadena, CA 91105   **(818) 796-5577**
This spa and mineral hot springs resort in Guadalajara, Mexico, is lacto-ovo vegetarian.

Royal Caribbean Cruise Line
1890 Park Marina Drive, #107, Redding, CA 96001   **(800) 852-3268**
The cruise line now offers vegetarian cruises to the Caribbean.

The Safari Connection
245 E. 35th Street, Ste. 5G, NY, NY 10016   **(800) 245-9234**
Arranges safaris to Africa . . . and beyond. The organization will cater to vegetarians upon request, and can easily arrange a tour for a large group of vegetarians.

Sea Quest Expeditions
Zoetic Research, P.O. Box 2424
Friday Harbor, WA 98250   **(206) 378-5767**
Experts in the field lead whale-watching trips. Kayaking expeditions in Washington and Mexico, some of which are parts of research projects, are also offered. All meals are vegetarian; much of the food is organically grown.

Sivanda Yoga Vedanta Center
243 W. 24th Street, NY, NY 10011
The center will connect you with ashrams around the world. Accommodations are strictly lacto-vegetarian. Camping is available.

Southwind Adventures
P.O. Box 621057, Littleton, CO 80162   **(303) 972-0701**
Vegetarian and vegan diets are accommodated on trips to the Andes and Amazon.

Tigh-Na-Mara
The Shore, Ardindrean, Loch broom
Wester Ross, Scotland IV23 2SE   **0854 85 282**
This guest house is close to many Scottish attractions and serves principally vegetarian meals. Some vegan and seafood entrees are offered.

Tivoli Ltd.
Merkazim Building, P.O. Box 2045, Maskit Street 5, Industrial Area

Herzliya, Israel 46120 052-557108

This organization books hotels and tours that cater to vegetarians.

Transitions Abroad Magazine

18 Hulst Road, Box 344, Amherst, MA 01004 (413) 256-0373

This is an international resource guide for educational and socially responsible travel.

Wildland Adventures

3516 NE 155th St., Seattle, WA (800) 345-4453

Wildland specializes in "authentic, worldwide expeditions." Some of the proceeds go to local conservation groups. The organization is always able to provide alternatives to meat-based diets; 60 percent of the clientele request alternatives.

Yin Yang Tours, Inc.

PO. Box 952, Glenwood Landing, NY 11547 (516) 759-3152

Specializing in macrobiotic cuisine, Yin Yang offers tropical expeditions around the world.

LOCAL CONTACTS FOR MORE INFORMATION

When traveling, you may want to contact the following groups for the latest information about restaurants in their areas. Our thanks to many of these contacts for helping us locate information for this guide and apologies to any group that we may have accidentally failed to acknowledge.

For updated information about local groups or to ask questions about vegetarianism, contact The Vegetarian Resource Group, P.O. Box 1463, Baltimore, MD 21203, or call (410) 366-VEGE.

UNITED STATES

ARIZONA

Jewish Vegetarians of Arizona
P.O. Box 32842, Phoenix, AZ 85064   (602) 840-7142

CALIFORNIA

Bay Area Jewish Vegetarians
303 Adams St. #201, Oakland, CA 94610   (415) 465-0403

EarthSave
706 Frederick St., Santa Cruz, CA 95062   (408) 423-4069

EarthSave Orange County
P.O. Box 15131, Santa Anna, CA 92705   (714) 835-1775

Los Angeles Vegetarian Association
505 S. Beverly Dr., Suite 690, Beverly Hills, CA 90212   (213) 964-4FUN

Peninsula Vegetarians
284 Margarita Ave., Palo Alto, CA. 94306   (415) 493-0211

Sacramento Vegetarian Society
P.O. Box 163583, Sacramento, CA 95816   **(916) 446-9334**

San Francisco Vegetarian Society
1450 Broadway #4, San Francisco, CA 94109   **(415) 775-6874**

COLORADO

Vegetarian Society of Colorado
P.O. Box 6773, Denver, CO 80206   **(303) 777-4828**

CONNECTICUT

ARIES (Animal Rights Information and Education Service)
P.O. Box 332, Rowayton, CT 06853

Friends of Animals
P.O. Box 1244, Norwalk, CT 06856   **(203) 866-5223**

DISTRICT OF COLUMBIA

Vegetarian Society of D.C.
P.O. Box 4921, Washington, DC 20008   **(301) 589-0722**

FLORIDA

I CARE
P.O. Box 279, Osprey, FL 34229

Vegetarian Gourmet Society
P.O. Box 8060, Hollywood, FL 33084   **(305) 791-1562**

Vegetarian Society of Southern Florida Environmental Center
11011 SW 104th St., Miami, FL 33176-3393   **(305) 347-2600**

GEORGIA

Vegetarian Society of Georgia
P.O. Box 2164, Norcross, GA 30091   **(404) 447-5561**

HAWAII

Vegetarian Society of Honolulu
P.O. Box 25233, Honolulu, HI 96825   **(808) 395-1499**

ILLINOIS

Chicago Vegetarian Society
P.O. Box 6154, Evanston, IL 60204   **(312) 764-VEGY**

Vegetarians in Motion
P.O. Box 6943, Rockford, IL 61125   (815) 397-5579

IOWA

Heartland Products
P.O. Box 218, Dakota City, IA 50529   (515) 332-3087

MAINE

Maine Vegetarian Resource Group
RFD 2 Box 194, Belfast, ME 04915

MARYLAND

Bowie Area Vegetarian Society
P.O. Box 1478, Bowie, Maryland 20717   (301) 249-7926

Jewish Vegetarians of North America
6938 Reliance Road, Federalsburg, MD 21632   (410) 754-5550

The Vegetarian Resource Group
P.O. Box 1463, Baltimore, MD 21203   (410) 366-8343

MASSACHUSETTS

Boston Vegetarian Society
P.O. Box 1071, Cambridge, MA 02238   (617) 625-3790

Cape Cod Vegetarians
P.O. Box 243, Sagamore Beach, MA 02562   (508) 888-2106

New England Anti-Vivisection Society
333 Washington St., Suite. 850, Boston, MA 02108

MICHIGAN

Michigan Vegetarian Society
P.O. Box 258, Clawson, MI 48017   (313) 435-3514

MINNESOTA

Vegetarian Information Service
5049 Thomas Ave., S., Minneapolis, MN 55410   (612) 920-6412

Vegetarian Society of Southern Minnesota
P.O. Box 1774, Mankato, MN 55345   (507) 625-4448

NEBRASKA

Nebraska Vegetarian Society
P.O. Box 30631, Lincoln, NE 68503-0631   **(402) 476-7252**

NEVADA

Sierra Vegetarian Society
15425 Fawn Lane, Reno, NV 89511-9068

NEW JERSEY

American Vegan Society
501 Old Harding Hwy., Malaga, NJ 08328   **(609) 694-2887**

New Jersey Animal Rights Alliance (NJARA)
P.O. Box 174, Elizabethtown, NJ 07726-0174   **(908) 855-9092**

Vegetarian Society of South Jersey
P.O. Box 272, Marlton, NJ 08053   **(609) 983-3964**

NEW MEXICO

Sangre de Cristo Animal Protection, Inc.
P.O. Box 5179, Albuquerque, NM 87185   **(505) 983-2200**

NEW YORK

Binghamton Area Vegetarian Society
P.O. Box 614, Vestal, NY 13850-0614   **(607) 757-9463**

Long Island Vegetarians
P.O. Box 1146, Huntington, NY 11743-0656   **(516) 349-8639**

North American Vegetarian Society (NAVS)
P.O. Box 72, Dolgeville, NY 13329   **(518) 568-7970**

Rochester Area Vegetarian Society
P.O. Box 20185, Rochester, NY 14602-0185   **(716) 381-5780**

Vegetarian Society of New York
P.O. Box 1518, New York, NY 10028   **(212) 535-9385**

NORTH CAROLINA

Mecklenburg Vegetarian Society
7302 Lancashire Dr., Charlotte, NC 28227   **(704) 545-3796**

Triangle Vegetarian Society
P.O. Box 61069, Durham, NC 27705-1069   **(919) 471-4453**

Vegetarian Society of the Lower Cape Fear
P.O. Box 3411, Wilmington, NC 28406   **(919) 791-4907**

Very Vegetarian Society
620 Bellview St., Winston-Salem, NC 27103-3502   **(919) 765-2614**

OHIO

Vegetarian Club of Canton
P.O. Box 9079, Canton, OH 44711   **(216) 497-2859**

The Vegetarian Society of Greater Dayton Area
P.O. Box 404, Englewood, OH 45322   **(513) 429-9163**

Vegetarian Society of Toledo and Northwest Ohio
2655 Calverton Rd., Toledo, OH 43607   **(419) 536-4073**

OREGON

Portland Vegetarians
P.O. Box 19521, Portland, OR 97219   **(503) 223-5596**

Salem Vegetarians
P.O. Box 13932, Salem, OR 97309-1932   **(503) 585-1829**

PENNSYLVANIA

Lehigh Valley Vegetarians
1035 Flexer Ave., Allentown, PA 18103   **(215) 437-3278**

Mobilization for Animals, PA, Inc.
P.O. Box 99762, Pittsburgh, PA 15233   **(412) 232-5106**

Vegetarian Education Network
P.O. Box 3347, West Chester, PA 19380   **(215) 696-VNET**

Vegetarian Society of Central Pennsylvania
P.O. Box 11066, State College, PA 16805-1066   **(814) 238-2239**

The Vegetarians of Philadelphia
P.O. Box 24353, Philadelphia, PA 19120   **(215) 276-3198**

RHODE ISLAND

Rhode Island Vegetarians
P.O. Box 716, N. Satuate, RI 02857

SOUTH CAROLINA

South Carolina Vegetarian Society
P.O. Box 1093, Lexington, SC 29072   **(803) 957-8155**

TENNESSEE

East Tennessee Vegetarian Society
P.O. Box 1974, Knoxville, TN 37901   **(615) 522-5555**

Tennessee Vegetarian Society
P.O. Box 854, Knoxville, TN 37901   **(800) 280-8343**

TEXAS

Austin Vegetarian Society
P.O. Box 2335, Cedar Park, TX 78613   **(512) 331-5287**

Denton Area Vegetarian Organization
2040 West Oak, Denton, TX 76201   **(817) 383-3858**

San Antonio Vegetarian Society
P.O. Box 790391, San Antonio, TX 78279-0391   **(512) 646-7432**

Vegetarian Society of Houston
P.O. Box 980093, Houston, TX 77008

VERMONT

Vermont Vegetarian Society
RR1 Box 1797, N. Ferrisburg, VT 05473   **(802) 453-3945**

VIRGINIA

Virginia Vegetarian Society
6451 Cotton Hill Rd., Roanoke, VA 24018   **(703) 772-3316**

(See also D.C. Vegetarian Society)

WASHINGTON

Animal Advocates of the Inland Northwest
P.O. Box 4262, Spokane, WA 99202   **(509) 459-8502**

CANADA

Canadian Vegans for Animal Rights
620 Jarvis St.,Ste. 2504, Toronto, Ontario
M4Y 2R8   (416) 924-1377

Ottawa Vegetarian Society
P.O. Box 4477, Station E, Ottawa, Ontario K1S 5B4   (613) 521-0443

Toronto Vegetarian Association
736 Bathurst St., Toronto, Ontario, M5S 2R4   (416) 533-3897

Vancouver Island Vegetarian Association
529 Stornoway Dr., Victoria, British Columbia
V9C 3G8   (604) 478-8477

Vegetarians of Alberta
9211 72nd St., Edmonton, Alberta T6B 146   (403) 469-1448

Camps Offering Vegetarian Meals

When the cry of "School's out for the summer" echoes across North America, legions of youngsters trade their school jackets for camp tee-shirts. Happily, vegetarian youngsters can find a variety of camps that will cater to their diets.

The Vegetarian Resource Group conducted a mail survey of more than 2,000 camps throughout the United States and parts of Canada. In addition to completing the survey, many camps ordered recipe packets and subscriptions to *Vegetarian Journal*–a sign of their commitment to the vegetarian lifestyle. The survey asked each camp whether it offered vegetarian meals, either upon request or as an option at every meal. The same question was asked with respect to vegan meals and kosher meals. We also asked camps to list some of the vegetarian dishes they prepare and to note whether they will cater to special dietary needs.

The following is a summary of the responses we received from this survey. Since we intend to keep this list updated, we'd like to hear about your experiences obtaining vegetarian meals at the camps listed. We'd also like information about any other camps that serve vegetarian and/or vegan meals.

VEGETARIAN CAMPS OR CAMPS WITH A LARGE VEGETARIAN CLIENTELE

NEW YORK

CAMP TE' YEHUDA located in New York City offers vegetarian/vegan/kosher meals as options at every meal. Regular vegetarian food service is available for those campers who register as vegetarians. For further information write to Camp Te' Yehuda, 50 West 58th Street, New York, NY 10019, or call (212) 246-9215.

VERMONT

CRAFTSBURY SPORTS CENTER offers programs in running, sculling (rowing), weight loss, walking, bird watching, swimming, guided nature walks, etc. (Beware that fly-fishing is also taught.) All ages and abilities are welcome.

Vegetarian meals are always offered as an option. Dishes served include Mushroom-Tofu Stroganoff, Spinach Casserole, Ground Nut Stew, Lasagna, Pizza, Chili, Hummus, Mushroom Paté, seitan, and homemade breads, salads, and soups. The camp frequently accommodates those who eat fat-free or yeast- and gluten-free diets, diabetics, and vegans. For information write to Craftsbury Sports Center, P.O. Box 31, Craftsbury Common, VT 05827, or call (802) 586-7767.

KILLOOLEET says that 20 percent of its campers sign up for vegetarian dinners and that all other meals are vegetarian. Some of the dishes served include Vegetable Lasagna, Chili, Stuffed Peppers, Quiche, Pita with Hummus, and Zucchini Fritata. Killoolet will cater to campers who are allergic to milk, milk products, and/or wheat. Write to Killooleet, Hancock, VT 05748, or call (802) 767-3152 for further information.

VIRGINIA

LEGACY INTERNATIONAL is a nonprofit, educational organization, affiliated with the United Nations Department of Public Information as a non-governmental organization. The camp offers vegetarian meals primarily, but will occasionally serve meat dishes, too. Many international vegetarian dishes are served, prepared with foods such as whole grains, legumes, breads, a variety of vegetables, some dairy products and eggs, fruits, and nuts. The camp is happy to accommodate non-dairy or non-wheat diets.

Campers aged eleven through eighteen come from around the world and have ample time to enjoy Legacy's various workshops, including "Intrigued by International Affairs? — Leadership and Global Issues"; "Motivated to Help the Environment?"; "Concerned about Resolving Conflicts?"; "Inspired to Promote Global Thinking through Theater Arts?"; and "Attracted to Serving Others?" For information write to Legacy International, c/o Mary Helmig, Route 4, Box 265, Bedford, VA 24523, or call (703) 297-5982.

CANADA

QUEBEC

AU GRAND BOIS is a nonprofit camp and resource center located on 565 acres of rolling hills, woods, fields, streams, and ponds in Quebec, Canada. The camp serves vegetarian meals including grains, beans, vegetables, nuts and seeds, fruits and a few dairy products. No eggs are used. Campers may also choose non-dairy and macrobiotic meals. An organic garden supplies the camp with fresh greens and some vegetables.

Au Grand Bois accommodates children and teens between the ages of eight and sixteen. Since it is a small camp with approximately fifty children per session, everyone gets to know one another and some nice friendships are made. Activities reflect the camp's desire to encourage respect for others and an understanding of our natural environment. For further information write to Lenny and Arleen Prost, Au Grand Bois, Ladysmith, Quebec J0X 2A0, Canada, or call (819) 647-3522.

CAMPS OFFERING VEGETARIAN MEALS AS AN OPTION AT EACH MEAL

CALIFORNIA

BOYS AND GIRLS CLUB OF HOLLYWOOD CAMP offers vegetarian meals as options at each meal and vegan meals are available upon request. For information write to Boys and Girls Club of Hollywood Camp, 2103 Wilderness Road, P.O. Box 751, Running Springs, CA 92382, or call (714) 867-2155.

MONTECITO-SEQUOIA FAMILY VACATION CAMP offers vegetarian meals as options at each meal and vegan meals upon request. Dinners are served buffet-style, and a salad bar is available. Write to Montecito-Sequoia Family Vacation Camp, Box 858 Grant Grove, Kings Canyon, CA 93633, or call (209) 565-3388 for information.

COLORADO

TROJAN SUMMER CAMP has vegetarian meals as options at every meal. Write to Trojan Summer Camp, P.O. Box 711, Boulder, CO 80306, or call (303) 442-4557 for details.

CONNECTICUT

CAMP HORIZONS, a camp for people who are mentally handicapped, offers vegetarian meals as options at every meal. Mexican dishes and other homemade vegetarian dishes are prepared. Meals are served family-style. For more information, write to Camp Horizons, P.O. Box 323, South Windham, CT 06266, or call (203) 456-1032.

INDIANA

CAMP ALEXANDER MACK offers both vegetarian and vegan meals as options at every meal. Diabetic campers or those needing low-cholesterol, or low-sodium diets can be accommodated. Write to Camp Alexander Mack, P.O. Box 158, Milford, IN 46542, or call (219) 658-4831 for information.

MAINE

CAMP MATOAKA FOR GIRLS offers both vegetarian and vegan meals as options at every meal. The camp will cater to campers who are lactose intolerant and to dieters. For details, write to Camp Matoaka for Girls, RFD 2, East Lake, Oakland, ME 04963, or call (407) 488-6363.

KINGSLEY PINES CAMP offers both vegetarian and vegan meals as options at each meal. Italian and Chinese dishes are sometimes available. Write to Kingsley Pines Camp, 113 Plains Road, Raymond, ME 04071, or call (207) 773-4621 for further information.

MASSACHUSETTS

ROWE CAMP for adults, young people, and families is located in Rowe, Massachusetts. It offers vegetarian meals as options at every meal and vegan meals upon request. The camp uses as many regional and local foods as possible and fresh baked goods are offered at most meals. The camp will try to accommodate all dietary needs. For information, write to Rowe Camp, Kings Highway Road, Rowe, MA 01367, or call (413) 339-4954.

MICHIGAN

CIRCLE PINES CENTER offers vegetarian meals as options at every meal and vegan meals upon request. Meals are served family-style, and locally grown organic produce is used as much as possible. For information, write to Circle Pines Center, 8650 Mullen Road, Delton, MI 49046, or call (616) 623-5555.

NEW HAMPSHIRE

INTERLOCKEN INTERNATIONAL SUMMER CAMP offers vegetarian meals as options at every meal and vegan meals upon request. Meals include meatless pizza, chili, and lasagna. A salad bar is available along with fresh breads. Campers can choose what they wish as they go through the meal lines. For information, write to Interlocken International Summer Camp, RR 2, Box 165, Hillsboro, NH 03244, or call (603) 478-3166.

NEW JERSEY

CAMP DARK WATERS offers both vegetarian and vegan meals as options at every meal. Write to Camp Dark Waters, P.O. Box 263, Medford, NJ 08055-0263, or call (609) 654-8846 for further information.

NEW YORK

CAMP KINDERLAND is located in New York City. Vegetarian meals are offered as options at every meal. For details write to Camp Kinderland, 1 Union Square West, New York, NY 10003, or call (212) 255-6283.

CAMP REGIS-APPLEJACK, located in White Plains, New York, offers vegetarian meals as options at every meal. For information write to Camp Regis-Applejack, 107 Robinhood Road, White Plains, NY 10605, or call (914) 997-7039.

CAMP SOMERHILL is situated in the Adirondack Mountains near Lake George, New York. The camp offers both vegetarian and vegan meals as options at every meal. A salad bar is available and cafeteria-style service is provided. For information write to Camp Somerhill, 20 Huntley Road, Box 295, Eastchester, NY 10709, or call (914) 793-1303.

NORTH CAROLINA

CAMP JUDAEA offers kosher vegetarian meals as options at every meal. Vegan meals are available upon request. Vegetarian dishes include falafel, vegetarian hot dogs, and lasagna. For details, write to Camp Judaea, Rt. 9, Box 395, Hendersonville, NC 28739, or call (404) 634-7883.

PENNSYLVANIA

KEN CREST offers vegetarian meals as options at every meal and vegan meals upon request. Different combinations of pasta and quiches, plus much more are offered. Write to Ken Crest, Rt. 29, Mont Clare, PA 19453, or call (215) 935-1581.

VIRGINIA

CAMP HANOVER offers vegetarian meals as options at many meals and upon request. Dishes served include lasagna, chili, and squash/zucchini casserole. A sandwich and salad bar is also available. Freshly baked bread is offered. For further information write to Camp Hanover, Rt. 1, Box 492, Mechanicsville, VA 23111, or call (804) 779-2811.

WEST VIRGINIA

CAMP ALLEGHANY offers both vegetarian and vegan meals as options at every meal. Camp cooks bake their own bread. Write to Camp Alleghany, Greenbrier County, Lewisburg, WV 24901-0086, or call (304) 645-1316.

WISCONSIN

CAMP INTERLAKEN offers kosher vegetarian meals as options at each meal and vegan meals upon request. Write to Camp Interlaken, 6255 North Santa Monica Blvd., Milwaukee, WI 53217, or call (414) 964-4444.

MENOMINEE SPORTS CAMP FOR BOYS offers vegetarian and vegan meals as options at every meal. For information, write to Menominee Sports Camp for Boys, 4985 Highway D, Eagle River, WI 54521, or call (715) 479-CAMP.

CAMPS OFFERING VEGETARIAN MEALS UPON REQUEST

CALIFORNIA

CAMP A-LOT
5384 Linda Vista Road #100, San Diego, CA 92110   (619) 574-7575

PILGRIM PINES
39566 Clearwater, Yucaipa, CA 92399   (714) 797-1821

SKY MOUNTAIN CHRISTIAN CAMP
P.O. Box 79, Emigrant Gap, CA 95715   (916) 389-2118

COLORADO

CHELEY COLORADO CAMPS, INC.
P.O. Box 6525, Denver, CO 80206

COLORADO LIONS CAMP
FOR THE HANDICAPPED
P.O. Box 90434, Woodland Park, CO 80866   (219) 687-2087

PRESBYTERIAN HIGHLANDS CAMP
P.O. Box 446, Allenspark, CO 80510   (303) 747-2888

GEORGIA

CAMP PINE ACRES
100 Edgewood Avenue, Suite 1100, Atlanta, GA 30303   (404) 527-7500

ILLINOIS

CAMP MEDILL McCORMICK
P.O. Box 1616, Rockford, IL 61110   (815) 962-5591

WOODLAND FOR GIRLS
AND TOWERING PINES FOR BOYS
242 Bristol Street, Northfield, IL 60093   (708) 446-7311

MASSACHUSETTS

CAMP YAVNEH
43 Hawes Street , Brookline, MA 02146   (617) 739-0363

MICHIGAN

JUDSON COLLINS CAMP
1000 Hane Highway, Onsted, MI 49265   (517) 467-7711

PRESBYTERIAN CAMPS
631 Perryman Street, Saugatuck, MI 49453   (616) 857-2531

MISSOURI

SALVATION ARMY CAMP MO-KAN
16200 East 40 Highway, Kansas City, MO 64136   (816) 373-4153

NEW HAMPSHIRE

WAUKEELA CAMP
Rt. 153, Eatoo Center, NH 03832   (603) 447-2260

NEW JERSEY

CAMP TECUMSEH
4 Gary Road, P.O. Box 3170, Union, NJ 07083   (908) 851-9300

NEW YORK

BACO/CHE-NA-WAH
80 Neptune Avenue, Woodmere, NY 11598   (516) 374-7757

CAMP MONROE
P.O. Box 475, Monroe, NY 10950   (914) 782-8695

NORTH CAROLINA

CAMP ELLIOTT
601 Camp Elliott Road, Black Mountain, NC 28711   (704) 669-8639

CAMP NEW HOPE
4805 Highway 86, Chapel Hill, NC 27516   (919) 942-4716

OHIO

CAMP ALLYN
1414 Lake Allyn Road, Batavia, OH 45103

OREGON

TILIKUM RETREAT CENTER
15321 NE North Valley, Newberg, OR 97132   (503) 538-2763

PENNSYLVANIA

CAMP BLUE DIAMOND
Box 240, Petersburg, PA 16669-0240   (814) 667-2355

CAMP EDER
914 Mt. Hope Road, Fairfield, PA 17320   (717) 642-8256

WASHINGTON

BUCK CREEK CAMP
67404 S.R. 410 East, Enumclaw, WA 98022   (206) 663-2201

RESTAURANT SURVEY FORM

Restaurants continually change locations, new ones open, and others close. Please help us to update the next edition of this book by returning this survey with any new information we should have. Feel free to make copies of this form. Your help and support are greatly appreciated.

Return to Restaurant Survey, The Vegetarian Resource Group, P.O. Box 1463, Baltimore, MD 21203. Please include a menu. Call (410) 366-VEGE.

RESTAURANT NAME:_____

STREET ADDRESS: _____

CITY:_____

STATE OR PROVINCE:_____ ZIP:_____

TELEPHONE NUMBER: (_____) _____

Please circle choice(s):

TYPE OF RESTAURANT: Vegetarian (no meat, fish, fowl); Vegan (no meat, fish, fowl, dairy, eggs); Natural Foods; Macrobiotic; California style; American; Juice Bar; Juice Bar in Natural Foods Store; Take-Out Only; Italian; Chinese; Indian; Thai; Middle Eastern; Mexican; Other: _____

DESCRIPTION/SPECIAL FEATURES (examples of dishes, special foods, decor, music, view; what makes this place special?):

_____

_____

_____

Formal restaurant (you need to dress up); Typical, informal; Suitable for business entertaining; Earthy; Totally non-smoking

HOURS:_____

MEALS SERVED: Breakfast   Lunch   Dinner
Late evening service   Sunday brunch   Open 24 hours

TYPE OF SERVICE: Full service (regular table service); Cafeteria; Take-out; Take-out only; Limited service (order at counter, but food taken to table); Counter service (eat at counter); Catering

RESERVATIONS: Required; Recommended; Not needed; Not taken

OPTIONS: Vegan (no meat, fish, fowl, dairy, eggs); Macrobiotic; Vegetarian

BEVERAGES: Juices made in the store (e.g. carrot juice); Espresso; Cappuccino; Non-alcoholic beer or wine; Smoothies; Soy milk; Special drinks; Beer; Wine; Alcohol

CREDIT CARDS: Visa   Mastercard   American Express
Discover   Diners Club

COST: $–less than $6 ; $$–$6–$12; $$$–more than $12

Should this restaurant be given a four-carrot rating? _____

NAME OF READER:_____

ADDRESS:_____

CITY: _____

STATE OR PROVINCE:_____ **ZIP:**_____

TELEPHONE NUMBER: (_____ **)**_____

Attach to this questionnaire any additional comments you may have.

VEGETARIAN JOURNAL

The practical magazine for those interested in health, ecology, and ethics.

Each issue features:

- **Nutrition Hotline** -- answers your questions about vegetarian diets.
- **Low-fat Vegetarian Recipes** -- quick and easy dishes, international cuisine, and gourmet meals.
- **Natural Food Product Reviews**
- **Scientific Updates** -- a look at recent scientific papers relating to vegetarianism.
- **Vegetarian Action** -- projects by individuals and groups.

VEGETARIAN Journal ISSN 0885-7636 is published bi-monthly by the independent Vegetarian Resource Group.

To receive a one year subscription, send a check for $20.00 to The Vegetarian Resource Group, PO Box 1463, Baltimore, MD 21203. Canadian and Mexican subscriptions are $30.00 per year and must be paid in U.S. funds. All other foreign countries subscriptions are $40.00 per year and must be paid in U.S. funds.

Name: _____

Address: _____

_____Zip: _____

Other Books Available Directly From the Vegetarian Resource Group

If you are interested in purchasing any of the following five VRG titles, please send a check or money order made out to Vegetarians (Maryland residents must add 5% sales tax) and mail it along with your order to: The Vegetarian Resource Group, Box 1463, Baltimore, MD 21203. Make sure you include your shipping address.

MEATLESS MEALS FOR WORKING PEOPLE
Quick & Easy Vegetarian Recipes
Debra Wasserman and Charles Stahler

Vegetarian cooking can be simple or complicated. The Vegetarian Resource Group recommends using whole grains and fresh vegetables whenever possible. However for the busy working person this isn't always possible. **Meatless Meals For Working People** contains over 100 delicious fast and easy recipes—recipes that tell you how to be a vegetarian within your hectic schedule using common convenient vegetarian foods. This handy guide also contains spice charts, party ideas, information on fast food chains, and much, much more.

Trade Paperback, $6.00

SIMPLY VEGAN
Quick Vegetarian Meals
Debra Wasserman

Simply Vegan is an easy-to-use vegetarian guide that contains over 160 kitchen-tested vegan recipes—included are vegan menus and creative meal plans. It is also a guide to a non-violent, environmentally sound, humane lifestyle. It includes a comprehensive list of mail-order companies that specialize in selling vegan food, natural clothing, cruelty-free cosmetics, and ecologically-based household products.

Trade Paperback, $12.00

THE NO CHOLESTEROL
PASSOVER RECIPES
100 Vegetarian Passover Recipes
Debra Wasserman and Charles Stahler

For many, low-calorie Passover recipes are quite a challenge. Here is a wonderful collection of Passover dishes that are non-dairy, eggless, low-cholesterol, and vegetarian. It includes fool-proof recipes for eggless blintzes, dairyless carrot cream soup, festive macaroons, apple latkes, sweet and sour cabbage, knishes, broccoli with almond sauce, mock "chopped liver", no oil lemon dressing, eggless matzo meal pancakes and much more. This handy little book is a must for every home that wants to celebrate a healthy and ethical Passover.

Paperback Booklet, $5.00

VEGETARIAN QUANTITY RECIPES

FROM THE VEGETARIAN RESOURCE GROUP

VEGETARIAN QUANTITY RECIPES
From The Vegetarian Resource Group

Here is a unique vegetarian-oriented kit for people who must cook for large groups and institutional settings. It includes 28 vegetarian quantity recipes including main dishes, burgers, sandwich spreads, side dishes, soups, salads, desserts, and breakfasts—each printed separately on large index cards. Each recipe provides a serving from 25 to 50 people. It includes a nutritional analysis of all recipes, preparation tips and helpful time-saving suggestions. It also includes a iisting of over 70 companies offering vegetarian food items in institutional sizes.

Recipe Kit Folder, $15.00

I LOVE ANIMALS AND BROCCOLI

By Debra Wasserman
& Charles Stahler

A Children's Activity Book

Preface By Ruth Ransom, R.D.

I LOVE ANIMALS AND BROCCOLI
A Children's Activity Book
Debra Wasserman and Charles Stahler

I Love Animals and Broccoli is a fun-filled children's book that will help your child develop a better understanding of good nutrition—in a painless and highly entertaining way. This book, chocked full of creative nutrition and animal rights activities, is designed for children of all ages. It covers such diverse areas as food labeling, world hunger, zoos, animal experimentation, and healthy eating—all presented in a way sensitive to children's feelings. Here is a great teaching tool for socially conscious parents and educators.

Paperback Workbook, $5.00

Other Books Available From Avery Publishing Group

COOKING WITH THE RIGHT SIDE OF THE BRAIN
Creative Vegetarian Cooking
Vicki Rae Chelf

This book provides wonderfully imaginative meals with easy-to-follow instructions. With over 500 mouth-watering recipes, you can choose from the many creative breakfasts, lunches, and dinners that abound in this attractive book. From a simple family dinner to an elegant extravaganza, this complete cookbook will provide you with all the ideas you'll need. Step-by-step illustrations will guide you through even the most complicated procedures, while color photos of prepared dishes will fire your creative spirit.

Trade Paperback, $14.95

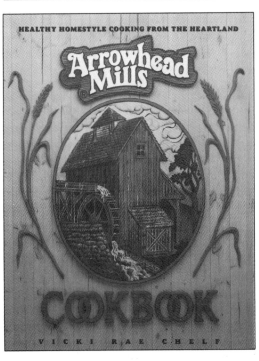

ARROWHEAD MILLS COOKBOOK
Healthy Homestyle Cooking From The Heartland
Vicki Rae Chelf

This cookbook provides a complete variety of natural fare from breakfast to dinner and from appetizers to desserts. The author presents dishes that are rich in flavor, visually appealing, and utterly satisfying. Her detailed instructions guarantee confusion-free cooking every time. With a little practice, it is possible to make the majority of her tempting creations in less than thirty minutes. Insets throughout the book highlight useful cooking tips and intriguing food facts.

Trade Paper, $14.95

DEAF SMITH COUNTRY COOKBOOK
Natural Foods For Natural Kitchens
Marjorie Winn Ford, Susan Hillyard, and mary Faulk Koock

The **Deaf Smith Country Cookbook** offers dozens and dozens of hearty and satisfying new recipes for you to try. It also suggests simple but tasty substitutions in more traditional favorites, ranging from appetizers to desserts, breads, beverages, and more.

Written by Marjorie Winn Ford, cofounder of the Arrowhead Mills Company and natural-foods cook extraordinary; Mary Faulk Koock, food editor of The Texas Star newspaper as well as author of several other cookbooks; and Susan Hillyard, a professional photographer and natural-foods cook, Deaf Smith can clearly show you a better way of preparing family dishes.

Trade Paperback, $11.95

THE GARDEN OF EARTHLY DELIGHTS COOKBOOK
Gourmet Vegetarian Cooking
Shea MacKenzie

In this book, the recipes begin with a wonderful variety of delectable soups, followed by tempting salads, enticing hors d'oeuvres, and fresh breads. For the evening entree, there are inviting centerpieces of beans, and a cornucopia of vegetables and side dishes. Topping off the evening are sensual desserts.

Detailed instructions lead the novice gourmet through each and every step. Author Shea Mackenzie, a talented artist, provides dozens of clear illustrations throughout the book to make complicated procedures easy to follow.

Trade Paperback, $14.95

SWEET TEMPTATIONS NATURAL DESSERT BOOK
Delicious Desserts Without Cooking
Frances Kendall

Frances Kendall has perfected the art of creating sweet surprises for dessert lovers who care about their health. With **Sweet Temptations** you can have your cake—and eat it too!

This collection of kitchen-tested recipes will sweeten your life in more ways than one. Each recipe is as you like it—easy to prepare and naturally delicious. For many years a chef extraordinaire at Hippocrates Health Institute in Boston, Frances Kendall shows you dozens of creative ways to combine fresh natural ingredients—without any cooking at all. And, without any added sugar or salt.

Trade Paperback, $7.95

CLASSIC AMERICAN NATURAL DESSERTS COOKBOOK
Delicious, Healthful Treats & Goodies
David Smither

Classic American Natural Desserts Cookbook brings you allergen-free, low-fat, high-fiber goodies that taste great—without refined sugar, overly processed flours, preservatives, or dyes. This book provides a wide selection of kitchen-tested treats from cakes, cookies, pastries, and pies, to puddings, mousses, and holiday punches. The author's easy-to-follow instructions include recipes for pie crusts, frostings, and glazes. Dairy-free alternative ingredients are also included for those with lactose intolerance.

Trade Paperback, $11.95

NATURALLY SWEET DESSERTS
The Sugar-Free Dessert Cookbook
Marcea Weber

This book shows how desserts can be prepared in a healthy and delicious way. None of the recipes uses a speck of refined sugar or processed foods, and most use very little, if any, dairy products. Sweetners come from natural sources throughout.

Beautifully illustrated with color photographs and drawings, **Naturally Sweet Desserts** contains a wealth of information on natural ingredients, utensils, baking, and preparation. It also includes a glossary of natural ingredients and suggestions on where to get them.

Trade Paperback, $12.95

DIET FOR A GENTLE WORLD
Eating With Conscience
Les Inglis

As the demand for animal-based products has grown, the idyllic family farm has been replaced by the corporate factory farm. As the growth of degenerative diseases has soared, so has the number of studies linking these chronic illnesses with the food we eat. This book looks at how animal-based food consumption is truly hazardous to our health. It also examines our factory farm system's insensitivity to the animal's pain, fear, and suffering. Further, it provides a startling picture of the under-publicized devastation being inflicted on the environment. But this book goes beyond just examining the problems. It offers many practical, inexpensive, and simple solutions that everyone and anyone can follow.

Trade Paperback, $7.95

Available at your local bookseller.
For a complete catalog of our books, call us at 1-800-548-5757.